On My Way to Heaven

In Loving Memory of

Victor K. Ziegler

November 11, 1932

December 5, 2004

THE GIDEONS INTERNATIONAL

Jubilee Ministries

SVPS
SUSQUEHANNA VALLEY
PREGNANCY SERVICES

The Celebration of Life

for

Victor K. Ziegler

at

Richland Church of the Brethren
December 11, 2004 11:00 a.m.

Piano Music .... Judy Whitman

The Opening Sentences and Prayer .... Pastor Jim Bauer

The Eulogy

The Hymn "What A Friend We Have In Jesus"
.... Congregation

A Time of Sharing – Family
The Solo "How Beautiful Heaven Must Be"
.... Phyllis Oxenreider

Selected Scriptures
The Prayer .... Rev. Amos Cunningham

Hymn "I'll Fly Away" .... Congregation

A Time of Sharing – Friends
Solo "The Lighthouse" .... Kay Weaver

The Meditation "Ultimate Healing" ...... Pastor Jim Bauer

The Hymn "When We All Get To Heaven"
.... Congregation

The Benediction

Grandson Ushers
Nick Hower   Ryan Ziegler
Jordan Martin   Eric Ziegler
Keith Myer

A noon luncheon will be served here following
the service of celebration for Victor's life. All are
invited to stay. The family deeply appreciates all the
expressions of love and caring during Victor's time

August 24, 1952
Mt. Zion Road

On My Way to Heaven
Traveling with Grace

The Life of Victor K. Ziegler

---

by Vivian S. Ziegler

First Page: The Memorial Service brochure
        Front Left: Top – Grace and Victor Ziegler
                Center – Celebrating 50 years of marriage, August 24, 2002
                Bottom – The farmhouse at Villa Pine Farm
        Front Center: Grace and Victor and their children:
Ron and Bonnie Myer
Dennis and Sharon Martin
Theresa and Mark Wickert
Kathleen and Lynn Ziegler
Leon and Donna Ziegler
        Surrounded by logos of organizations in which Victor was active.
        Front Right: Victor K. Ziegler

Second Page:
        Left: Wedding day of Victor and Grace – August 24, 1952
        Center: Program for the Celebration of Victor's Life, Dec. 11, 2004
                In background, Victor on his dairy farm
        Right: Top – Victor's high school graduation picture, 1950
                Bottom – Our marriage got off to a "flying start!"
           (August 24, 1952)

On My Way to HeavenTraveling with Grace

Second Printing - 2006

Copyright © 2005
by
Vivian S. Ziegler
3001 Lititz Pike, P.O. Box 5093
Lancaster, PA 17606-5093
evzieg@verizon.net

Although this is a biographical work, some of the names have been changed.

Library of Congress Control Number: 2005931012
International Standard Book Number: 1-932864-33-4

Published 2005

Masthof Press
219 Mill Road
Morgantown, PA 19543-9516

CONTENTS

Frontispiece

Preface and Acknowledgements

Chapter One: God Opens Doors in the Soviet Union 1

Chapter Two: On the Way to Becoming a Man. 19

Chapter Three: My Life as a Dairy Farmer 42

Chapter Four: Preserving the Earth's Resources. 71

Chapter Five: Buying and Selling Farms 89

Chapter Six: Financial Trouble-Shooting and Betrayals 113

Chapter Seven: Committing My Finances to Christ 141

Chapter Eight: Miracles in Cuba 161

Chapter Nine: Traveling Around God's World 176

Chapter Ten: Managing a Nursing Home at Villa Pine Farm. 197

Chapter Eleven: Sponsoring Refugees. 203

Chapter Twelve: Endorsing Natural Healing Concepts 215

Chapter Thirteen: Helping Others Through Christian Organizations. 247

Chapter Fourteen: Witnessing in Words and Deeds!. .273

Chapter Fifteen: Being a Community Leader 292

Chapter Sixteen: Living With My Amazing Grace 305

Chapter Seventeen: Being a Father and Grandfather 324

Chapter Eighteen: Our Children Remember Their Growing-Up Years. 353

Chapter Nineteen: My Foundational Beliefs and Rules of Life 364

Chapter Twenty: Battling Lymphoma 378

Epilogue. 404

"Victorisms" and Anecdotes 410

In Appreciation to Those Who Shared Memories 426

Chronology of Events in the Life of Victor Ziegler 428

PREFACE AND ACKNOWLEDGEMENTS

Until the time of his death, Victor K. Ziegler, was my brother-in-law for fifty-three years. Being four years younger than my husband, Earl, he was not only a brother but also our best friend and confidant, the best man at our wedding.

When Earl needed someone to drive him to the Philadelphia airport for a morning flight, Victor was at our door promptly at 3:30 a.m. to do it. If we had some doubts about a financial transaction, we often checked to see what Victor's thoughts were about it. We felt free to share with him, because we knew he kept confidences.

At a family gathering, in a travel tour group, or after a church meeting, Victor always had people around him being entertained by his stories. About ten years ago I began kidding him, although we both knew I *meant* it, that he should record his stories or get them preserved on paper, so that when he would be gone, they would not be lost. He agreed in spirit, but never took the time to do it. About three years ago, *he* approached *me*, reminding me that we never began that project. I suggested that he put a tape in his car or truck and when he was on long trips, tell his stories to the tape. He *did* begin that, but only got one side of one tape finished.

In early March, 2004, when he knew he was fighting lymphoma, he told me he is now ready. So was I, so I began visiting him twice a week for two-hour sessions when he would tell his stories and I recorded them on tape. Before almost every recording session, one of us would lead in prayer. We both agreed completely that this was to be a project solely for the honor and glory of God. In the next several months, I recorded 25 hours of his stories and my interviews with him.

Those of you who knew and remember Victor, are aware that he spoke with a very pronounced "Lep-a-none Cahn-tee" (Lebanon County), Pennsylvania Dutch accent. In addition to that, he butchered the English language with frequent "he don't's," "I done its," "I seen," "ain'ts," and used countless Pennsylvania Dutch expressions and colloquialisms. Having been an English major in college, I couldn't resist correcting much of his language instantaneously as I transcribed the tapes to my computer. However, in writing this book, I allowed a few examples of his speaking style to remain, (even though *I know* they are grammatically incorrect), so it would still *sound* like Victor speaking.

On Sunday, January 16, 2005, I was listening to the Hour of Power and Dr. Robert Schuller's guest was Chuck Yeager, age 82. In his interview, Chuck Yeager said, *"I say things the way I remember them, but that's not necessarily the way it happened."* The reader should regard Victor's recollections the same way. These are *his* stories, *his* viewpoints, *his* memories and understandably the facts may seem to be not 100% accurate to those who were present. However, this is the way *he* remembered it.

Nevertheless, what does come through, loud and clear, is that Victor loved his Lord, his "Amazing" Grace, his family, people in general, and working outdoors in partnership with God, nature, land, and animals. Sprinkled through each memory is his evangelistic fervor, commitment to helping others, financial savvy, common sense approach to solving problems, and his positive outlook on life, all interspersed with his delightful and contagious humor. He was a multi-faceted person, and I have divided the chapters to separate and highlight his many interests. Even though Earl and I thought we knew him *very* well, we have been amazed at how energetic and involved he really was and cannot imagine how he juggled all these interests, projects, board meetings, mission trips, family life and farming all at once!

His deep faith, tried in the furnace of adversity and disappointment, and his close prayer relationship with God combined to give him the courage to witness to strangers in an open, uninhibited way. He put his faith into action through his life experiences, his forgiving heart, his willingness to give people "second chances," and his commitment to share so generously of his time and resources. He definitely "put his money where his mouth was!"

The title of this book, *On My Way to Heaven*, is from one of Victor's frequent quotes. If he walked into a garage in Lebanon and someone would ask, "What are you up to today, Victor?" his frequent response would be, "Well, I'm *on my way to Heaven*, but I just stopped in Lebanon this morning to get an engine part that I need." If he walked into the post office in Schaefferstown and someone would ask, "What are you doing in town this morning, Victor?" he would answer, "I'm *on my way to Heaven*, but I wanted to mail a few letters here."

Since Victor always credited his wife, Grace, as the secret behind his many successes, the subtitle is *Traveling with Grace*. Together they traveled life's road for 52 years, raising a family, sponsoring refugees, traveling, and marketing nature products as a team. Victor often used the word "grace" with a triple meaning, referring to his wife, to the grace of God, and to the personality trait of being kind, considerate or thoughtful. In this subtitle, the reader may interpret it all three ways. They all are true.

My prayer is that while you may smile at his antics and "learning experiences," they may serve as models for *you* to better experience *the same joy* he knew in serving Christ using *your* gifts and abilities. May these stories motivate you and instill in you the courage to share your faith and resources with others as *you* are on *your* way to Heaven. If that happens, our prayers, that God may receive all the honor and glory, will have been answered.

Before you begin reading, I would like to make a few acknowledgements.

First, I want to thank God who planted the idea for this book and its title and gave me the health, time, abilities and opportunities to record Victor's stories. If there is any glory or praise, it should *all* go to Him.

Second, a big thank you to Grace who has cooperated

and supported me in each step of this project, sharing her own memories, correcting name spellings and facts, and providing photographs. Her willingness to share openly about her painful past shows the depth of her love and desire to help and encourage those who may still be trapped in similar circumstances. Victor wasn't just kidding when he referred to her as "amazing!"

Third, this would have been impossible if Victor hadn't shared so freely, openly and honestly, searching his memory for the humorous, inspirational, miraculous and painful happenings to include. At the end of several recording sessions, he exclaimed, "This was *fun*! I never expected it would be, but I am *really* enjoying this." Because he never doubted my ability to do this, his trust spiked my confidence.

Fourth, my long-time friend and current next-door neighbor, Gwen Miller, a writer and professional proof-reader, has graciously and meticulously read my manuscript, making valuable punctuation corrections and suggesting improvements in the choice and order of words. Thanks soooo much, Gwen.

Last, but not least, words are inadequate to express my gratitude and love to my husband of 54 years, Earl. He is my best friend, supporter, sounding board, inspiration and encourager. With a keen sense of what sounds best, he has been ruthless in deleting, prolific in offering suggestions and advice, as well as quick to praise, and has given me the compliment of saying, "Each chapter makes me feel as though I've just had a visit with my brother, Victor. It sounds just like him!"

Vivian S. Ziegler

August 2005

Chapter One

God Opens Doors in the Soviet Union

"With men this is impossible; but with God
all things are possible." —Matthew 19:26 (KJV)

"How about going along with us to the Soviet Union?" our friends asked.

It was 1981, Ronald Reagan was our President, and the United States and the Soviet Union were locked in a Cold War. I was having a phone conversation with our good friends, Vernon and Florence Wolfe, dairy farmers in Maryland, and when they asked me this question, I almost dropped the phone!

They went on to explain that they were planning to go on a three-week trip with a group called "Promoting an Enduring World Peace" with its headquarters in Woodmont, Connecticut. Thirty-three people had already signed up, and the anticipation of spending that time with the Wolfes and sharing travel experiences with them was a strong motivation. It didn't take long for Grace and me to decide to join them and send in our reservation.

Ironically, during the week before our departure date, one of the Wolfe's parents became critically ill and died and they had to cancel out of the tour. However, Grace and I decided to go anyway.

Upon arriving in Moscow, we were met by a 25-year-old

woman named Marcia who was to be our tour guide for the next three weeks. In obedience to the Communist party line, she took us on their prescribed city tours. We saw many massive buildings, beautiful churches, well-constructed stone sanctuaries, and impressive statues, the majority being of Lenin, but we saw most of these buildings only from the outside. We did notice that many had beautiful red doors. Of course, the churches were not used anymore for worship. Some were museums, others were being used for dramatic performances, and many appeared to be just empty structures, silent testimonies of a long-lost faith. Much of what we saw was gray, dead, and cold-looking. At that time, any Christian believers who did not belong to the Russian Orthodox Church, the state-approved church, had to go underground.

At the end of the day's tours, most of the group would go to their rooms to watch television, hand-wash laundry, or to rest. I figured I hadn't come to the Soviet Union to do those things, so I would go out on the street alone hoping to meet the locals. I'll never forget one encounter I had with a man who appeared to be in his late thirties. He approached me on the middle of the sidewalk as I was about to cross the street. In fairly good English he said to me, "I believe you are a Christian man from America, aren't you?"

I was puzzled, but interested, so I cautiously said, "Yeah."

After looking around, he said, "Could I talk to you a minute? I am one of the pastors of the underground church here and I'd just like you to ask your friends back home to pray for us. We are really 'under the gun' here. If I would be caught having a Bible Study or preaching the gospel of Jesus Christ, I could be arrested, put in jail, lose my job, and perhaps even be tortured or killed. Because of this, our church has just disbanded." All during our conversation, his eyes darted here and there to see if anyone was noticing us talking there. With tears in his eyes, he shook my hand, and I promised him we *would not* forget him. To this day, I often think of that request and do remember him often in my prayers.

On another occasion, I met another underground pastor who said he had had a group of young people meeting in the woods in secret. They would sing softly and had a Bible study there. They thought they were at a safe place and alone, but one time they heard some noises that seemed to be coming closer and closer to them. Suspecting the worst and since there was nothing they could do, they simply formed a circle, held hands and prayed that God would keep them under His protection from the enemy. The next day they found out that the KGB had discovered their meeting place and *had been there* the day before, but had walked away. Someone asked an agent why the group hadn't been arrested. He explained, "We intended to arrest all of you yesterday and take you in, but as we got closer to you, we saw you were surrounded by fiery beings like angels, so we all walked away."

Talking to people like this were really heartwarming experiences for me. I found the courage and faith of these believers, who were living daily under the threat of persecution and even death, to be a real inspiration and challenge. Some of our days had a fairly light schedule of planned activities, and I was glad it was that way. That gave me more time to have these wonderful "learning experiences" on my own on the city streets.

After we toured around for a whole week, I noticed we were seeing the same things again and again. Marcia kept telling us in many different ways how wonderful their country was. I always tried to be positive, commenting on the good things I saw and congratulating the citizens there. I was especially surprised at the respect the young people had for senior citizens.

One example of this occurred when several of us were walking at dusk in a park area. One American woman, who was in her early seventies, dropped her scarf, but none of us noticed it. A teenage Russian boy came behind me, tapped me on the shoulder and said, "Sir, I believe that lady dropped something." He pointed to where the scarf was lying and explained that if he had picked it up and someone would have seen him with the scarf in his hand, he could have been accused of snatching it. For fear of being arrested, he wouldn't touch it, but he did *care enough* to tell us about it. I asked him how he had learned English so well, and he said that after 4th grade, English was compulsory. I responded by saying, "That's interesting, but I guess if Americans are considered to be the enemy, your country would want their young people to learn our language so they could combat us!"

On another of my evening walks in Moscow I met a young fellow who was carrying a knapsack. He told me that the next morning he was going to visit his grandparents who lived 90 kilometers away (about 60 miles). I gave him a broad hint of how I felt about that when I said, "I would love to go on a visit like that, especially with a translator who is as good at speaking English as you are."

He caught it and responded, "Why don't you go with me? I'm leaving tomorrow morning at eight o'clock."

"Wonderful! Where shall I meet you?" I asked.

"Right here at this corner near your hotel," he replied.

When I went out the next morning, he was there waiting. With a look of concern, he said to me, "Victor, I must warn you about one thing. It is really illegal for me to take you along with me. Even when I am traveling alone, if I go more than 10 or 15 miles or if I simply go out of the city, I am required to have a permit. However, I know all the bus drivers, and when I get on their bus, they just smile and say nothing. If somebody would ever tip off the KGB, they might kick me off and get a little rough on me and penalize me."

In spite of that, he was willing to risk it, but I said to

him, "I am disappointed to not be able to go with you, but I don't want to disobey the law. I don't want to ruin my testimony here. If I hadn't been told, I might have gone in ignorance, but I really appreciate your honesty in forewarning me. While I am in your country, I want to honor your law."

He said he understood that and that's why he told me. So, I wished him well and told him to tell his grandparents that I'd be thinking about them and that I hoped he would find them well. So, that little trip never happened and I never talked to him again.

One evening after dinner at our hotel, a middle-aged guy approached me and in a conversational tone asked, "You folks are visiting?"

I spoke up and answered, "Yes, we are part of a small group of thirty-five Americans who have been enjoying seeing the countryside and learning about the history of the Soviet Union."

Then he told me, "I am a reporter from the Moscow News. Could I meet you here in the lobby at 6:30 tomorrow morning?"

Since we had nothing scheduled before 7:30, I figured nobody would be around, so I replied, "I'd be more than happy to meet with you. I get up early anyhow."

The next morning he was there at exactly 6:30. He questioned me as to what I liked about the Soviet Union and what I didn't like. I have always tried to avoid bad-mouthing any person or country because I believe God's handiwork makes something beautiful everywhere. So I told him that I had met such warm-hearted people here and had observed that the countryside was beautiful and had so much potential. (I *didn't* tell him that they weren't using it to the fullest extent because of his government's policies.)

I truthfully said that I've enjoyed the day-trips our group had taken and I've learned a few helpful things here that

I am going to take home to share with my fellow Americans. I added, "And I believe there are a few areas here, such as the government, agriculture, and education, that could be improved and your country would be blessed by the sharing of some of *our* ideas."

"Well," he said, "could I ask you a question? What do you think of President Reagan?"

"I think he's doing a pretty good job," I replied. "You know, it's tough for the average person to really know what is going on internationally, because there is so much going on behind the scene that isn't fully reported and that we can't understand." Then I added, "The nicest part, the thing I really DO like about the country of the United States is that I can say what I want about our president and nobody blinks an eye. Nobody says, 'Hey, Victor, if you don't retract that statement, we'll lock you up and analyze you!' That's one thing I like. We call it 'freedom of speech,' but when it is taken too far, even this freedom can be a curse. People sometimes express themselves in the wrong ways."

We spent about twenty minutes talking together. At the end, I said to him, "Talking with you was very interesting. Thank you for the interview, and perhaps we'll meet again sometime." I had *no idea* what was about to happen.

My meeting with this guy had ended before seven o'clock in the morning. By noon time the Moscow News had printed an edition with the headline: "35 American Citizens Here Blasting President Reagan." The word "BLASTING" was in big letters.

This article was based on my remark that I could say what I wanted about our President.

When the other members of the group saw the newspaper they came to me and asked, "What does this mean?"

I explained that I had met with the reporter that morning and then told them what I had said. To clear the air, we met together and discussed it at length, concluding that the media in both countries are frequently guilty of twisting the truth and this was just another example of it. Fortunately, we were all able to shake our heads in disbelief and smile about it, and it didn't become an "international incident."

One of the items on the itinerary that had really attracted me to taking this trip was that we were to visit a fruit farm and a dairy farm. By the end of the second week, I didn't see any signs that it was going to happen. One day I had a little talk with Marcia, our guide, and told her that I was a "born" farmer and I really enjoyed seeing the countryside with its animals and plant life. I explained that we had been promised that we would get to visit a fruit farm and a dairy farm.

"Well, that isn't going to happen," she snapped. "There is nothing there to see."

I kept pushing by saying, "Marcia, I was *promised* that —unless somebody mis-communicated something. I don't want to go home until I get to visit some farms. I hope you can do something for us, because you are the one who knows your way around. *You are the tour guide!*"

In a reluctant and sarcastic tone, she conceded, "I'll see what I can do."

I knew I had rubbed her the wrong way and it was very obvious that she didn't *want* to do it. I was also aware that as a tour guide, she had been ordered to not let us see anything antiquated and the like.

However, the next day when she got on the bus, she looked directly at me and announced, "I have made a reservation, and tomorrow morning we are going to visit a fruit farm and tomorrow afternoon, a dairy farm." Upon hearing that, everybody clapped.

I smiled and said, "Thank you, Marcia." I knew she wasn't pleased to do it.

When you visit their farms, you quickly understand

why they don't want to show them to you. They are such a contrast to what we see here in the United States on a well-run farm: the signs of productivity, green fields, and fields ready to be harvested.

On one farm we visited, the farm workers who chose to do so could have a little section of land–about one-fourth of an acre–around their house to produce fruits and vegetables for themselves, truck cropping. Many of them were surrounded by a picket fence and in order to see over it, you really had to stretch.

I called Marcia, "Come over here. I want to show you something." (I tried to be nice about it). She looked over the fence and saw the bountiful gardens with their beautiful fruit-laden trees and neat rows of vegetables soon ready to be harvested. This scene contrasted sharply with the land outside, where the farmers were being paid to work for the government. Here they were getting *only twenty percent* of the productivity that they were getting on their own little plots of land.

I exclaimed, "It is amazing to see the difference that personal initiative and ownership of land makes. Here is living proof. If your people could get motivated, your country would really grow."

Continuing, I added, "Marcia, back home in America, if farmers were paid by the government and were told to plant corn on May 6, they'd go ahead and plant it in rain, in snow, in mud, in any weather. When you do that, your crop just doesn't produce. To get good crops, your soil condition has to be just right, the weather warm, the seed good. If the farmer is getting paid by the government, regardless of whether he does his job right or wrong, he is going to just go through the motions to report it done. The end result *for him* is the same. On the other hand, if his family's income and survival depends on what his land produces, he will do the right things so he will get the greatest return. If the leaders of the Soviet Union could understand this, that would really be a PLUS for them."

Marcia didn't seem too happy with my explanation. I tried to soften it by adding, "I think your country *will* get there. Some changes take a lot of time."

Even though our three weeks were winding down, there was never a dull moment. When we'd be driving through the countryside, we'd start singing on the bus and have moments of sharing. Whenever we brought up the subject of Christianity or religion with Marcia, we could tell she didn't want to hear anything about it. On the last day though, she did accept a Bible from Grace, and we hoped it meant something to her when she got home and was alone. That's something we will never know.

We were scheduled to leave from our hotel on a Sunday afternoon about 1:00 to go to the airport to fly back home. However, there was one more thing that I had hoped to do before leaving the Soviet Union: I wanted to visit the American Embassy, but I didn't even know the ambassador's name! That was poor planning on my part. I asked Marcia if it would be possible, and her response was, "He's busy. He doesn't have time to talk to you. He doesn't waste time talking to people like you!"

I told her, "Well, I help to pay his salary. He'll talk to me if I go to visit him."

I could see I wasn't going to get any help or encouragement from Marcia if I pursued this venture.

Early Saturday morning I went to the hotel desk and asked them to write down in English and in Russian the name and address of the American Embassy and the ambassador's name. I asked the clerk the easiest way to get there and could I walk there.

She said, "You might want to take a taxi. The drivers all know where it is and they won't charge you much of anything to get there." (As it turned out, they charged me double and triple the usual price, but that was all right.)

In our travel group was a man in his mid-seventies, a retired school teacher from Florida. As I was going out to get a taxi, he called, "Hey, Victor, where are you going?"

I said, "Our itinerary for this morning is to take a final bus tour around the city, but I want to have a *real learning experience*, so I am going to try to visit the American ambassador, if I can find him."

Eagerly he asked, "Could I go along with you?"

"Sure," I responded, "I'd be more than happy to have someone else go along."

So he jumped in the taxi with me.

We were taken right to the edge of the embassy building. We could see the metal fence, the American flag, the pillars and something written (mostly in Russian) about the embassy on the steel gates. At the very front, the taxi stopped and we got out.

Directly between us and the main gate were two Russian guards standing about five feet apart. We tried to say "Good Morning" to them and to begin walking toward the gate, but they closed in and wouldn't allow us to go through. With their billy clubs hanging on them, and we presumed loaded guns in their holsters, they *were* somewhat threatening, to say the least! They kept saying, "No, No, No," and pretended that they couldn't speak or understand English, although we suspected they probably did have *some knowledge* of English.

During our time in the Soviet Union, I had heard different locals refer to us as "American-ski," so I said to the guards as I pointed to myself, "I–American-ski." (I would have shown them my American passport, but it, along with those belonging to all the others in our group, had been collected and kept by our hotel. That was their way of guaranteeing that we wouldn't disappear and that we would return to get them.) But they still shook their heads and said, "No, No!"

I decided to try a different tack. Pulling out my hotel identification card, I showed it to them and tried to explain that

I was an "American-ski" staying at this hotel, and I MUST see the American ambassador. They continued to shake their heads, "No," and to look really stern and tough.

Turning away from facing the guards, I turned my head toward the gentleman who had come with me. Without making eye contact with him, I just said a prayer aloud.

"Lord, you parted the Red Sea, please make a way for us now!"

Without asking the guards for permission, I took one step forward and they went back a step. I just continued on walking and my companion followed me. After we were through the steel gates, we looked back and they were watching us over their shoulder. They were frowning and looking ugly and mean. We didn't smile either, but just kept moving on.

I said to my partner, "I think international law states that they couldn't stop an American from visiting an American ambassador. Scaring us or pretending to rough us up is okay, but they aren't allowed to touch us. *After we prayed and then stepped forth in faith,* they just separated.

The gentleman with me said, "Well, Victor, we got in, but I don't know if we're getting out!"

It was Saturday morning, and we had no idea where we were going. We found ourselves in a spacious courtyard and started roaming around. I spoke to the man with me, and tried to say it casually, "You know, there is a Christian family living in the basement of the American Embassy."

They were called by the media, "The Siberian Seven," and were members of the unregistered church, a Pentecostal group. Although they would have liked to annihilate them, the Soviet Government knew they couldn't do that without causing a public uproar.

So, temporarily, they were being fed, sheltered and protected in the basement of the American Embassy. They had come from Siberia to find religious freedom in some other country and had pleaded to come to the United States, but were denied passage. After being turned away from the embassy twice, on their third try eight of them actually rushed the guards and got through the gates. Once they were inside, the guards couldn't touch them. They looked back and to their horror discovered that one of them, a seventeen-year-old son, was still outside on the sidewalk being beaten mercilessly by the guards. (His mother told me she had thought he was dead, but he was later treated for his bruises and did live.)

To see them was my *real* purpose in coming to the embassy. I hadn't mentioned this to the guards outside, because I thought I had a better chance of getting in by saying only that I needed to see the Ambassador. In the back of my mind, I was also thinking that if I were able to meet with the Ambassador, perhaps in some way I could plead their case. I hadn't even told the gentleman who was with me that that was my *real* intent. We knew they were living in the basement, so we decided to walk around until we could find a stairway that went down.

About that time, a young Russian man, who appeared to be about twenty-five years old, came walking across the courtyard. I said to him, "We'd like to meet with the ambassador. Can you help us?"

Somewhat surprised, he said, "Oh, you are from the United States?"

We said, "Yes."

Then he explained, "Since this is a Saturday morning, he might not be here, but there is a telephone over there under that dark stairway. Dial his number, and his receptionist or someone will give you an answer."

So, we tried that. His secretary's response was, "It's Saturday morning. Come back on Monday."

"We're leaving for New York early tomorrow morning, and we *can't* come back. We so desperately wanted to talk to him for at least fifteen minutes."

After a slight pause, she answered in a more reconciliatory tone, "I don't know if that is possible or not."

Sensing her change in tone, I added, "Ma'am, maybe I should have told you, we are in the building NOW. We are on the edge of the courtyard under the stairway using *your* telephone."

"Oh!" she said. "You're right here! Hold on a minute. If you have a couple of hours, he'll probably be back and can meet with you then."

"Fine! With your permission, we will just visit around here in the courtyard and in about ninety minutes, I will call you again and check with you." When I hung up, I said to the guy with me, "Boy, that gives us almost two hours to hunt and visit with the 'Siberian Seven.' We couldn't have planned it any better!"

As we resumed our search for a stairway, we saw a teenage Russian girl walking.

I approached her and said, "Miss, we would like to visit the family living here under the protection of the American ambassador and known in the American newspapers as the 'Siberian Seven.' Could you direct us to where they are?"

To our surprise and delight, she said, "Follow me. I am one of them."

She took us down the stairs to a room that was about ten by sixteen feet that had in it a bed, cots on the floor, a little cook stove, and a few other bare necessities. When we entered, she started introducing us to the other six family members. I don't recall what their relationships were but I think one was her mother, her father, an aunt, and others.

After she had spoken only a few minutes, her father interrupted her by saying, "You MUST tell these men to thank the American people for having an ambassador who so much expresses the love of God in his life by allowing us to live here." He was *so grateful!* Tears flowed down his cheeks as he opened his arms to hug us. His gratitude was expressed in *a language we would never forget!*

At that point, the ambassador had been providing food, clothing and protection for them for about three years. *All of them* were so very appreciative. The father added, "The world can say what they want about your country, but we *know* Americans *do* go out of their way to help those who are hurting and in need."

Several of the younger family members spoke fluent English. The older people just listened and now and then would tell the younger ones what to say, and they would interpret. We had a meaningful visit for almost two short hours and then realized that we needed to call back the ambassador's secretary. If he had returned, we didn't want to miss him.

Before we left, the seven family members, my friend and I joined hands in a circle and prayed in English and in their language. They just couldn't get done hugging us.

All this time, this retired teacher was with me. He was at least six feet tall, thin, lanky and very friendly. When we left there, he said, "Victor, this experience today has made the whole trip worthwhile!"

During our half-hour visit with him, the ambassador asked us, "How did you get in here?"

"Well," I said, "it wasn't easy!" I told him I'd give the credit to prayer, as the guards had given us a really hard time.

"They knew that since you were Americans, they couldn't legally stop you by using force," he explained.

I replied lamely that "I *thought* I was aware of that, but I wasn't *absolutely* sure."

We all laughed.

The ambassador told us that when a tourist like myself keeps asking questions everyday, by the third day he is "pegged" and the KGB is notified. They spread the word to their agents: "Look out for this guy. Watch him." He added, "If you would have made ONE MOVE, they would have loved to nab you and lock you up. After sending the rest of the tour group home, they would give you a hard time for months." I said I could often sense that someone was watching and even trailing us, and tried very hard to be careful.

We chatted about various topics and had a nice visit. He did say he felt so good to be in a position where he was able to help people. Sadly, I don't even remember his name.

When we left him, my friend asked, "Do you think we'll get out alive?"

"Yep," I said. "The Lord brought us this far; blessed be the name of the Lord!"

He replied, "Well, you lead the way and I'll follow. I'm not going first!"

So we retraced our steps and went through the courtyard toward the gate. The same guards were still on duty, and I tried to smile at them. However, they avoided any eye contact and still looked stern, but they did allow us to go through. We went to the sidewalk and within a couple minutes had flagged down a taxi to take us back to the hotel. From that moment on, my friend was so excited I didn't have to talk a bit!

In reporting to the group about our morning's escapade, he said, "All of you should have been with us visiting the 'Siberian Seven' and the Ambassador. You know, for the last three weeks, Victor has been telling us that we shouldn't be so gullible. We should look *beyond* what we are being shown—not to attack anyone—but to learn what is *really* going on. We were led around like sheep to the slaughter as they showed us all the things they wanted us to see. We saw all the wonderful things that the Soviet Union is doing, but we didn't really learn a thing. We are going home as blind as when we came, except for THIS experience."

Our final dinner in the Soviet Union occurred on that Saturday night and was hosted by Orthodox priests wearing black robes and caps. Included in the menu were all kinds of beer, wine and vodka. A young United Methodist minister from Milwaukee, a member of our group, noticed that I didn't drink any of these alcoholic beverages.

"Victor, aren't you going to drink any of these?" he inquired. "Don't you think you'll hurt their feelings?"

"No, I don't want to drink any of them. I'll explain to them that I am not used to drinking alcoholic beverages and I don't want anybody to be upset about it. When a person isn't used to them, foreign things like that can make him or her sick."

"Oh," he teased, "you must be one of those 'goody-goodies' from the old Brethren church who don't believe in drinking and can't even take a social drink."

"No," I answered. "I am not a 'goody-goody.' I'm just trying to do what's right."

At the dinner that evening, he and several others overindulged in their drinking, and the next morning when it was time to leave for the airport to come home, he was so sick that they actually thought he might die. A government doctor was sent to the airport to care for him. Our takeoff was delayed, and two hundred people had to sit waiting on the plane for almost two hours because of this one American person who was so sick.

Instead of boarding the plane and waiting, we took advantage of those two hours by walking around in the Moscow airport talking to people. After awhile, we started singing all kinds of gospel hymns so that the Moscow airport was "ringin' with gospel singin'." I especially remember everyone singing, "When we all get to Heaven, What a day of rejoicing that will be! When we all see Jesus, We'll sing and shout the victory!" What a thrill to sing that old hymn in that location surrounded by such a mix of cultures and races. I wondered how many of the people in that foreign airport really understood it.

Finally, the announcement came that we were to

board the plane. The United Methodist pastor was so sick he was brought out on a stretcher. His wife, who was somewhat highfalutin had also teased me the evening before about being a "goody-goody." Lo and behold, now this same woman asked me if I would help to carry him up the steps into the plane. After laying him across six seats in the first class section, they placed cold packs on his head, covered him with blankets, and even sent a nurse along as far as Frankfurt, Germany, where we were going to change planes.

What really amazed me was the irony of the situation that this woman, this pastor's wife, who had laughed at me less than 24 hours earlier for being a total abstainer, now asked me if I would pray for her husband, the pastor. This incident just verified again that the Lord will never let you down. If you defend the truth, you'll always be repaid for it—not in dollars and cents—but in blessings beyond measure.

I was so thrilled just to be able to be of help to them. I was invited to sit up in the luxury of first class with them, and every once in a while, she would ask me something. "He's going to make it," I assured her, "because we are praying for him. Some guys simply got carried away last night and did something stupid. He is paying a big price for doing something that he knew better than to do." She just smiled and nodded that I was right.

And you know, I never heard from them since. We had a smooth flight home, and all the way, the group who had witnessed all this in the Moscow airport marveled that during all our singing there, nobody stopped us, told us to shut up, or even approached us. Everybody just stood around and listened. It was truly a spiritual learning experience, one I wouldn't trade for anything.

Two years later, one of the boys who was part of the "Siberian Seven" got to America, and I heard he was speaking in a Philadelphia church, so I went to hear him.

I walked in the church and spotted him and thought to myself, "I believe that's the guy."

After he gave a forty-five minute speech about the status of Christian churches in the Soviet Union, the role of the Russian Orthodox church, and the persecution that is occurring there, I waited around to talk to him. He remembered me from having met with them several years before and together we recalled the wonderful time we had.

That was the final episode of our Soviet Union experiences.

When you have had so many good experiences, you can hardly say no to the next one because each time you just get so blessed. It's like you want to jump into the warm water of a swimming pool again and again because it feels so good!

Note: For more information about the "Siberian Seven," see *The Last Christian: The Release of the Siberian Seven* by Timothy Chmykhalov, with Danny Smith, Zondervan, ©1986.

Chapter Two

On the Way to Becoming a Man

VICTOR: *"One that defeats an enemy or opponent . . . a winner."*
(Merriam-Webster's Collegiate Dictionary)

On November 11, 1932, Abraham Hoffman Ziegler and his wife, Rhoda Bucher Keller Ziegler, welcomed the fifth child into their family, and that one was me! At the time of my birth, my oldest sister, Ada (now Mrs. Monroe Crouse Good), was just a week short of being seven years old, my sister, Mae (who married Wayne Patches), was just a week short of being five years old. These two sisters were born on the same day, November 17, but two years apart. My brother, Earl, was third, born on March 4, 1929, so he was about 3 years and 8 months old at the time of my birth, and my sister, Verna (Mrs. Norman Kline), born on August 4, 1930, was 2 years and 3 months old. After my birth, my parents had three more children: Lee, born on February 4, 1934, Lena (now Mrs. Irvin Kreider), born August 29, 1935, and Glen, born on May 16, 1939. The place of my birth was a little farm on North Race Street in Richland, Lebanon County, Pennsylvania, the first farm at the edge of the town.

Although my parents had the responsibilities of raising eight children, I must say that if I have done anything worthy of note in my lifetime, it would have to be a tribute to my mom and dad. We always called him "Pop," and he always smiled and enjoyed it. I don't believe anyone ever experienced more shared love and devotion within a family than we did. It wasn't a wordy or emotional thing, but actual daily demonstrations of prayer and concerns for their family, neighbors and community. Helping others was not only spoken about or done *within* the family but it went out in circles far beyond. We children saw this modeled for us daily by our parents.

Just as the names given to children in the Old Testament often seemed to describe their personality later in life, I feel my parents experienced Divine Guidance in naming me, "Victor." Because of the coincidence that I was born on Armistice Day, the day commemorating the truce at the end of World War I, a war in which the United States was one of the Allies on the winning side, my parents probably had that in mind when they named me. However, I feel having a positive name like that, the name of one who wins, helped to give me an optimistic outlook, to rise above discouragement and defeat, and to view all of life with an overcoming, *victorious* attitude.

My earliest memory, the one that stands out most vividly in my mind, is the death of my younger brother, Lee. At the time of his death from spinal meningitis on June 25, 1936, he was about two and one-half years old and I was a little more than three and one-half. I remember that Lee was in the hospital in Reading, Pennsylvania, and Mom stayed there with him day and night for several weeks before he died.

Because of their deep faith in God and in the power of prayer, I never saw my parents "fall apart" when Lee died or when they had financial hardships later on. They believed the end result was the same: "Heaven now or Heaven later," you know. In fact, I never saw my dad really discouraged. He was very verbal and also very physically expressive, a great "hugger." My mother's personality was sweet and quiet, and like sunshine, it just soaked into us. She didn't always have to pray eloquent or even audible prayers, but boy, I will never forget them! During my school years, my mother and dad's prayers were like guardrails. I knew I could only go so far. I couldn't get into trouble because I knew Mom and Dad were concerned and *their goal was that their children were to be an honor and glory to God.*

We walked a mile to school and came home for lunch and then walked back to school again for the afternoon. My dad used to say, "Well, the only time you can carry your lunch to school is on a rainy day. Then you won't get into trouble in school." So on most days, we walked home for lunch. Mom would have it made and we would gather around the table. It was a wonderful daily family experience.

I'll never forget when I was in third grade, and of course, back then, gas was rationed and money was tight. We'd walk to school to save the gas and the money, as we wanted to be sure we wouldn't run out of gas and then be unable to run the farm machinery. We would sometimes ask Dad, "Must we walk to school today?" and he replied, "No, today you can run!" Off we went with a smile and never a negative thought.

An interesting thing happened when I was in first grade. Miss Frances J. Weik was my teacher. She was a great disciplinarian and a lovely person. Over the summer, before my second grade, she got married, and her name was now Mrs. Wolf. Some of us boys went back in the corner of the room and griped, "That's stupid. Why must we call her Mrs. Wolf?" We just couldn't comprehend that marrying her husband would change her name. It took a while to sink in, but you know, those things are what one remembers. We had fun with her name and said, "We are not dealing with the fox, and now we are stuck with the wolf!" We were always up to something; there was never a dull moment. There were fifteen in each grade and two grades in our one room, so Miss Weik had about thirty students total when you added together both grades.

Being born and raised on this small dairy farm of 120 acres, we had 42 dairy cows. We milked them by hand, and when I was about six or seven years old, my dad was one of the first farmers in the area to get an electric milking machine. That was a real God-send! My dad told us, "You have to learn how to milk a cow by hand so you can get a 'feel' or a 'touch' for it before you can operate the machine." That was good advice. By the time each of us was seven years old, we were all involved in the milking. This was also good "family time," because Mom and Dad were both helping plus often at least one outside paid helper, sometimes two. Since Dad was the kind of guy who never got tired, he farmed a neighbor's farm also. He never would quit but would sweat and continue working and just say, "It feels good," you know. He was very positive.

My Parents, Abram Hoffman Ziegler, 1903-1985, Rhoda Keller, 1906-1993. 50th wedding Anniversary photo Nov. 18, 1974.

When I was eight years old, my older brother, Earl, and I would help cut corn by hand to fill the silo, and every day my dad would generate an attitude of enthusiasm by creating a race. He'd say, "Let's race to the other end of the field. I'll cut two rows of corn off to the end of the row by the time you boys cut one row." And you know, *he did it!* He stayed right with it. That taught us that when you develop a spirit of competition and enthusiasm, you get things done. When you do things that way, no one has time to sit around and complain. At the end of the day, you felt good looking back at what you have accomplished and thinking about what a wonderful time you had. You *are* tired, but if you had been working out or practicing football or soccer, you would also be tired. We got our exercise in a productive way by contributing to the economy of the family.

From about 1930 to 1941, my parents processed and sold all their own milk. Everyone at that time sold raw milk under a state health license. We had a veterinarian come twice a year and give health exams, TB (tuberculosis) tests, and blood tests. My dad always prayed hard that the blood tests would be clear, because if a person would get one reactor, you couldn't sell milk to the public, and that was our livelihood. That's what kept us going financially. Every day we sold about 200 quarts of milk, delivering seven days a week. We would milk the cows from 4:45 a.m. to 6:30 a.m. and Mom would run the bottling machine, so that by 7:00 a.m. we had 200 quarts of milk cooled and bottled and ready to go on the truck. Mom was skilled in making the best mixture of chocolate milk. All over Richland, (as I remember it), people would rave, "If you want good chocolate milk, you've got to get it from the Zieglers."

Our business was called Richland Dairy. Because the name, "Abraham Ziegler," was too long to print on the bottle, we simply put on "A.H. Ziegler." By the time I was in second grade, I was allowed to go along on the milk routes on Saturday and Sunday. Through the week, I wasn't allowed to skip school to deliver milk. My dad started out delivering milk with a horse and wagon. He would give me a quart in each hand as that was all I could handle. His older helper carried a whole basket with 6 quarts in each hand. Dad knew everybody by name in the whole village, and he'd tell me to put two quarts on that porch and one quart goes on that next porch. We'd never look back, and the horse would watch us and stay right with us as we went from house to house. I think that must be where the term, "horse sense," comes from. Horses have more sense than some people! They're not as dumb as we think!

Around 1938, when I was six years old, we got a new Ford panel truck. On the third or fourth day of using the truck, my dad commented, "We should have kept Old Pete, the horse, and the wagon. Now we have to keep running back to bring the truck up to where we are." I was so little, but I *really* wanted to drive this truck. I had figured out how to do it, but my dad said, "No, you can't handle that." Well, one time I proved to him I could. I put it in gear and because I was too short to see out the front window, I looked out the side door to watch that it was still on the road and was able to keep up with the man delivering the milk. At that time, some of the main streets were black topped and the rest were gravel. Traffic at that hour of the morning was so light that it wasn't a big deal, but it was a BIG DEAL to me! I used to love doing that. I was sure glad my dad *didn't* keep the horse because this was fun. We often delivered milk like that and had many interesting experiences.

After we did all these milking chores, we would hurry into the house and change clothes, (but not bathe or take showers as people do today), have family devotions and eat breakfast. Then it was time to walk to school. Although I never detected my classmates snickering or making fun about it, I have often had to wonder since about how these Ziegler children must have smelled! However, my suspicion is that nobody detected it because in this rural school, almost everybody smelled the same!

My dad always ran, rather than walked, whenever he went anywhere. One morning an elderly woman heard him on her porch putting the bottles in her milk box. Before he left, she came out and called after him, "Abe, what are you running for?"

He replied, "I'm trying to stay ahead of the sheriff!" And, you know, while it was a funny answer, there was some truth to it. He had bought the farm before the 1929 crash, and there were a couple years he couldn't pay any interest on the principal. His banker advised him to "keep on farming because nobody wants your farm; nobody else has any money either!" The guys who had money didn't want to do the work, so they didn't want a farm. The banker added, "This will turn around sometime, and then you can start paying us back." A few years later, it did, and things started to change.

As I said before, we delivered milk seven days a week. Nobody had electric refrigerators. If a family was lucky enough to have a refrigerator, it was literally an ice box, cooled solely by a block of ice. Our fresh milk was delivered each day within three hours after we were finished milking. Yet, every Sunday morning at 9:00 a.m., our whole family would go to Sunday School at the Richland Church of the Brethren, and we were never late. I can still hear some of the people from the church commenting to my mother and dad: "We have no Sunday morning chores and still have trouble getting here. How do you do all this farm work, get seven children ready, and are here on time?" Well, it took organization, time management and just making up our minds. We never forgot that.

In 1941, my dad met with Sam Wengert from Lebanon who had a milk route similar to ours and wanted to expand it. They were sitting around our dinner table, and Sam said, "Abe, I'd like to buy your milk business. Would you consider selling it?"

Dad answered, "I *am* really busy. Maybe if I would sell, I could concentrate more on my farming." That night they negotiated for the price and settled on $1,100. (I was a little sad because I knew I would miss riding along to deliver the milk.) Wengert's Dairy became one of the largest dairies in the east, but now it has been sold to Dean Foods from Chicago.

My teacher for third and fourth grade was Miss Margaret Klopp and in 1942, in fifth grade, I had Irene Klopp. My record in school wasn't too bad if you consider the little amount of effort I put into my studies. Because I just loved the outdoors and doing physical work related to animal or plant life, I was constantly looking for excuses, not to play sick, but just to stay at home. If my dad happened to say, "I have a lot of work I would like to do today," I would be quick to suggest to him, "Well, if you'd give me an excuse slip, I could get out an hour early." Or if I was aware that what we were going to be doing at school that afternoon wasn't too important, I would ask the teacher if I could be permitted to leave early. She would often say, "Yeah, you can go!" I did those kinds of things as much as I could.

A poverty-stricken family who lived on North Race Street had a son, John Auchey, who was like me in that he didn't like school and liked to have fun. He was close to my same age and could act like a dunce, doing awfully stupid and funny things. One day we were in the back of the room carrying on, and the teacher came back and grabbed John.

(She didn't grab *me* because my dad was on the School Board!) She shook John and said, "You are the dumbest little boy. You will *never* amount to anything!"

Coincidentally, John died recently at the age of 71 and was a multi-millionaire! He had one of the largest cabinet companies in the east, Plain and Fancy Kitchen Cabinets, located along Route 501 in Schaefferstown. His son, John Jr., is keeping the business going, and they have trucks delivering cabinets all the way to California.

But that teacher had said to him, "You'll never amount to anything." When she called him "the dumbest little guy I ever met," he would just smile. He was a very low-keyed guy until the day he died. I talked to him just a month or two before he passed away. We were never very close after our school days, as he went on and got into kitchen cabinet making and made a *real* success of it.

When I was in fourth grade in 1941, after a test of my vision, I began to wear eyeglasses. That same year I also remember that we were on our way home from church on December 7 when we heard the news that Japan had attacked

Pearl Harbor. Being very young, World War II was very impressive to me. I remember vividly the air raids and how we were supposed to have every light out and every shade pulled. Gas, meat, and sugar were rationed. During that time, we learned to be very conservative with what we called the "good things of life" because they were very limited. In retrospect, a good result was that we ate healthier foods, such as more fruits and vegetables, less sugar, and less high calorie baked goods.

The Richland farm where I was born in 1932. The Ziegler family lived there until 1946.

I also remember that sometimes we would run out of gas. Whether it was because of the rationing or because of our shortage of money, I'm not sure, but the result would be that our family would walk to church. Even that was a good experience.

In school, at times there would be daytime air raid tests, and we would either have to hide under the desks or we would be given 20 minutes to get home and not be seen anywhere on the streets. Everything got quiet. It was *really* emphasized at night, because it was believed that a "total black-out" would save our town from being blown up. I'm sure these measures would have made a big difference, but by the grace of God, we, who live on United States' soil, were spared from that.

When I was eleven years old and in sixth grade, Rev. Jessie Whitacre, an evangelist, came and held a week of meetings in our church. During his ministry my heart was touched, he "led me to the light" and I accepted Jesus Christ as my Lord and Savior. Shortly after that, I asked the Lord to save me from failing an arithmetic test (known today as mathematics), and he answered my prayer! That following January 23, 1943, I was baptized at the Keller Brothers' Farm pond at Buffalo Springs, but they had to break through the ice to do it! Chunks of ice were floating on the water.

During the time I was in seventh grade, in 1944, we raised ten Holstein heifers on our farm for Heifer Project International. They were sent to Germany to bombed out families as a way to show our compassion and to help them get started again after World War II.

The next year while my dad was helping a man out of a snow bank on the Richland to Millardsville Road, he broke his leg. All of us had to pitch in a little harder to get the work done through his time of healing.

My dad had been helping my uncle Wayne Keller (his brother-in-law) to finance an out-of-town project and someone ran off with the money. Because he had signed for him, my dad was advised to sell his farm to cover the bad debts accrued by uncle Wayne.

When I was in eighth grade in April, 1945, my dad consented to sell the Richland farm for $27,000 to Paul E. Barry, an excavating contractor, with the privilege of continuing to live on the farm for two years more rent free. By October, 1945, in some miraculous way, Dad had satisfied all the creditors for whom he had signed for uncle Wayne.

With renewed vision and enthusiasm, he went to a farm sale that same month and purchased the 160 acre Long's Mansion Farm at Reistville, and in March, 1946, we moved there with all our livestock and farm equipment. This farm was named after Isaac Long who built the mansion first and then the white concrete farmhouse where members of the Ziegler family live to this day. Today it is called the Villa Pine Farm and is located near the ELCO (Eastern Lebanon County) High School on Weavertown Road.

In this new location I had to change schools and began going to the Newmanstown High School in Millcreek Township where I was introduced to an agriculture course and joined the F.F.A. (Future Farmers of America). Studying plant and animal life and learning the basics of farming and veterinary medicine were fascinating to me.

The Sears & Roebuck Company sponsored a $100,000 foundation which gave a dairy heifer as a free gift to every boy between 15 and 17 years of age who met their qualifications. It was a program somewhat similar to today's Heifer Project International in that when she had her first heifer calf, it was to be passed on. I qualified, was given a heifer, and was allowed to go to the Pennsylvania Farm Show at Harrisburg. There I got the PA Grand Champion Dairy Cow Award for three years in a row with the same animal. The beef animals are sold annually, but the dairy cows are kept for reproduction and milk production. The same animals are allowed to be brought back for three years. So, for those three winters, I slept on the straw at the PA Farm Show, and I enjoyed that. The experience of showing a dairy animal was entertaining, good clean fun, a wonderful chance to make friends from all over the state, and coming home with a purple ribbon each year was just the "icing on the cake."

Six months after we had sold the Richland farm but hadn't moved to the new one yet, my dad was beginning to see light at the end of the tunnel of debt he had assumed to cover my uncle Wayne's losses. Incredibly, about that time uncle Wayne came to him once again requesting yet another $500 loan. He pleaded for the money "one more time," because he felt *sure* that would make the difference and then he would recover financially. This would be the *final* time, he promised.

Pop had just bought a brand new manure spreader for $500. It had rubber tires and was the most modern one around. He had only owned it a week, and during that time, I hooked it up one time with the horses and a few days later with the tractor. I thought it was *really* nice.

Uncle Wayne's latest request really bothered Pop as he was reluctant to give uncle Wayne any more money fearing he would just lose it. That morning, when he went out to the field, he kept pondering, "Should I help uncle Wayne or not?" He had such mixed feelings. Finally, he stopped and dropped to his knees right there in the cornfield and holding on to a cornstalk prayed, "Lord, if you send me someone who will give me $500, I will sell that new manure spreader even though I need it so badly, and I will weld together the old one and try to make it do for another year until we get turned around."

Two hours later, two men, who were strangers to us, drove in and asked if we might have a manure spreader for sale. They offered Pop $500 in cash, and he said, "What could I say?" He sold it, and I was so disappointed

Children of Abraham and Rhoda Ziegler. Standing left to right: Mae, Ada, Earl. Seated: Victor, Lena, Verna. Photo date: December 1936.

as I watched those men driving out the old dirt lane towing our new manure spreader hooked to their bumper hitch. I thought, "Oooooh, *why* did my dad do that?" What a lesson this became for me as a demonstration of a prayer of faith. I discovered my dad did a lot of that, you know, in secret. He told us later that his decision to sell had been based on that prayer.

When I was about thirteen years old, a tobacco buyer came to our farm one day to talk to Dad. He said, "Abe, I want you to consider growing twenty acres of tobacco. I can promise you that it will give you more income than a farm of 150 acres, because it will give a higher return per acre. Why are you raising tomatoes? That is such hard work. With all your children, you could utilize a lot of family labor harvesting the tobacco, as it involves a good bit of hand work."

My dad thought a moment and then responded, "You're right. It would be the biggest income I've ever had. However, all my life I've been teaching my children, my neighbors and their children the evils and the harm of alcohol and tobacco. *If I don't want my children to smoke it, I have no business raising it.* We're just determined to *live more with less.*"

And we *did* live more with less. We lived a healthier lifestyle, a happier life. We didn't have the money that the world had to offer, but we had a lot more than what money could buy. I never forgot that: "Living more with less." Happiness is not measured by dollars and cents. My mother was the best person at taking what the world calls "leftovers," putting them together, and making them taste better than the first time around. We used to say she watered it down, added bread or milk, and stretched out the soup, but I think it was an excellent lesson in diet and kept us from being overweight.

We weren't filling up on all those rich foods, and I've always considered it a real blessing.

My parents had the policy that all their children were to work at home until they were eighteen years old, putting any money they earned into a common family pool. Consequently, although I did have a savings account at the bank, by the time I was eighteen I only had about $50 in it.

When I was a high school senior, my ag teacher, Arthur Wolfe, said, "You know what, Victor? I think you ought to go to Penn State and study dairy husbandry." I was excited about that idea. However, this was after the war and there was just not much farm help available. My dad didn't want to say "No" to me, because that was the way he was natured. He wanted to help his children use their God-given gifts and achieve their goals. On the other hand, he realized I *was* eighteen, an age when many children leave home, get a job, go to school or whatever.

So, one day he came to me and said, "Why don't I sell you half the livestock and farm equipment and you could begin to do your own farming? We could do this 50-50; I would get half and you would get half."

I thought this sounded pretty good. I reasoned that if I would go to Penn State, there was a possibility that my dad *could* get discouraged with farming in three or four years and might decide to sell the farm. If he did that, when I came back from college, I would have missed out on this opportunity. So, I decided to accept his offer.

Dad and I proceeded with organizing the partnership with the advice of Lloyd Lebo, the vocational agriculture supervisor of the Lebanon County schools. To make it completely legal, my dad hired a lawyer, who drew up the necessary papers, and Dad presented me with the papers for my approval. In them, I got a half-interest in all stock and implements, an option on the purchase of the farm if anything should happen to Dad, and along with the interest, I assumed half of any loss and shared in any profits to the same extent.

At that time, I told a news reporter who wrote an article about our partnership, "My dad is the nicest man in the world to get along with, so why shouldn't I stay home and run the farm with him?" Very few parents would be this generous to a son eighteen years old. But then, my parents were the sort who would (as the Dutchmen would say) "give their shirts off their backs" to help someone and would rather skip a meal themselves than to see someone else go hungry.

Weighing in at 170 pounds and being 5 feet 10 ½ inches tall, I towered head and shoulders over my dad, but I knew very well that stature doesn't have anything to do with operating a farm. "He may be shorter," I would say, "but Dad can run rings around me in farming."

As we worked in partnership together, things went pretty well. I don't ever recall having an argument with my dad. I never said, "Aw, Dad, that ain't gonna work!"

I don't ever remember getting a good lickin', but one time—I don't recall if I had disobeyed my mother or what—but I do remember

Here I am (on the left wearing my new glasses) with my little brother, Glen, and my older brother, Earl. Photo date: 1943.

that my dad got the razor strap and wrapped it around my little behind, so to speak. It stung, but it didn't hurt, and he said, "Do you know what? This hurts me more than it hurts you. I *had* to do this because I love you." I never forgot that. Although to be honest, at that time I couldn't see much love in a razor strap wrapped around my butt a few times, but I can really understand it now. Looking back, I can see it was a *real gesture of love because he cared.* We also got our fingers slapped occasionally, but I never saw either of my parents discipline anyone in a spirit of anger. Along with the discipline, we could feel the spirit of love overriding it so much, we couldn't remember it!

My first cousin, Harold Keller, and I were both about the same age, in the same year in school and we spent a lot of time running around together. One day when we were high school seniors, he suggested, "Victor, let's have a little fun tonight. I dated this girl a couple times and she's a nice girl, but I'm not serious about her. Why don't you take my car and take her home from the basketball game, and I'll hide in the back on the floor of the car?"

Oh my!! Ha! Ha! . . . And I did this! When I asked her if I may take her home, I told her that "Harold gave me his car for tonight as his is a little nicer than mine." I also gave her the line that "It is nice to have a nice car for a nice girlfriend." She consented to go with me, and only I knew that Harold was lying on the floor in back of us.

I would purposely ask her dumb questions about my "stupid" cousin.

"Yeah," she agreed. "He's some guy!"

And I got her to talk. Harold said later, "I could hardly keep from laughing out loud as I was lying there on the floor in the back in the dark and hearing it all!"

I raised too many questions and then I had to quit, because I didn't want him to laugh out loud either! I don't think she ever found it out, but I don't really know. I said, "I'll walk along with you into the house, but then I gotta go home."

So, I did and said good night to her and then went home. She was a very pleasant girl, and it was kind of a mean trick, but it *was* funny.

On another occasion, Harold and I and another guy were having fun one night. Elmer Brubaker (who later became a preacher in the Church of the Brethren) was dating Alton Bucher's daughter, Rachel, whom he later married. We knew that when he was visiting her, he would park his car in their barnyard under a pole light that lit up the whole area and could be turned on and off by a switch on their porch. Our intent was to lift up Elmer's car and set it on cement blocks so he couldn't drive it away. However, we thought that first we had better screw out the light bulb because if we happened to make noise or laugh out loud, he'd turn the light on and catch us there in the barnyard. We found a ladder in a nearby shed and intended to climb to the top of the pole and turn the light bulb out. When we were setting up the ladder, working in the dark, we missed the pole and hit the light bulb and smashed it. We said, "Oh my gosh!" but we knew that at least, the light wouldn't be coming on! We had parked our car (I think it was Harold's car) about a quarter of a mile away across a field, so we had to run a nice distance on a dirt road.

Meanwhile, inside the house, Elmer became suspicious that something was going on. He went out and jumped into his car and arrived at our car just moments before we got there. We had left the keys in our car, and he quickly took out the keys and was waiting for us. When we arrived, panting, he said, "What are you boys doing here tonight? You act like you're lost."

"Oh, we just thought we'd have a little fun and say hello to a few neighbors," we said.

"Yes, and I'm the neighbor," he replied, adding, "where are you guys going?"

We just kidded around and said, "Oh, we don't know. We're just out having a little fun."

We edged slowly toward the car as we kidded around and then Elmer said emphatically, "You ain't going *anywhere!*"

Only then did Harold notice that the car keys were missing, and about the same time, Elmer dangled them in his hand. We had to apologize before he would give us our keys. We felt so bad about the light and had to confess to him what we had done.

The next day I stopped in to see Harold who was working at Keller Brother's Garage and told him I thought that it was my fault that the light had broken and that I would pay for it. A new bulb only cost around $.25, so we bought one and took it to Alton Bucher's farm and told him we had been out having some fun the night before and had broken the bulb and wanted to make it right. He allowed us to put the new bulb in for him and told us, "Yes, I knew who did it." Of course, Elmer would have told him. We had a lot of fun nights like that.

When John Kegerise was dating Helen Miller, several of us knew where Helen lived. One night Harold Keller, another guy and I went to her house when John was visiting her, and we lifted up his car and set it on blocks. We knew he couldn't drive it away quickly when it was jacked up like that. When he heard something going on, he turned on the light and we all went running. Once again, our car was parked across the field on a dirt road. In our hurry to get there, we went around the barn the wrong way and were surprised to meet a big police dog on a chain that floated pretty far. Harold was a tall guy with long legs, a fast runner, and the other guy was too, so I was left in the dust,

My dad Abraham, worked with us making work fun for Earl (center) and me (right).

so to speak. Fortunately, we scared the dog so bad that he didn't react immediately, and we all were able to get away. Had that dog been loose, he might have gotten us! It was a moonlit night, and I remember running across the cornfield among the shocks. The funny thing was that John, the very guy we were heckling, ended up asking me to be the best man at his wedding! We told him about it later on and he just had to laugh because sometimes he was part of the fun too!

One of our most unusual experiences occurred one night when we came up behind an Amish buggy. We thought it was Rueben Stoltzfus, a young fellow who was a year older than we were and one we knew real well. We decided we were going to have some fun. We turned the headlights off on our car and waited, allowing the buggy to move forward a distance from us. One person drove the car and one sat on each fender of the car. In the dark, we quietly and slowly pulled up to within five feet of the buggy. Suddenly the driver hit the brakes, and we slid off and grabbed the buggy's rear wheels, and the buggy started to slide into the ditch. About that time, a long buggy whip came flying over the roof, (it was one of those open, courting, dating buggies), and almost hit us. It missed us all, but we heard the whistle! Then the horse took off running! We thought, "Oh, my, this horse is going wild!"

We followed them for a mile or two in the moonlight with our headlights still off because we didn't want the horse to really get out of control and actually run away. Finally, he slowed down, so we stopped and turned around only to discover it was the wrong guy! It was an older couple who we found out later were from the Iona area that we never even knew. We had scared the wits out of them! I can still see that buggy! Whew! We were running the same speed the horse was when we grabbed the wheels of this buggy. When the buggy was sliding sideways, it *had* to scare them, because it must have felt to them as though it were going to upset . . . *and it could have!*

In growing up, we never had a dull moment, and we always had a lot of fun, but there was one thing we always kept in mind, and we thank our parents for that. It was okay to have fun, but we never really damaged anything or hurt anyone. Nothing we did cost people money or damaged their health or anything like that. We were pretty sensitive to that.

While I was a senior in high school, I was fortunate enough to receive the Pennsylvania F.F.A. Star Farmer Award. In

May, 1950, I graduated from Newmanstown High School and by August had finally been able to convince my dad to help me buy a 1939 bluish-colored Ford for $500. After the bank loaned me the $500 at 4% interest, I was to pay them $50 a month on the principle for one year. A lot of the other boys in my class smoked, but I saved my money toward my car. That Ford was a good little vehicle, and today a '39 Ford dressed up like that one was would bring at least $15,000.

I first met Grace Cox in November, 1950, at a church meeting. I'm not sure if it was a revival meeting or a special Saturday night youth meeting, but for some reason, she stood out from the rest in my view.

Grace is only six months younger than I am, but she graduated two years later because she started school two years later than I did. She was orphaned at the age of seven when her father died and her mother was institutionalized due to a mental breakdown. From that time she was pretty much on her own. An older sister, Evelyn, tried valiantly to keep the family together, but in time, Grace was placed in two or three foster homes, and finally ended up living with a family who moved from Lancaster County to Berks County where they attended the Mt. Zion Road Church of the Brethren.

On a Saturday afternoon in the spring of 1951 I attended the wedding and reception of Kenneth Edris at the old Myerstown Church of the Brethren. He was not a personal friend of mine, but I knew him, and his wife was a couple of years older than I was and had been a member of our youth group and Sunday School class at the Heidelberg Church of the Brethren. (After we had moved from the Richland farm to the Villa Pine Farm, our family began attending the Heidelberg Church of the Brethren, as it was closer.) The whole Sunday School class had been invited to the wedding.

Receptions in those days did not involve a big dinner but instead, often consisted of cake and jello or cake and ice cream, but they were fun. The girls from Kenneth's home church were serving the cake and ice cream, and Grace was one of them.

I knew the name (but not much more than that) of one of the girls, a friend of Grace's. When this girl came out with ice cream, I told her–nodding toward Grace–"If that girl would give me two dips of ice cream, I'd take her home tonight."

Lo and behold, a few minutes later, here came Grace parading out with one plate with a double dip of ice cream on it, and she handed it to me. She looked at me smiling expectantly, but I said, "Oh, do you know what? I forgot what I said." And I had a little fun teasing her, but before she walked away, I whispered to her, "I'll see you later. Don't eat too quickly as I want to talk to you." Something like that. However, some of the other fellows there, like Harold Keller and Kenneth Balmer, picked up on it. We were all in that age group. These guys were all saying, "She's not going to go home with *you*, Victor!"

"I believe she will," I replied. "If not, I'll try again next week." I did take her home that night, but I didn't hang around very long, as I was a little nervous.

I said something about coming around again the next Sunday night, but she hesitated and then said, "I don't think I am allowed to go out Sunday night because I must finish my studying to get ready for school Monday morning."

So I said, "Okay, is Saturday night a better night?" She said, "Yes," and the next Saturday night I went to see her and we dated six months like that. It was only after she graduated in the late spring that I went over to see her twice a week.

I must confess that occasionally I would drive on the road past her house and pretend I was on business. If I'd see her outside, I would stop and we'd talk a little bit, and that made the trip worthwhile.

About this time I sold my 1939 Ford for exactly the same price I had paid for it and then went up almost nine years by purchasing a 1948 club coupe Plymouth with an automatic shift, that had belonged to Ruth Miller.

During September and October of 1951, Grace had a number of things to think through, and we broke up. She was debating if she would go to college, go on some missionary project overseas for a couple years, or what she would do with her life. At the same time, although I was unaware of it, she was having problems at home with her foster parents and there was a part of her that was unconsciously looking for a way out of that situation. I thought it was merely that she was looking for "greener grass" and I prayed that somehow God would bring us together again.

Before my wedding—Aug. 24, 1952. Last minute preparations with my first cousin, best friend, and best man, Harold Keller, on the right.

After about six weeks or so, I thought I *must* find a way to get her to talk to me and about that time she wrote me a letter mentioning in it that I had left my ball point pen lay at her house, and she wanted to return it. My initial reaction was: "That's not a good reason to go back to her house–just to pick up a ball point pen–but it's a good opening for me!" I did go back and we started dating all over again, getting more serious all the time.

We dated all that winter and then the next spring was when I served as the best man at John and Helen Kegerise's wedding, and Grace went with me. Everybody said, "Well, it looks like Victor will be next!" I knew that's what *I* was thinking, but I was afraid to push *too hard*.

Everybody at Grace's house were fighting her, saying, "You can't get married until Christmas." The sad part, which I discovered later, was that she was doing all their dirty work, and they were not intending to give a penny toward the wedding. She sensed that, but didn't feel free to tell me at that time.

However, Grace Cox and I *did* get married on the beautiful Sunday afternoon of August 24, 1952, at the Myer Church of the Brethren. (Today it is called the Mount Zion Road Church of the Brethren.) Harold Keller served as my best man and Grace's sister, Winona, was her maid of honor. Officiating at the wedding was my older brother, Earl, who was an ordained minister attending Bethany Biblical Seminary in Chicago.

I used to kid everybody and say, "I never knew what that double dip of ice cream might cost me!" I heard later that Grace had read a book that said, "The way to a man's heart is through his stomach." All the other boys had gotten one dip and I got two.

I remembered Pop used to say, "Let your 'Nay' be 'Nay' and your 'Yea' be 'Yea,'" and I told my friends, I am *not* backing out! We had a lot of fun about that.

One of our most unusual wedding gifts was presented to us as soon as we exited the church from our wedding. Instead of a car with "Just Married" signs and tin cans dangling from it waiting to take us for a ride around several blocks with its horns blowing, when *we* came out of the church, there was an *airplane* waiting for us! Neither of us had ever flown before and Elmer Gibble, a deacon in the church there, had decided to give us a short airplane ride as his gift to us. What a different gift that was! Obviously, our marriage, having been joined together just moments before, was off to a flying start!

Chapter Three

My Life as a Dairy Farmer

"I feel so fortunate that I never worked a day in my life!" —Victor K. Ziegler

When I was eighteen, and we began farming together, my dad would sometimes set the guidelines by saying, "This is what I think we should do." At other times, he would ask for my input. On some occasions I would say, "Dad, I would really like to try this new method or approach, whether it be tilling the soil or feeding the livestock." Out of concern for my parents' feelings and future, I didn't want to make any large scale mistakes. We'd do many projects on a small scale first to be sure they worked before we would put it into general practice. I didn't want to be responsible for destroying all my dad had done in improving the farm.

I was eager to learn but must confess that I never enjoyed reading long books. However, I frequently read short articles that were published in farm magazines such as "Hoard's Dairyman," "American Agriculture," and others. Reading about what someone in Iowa or Nebraska was doing stimulated my thinking and if we thought it would fit our local operations, we would give it a try. Our success rate was about 90%.

Let me illustrate. After I was married and had been farming successfully about three years with my dad, I read about a farmer in Nebraska who was storing haylage and corn silage (as we would call it today) in a high moisture form. By doing it this way, you could beat the weather, take it off the field in half the time, and you didn't have to spend extra time and money to dry it. After much explanation, I finally convinced my dad to let me get a local contractor to come and dig a hole in the ground. We did this also on a small scale. In May, 1953, we took 30 acres and mowed the hay, and instead of drying it for the normal three or four days, we mowed it in one day. We cut it about an inch long and put it in a hole in the ground that was dug out 20 feet wide by about 50 feet long–just a pit.

People would warn my dad, "Don't let your boy ruin you or mess you up. That ain't gonna work."

I would say, "I remember hearing my grandparents talk about how they dug trenches and buried celery, cabbage, potatoes, and carrots, and they'd cover them with paper bags and newspaper. (They didn't have plastic yet at that time). Then they'd cover the trenches with ground and horse manure to insulate them. By January, they'd begin to dig out a few stalks of celery at a time, ten potatoes, cabbage for slaw, etc. Because of this fresh, nutritious food, they were really healthy. I began to think, if it worked for people, it has to work for animals. I always contend that the only difference between animals and human beings, since both were created by God, is that He breathed into us the breath of life, and He gave us the animals to use.

That first year, I forked out the silage by hand. Nobody had tractors with front-end loaders. My dad didn't comment much, but just smiled. That summer we had the healthiest herd with good milk production, and when September came, I said I'd like to fill the pit again with corn the same way. And I did. By June, we could look back on another successful winter in which we had enjoyed better herd health, better production, and it was obvious that the cows loved it. We did this four years, and remember, this pit had only a dirt floor with some stones to build up the side.

An overview of the Villa Pine Farm. Our new home was built in 1970 to the left of this photo.

Later, front-end loaders came into use, and I tried to use them as an easier way to take out the silage. That worked great for the first three or four weeks, but then it would start freezing and thawing. Because our tractors were old, the silage trench would get so muddy and ruts formed so that we couldn't work efficiently, and I would always have to finish taking it out by hand anyway. A year later, we graded the floor of the trench, stoned and concreted it. Then I thought I was in heaven! I could load all of it without losing or wasting any (because of the concrete flooring). We used that for years with just earthen sides. The important thing was that if you wanted to use that equipment, you had to have a concrete floor.

Another advantage with this method was that there was no danger of poisonous gases. On a fall morning, especially with corn silage, one could actually smell a little bit of gas at the lower end of the pit, but it was still safe because it was out in the open air. In a tall silo, a farmer has to be very careful, because he could easily get asphyxiated.

I was present one time when my dad almost got asphyxiated. He came down the chute and practically toppled over. He laid stretched out on the ground for almost fifteen minutes, gasping for breath. Finally, he came out of it and didn't seem to have any aftereffects, but he was very fortunate.

Those trenches were also very cheap to build. In fact, our first hole in the ground was contracted before hydraulic equipment was available. This guy had an old steam shovel and said he could do it for $300 or less . . . and he did. A silo would have been $3,000. There was always a 90% difference in price, depending on how sophisticated you wanted it. Over the years, it worked so well that we also figured out how we could put up nice concrete sides, so we wouldn't have to pick up dirt or stones that would occasionally fall in. Even with that, it was so cheap to construct, and my son, Leon, who now farms that property, still does it that way today. This was the best thing that ever happened, and a tremendous learning experience for us all.

After ten or fifteen years, some of the neighbors began to wise up and started to do it that way also. They discovered they could get the same residual income without spending a lot of money. After all, what's leftover . . . is what one has to live on. If a silo cost $3,000 versus what I could build for $300 or $400, and later on it was $30,000 versus $3,000 and the like, you can see what a farmer could save. It really took almost 25 years before people would quit laughing at me, and I was filling it (and saving all that money) for all those 25 years! The economy would no longer allow you to spend $30,000 to $50,000 for a big silo if you could build something for $3,000 to $5,000 that would facilitate the same thing.

I used to go around giving lectures about this concept. In fact, during the years of 1955-1965, once a year, the Penn State County Extension would bring a busload of farmers from New York, Maryland, and Virginia. It was so interesting to hear the leader, a good man, get off the bus and say, "Well, now, Ladies and Gentlemen, I must warn you that Victor is a little 'different.' We're not here to support or promote anything he does. Although it does work for him, we don't recommend it." It was so funny, and I couldn't keep from smiling.

We'd take a little tour, and people would ask questions such as, "How do you do this?" and "What are you doing about that?" And I'd say, "Well, you know, digging a hole in the ground doesn't impress my neighbor, but when I build a 75 foot high silo and put an American flag on the top of it, that's attractive and impressive! That's what many farmers used to do, but do you know what? I'd rather have my banker smiling at me than anyone else. After all, he might come to me and say, 'Hey, when you are ready, our bank will give you the money for a second farm.' The neighboring farmers look and wonder how you do it. Well, all the little things add up, and this helps you save toward a second farm. You are saving to put it back into the operations, and you're saving all that interest." I always tried to keep it low key, but I was the kind of person that liked to express enough to really generate discussion, you know. I used to look forward to those tour groups.

Once a year, a local farm group sponsored what were called "Farm-City tours." On a Saturday or Sunday afternoon, to promote good public relations, city couples were brought out to walk around on the farm and ask any questions. At that time we were milking several hundred cows, and a young, thirty-five year old woman from Lebanon with two little children asked, "Do you milk all these cows EVERY day?"

"Yes, we do it twice a day," I answered, "and sometimes even three times a day, but twice a day is the more normal practice."

"Not seven days a week?" she questioned, unbelievingly.

"Yeah, seven days a week," I replied. But then, her questions seemed so funny to me that I couldn't help adding, "But not for much longer. We just introduced a bill in Washington to ask Congress if we could shut down Saturdays and Sundays." . . . And she believed me!

She resumed the farm tour with her two small children. At that time we had about fifty baby calves under three months old, and the children were fascinated to see them. Before they left, I approached her and said, "I daren't let you go home believing a lie." I apologized to her and admitted to her that I had gotten carried away. I explained, "If we would shut down the cows on Saturday and Sunday, they would begin to dry up and they wouldn't have much milk on Monday. Think about how nature works. If you feed a human baby, and the baby stops nursing, God designed it that everything shuts down and you move on. Every cow will go through a dry period to get ready for the next baby calf." Finally, she understood it. I was surprised to have to spell it out for her as she was the mother of two, but she just never associated that aspect of human and animal life before. So many interesting things happened.

The secret and success in storing feed was to do the same thing they did with the sophisticated systems—keep out the water and the air. We'd cover the trench with plastic, making it waterproof, weighting it down with sawdust or even plain ground, limestone, or anything so we'd have the best feed, and the cows loved it. We were doing as well financially as anybody at half the expense and half the labor. I could take care of 100 cows easily, without hurting myself, by the time our neighbors took care of half as many. In this way, I doubled my income, and I loved what I was doing.

In 1950, I took over my dad's 28 cows, and by 1976, we were milking over 500. One year we had 578 cows and were milking 510 and 68 were dry, as we always kept about 10% of our herd dry. When someone refers to "dry" cows, they mean cows which are experiencing six to eight weeks per year of "vacation" (from being milked), a rest period. If a farmer is greedy, he can milk his cows year round, but he'll lose money in the long run. They'll do so much better if you milk them 10 months and give them a vacation or dry period, letting them rebuild their energy systems, and during the last few months of pregnancy, they will be building a nice, big calf. You'll get a healthier calf and better milk production year after year if you do it the right way.

The highest number of milking cows we had was 510, filling a tractor-trailer full of milk once a day. I always said, "I live in the land of milk and honey. The cows give me milk and Grace, my wife, is the honey!" Grace would often say to me, "Victor, are you crazy?" But I was having so much fun, and I can honestly say that I never experienced what the world calls stress. I would get tired, of course, but boy, after six hours of rest, I was regenerated every morning.

My day normally began at 4:00 a.m. and I kept working until 8:00 or 9:00 at night, usually going to bed around 10:00 p.m. I always liked to work, and there's not much on the farm that I didn't like to do. I often said, "I'd rather smell fresh-mown hay than go golfing!" And I always knew God was in it. In looking back, I can see that half your health is in your attitude and spirit. You praise God for what you've got and not for what you ain't got! The world looks at it the opposite way. They complain and count the sheep they've lost, but don't rejoice in the ones that are left.

I never believed in "crying over spilled milk." In fact, literally, one time I had two women milking during the day for seven hours and two men at night. I came in one day and these women were half through milking and two tons of milk were going down the drain! They had everything working perfectly but had forgotten to shut off the cooling or storage tank. The faster they were milking, the faster the milk was going down the drain.

Until I walked in at 4:30 p.m., they weren't aware of it. We had a policy that five minutes after you started milking, you were to check the equipment and be sure that nothing was leaking. It was always possible that one could hook up something wrong.

Anyway, somebody goofed, and within minutes, these good, willing and conscientious workers started picking on one another as to whose fault it was. To reassure them, I said, "It really doesn't matter who did it. We're not going to waste time crying over spilled milk, but this is a true learning experience for all of us. We will all remember this from now on and we won't let it happen again. And don't worry, I am not going to deduct any of your wages. In fact, you'll both get your bonuses, whatever it is. Since the Lord has allowed me to make so many mistakes and always took me back and continued to love me, I must forgive also and be at ease about it. This is something that will pass."

For an hour or two after that, they were still uptight. When the milking was finished and I started walking away, I reminded them – "One more learning experience!"

Victor in his milking parlor, surrounded by the milking machines manufactured in New Zealand.

About three years after I started farming with my dad, I got a phone call. "Hey, Victor, we need four or five boys from Pennsylvania to represent us at the National Future Farmers of America Convention in Kansas City, Kansas. With your track record, we think that you would be eligible and would be accepted."

So I thought, "Yeah, that sounds like fun." So I filled out an application. It asked what my interests were and what I had been doing the last four or five years. I had written a few speeches on production in agriculture, the changes we see coming, and how it might be different in 25 years. In those presentations, I emphasized the importance of not putting your head in the sand and kidded them that farmers need to sleep with one eye open so that they don't miss anything.

I was accepted, and if I remember right, they paid some of the cost of the trip. Because money was tight, Grace and I drove our old station wagon, taking a seat out in the back and putting a mattress in its place. That's where we slept on the way there, but in Kansas City, we stayed at a motel.

During that convention, I was honored to be one of eight or ten persons who received the "American Farmer Award." From these, one was selected to receive the "Star Farmer Award," and that was a young man from another state.

These events kinda triggered, enhanced, and multiplied my enthusiasm for farming.

I thought, "Those boys aren't dumb. All of us were taught much by our parents, and if we pick up where they left off, we should do even better. Starting from the base of their knowledge, experience, help, background and encouragement, we can add the new ideas we are learning and improve things even more, and it works, it works!"

Three days later, we left to return home. We stopped at a farm and parked in his barnyard and asked if we could sleep there overnight. With a big smile, he quickly said, "Yeah, we'd be more than happy." We visited and chatted with the farmer and his wife until eleven o'clock! We were picking their brains, and they were picking ours. It turned out to be a great experience as I was sure it could be. However, it takes a little guts to drive up to a farmhouse and ask to stay in their barnyard overnight. Sometimes I would tell them, "We're driving home from Kansas City, and we chose to go this way because we just got married. We don't have much money to spend, so we wondered if we could park here and sleep overnight?" At that time, motels were only fifteen bucks a night, but then even that sounded like a lot.

As I said earlier, right after I graduated from high school

in 1950, when I was eighteen years old, my dad made me an offer to enter a business partnership with him.

During the next four years, we only made $2,000 or $3,000 a year, which doesn't sound like a big deal, but at that time it was! Some farmers were making only about $500, and we were making four to six times that.

Having worked together successfully for four years, my dad really shocked me one day. While we were working, he casually said to me, "You know, Mom and I were talking about maybe getting out of farming. We are thinking you and Grace can do as well without us as with us."

Well, that almost made me fall to the ground! I didn't stop and shout, "Praise the Lord," but I know it really sent me for a spin internally. My first thoughts were: "After only four years, how can my dad feel so much confidence in me, have so much faith?"

But evidently, he knew what he was doing.

Dad called a couple of his friends who were considered to be good, honest appraisers. They said, "Well, right now, in 1954, your farm would fetch $50,000," but my dad said, "If I were to sell through a real estate firm, I would have to pay them commissions. If I have it auctioned, I would need to get an auctioneer and that could cost me $3,000 to $5,000 plus all the work and headache of having the sale. Would it be fair if we would take what I would

View of the dairy operation on Villa Pine Farm.

have paid to have a sale with all the commissions and subtract it from the farm and sell it to Victor for $45,000?" And that's what we did.

My dad had bought the farm in 1946 for $27,500 and I bought it from my dad in 1954 for $45,000. To arrive at that price, we added all the improvements he had made and considered a little bit of depreciation. I told him, "Well, Dad, you couldn't have been any fairer than that to me. Talk it over with the rest of the family."

I think he did with some, but I don't know how far he went with it. He said, "We have to do what is right in the eyes of the law, something we can justify, and seems right in the eyes of everybody."

I agreed by saying, "Well, I'm happy if everybody else is." And so the transaction was done, and we went on from there.

By 1959 I had increased my dad's herd from 28 head to about 72 head. There seemed to be a shortage of milk, and I had the help, material and feed resources to produce more. Enjoying the challenge, I confidently bought 5 or 6 dairy cows, unaware that one of them was infected with brucellosis, known in the dairy business as "abortion disease." The guy selling the cows had guaranteed their health charts and said everything was perfect. However he had switched their documents, and I was not aware of it. They were identified either by a tag in an ear or by documents and individual photos at the state office if they were registered animals. I bought these cows in August, 1960, and in only ninety days, by October, this dread disease had spread through the herd. I lost over fifty cows and only had twenty or so left. Consequently, I had no income.

I then sought the advice of Stuart Klopp, president of the Richland National Bank, saying, "Mr. Klopp, last night I considered my options. If I were to liquidate everything I have left and instruct my dad to either take the farm back or to sell it, I could repay my dad and mom and everyone else, but I wouldn't have more than ten cents left. However, I am willing to buy a lunch kettle and go to work and do whatever I can. I don't have much talent outside of agriculture, but in my mind, I know there is nothing you can't do when you put your mind to it. I could be a welder, a carpenter, or a house painter, and whether I liked it or not, I would do it to support my family." So I was gung-ho on this idea. In fact, I was determined that this was what I was going to do as I saw no other option at that point.

Mr. Klopp, who might have been about 56 years old at that time, leaned forward and looked at me and I'll never forget what he said. "Now, Victor, if you were to lose your pocket knife in a certain field, would you walk across the street to another field to look for it? Of course not. You'd go right back in the field where you lost it."

And do you know what? That struck me. In my mind, I was saying, "That's a profound statement!"

Mr. Klopp added, "If you had been a failure for the last five to seven years, that would be one thing, but this is just like a barn burning down or an accident without insurance, and you are only 28 years old. We want to help you start over again. What do your parents think about this?"

Sheepishly, I answered, "Do you know what? I never told my dad that I was thinking of selling everything, paying everybody off and going to work."

Nodding his head with understanding, Mr. Klopp advised me: "Go home, talk to your dad and mom, and let me know their opinion. If I could do it legally, I'd loan you 100% of the money you need, but my bank limits are 80% and I will need a co-signer."

"Well," I said, "my dad and mom have treated me so well over the years. When I was eighteen, I had no money, and they helped me borrow $500 for a car, which I then paid back. Later on, we went into partnership, and he signed a note for me for

$10,000 or $12,000. I've been working on paying that, and it's going well, but . . . oh, I just don't have the heart to ask Dad and Mom for the third time."

"I know," he assured me, "but their hearts are in agriculture, and this wasn't some foolish mistake you did or something stupid on your part. You simply got caught in the crossfire of this disease." Then he asked, "In your mind, what amount do you think you would need?"

"Between $18,000 and $20,000," (which would be about $180,000 or $200,000 today), I replied, adding, "I believe I could get by with that bare minimum and get going again."

That night I sat down with Pop and Mom. I told them what I had been planning to do and also the encouraging words Mr. Klopp had said. After they had heard the whole story, my dad asked, "How much money would I need to sign for to get you going again?"

"I would need a maximum of $20,000, but I think I could get by with $18,000."

"Well," he said, "you call Mr. Klopp and tell him we'll be in tomorrow morning, and Mom and I will sign for you."

Hearing that almost brought tears to my eyes! What a vote of confidence when everything seemed to be going wrong. I had such wonderful parents. They always came through, prayed for me, supported me, and gave of themselves, even when the going was tough.

At the same time that I was going through this time of trial, I received a second blow.

My wife, Grace, was hospitalized for a month and almost died of complications from a hysterectomy. We had five little children at home, all less than seven years old. In fact, Leon was only about seven months old. My mom and some neighbor girls helped us, and I had wonderful support.

I remember clearly one August evening in 1960. That day I had worked hard at baling hay, backed the equipment into the shed, jumped in the shower, and without taking the time to eat supper, drove to Lancaster to the hospital before visiting hours ended. Since I got there late, I cheated a bit and stayed overtime, past the 8:30 p.m. closing time.

I wasn't sure what was happening, but Grace didn't talk much and I could tell she was very weak. I was really concerned.

Before I left, I grabbed Grace's hand and assured her, "Everything will be all right."

Her response was, "Let's pray and live!" While still holding her hand, I offered a prayer and then went home.

When I walked into the kitchen, I noticed our old brown family Bible lying on the table. The first thing I did was throw off my coat and turn the Bible open. Amazingly, it opened to the book of Job. A passage in Job 2:9b appeared to me to stand out from the page in bold red letters. When Job was facing adversity, his wife advised him, "Curse God and die!" The significance of this message hit my mind so vividly. Just an hour earlier my wife had said to me, "Let's pray and live!" What a contrast in wifely advice! I thanked God then and there for having a wife like Grace who was such a tremendous blessing to me.

With that assuring message fresh in my mind, I went to bed and slept like a baby, without a concern or care. I knew in my heart that everything was going to be all right.

This was the turning point. From that night on, everything started changing–Grace's health improved, and my comeback in dairying grew from one success to another.

Sometime around January, 1974, I was at the Pennsylvania Farm Show admiring some new style milking machine that had been developed and manufactured in New Zealand. Its cost was half that of American models, and it was made simply, requiring very little maintenance. I told the salesman who was a native of New Zealand, "You know, that equipment is so simple that it can't work!"

With a confident grin, he quickly replied, "Man, if you'd give me a chance, I'd prove you are wrong."

He was a man, about sixty years old, whom I had never met before. For a few minutes, we had kidded one another and had a little fun, and then I made that remark.

I started to walk away, but turned back to say, "I take that back. I've been working at dairying all these years, and I'm still simple!" At that, he laughed.

In a more serious tone, I added, "You just might have something there (in that machine); I just don't comprehend it."

He suggested, "Would you let me try it in your milking parlor?"

At that time we were milking about 500 cows. I said, "Do you know what? That makes me nervous. What if it doesn't work and I would ruin 500 cows?"

"No, that won't happen," he assured me.

With my interest now aroused, I asked, "What's this going to cost me?"

"Well," he said, "it will cost you $12,000."

Still not convinced, I questioned further, "But what if it doesn't work?"

"Then I'll take it out and thank you for giving us the opportunity of trying it in your facility. We'll put all your old equipment back in, and we'll go home."

It sounded good enough to me, so I told him, "Well, if you are going to do all that, then I am going to give you a check for $500 as a 'good faith gesture' for your labor to install it." However, I still had another question: "Who's going to determine whether it works or whether it doesn't? My definition of something working or not is sometimes different from some of my neighbor's. They are often satisfied with something mediocre, but I am looking for something that will be a big improvement."

Again, he had that smile of confidence as he said, "I

know we will do just as well . . . and better!"

Amazed, I asked, "Do you really believe that?"

He quickly responded, "Yep!"

Well, that was the year I promised Heifer Project International that I would conduct a 12-member tour for them throughout South America. Within three weeks, the installers of this new equipment showed up at my place. They came one day before I was committed to leave for South America.

Never before had I bought new equipment and left home and let my employees stuck and possibly irritated with something with which I left them hanging. I just didn't operate that way.

At that time we had a wonderful woman living in the farmhouse with her six children. Although her husband had deserted her, she was a good Christian, a hard worker, and she alone supported her children, refusing to go on welfare. Her church had given her some help, in fact, one of the members suggested that she apply for work on our farm. She was really doing a great job for us and knew what was going on. She was good.

When the installers came, I told this woman named Julie, "Do you know what? I am committed to leave tomorrow, and I feel so bad about it. I will call you from wherever I am in the world in a day or so."

It took three days before I got back to her. I knew they usually finished milking about 7:15 a.m., so I called when I knew they would still be washing up in the milk house and could hear the phone ring. I said, "Julie, how's it going? This is Victor."

Her response was, "How are you doing?"

"We are having a good experience here. What's your experience like?"

I could tell she was smiling as she shared, "We're doing great! It's taking us ten minutes longer to milk, but we are getting 300 lbs. more milk every day!" Then she continued to tell me that the new heifers coming in (a heifer is always somewhat scared and more sensitive to being milked) are seeming to enjoy the milking process, as it has a 'softer touch.'"

Breathing a sigh of relief, I replied, "What a blessing, Julie. You've told me enough. I just didn't want you to get discouraged."

"No, things are going just fine. I think we are on the right track," she responded.

To assure her, I said, "Well, I told them we would try the new equipment for sixty days, and if either you're not happy or I'm not happy, we'll tear them out."

"The way it looks now, you're not going to tear them out. If they leave, I leave!" Then she laughed.

When I heard that, a warm feeling swept over me. And you know what? They did work . . . and we are still using them today! The company has added improvements, and my son, Leon, updated them, but they did us so much good that our income increased as our expenses went down. They required 90% less servicing than any other machine. They are so simple that there's not much that can go wrong. It's almost the equivalent of the old cars that had an engine, transmission and clutch. The new cars have computers, all kinds of gimmicks, and you take them to a garage that sends you a bill for $500 and haven't fixed anything! I said, "Man, if we can use such a simple piece of equipment to increase our milk production and herd health, that means we will be giving less to the veterinarian and our net income will grow." So that new idea was another blessing!

The New Zealand salesman stopped in once a week to check how things were going.

One day he said, "Victor, I'm going to give Julie my phone number in my motel and in my car. You tell her that if anything ever goes wrong, I will come here to help her milk. I'm not going to let her down when you're not at home."

That seemed to me to be a real vote of confidence.

After I came home from South America, I gave Julie a couple days off and helped to do the milking myself. I thought, "This IS kinda nice!" So, I called the salesman and told him, "You can come and pick up your check of $12,000 any time."

That was a real venture of faith. "Nothing risked, nothing ventured, nothing gained," they say. Right? However, I always had to fight the thought that three or four employees might be saying, "Aw, Victor's making another change, now what?" But, do you know what? They'd always come back a week or so later and admit, "This is working!"

The salesman always gave me enough assurance that I knew we were not going to go backwards. I told him, "What convinced me to do it was that most people, salesmen or customers, are not willing to put their money where their mouth is. Those that do, often can't back it up. But you were willing to give me all this equipment free of charge for just my $500 'good faith' deposit! You may keep that for your work, and I will chalk that up to my education."

"No," he replied, "I'll return it to you if you are ever not happy, but I know I'll never give it back."

And he was right! That happened about 1975, and we're still using it today, and Leon is doing as well as anybody. His is not the highest producing herd in the county, but he has one of the highest dollar returns versus his expenses.

For eighteen years, I was on a regular monthly program with the (DHIA) Dairy Herd Improvement Association who tested our cows, butterfat, weight and content. I don't remember how much it cost each month, but finally I got so good at it myself that I could almost predict within 5% or 10% what the final records were going to be. I decided to save that money.

What I did was I milked all these cows myself every two weeks. I became so very well acquainted with my cows that I never needed to call the veterinarian, even for a pregnancy test. By just looking a cow in the eyes, looking at her stomach and observing her closely, I could almost guess (as well as the veterinarian did with his examination and pregnancy test) whether a cow was pregnant for five months or seven months.

For about a year, I wrote all these cows down and their numbers, and I'd say, "The vet is coming today, and I am going to have him check these twenty cows." Then I'd get my paper out and say, "This one appears to be pregnant six months, and that one five months, and that one seven months." And I was always 99.5% right! Even the vet misses it too, now and then. So, I quit spending that $10 per animal. Well, with 500 animals at $10 each, that is $5,000, isn't it?

And we would do it on our own time. In fact, I would do it when I would go to the milking parlor. We didn't have to spend a whole day rounding up two helpers to do all this extra, you know. It just helped to make all these efforts more efficient. We enjoyed it. And, well, it was like any specialty; after you do it for many years, you kinda get a "feel" for it. I loved what I was doing. I loved the challenge!

It was funny. We had a good veterinarian, a Christian man, whom I'll never forget.

He said to me one day, "You know, Victor, if I had to count on making my living off you, I'd starve. You give me less money with your 500 head of cattle than most of your neighbors with 50!"

"Well," I said with a smile, "I don't want to see you starve. I'll send you a love offering." I used to kid him and he'd say, "You'll make it." He was very successful in his profession. He's retired now and came to visit me not long ago.

People, animals and plant life were so interesting, they just got my blood flowing.

I'd go down the road and see people doing everything wrong, and I could almost cry. I would think, "What's wrong with that guy? He could save himself lots of money. He could have an easier life and a better income for his family."

Occasionally, I'd try to inject a few thoughts to neighbors and strangers. Sometimes I hesitated talking to them because I was afraid it might arouse a spirit of jealousy. One guy responded to me, "Oh, I'm doing all right."

"That's all that matters. If you're happy, I'm happy," I answered. I'm the kind of guy that if I enjoy something, I like to share it. If it is not received, I let it go. In a few cases, some persons have expressed their gratitude years later.

Some mistakes that we make can directly affect our health. One that I made occurred on a wintry day when I was plowing snow using my tractor with its blade in front. As a windbreak against the wind and snow, I had made a homemade wrap-around cover and attached it to a plywood "roof" so that it looked something like a golf cart. I was working at this from 5:00 a.m. until around 8:00 a.m. to open up the road for the milk truck to come into our farm, totally unaware that I had an exhaust leak and was breathing in carbon monoxide.

In the house, Grace got a phone call to let us know that someone was coming with a payloader in about ten minutes to open our road. She knew they could do the job with much less time and effort and because she wanted to be nice and lessen my work, or perhaps because she was prompted by God, she grabbed her coat and came running out to tell me. When she got to me, I was sitting on the tractor (with the wheels spinning in low gear, just digging away), slumped over the steering wheel with my head hanging down. When she hollered at me, I came to. I remember kicking it in neutral, jumping off the tractor, and falling over into the snowbank, and then I passed out. At first, Grace reprimanded me, thinking I was playing a trick on her to scare her. She said, "Come on, Victor, you are carrying this too far."

However, she soon recognized that it was not an act. Fortunately, in a few minutes I became conscious again. Only then did I realize what a stupid thing I had done and how close I had come to being overcome by the subtle, odorless gas of carbon monoxide.

I was so fortunate that my life was spared that day. I feel it was a miracle of God that the person called when he did, and that Grace came out to me at that exact time. However, I did have one interesting aftereffect. Ever since that incident, I have been extremely sensitive to certain odors. I am practically allergic to most perfumes and hairsprays. When a woman enters a room where I am, I can tell immediately if she is wearing hairspray, and when I am driving and there is a traffic light ahead, I hang back several car lengths from the car in front of me, as I don't want to smell its exhaust.

One of the most dramatic experiences related to farming occurred when a gentleman and his friend drove past my place on a Sunday afternoon as they were enroute to a restaurant for dinner. He told me 35 years later that he had remarked to his friend that day, "That young Ziegler boy will never make it in farming!" Thirty-five years later, he went bankrupt, and I bought his farm from the bank! That was an unusual turn of events but I had to give the guy credit for admitting to me his mistake in judgment all those years later.

When the bank called me and asked if I would be interested in his farm, I made them an offer and they accepted it. At that time he was so poverty stricken that I told him, "I'll let you keep your mobile home on the farm as long as you live, and when you're no longer here, it reverts back to the farm." He was courageous enough to confess to me what he had said 35 years earlier. In looking back across the years, I just had to smile. I always try to refrain from saying, (whether it is to an employee or a family member), "I told you so." I always loved when people tried something different. Even if it didn't work, I learned something from it, and we all grew together and would go on from there.

We once had a neighbor who returned from World War II and even though he knew nothing about farming, his dad bought him a farm near ours. He hired an older man to do the actual hard and dirty farm work, and he became what is called a "gentleman farmer."

His specialty was what he called his "best and prized" Angus cattle, but he had a problem because these cattle were always breaking out. His old fence wasn't strong enough to keep them in, and they'd wander across our property line.

One day I approached him and said, "Mr. Yingst, if you want me to, I will install an electric wire. Since I don't have the money to put up a big new permanent fence, I am willing to put in a 'hot' electric wire fence eighteen inches from the old fence. Your cows will be able to graze the grass under the fence, but when they touch that electric wire, they are going to back off. If I do this, your old fence will last another twenty years because the cows won't be able to push or break it."

"Nope," he replied. "I want it done right. We'll order a permanent fence, and you can pay for the stretch between your farm and mine."

At that time, I had no money and couldn't afford to spend $10,000 or even $5,000 for fencing. "I can't handle that right now," I admitted honestly.

"Well, I'll do it, and you'll pay for it," was his gruff reply.

"Then we'll just have to go on from there," I said as we parted. He was a rough character and spent eighteen years fussin' and fightin'. He'd go to a local restaurant and say, "That Ziegler don't know what he's doin'. He's farming over there . . ." He was the kind of guy who would cuss about everything.

After 18 years, Mr. Weidman, the old guy who actually did the work on his farm, came to him one day and said, "I'm quitting!"

"Then what am I going to do?" questioned my neighbor.

"If you'd be smart, you'd ask Victor Ziegler and his boys to farm your farm."

Mr. Yingst hung his head and said, "I don't know what to do now. If you're really quitting, okay, would you go and talk to Victor for me?"

So, Mr. Weidman came and told me, "Victor, John Yingst wants to talk to you. He's looking for a farmer."

My immediate response was, "John doesn't want me! I never could do anything to please him." When his cattle broke out, I used to tell him, "We'll help you, you know. We'll be glad to help you get straightened out." But he was so irritated and mad, he wouldn't even answer or look at me.

In fact, one Sunday morning forty of his beautiful Angus broke out and they all came through my cornfield. Fortunately, they walked between the rows and didn't ruin much.

We rounded them up in another neighbor's barnyard and took them home. In the whole process, he never showed up. He sent his wife with a truck and made her do the dirty work. Since nothing suited him, she must have had a lot of patience.

They had gotten married late in life and had two small boys under six years old.

During the heat of his terrible attitude, one Sunday while we were eating dinner, Mrs. Yingst called. I could hear the fear in her voice as she said, "Victor, we hate to bother you, but we are missing our three-year-old and our six-year-old sons. We can't find them anywhere. Have you seen anything?"

I said, "No." Our own children were all small at that time, and I sympathized with her. I added, "Hey, we're just about done with our dinner here, and our children are about ready to take their naps. Grace and I will be there shortly to help you hunt for your boys."

To get to their place, we walked down through the woods, and there we met Mr. Yingst. When he saw me coming, he pulled his hat down over his eyes. Ignoring that, I asked him, "What's the situation?"

"There's no sign of them," he answered softly, and I could tell he was upset.

"We can't give up," I said to encourage him.

We searched for awhile and found nothing and then went back home. Mrs. Yingst phoned us about two hours later to tell us they had been found. It turned out that the boys had been playing in the hay in the barn and had fallen asleep for three or four hours. So, everything was just great, and of course, she was very happy.

Anyhow, after his old farmhand had visited me, I went to see John. He said, "You know, Elmer Weidman says he is too old to work on my farm so he is quitting, giving it up, and he says he thinks you should be the one to farm it."

It was kinda awkward, because I knew how he felt, so I responded, "Well, I don't know. I've never given that a thought."

He pursued it with the question, "What do you think?"

"Let me talk to my boys." My sons were getting a little older, and I liked to get their suggestions and input, even though I was deciding everything myself, you know. They would give honest answers. If I'd ask, "Do you think it would be too much work?" They'd say, "Aw, we'd get it done. It would be fun to work with this rough character."

(My boys were a little bit like me, I guess.) The boys and I decided we would offer him $7,000 a year rent for the barn and the land because we knew we could come out ahead at that price.

So, I went to meet with him again and offered, "Mr. Yingst, what were you thinking of charging? If we can afford it, we'll farm it for you, but if we can't afford it, you'll have to get somebody who is better than we are."

He hesitated and then replied, "Well, I was thinking of

about $6,000 a year."

"That sounds fair between neighbors," I agreed. "We'll do it for you. How do you want to be paid?"

"Pay half on April 1 and the second half on October 1," was his prompt answer.

And do you know what? From that day on, he became my best friend!

A few of the next generation—in 1958. Back, left to right: Peggy Keller, Karen Ziegler, Bonnie Ziegler, Randy Ziegler. Front: Patsy Keller, Sharon and Theresa Ziegler, Doreen Ziegler. Children of Harold Keller, Victor Ziegler and Earl Ziegler.

One of my innovative projects was developing an automatic washing system so the cows could come into the milking parlor, be washed, and you would just wipe them dry and attach the milking machines. When we had these, (they looked like a dinner plate upside down with a half dozen nozzles in it), we discovered the idea was great, but the cow's tail got soaked in the process. A cow with a wet tail will always swing it, you know. So, for the person milking it was no fun getting a wet tail in your face! We tried to think of a solution, and one day I said, "We could correct this by bobtailin' them all!"

We had one cow, in particular, who, if her tail got wet, would hit you in the eyes every time she came in to milk. One night she happened to do it when I was the milker, and I said, "This is the last time she will ever make anybody's face or eyes burn from her wet tail!" I put a tourniquet of baler twine on the thinnest part of her tail, about half-way down, and clipped the bottom part right off. There was no indication that the cow felt it; it never affected her production, and the next day when she came in, it was so nice because she didn't have a wet tail!

At that time we had a couple guys and one woman helping us with the milking. The woman remarked, "That's the way they all ought to be; all the cows should be bobbed like that." So, we did dock several hundred of them and discovered that the cows looked better, cleaner, and were more pleasant to work with. Only two, of all we docked, had any significant bleeding. None of the cows showed any ill effects of the amputation.

Of course, when the word got out, there were some raised eyebrows and opposition.

Some friends warned me, "Be careful, Victor, some people will think that is cruelty to animals. The Humane Society will be coming after you."

"That will be fun if someone takes me to court for bobbing the cow's tails," I responded. "If that happens, I'll show up in the courtroom with a little rat terrier dog with his tail bobbed, a bull dog with his ears clipped so they stand up nicely, a steer, and a castrated bull, and then make the jury decide who is the crook."

After World War II, milk testers were needed desperately. My cousin, Harold Keller, had the choice of being drafted into the army or entering CPS (Civilian Public Service). Harold said, "Do you know what? I could spend a year or two working with the farmers," so he decided to join CPS. He was assigned to be a milk tester in the community of Thurmont, in Carroll County, Maryland. Among the farms where he worked was one owned by Vernon and Florence Wolfe. Harold would weigh their milk and test it for butter fat and other various proteins.

One day Harold said to them, "Someday I am taking you up to Lebanon County, Pennsylvania, to visit my cousin, Victor. You two guys do a lot of things alike. Both of you are always trying something new." They agreed to go with him.

However, instead of the Wolfes coming to see us, we got an invitation to the Meadow Branch Church of the Brethren where they attended. We packed up early one Sunday and went down. We had three little girls, Harold and his wife, Helen, had three little girls, and Vernon and Florence had three little girls. We met the Wolfes at their church and they invited us all to their farmhouse for dinner. There were nine little girls around the table. It was kinda interesting! That was the beginning of our friendship, and it never ended. We still get together about once a year.

Vernon was not a real aggressive farmer, but he was creative and enjoyed trying new things and making them work. Many of his innovations were short-cuts to labor, making it easier, and brought in a nice income.

He and I were some of the first dairymen to feed our cows only once a day. Everybody else would feed two or three times a day, thinking that to do any less would diminish the milk production. We found that the extra expense and labor of doing that were just a big headache and didn't give an adequate return for the extra time and cost. I said, "I don't want to be a slave to the cows. I would rather have the cows be a slave to me!" So we began doing things that brought the optimum return for the dollar but not always the optimum in production. Vernon and I thought alike. Neither of us cared about being the first, the blue ribbon winner, in production in our counties. Our main concern was getting our farm mortgages paid and supporting our families. That makes a big difference.

Because of our similar interests, our friendship deepened and continued. Through them, we met many others. Twenty-five years later, after I left the Lehigh Valley Milk Producers, I was called from Maryland to serve on their Milk Producer's Board. For about six years, I spent two days a month working with them in Baltimore. That was interesting.

First of all, Maryland was paying ten cents per hundred pounds more for milk. However, some things in the organization were not quite right, and rather than challenging or fighting with people, I just said, "Do you know what? I can just accept the additional ten cents and sit back, breathe easily and relax." They didn't want to hear that.

Instead, within six months I was on the board of directors of the Maryland Milk Producers Cooperative. The guys that knew me understood that I was very outspoken and the kind of person who defended what I believed and spoke out against what I opposed, even if I spoke alone. They said, "We don't need 'Yes Men.' We need someone who will challenge our thinking and won't be angry with anybody regardless of how it turns out." So, that was another good experience.

During the years from 1960 to 1998, I served on the boards of many different farm organizations. (See the Chronology for the full listing.) By interacting on all these boards, I started knowing many of the farmers in Pennsylvania, Maryland, Virginia, and across the country. Most of them knew me, but I couldn't say their names. If I took their per diem recompense, I wouldn't have had much for all the troubles and headaches we handled, but I felt I was serving the farm community, helping to make it better for everyone, and that was the bottom line.

One time I wanted to have some fun with the local banker. I went into the bank and announced, "I want to borrow one million dollars!" He looked up at me in surprise and asked, "What for?"

"I love farming so much, I am going to farm 'til it's all (gone)!" We both had a good laugh and then got on with business.

I remember telling a guy, "I feel so fortunate that I never worked a day in my life!"

The man stopped in his tracks and turned toward me and said, "Victor, why would you lie to me?"

I said, "What do you mean?"

"All I know about you is that you work, work, work, and nothing stops you," he replied.

"Ooooooh, now wait a minute," I interrupted, "maybe I should clarify my definition of 'work'. If you are going golfing, do you tell your wife you are going to work?"

With a puzzled look, he responded, "No, I tell her I am going golfing."

Then I explained, "When I went out on a Saturday night and mowed 20 acres of hay to put in on Monday, and I would watch the sun going down while I am smelling the fresh-mown hay, I couldn't help but think 'how beautiful what is coming must be!' That wasn't like work to me. When I go out and work on my farm, I get the same feeling that you get when you go golfing. I love my work."

Chapter Four

Preserving the Earth's Resources

"Stewardship is so important. Whether it is our own physical lives or the earth's resources, God created them and showed us the path to walk down, and it is our job to make it better for the next generation." —Victor K. Ziegler

When my dad moved his family to the Villa Pine Farm in 1946, there was no fresh water lake on the property, and I used to dream of having one. If there had been a fire, we would have had nothing with which to fight it except a water hose and a well hydrant.

One winter I was watching the January thaw. On this particular farm, about 800 acres of water actually drained from Reistville, past the Heidelburg Church of the Brethren and the ELCO (Eastern Lebanon County) Medical Center, and it all drew down to one given point. I said to myself, "Here is where I am going to put a one acre lake." Even though no known springs were around, I believed I could save enough water from a flash flood or a melting snow to create something that would work well.

So, about 1962, I built a lake, but I did it on a small scale, only about half the size it is today. When we excavated to about ten feet deep, we hit a loamy gravel that leaked and wouldn't hold water. To solve that problem, I put a water tank in the excavated area and had 75 dairy heifers come in there for six months. I also put in a water hose and allowed it to trickle, so this became a real mud hole. They trampled in this so it got tight like concrete, and by the following year, it didn't leak. As the cattle came in there for water a couple times a day, they continued to tramp it until everything was tight.

Before I put the cows in, I invited some professionals to come and examine the possibilities, and they strongly advised against building the lake. "You're wasting your money here. You'll never get any water here, and if you do, it'll never hold it," they warned.

Once again, they were proven wrong, because it is the little things that make the difference! If I wouldn't have sealed it in some way first, even using something as simple as letting the cattle tramp it, it probably wouldn't have been successful. I could have concreted the floor of the lake for between $5,000 and $10,000, but I didn't have that kind of money then, so I did the next best thing, and it worked!

When my son, Leon, moved into the farmhouse, I suggested, "Let's double the size of this lake" . . . and we did. We tapered it from four feet deep down by the road to twenty-four feet at the lower end. That was another funny experience!

The reason we enlarged it was that we were grading and landscaping around a new barn we had built and needed several thousand tons of fill to put around it. We reasoned, "Now we can 'kill two birds with one stone.' We'll double the size of our farm pond and get all the fill we need, and we won't waste the effort, time and cost of hauling it far. In this way, we'll get two things done at one time for the same amount of money."

Now, twenty-four feet is pretty deep! When we got down that far, you couldn't even see the earth pans and the bulldozer working.

Some neighbor boys came by one day and laughed and said, "Hey, Victor, do you think you'll get that full of water in twenty years?" They liked to needle me, and we always had fun.

"You might be right; it might take twenty!" I replied. "The Lord only knows."

Lo and behold! We finished digging it out on the last day of April. I remember disking and grading around it, raking it off and spreading grass seed. And you know, within three days it started to rain. It was the wettest spring we had in a long time. In three weeks, we had the pond filled twenty-four feet deep, so that it was actually spilling out a little bit over the overflow.

The same boys stopped by again to see me. "What did you know that we didn't?" they asked.

"Well," I answered, "you should know that Noah spent 120 years building the ark, and everyone laughed at him, but when the rains came, he was ready. I just knew by faith it was gonna fill up, but I didn't know when!"

That lake has been a real blessing. It has been used at least a dozen times for fire protection in our community . . . at the school, at a barn fire, a house fire . . . We put in several gates to make it more accessible. I even put stones all the way around it so fire trucks could drive in a circle and come in one way and leave by another.

One night about a million gallons of water were hauled out in a couple hours to save a barn that was burning. The barn was too far away to pipe water to it, so they trucked it. On the premises there was a big plastic swimming pool that could hold a truckload of water. As fast as the trucks came and pumped water out of our pond, they would haul it to their swimming pool, empty the water into the pool, and the fire trucks would pump it out on the fire. They did this over and over.

At that time a Catholic family was living in the farmhouse. During this process, the mother came down to the pond and was alarmed to see that the water level had dropped sixteen or eighteen inches. She said, "Victor, are you going to let them take all your water?"

"I don't think they will take it all," I replied confidently.

"I don't think I would give so much to them," she advised.

In response, I said, "Okay, I'll tell them to stop pumping if you will answer one question for me: If it were your house on fire, should I let them pump water out of our pond to save it?"

She smiled sheepishly and acknowledged, "You'd better just let them keep those pumps going."

Then I reminded her, "The Lord restores to us what we give. You watch; it will be filled up again in no time."

In less than a week, after a couple days of nice steady rain, the water level was up a foot and one-half.

Later, she stopped in especially to apologize and exclaimed, "Isn't that something . . . the way God rewards you! You gave up over a million gallons of water, and you have it all back in less than a week!"

And it was amazing! That summer and many times since, I have looked back and thought, "How could that happen?" God just performs one miracle after another! It never ceases.

I am so convinced that even when you make a mistake, if your heart is right, God will honor the mistake. If you get off the beaten path, but your heart is right, I believe God knows the intent of your heart and will honor it. The world may say your actions look like those of a fool, but God can turn things around so that you come out of the experience "smelling sweet as a rose." After you've experienced that a few times, you can just sit back and smile when people are critical and give you a hard time. This happened to me time after time. It was really amazing!

Since my farm pond turned out to be so successful, I approached a neighbor and said, "When I get time, I'd like to build two ponds on your farm to make it more beautiful, more valuable, more water accessible, and provide a few possibilities for recreation."

He looked at me with a doubtful and puzzled expression and said, "Well, that is going to cost you a lot of money."

But he did give me permission to do it. In essence, I spent $2,000 to $5,000 out of pocket, but one summer, during a dry spell, we used one of them for irrigation, so we got a little benefit out of it.

The funniest thing was that so many people, especially other neighbors, would say, "Why would you do that for that guy? He's such a miserable person."

"Well, we always got along with him okay," I explained, "and we like to go the second mile and even beyond. I know he appreciates it. He just doesn't have the ability to express it yet."

It all boils down to another "big-little" principle: "If you wanna get, you gotta give!" We must be reminded all the time about how sowing and reaping work. We want the harvest before we plant the seed or give anything. It doesn't work that way. Some people go through life and miss the whole blessing, all the joy of living, because they are either self-centered, or they are blinded to the right and wrong ways of doing something. We were taught to think for ourselves and be creative, and observed the parental example of always looking out for the other person, regardless of the cost to ourselves. That's what motivates us to do what might help somebody else and make life a little better. In my case, it was making a farm pond for somebody so that their family could enjoy it.

We only had one well on the farm and had over 500 head of cattle. One day I got to thinking, "I could be in trouble some day because I don't have a lot of water here." So, I built a 20x50 foot swimming pool, tapered from eight to ten feet deep, and put it up on the hill. I installed a two-inch gravity flow line so I could run water over the whole farm in case of an emergency. Our family used it as a swimming pool, and fortunately, never needed it for an emergency.

Later on, I dug another well so then I had two good wells that produced fifty gallons of water a minute. We still had the pool and were using it regularly. In time, it started to leak, so I put a liner in it, and we used it several more years.

One day we noticed that the liner had a crack in it, and all attempts to repair it failed. I called the company about the warranty, and they said it would cost $7,000 to redo it. Meanwhile, our children had gotten older. We did have the problem of neighbor children coming and using it, but that was fine with us.

However, one Saturday night when no one was home, a couple girls, whom we never knew, came here with some fellows. Both girls jumped into the pool, but the one didn't come out. The fellows finally were able to get her, but she almost drowned.

With the cracked liner and now with this happening, I remember saying to Grace, "We could spend $7,000 for a new liner, and the next day somebody could drown in here. Then we could be sued for a million dollars for negligence." I added, "Do you know what? We have two wells now so we don't need it anymore for a water supply." Besides that, Grace was doing all the dirty work for it, keeping it clean and in good shape, and there was a lot more work involved than I had ever anticipated.

I did a few calculations and told Grace, "With all the chemicals you have to buy and all the labor you put into it, we could afford to buy every neighbor a $75 ticket to the Community Swimming Pool where they have a lifeguard. They have strict regulations there and then we wouldn't have these worries. I am going to fill it up with ground."

By this time, we had a few grandchildren around and some small neighbor children and when they heard of my plan, they pleaded, "Oh, you shouldn't push the pool shut. It is too much fun!"

However, one morning I had trouble sleeping and got out of bed around 1:00 a.m. By daylight, I had the whole swimming pool bulldozed shut. By the time everyone woke up, I had it all leveled and graded. I knew that if those kids would show up, they would beg me not to do it, and I might break down, get softhearted, and give in to them. Doing it this way worked out well. It was a lot less work for Grace, a lot less responsibility, and a lot less liability. We seeded a lawn on it, and that was the end of it. It was one less headache.

In the late 60's and early 70's, people would farm thousands of acres and would plow every acre. One day I began thinking, "Why do we go through all these motions, spending all this money on labor, equipment and diesel fuel to do what God intended us to do—put seed in the ground and plant it?"

In 1972 I bought a big off-set disk, which would only cut in the ground about six inches. But again, being a little conservative, I tried using it on little areas at a time. For four years, I would plow one-fourth of my land, disk one-fourth of my land, and on one-fourth I practiced what was called "minimum tillage." For that, you would just plant the seed in the hard ground through a planter. On the last one-fourth, I used a chisel plow that would go down into the ground twelve to fourteen inches. This was the favorite way of the older farmers who believed, "You must help the plant heart to get a good crop." I never quite believed that though.

After my four-year experiment, I discovered that using the disk, the method on which I had spent the least time and money, produced as good a crop as any of the others. Through trial and error I discovered why.

The plow would always turn under all the residue creating a very nice-looking field. On the other hand, the disk, instead of burying it, would mix the trash, root zones, residue cornstalks, straw, liquid manure and whatever else. When all this residue was mixed with the top four inches of soil that really mattered, it worked like a sponge. When heavy rains fell, that soil was open just a little better. If you had a three-inch rain in an hour, there would be no run-off.

Through the years we raised approximately one-half to two-thirds of our roughage requirements with our main crop being no-till corn. I generally liked to disk the land one time before planting because of these advantages: better conservation, accepts rain more readily, no trash floating or accumulating in low areas of the fields, less chemicals are needed for weed control, no army worm problem, and in short, over-all easier management. The only other crop we raised was alfalfa mixed with orchard grass. We have not used a baler for years, as I discovered that two men can handle the same amount of haylage as four men can handle in bales.

Over the years, I've noticed that farmers often responded when some rich company salesman told them, "You've got to buy this new product or tool," such as the chisel plow which would go down into the ground twelve to fourteen inches, tearing up every limestone on the farm. Then they would have to spend a whole week picking up and hauling away rocks from the farm.

My experience was that if I could keep the limestone rocks in the soil, more moisture would be retained. When limestone rocks retain moisture, they are enhancing the productivity of the soil. You don't want to have the rocks in your top four inches of ground, though, or you will always be busting up your equipment.

What a contrast it was between our methods and those of the guys who used deep tillage tools. They would spend a whole week hauling rocks, dumping them in a stone quarry or along the fencerows. We would just disk the field one day, plant the corn the next day, and our corn was up before they got started. By harvest time, we had as good or better crop than anyone.

The farmhouse at the Villa Pine Farm with the pond in the foreground. I lived there from 1946 to 1970.

For five or ten years people kept telling me it wasn't going to work, but it HAS worked for 28 years, and we are still doing as well or better than anyone. (This is using a heavy, plate-like disk. We did have one 28 feet wide, but that was more for a farm of 500 to 1000 acres, and we scaled back a little. Now we use one that is 14 feet wide which cuts down 6 inches at the most.)

What we were most concerned about was the top 4 inches. What most people don't realize is that the "life" of the soil is in the top three or four inches.

This is where the soil life, the bacteria, live and where the sun, wind, rain and air hit. God created the sun, wind, air and bacteria, and it doesn't matter what you put in that top four inches, if you give the microbes time to work, many problems will be corrected.

A cornstalk will go down into the soil for eight to ten feet, while an alfalfa plant will go down as far as 18 to 20 feet. The root zones of these crops contain numerous web-like or hair-like branches, which all serve to aerate the soil.

They do the same job that farmers are spending thousands of dollars to get deep tillage and then paying laborers to haul away the rocks, taking away some of their water-holding capacity.

It wasn't that I was any smarter than anybody else, but I was willing to look and listen, and there was much Divine intervention. Things worked. It was so much fun seeing it work, and the more it worked, the more I wanted to try. When I was 35 or so years old, I loved to listen to the old 60 and 70-year-old farmers who said, "Aw, Victor, that ain't gonna work. When are you gonna learn?" That was fun!

Since I was active in promoting soil and water conservation on agricultural land, it always troubled me to see a farmer plowing downhill when I knew there was a better way that could have given him higher production. However, some farmers insisted on doing it the same way it's been done for the last hundred years.

Beginning when I was in high school, I took a keen interest in conserving the soil and water because they are God-given resources. If we don't take care of them, we could contaminate or destroy them, losing them for the use of the next generation. Courses in high school taught me better methods of protecting our water, our springs and our reservoirs. Most people take a pure and efficient water supply for granted. Their experience is that when they turn on the spigot, the water just flows. Until there is a serious drought, people don't even think about it.

As I took these courses, I applied what I was learning to our farm. I convinced my dad to let me try contour farming, which means that instead of plowing up and down a hill, one follows the contour of the land and you might have a long "S" curve. That makes such an amazing difference that I had a hard time believing it myself. I had to do it to prove it and also to prove it to Dad and to our neighbors.

I'll never forget that when we began doing it, once again some of the old-timers in the neighborhood warned my dad, "Your boy's going to ruin the whole farm!"

After we actually practiced contour farming for several years, they saw the results. What they didn't understand was that when one plows, cultivates, or uses a corn planter in a contour pattern, a little furrow or channel is created. It is all on the level, so when it rains, the water just stays and soaks in instead of running down into a valley and creating a flood. Even more valuable than that is that when the water stays, it is absorbed in the earth and is not carrying your topsoil away. During a dry summer, much more water remains on your sloped areas giving you better crops.

One time when I was cleaning a fence row, a neighbor stopped and yelled at me, "Hey, you gotta stop; you can't do that!"

"Okay, you tell me why, and I will stop," I responded.

"Well, I don't want all my topsoil down in your field," he answered, since my field was below his.

Nodding in agreement, I pointed out to him, "Well, it's already down. Here at the fence row it is six foot deep and up on the hill it is two inches."

Then it finally registered with him that he was doing it the wrong way, and I was able to convince him of the value in farming across the hill rather than up and down the hill.

Once again, we started our contour farming on a small scale, and every year we added more and more. Slowly, the neighboring farmers caught on, but it took a long time, like 10 or 20 years, before it was generally practiced. They would say that we had a few skipped corners. Traditionally, we'd start planting corn at one side of the field and continue planting across. Then we would finish with a whole bunch of short rows. However, when we planted in a contour, we farmed in 120 foot strips and planted around them. We finished with the excess short or odd rows in the middle. When we were harvesting, we didn't need to drive around the outside to get a couple short rows. Instead, we just spinned around, saving a lot of time, fuel, and excess wear on our equipment. It was amazing, but one only realized the difference after the fact.

Since I had such a love for the land, I enjoyed buying a farm nobody liked, one that was run-down and forsaken, and within three years, I could always double the production, if I did it right. After I got everything in order and working, it was fun hearing the neighbors talk about how nice it looked. When they commented about it, I told them, "In a sense it is just being good stewards. Stewardship is so important. Whether it is our own physical lives or the earth's resources, God created them and showed us the path to walk down, and it is our job to make it better for the next generation. If each one of us deteriorates it a little bit, and we keep doing that for ten generations, what future do they have to look forward to?" Of course, about this time, the government started getting involved in conservation also and began promoting it.

About 10 years ago the DER (Department of Environmental Resources) came into being. Their slogan of "Everything In Balance" is a great concept, but if it is carried too far, it tends to cause self-destruction.

One of the small farms I had bought just to rebuild and help it to recover was located near Bethel, PA. It was in a beautiful hollow where one could have made a perfect one-acre natural dam. I often drove over there after a heavy rain and watched all the water coming down through the valley and thought, "Boy, why don't we save all that water for fishing, wildlife, and above all, for fire protection?"

There was no water source in that community for several miles. If there had been a house or barn fire, there would have been no place to go for water.

So, I decided to build a small dam inside the road, using the road for a natural dam breast. My purpose for that was so that a fire truck could come down the road, drop a hose in the pond, and help somebody in an emergency. About three-fourths of an acre was flooded to about 12 to 14 feet deep, and it was working real nice.

Then I was approached by a man from the Pennsylvania Department of Environmental Resources who said a neighbor had complained because I had destroyed some wetlands. I never knew if that was true or not, but it could have been possible. They insisted that I had to lower the water level and this and that.

Another thing I had done was that in the streams on that particular farm, I had put in a pipe big enough to carry double the normal flow. If a 4-inch pipe would handle the normal flow, I'd put in an 8-inch pipe, so it could handle a heavy rain These pipes were put in a pasture area. It was interesting that when I put a pipe in at the one end of the farm, one in the middle, and one at the other end, the animals would always cross over on high ground.

One official threatened me by saying, "You must put everything back the way it was, and until you take those pipes out, we are going to fine you $10,000 per day."

I did not budge but replied, "I won't take them out, because that is so contrary to what's right! You don't understand that animals will not walk through muddy water unless you force them to do that. If you would understand 'cow psychology,' you would know that when animals are forced to go through the muddy water of a stream, 50 percent of them will stop and urinate or defecate and then walk on. That's polluting the water. The way I've designed this, that won't happen. All of that refuse stays on the land where it should be, helping to build the soil, protecting the water supply and making the whole community healthier."

I added, "Furthermore, if I'd do it your way and take a farm manure spreader through six or eight inches of water over a concrete pad, every time I'd do that 10 pounds of manure would wash off the tires. If you do that with 100 loads a year, and every farmer would do it that way, you'd get hundreds of tons of manure going into the Chesapeake Bay. And that's all because it is being done wrong!"

I kept arguing this position, from the point of common sense, and they said, "Well, that ain't what the books say. You've got to tear this out and do it differently. You're gonna have to change what you've done here!"

They sent me 12 to 15 registered letters reiterating the threat of the $10,000 per day fine and even threatening me with a jail term. At one point, they sent three people out to the farm, and I explained it all to them again.

On this particular time, one member of the team was a young woman who had just graduated from Delaware Valley College having majored in agricultural conservation practices. After hearing my story, although she was a trainee, so to speak, she turned to the two officials, her bosses, and said, "You know, Mr. Ziegler is doing everything right!"

Although I could see that they were irritated at her because she wouldn't listen and be quiet, I responded, "Well, I know it, because I have been observing and practicing this ever since I was in high school."

However, the two officials would not back down.

I continued, "Well, it's as simple as this. I am not going to pay the $10,000 a day fine, but I'd be happy to go to jail for you guys! I have spent 20 some years supporting prison ministries, and that way I'd have a legitimate excuse to check the system from the inside out! I know one thing: I'd only be in for one night. The next day I'd be out again, and when I tell my side of the story, if you don't back down, you guys will be in for life! I can prove what I am saying, but you can't."

Finally, they did soften up a little bit. They called me to a hearing in Harrisburg where there were five people accusing me along with the woman attorney representing them. When I entered the room, she said, "Mr. Ziegler, don't you have an attorney to represent you?"

"Nobody told me I had to. I wasn't aware that I needed an attorney," I replied.

Shrugging her shoulders, she commented, "Oh, well, legally you don't have to have one. You can represent yourself."

Then I asked her, "Tell me, ma'am, why would I pay $100 an hour to hire an attorney who only knows half as much as I do about this situation? He couldn't answer any questions. I have studied this since I was in high school, and have put these principles into practice for the last 50 years. I have built farm ponds, rebuilt springs, and corrected waterways from the seat of my own bulldozer. We have accomplished so many things, and there's not a question that you can ask me about soil and water conservation that I won't be able to answer or defend."

After much discussion, I finally asked, "What can I do to appease you guys? If I need a $50 permit, just tell me."

"Well, that dam you built is two feet too high, so we're going to get an engineer to redesign it," they replied.

I conceded, "If that would make you happy, I'll do that much for you."

I'd had that dam built and working beautifully for three years prior to this, but I fulfilled my promise, and we spent $400 to have a licensed engineer redesign it. Lo and behold! The first flood we had tore the whole dam out!

That had never happened before. I had lined it with heavy rocks as a spillway and the like, and it had worked fine. I wasn't going to let that rest. I told them, "We did it your way, and it didn't work. Now, I will do it all over again my way! There are certain times when you just have to use plain common sense, and this time, you missed it. I knew it wouldn't work, but I was willing to waste my time and money just to get you guys to learn something!"

We continued our discussion, and after I agreed to do a few little things, they said, "Well, if you are going to do that, we are willing to drop all the charges."

One should always give and take a little bit where it doesn't really matter so that the other person feels a little better when he walks away. I have always tried to do that. My goal was never to make a professional person look like a fool but to make them think so that they can do a better job next time. I tried to maintain a friendly demeanor, but of course, all the while, I was praying between my smiles. I kept reminding myself that "a soft answer turneth away wrath." (Proverbs 15:1a, KJV) After all, I didn't want to make any enemies.

When the case was dismissed, I went around shaking hands and thanking all these people. I shook hands with the woman attorney last telling her, "You know, I am so glad that you called me in, because now I have five new friends!" They weren't sure how to react to that or even if they should return my smile or not, but it worked. I told them I supported their cause 100% and that I am very much for regulations. I don't want anybody dumping chemicals and manure in a stream or creek and polluting everything. We must all work together to see that they get cleaned up.

Of course, word about this case got around. Over the years I got calls from different farmers and landowners facing similar opposition in several counties. The last one was only a year or two ago and involved a young Mennonite farmer who had built a beautiful farm pond. The DER (Department of Environmental Resources) came in about a year later and told him he had to bulldoze half of it shut because he got into a little wetland at the one end. He was being threatened with fines through numerous registered letters, just as I had been, and he got shook up and called me.

"Just sit tight," I advised. "They are not going to move fast. They are kinda afraid."

He asked me if I would go along with him to his hearing and represent him, as he didn't want to hire an attorney, and I agreed to do it.

After some discussion at the hearing, one of the DER officials said to me, "Where did I meet you before?" He was one of the guys who had been present at my hearing four or five years earlier, and he finally recognized me.

I said to him, "Do you know what's interesting? This guy took an old mud hole and made a beautiful three-fourth acre lake for fire protection, fish, recreation and beauty. You want to make him spend all his money, push it shut, and do it over because you said he got in a little wetland. Previously, he had one inch of muddy water, but now he has nine feet of fresh, clear water. He made more wetland and is saving more water. Furthermore, if you guys insist that he push it shut and make it the way it was, we're going to take you to law. If the legislators would know what's going on, you would all be locked up. Mosquitoes breed in a swampland; everybody knows that. This man took one-half acre of swampland, converted it to a fresh water supply, planted nice grass around it and got rid of all the mosquito nests.

"In one state organization we are paying people $50,000 per person in salaries to eliminate mosquitoes. To do it, they are spraying swamps, cleaning up piles of old tires where mosquitoes breed, and that's all right. Here you have a guy who did it voluntarily, and you are penalizing him for it! You ought to go to jail for advocating the breeding of mosquitoes!"

I have often thought I would enjoy being my own attorney in court. I know I'd win because one never loses when his argument is plain common sense. It's when they bring in all that technical stuff that a person becomes confused. The sad part is that most people are afraid to defend themselves. Every time I get cornered, I think of another Biblical principle: "Ye shall know the truth, and the truth shall make you free." (John 8:32, KJV) And it works every time if you are willing to go through the mill and sweat it out. If I were the attorney, I'd say, "The reason you have this trouble is because you don't know the truth. I am going to share it with you and then we'll all be all right."

When they raised the question about why I feel so strongly about protecting the environment, I said, "Well, I want this country to be a better place when I leave than when I came."

When I sat in high school, I saw some of my older friends go off to fight for this country in World War II and some of them didn't come back. I'll never forget that.

Chapter Five

Buying and Selling Farms

"If you have everything to gain and nothing to lose, DO IT!" —Victor K. Ziegler

An old auctioneer was in the hospital, and as a Christian friend, I paid him a visit. During our conversation, he asked me, "Victor, are you going to the farm sale next Monday?"

"I wasn't planning to," I answered.

"You ought to be there. That's a good farm, and you really ought to look at it," he advised.

Because he said that, and since I loved the land, I felt *I had to look at it.* I never told Grace about this farm, because I never really intended to buy it. Grace and I very seldom went shopping together, but that Saturday afternoon we did go to Lebanon for something and on the way home, I asked Grace, "Would it be okay if I'd just take 15 minutes to swing in here and make a quick U-turn to look at this place?" Of course, I was never in the farmstead itself.

Suspecting my intent, she replied, "What do you want to do that for? You don't want to buy another farm."

"I know that, but it's fun to look, and the time to look is before it's sold. It's just like getting married. You look around first and then decide which one is your wife-to-be!"

So, she smiled and cautiously agreed, and I didn't say much more about it.

On the day of the sale, we were in the midst of harvesting corn as it was in the fall of the year. At lunchtime, I said to my boys and two other men who were helping me, "Take an hour break. I'm going over to a farm sale, but I'll be back in one or two hours, depending on how it goes."

I ran over to my pickup truck and jumped in. I noticed my dad was out back cleaning up, and I called to him, "Hey, Pop, jump in my truck and go along with me to the sale. We want to see if they sell this farm."

When we were driving down the lane, Pop reminded me, "Now Victor, remember, we are going to *look;* we're not going to *buy* anything!"

"Okay, we'll just look," I responded.

When we arrived, I must confess that I was thinking that if that farm didn't bring $130,000, it would be going cheap, kind of a "steal," a give-away. So, when my dad wasn't around, I told the auctioneer that if I wanted to bid on the farm, I'd have a toothpick in my mouth. He said, "We're going to put spoons up for sale in ten minutes, but I'm going to go to town and get a pack of toothpicks in case you get nervous and drop yours, and then I'll give you another one." He had a little sense of humor.

When it came time to sell the farm, the bids were slow in coming, so the auctioneer came up to me and said, "Even if you aren't going to buy it, at least help me start it."

So I said, "Yeah, start it out at $90,000."

"Okay," he replied gratefully, and the sale began. Meanwhile, I walked through the crowd, visiting with people for the next hour, and seemingly ignored what was going on. The bids got to $120,000, $122,000 and $124,000, and started to slow down. I thought, "Boy, I wonder if it ain't going to make it to $130,000!" When the bid reached $127,000, nobody would budge, so I said to my Pop, "I'm ready to go."

But, before I got in my truck, I put the toothpick in my mouth and looked at the auctioneer, and he quickly called out $128,000! We got in the truck and started driving out the lane. I thought surely my bid would motivate someone else to top that. We drove past the house and could still hear clearly the echo of the auctioneer's call. I stopped the truck and rolled the window down.

"What are we waiting for?" Pop asked.

"Well, that $128,000 was my bid," and I looked at him and smiled.

"Really?"

"Yeah." I parked the truck in back of the house on the lawn as there were cars parked all over the place. I decided I'd better walk around and see what was happening. The auctioneer was struggling for a few minutes as he was ready to knock it off as sold, but couldn't find me. When I came around the house, I saw his face light up. He was afraid I had gone home.

He said, "It's going, this is your last chance. I'm calling one more time, and then it will be sold in thirty seconds." After giving everyone a fair warning and an upward fling of his arm, he shouted, "Sold!"

He didn't announce my name, although by that time, he knew who I was. It was really only the second time I had ever met the auctioneer, John Martin, so we had no prior personal relationship.

When I went to see him, he said, "Boy, Victor, you had me sweating for awhile." (He could have been accused of taking a false bid, you know.)

"No," I assured him, "I wouldn't do that to you."

I walked by some fellows who were discussing the sale, and I heard one rich guy from Philadelphia say, "Starting the bidding at $90,000 was the dumbest thing that auctioneer could have done. He scared all the bidders off by starting so high! He should have started lower and got them all cranked up."

But he didn't know much about farming.

Finally, you know how they do, the auctioneer introduced the buyer.

A couple guys said, "How were *you* bidding? You were talking to us all the time." So, we had a lot of fun out of it.

Because I had a line of credit at the bank, I was able to give a check for 10% of the cost. Although I hadn't really talked to any bank about it, I knew just about where I stood and what my limits were. We settled for it in the next week or two.

We had that farm for five years, fixed it up, cleaned it up, and remodeled the house. I bought it for $128,000 and sold it for $325,000, but I spent about $150,000 improving it. Over the five-year period, I only made about $40,000 to $50,000 on it, which wasn't a big deal. Figuring in my time, if I would have charged for that, I would have had barely $25,000. Be that as it may, I was enjoying it.

When I was ready to sell that one, I had it priced originally at $350,000. A young man, whose father lived in Lebanon, wanted to start farming and came to inquire about the farm. He and his wife seemed to me to be a young couple who were honest, hardworking but struggling to make ends meet.

I decided to make them an offer and said to them, "Do you know what? If you want to buy the farm and pay me off with no strings attached, I'll sell it to you for $325,000 so you can get started."

"I'll have to talk it over with my dad," he said. He was working with his dad, sharing livestock and equipment, just like I began farming in partnership with my dad.

Soon after that, I received a phone call from his dad, Myron King, who surprised me by saying, "Hey, Victor, I want to sell *my* farm where my son and I have been working."

He wanted $485,000 for it, and I declined, saying, "$485,000 is just too steep for me at this point. I would have to get too much money from the bank, and I don't want to pay all that interest."

"Well," he persisted, "why don't we do it without getting any money out of the bank? I don't need the money." Then he gave me a good interest offer in that he suggested just deducting the mortgage for his son's farm of $325,000, and leaving the rest of the money in it at whatever interest rate I would want to make it work.

His offer sounded so fair to me that I accepted it! So, within two weeks after selling that farm, I owned another one!

We were debating how we were going to get the paperwork done for the IRS to make everything look right. Then I said, "I can't give you a $100,000 check because that is too much for me to ask for at the bank in one lump, you know. But what I *can* do is give you a $100,000 down payment if you'll give me a $100,000 loan for 30 days, and he said, 'I'll do that.'"

A few moments later, he looked at me with a puzzled expression and asked, "How's that going to work? If you give me a check of $100,000 and I give you a check of $100,000, that's going to raise a red flag at the bank."

I explained that it *would* work, only that we couldn't go to the bank on the same day. A person can deposit $100,000 and then later write a check for the same amount, providing the deposit has been processed first. The bank will give a grace period of several hours in between.

Still hesitating, he said, "This isn't going to work, Victor. One of us will end up being charged with fraud or something."

"No," I assured him again. "It *will* work." We did it and the bank teller just smiled.

Over the next 10 years, I made payments to him, and the last one I gave him was when he was on his deathbed. I visited him in the hospital and he was dying of heart disease or cancer . . . I forget which. He was an Old Amish Mennonite and was only about 75 years old.

After I had visited and prayed with him, I said, "Well, Mr. King, I don't know when I'll get back again, but one thing

I know. We *will* meet again, either here, over there, or in the air with the Lord, you know."

His wife followed me out in the hall and whispered to me tearfully, "Victor, I have a $25,000 hospital bill still to be paid and we have no insurance."

I could tell she was really worried about this, so I asked, "Mrs. King, are you aware that I still owe you a little *more* than $25,000, and the final payment is due within six months?"

"Myron usually took care of all that, and I didn't even look at his accounts," she explained.

So I said, "Mrs. King, I'll tell you what. When you get home tonight, give me a phone call, and I'll come over and give you a check for $25,600, or whatever the exact amount is, and then you can pay the hospital bill and sign off for the farm."

So, that's what we did, and oh, she was as happy as a lark. She was so relieved that it had all worked out so well. For her peace of mind, she needed the bill paid, not the money. She assured me she had enough to live on comfortably.

One day, in reading a farm magazine, I saw that there was to be a bankruptcy sale near Huntingdon, Pennsylvania. The name of the man whose farm was being sold was "Ziegler," which caught my attention. So, on the day of the sale, I decided to take the day off and told Grace, "I think I'm going to that sale."

Enroute to the sale, I stopped at Philhaven, a Christian mental health facility, to visit a friend of mine from Franklin County who was a patient there recovering from a nervous breakdown. During my visit, he said to me, "Well, Victor, you are always up to something. What's next for today?"

"I'm on my way to a farm sale where a poor family is being sold out. I don't know if I can do anything more than give them a word of encouragement as I sure don't have any money right now," I replied. (I had just spent a couple hundred thousand dollars!) I added, "It's just kinda fun to watch and makes my day, even if I don't spend one dollar. I'm just going there to stop, look, and listen and see what I can do. Maybe at least I can give them a little encouragement and hope so they can see the light at the end of the tunnel after everything has seemed to go wrong."

Then he really shocked me. He said, "Well, Victor, you've got the time, and I've got the money."

And do you know what he did next? There in the hospital, he wrote out a check with my name on it for the amount of $200,000 saying, "Here, take this along in case you see an opportunity to help somebody."

There were no strings attached. No conditions. Then I *really* got nervous! He and his wife were a nice Brethren in Christ couple and we had visited in their home several times. I took the check because I didn't want to reject him.

The day went on and I attended the sale. Things went smoothly and I didn't see a desperate need there. When I got home that night, I said to Grace, "Do you know what? You're not going to believe this, but I have a check for $200,000 in my pocket!"

Of course, she was shocked, and I told her what had happened concluding, "I'm wondering about this. There are two things that don't add up. First of all, the guy is in a mental hospital. Secondly, his wife's name ain't on it."

If he would have signed it, she, too, should have signed it, adding the note "memo to be used at your discretion." That would have been okay. Otherwise, his wife could have contested it at some point in the future.

"I just don't feel *right* about this," I said. "I'm going to tear up this check and tomorrow morning I'll call up his wife and tell her about it."

It was about 10:30 at night, and right after I said that, our phone rang. It was this man's wife and she said, "Oh, Victor, *I am so glad* I got a hold of you. My husband wrote you a check for $200,000, and that thing'll bounce! However, we do have that much in stocks and bonds which we could cash in if necessary."

"Well, I stuck it in my pocket, and after I thought it through, I decided I wasn't going to act upon it without talking to you or your son," I assured her. "Your husband has a heart of gold and meant well, but was just under stress. I'm so glad you called. I'll tear the check in half and write 'Void' on it, put the pieces in an envelope and send them to you."

"Oh, thank you!" she said gratefully. "I'll surely sleep much better tonight!"

Since then, we visit them about once a year, but we never talk about that incident. He never gave me a smaller amount, nor did I ever ask him to give me anything toward any charitable cause.

Since then, when I thought about that incident, I had mixed feelings. First of all, it warmed my heart because, in a sense, he was giving me a vote of confidence. But secondly, it made me sweat because of the tremendous responsibility that he placed on me. People are sensitive when it comes to their pocketbook. Therefore, I didn't want to do anything that would destroy my integrity causing people to lose faith in me.

In an extreme case like that, I would always think about the verse, "There is wisdom in the counsel of many" (paraphrasing Proverbs 15:22). Then I would check with two or three friends for their input before deciding what action I should take.

We have to be aware that there is a constant tug of war going on between the Lord and the devil. When you move with that volume of cash, you don't want to yield to temptation and let the devil get his foot in the door. You have to weigh your actions carefully or he'll destroy you, take all your own savings, all your friends, and destroy your reputation. That's why at times you must move awfully slow. *It is one thing to bump your head, but it is another thing to have a fatal crash. In a fatal crash, there are no second chances!*

I can honestly say I never lost an hour's sleep over financial matters. When I went to bed, I would just pray, "Lord, you got to tell me what to do as I *have to act* on this tomorrow." If there were no definite answer or no strong feeling of direction, I would just sit on it for a couple days. I'd always say, *"You never make a drastic move unless the house is on fire or it is life threatening!"* You *might have to* throw a child out of a window if he is going to die . . . *to save him*, but you don't do that when it is not necessary. Events like this sure did add excitement to my life!

In the mid-1980's, the interest rate kept climbing from 8% to 10% and for a period of time was as high as 20%. About that time, I heard that a beautiful farm in a valley in Bedford County was being sold. I knew there was excellent farmland in this area because my brother, Earl, had been a pastor near there thirty years earlier and had taken me around. The property being considered was called the Baker farm and consisted of three farms totaling 380 acres which were to be sold at a "sheriff sale" or bankruptcy sale.

I phoned a friend of mine, Bob Baker, who had moved east from that area and asked, "Are you familiar with this farm?"

"Yes, I was born on the adjoining farm," he replied, adding, "I know where every fencerow and everything is on that farm."

"Well, I'd like to take a day off and go to that sale and see what happens," I said and invited him to go along with me.

We left in the morning at 5:00, driving west on the turnpike. Enroute Bob asked, "Are you interested in buying the farm?"

"No, not really," I answered truthfully. "Interest rates are so wild right now. It would have to be unusual before I'd be interested or even consider it."

We stopped to have breakfast at one of the restaurants along the turnpike, and were just finishing eating when two men entered. I recognized the one as Mark Bushong, whom I'd learned to know when he worked in public relations for Elizabethtown College but was now working for a Pennsylvania bank. His companion, I discovered, was the loan officer who was responsible for the farm that was to be sold.

When I saw Mark, I said, "What in the world are you two guys doing? I can't believe that two bankers are out at 5:30 in the morning!"

Mark instantly replied, "I was just telling my buddy here, I hope Victor's going to be at the sale. It might help us."

"We're just going to look and listen."

"Well, then, we'll see you out there," they responded.

When we arrived, we discovered the owner had just spent $100,000 remodeling the whole house, the swimming pool, and had just put in a whole new dairy system costing half a million dollars. He had installed an elevated milking parlor, built three of the big expensive blue silos, and everything one might want . . . and then went broke!

Some guy, a short, stocky fellow about 55 years old and wearing a crew cut, came to test me by asking, "Hey, Victor, what's this farm going to bring today?"

I responded with a question, "Do you want to know what it's going to sell for or what it's worth?"

"What do you mean?"

"Well, it's not going to sell for what it's worth for several key reasons. First of all, there's the current farm economy. We've just had two or three years that were very dry, so some guys have only had a 50% crop, and some even just 30%. Those guys are hurting a little bit. And then there's the problem of the high interest rates. I think the combination of the economy, the drought, and the interest rates will kill the sale. Farmers are tired of sweating, digging holes and scratching to make a living and then giving all their money to the bank. They're all going to sit tight for a year or two and see what happens. I think it might bring about $400,000, and I've heard they need $600,000 to pay off their bank."

And that's exactly what happened.

When an auctioneer has three farms to sell, they first try to sell one, and then the other, holding the bid and trying to put them together, and that's what they tried here. I wasn't going to bid up each individual parcel because that would have made the total package higher. So, I just watched everybody, and they bid them up until it was announced that they would sell them individually for a total of $398,000 unless they got a bid of $200,000 or more for the whole package. In other words, they would sell the three farms together to one person, but don't bid unless you have at least a $200,000 offer. If they get none, they will sell the farms individually. He tried for 15 minutes, but nobody bid.

When I saw he was winding down, I caught his eye and nodded and he said, "$400,000!" I thought surely somebody would make a bid then, but everyone got quiet. He tried for another 15 minutes to get a higher bid, checked with someone in the house, and came out and said, "It's sold for $400,000."

Then I had three more farms with 380 acres in Bedford County!

However, the day wasn't over yet. I always looked in my wallet whenever I went far from home, and I knew I only had $10 in cash, but I knew I had my checkbook in my pocket. When I looked in my checkbook, I had only one check left. I laid the checkbook on the hood of my car and wrote the check for $40,000 or 10%. When I raised my hand after writing the check, didn't the wind bring a little gust that blew the check up in the air! I had no idea where it went! I bowed my head down against the hood of the car and prayed, "Lord, I'm in trouble. Help me to know what to do. I know Mark Bushong knows me and can vouch for me, but this is *so* embarrassing. What am I going to do? I have no more cash and no more checks. I have nothing to give them to pay for these farms."

As I raised my head from praying, a young fellow about 25 years old walked past. He walked with a very noticeable limp, as though he had been crippled by polio. Coming closer, he said, "Hey, Sir, did you lose a paper? There's a piece of paper down under your car, right about in the area of the transmission."

Of course, I couldn't burst out with a loud shout but under my breath I said, "Praise the Lord! Thank You, Lord, for saving me again from a terrible disaster!"

So, with the check in hand, I went in and made the down payment. When I came out, a young female news reporter from the Bedford Gazette said, "Are you the man who bought the farm?"

"That's what they tell me."

"May I ask you a few questions?"

"Yeah, I'll answer anything I can."

"Do you plan to move your family here?" she asked.

"Well, you're not going to believe this," I replied, "but I came today with *no plans*. Back home I already have several farms, and I don't really *need* another one. However, this is a beautiful farm with lots of potential, and two years from now someone will wish they had bought it today." I added, "I know one thing: my youngest son would be interested in moving here if I would give him that opportunity, but right now, I really have no plans. Within a week, I'll know."

When the reporter left, another fellow approached me. "Victor, would you consider selling this farm?"

"Well," I said, somewhat curious, "I wouldn't know why not; I don't *really* need it. What do you have in mind?"

"I know a guy in Lancaster County who would buy it, so what do you want for it?"

I said, "Well, if I go back to Lancaster and Lebanon

Counties and make ten phone calls, by tomorrow I can get $50,000 more for it than what I paid today." (I found out later he had just started in the real estate business and was struggling so much he didn't have enough income to feed his family or pay his rent!)

Continuing my conversation with him, I added, "I'll tell you what. I always believe in 'living and let live.' So, if you come up with $25,000 within 24 hours, I'll sign off if I have no more obligations."

Eagerly he said, "Okay, will you wait here for ten minutes?"

He went into the house and made a phone call to the fellow who wanted the farm. That guy told him he'd give $450,000 for it, so the salesman got $25,000 and I got $25,000. Before we parted, I reminded him, "This agreement is only in effect for the next 24 hours. If somebody–you, your agent, the purchasing guy or someone from your bank–doesn't show up at my house with a check for $25,000 by 12:00 noon tomorrow, the deal is off, and I am going to settle for it and we'll go on from there."

He showed up at 11:00 a.m. the next day with the check. We signed all the papers, and he took it and went, and this was the beginning of November.

The interesting thing was that just a week before that I had said to Grace, "We still have over $12,000 of good faith commitments to make up for this year and we don't have the cash flow to handle it. What are we going to do about this?" In only about 72 hours later, I had this check for $25,000!

That night I sat down and wrote checks for over $12,000 to charities and missions, $7,000 to the internal revenue, and I had about $6,000 left for myself. That was pretty good for one day's work! If that hadn't happened, I would never have been able to pay those commitments in that year because we were paying too much in interest and it had been a dry year. As it was, we paid all our commitments in one day! It was amazing how it worked out. This was just another instance of God's miracles in my life.

About three years later a local realtor called me and said, "Hey, Victor, you're good at cleaning a place up and doubling its production in three years. You ought to buy this farm north of Myerstown in Berks County and make something out of it."

Being uninterested, I said, "Naw, sell it to the family or the neighbors. If neither the family nor any of the neighbors will buy it, you can let me know."

A week later he reported that he had talked to the family and none of them had any interest in it. One neighbor showed interest but couldn't buy it because his bank wouldn't give him a loan. So I asked, "What do you want for it?"

"We're asking for $450,000 for 330 acres."

"Okay, I'll tell you what," I said. "I'll give you $400,000 if you're willing to come down to that." The owner was an old man who drove an old truck and hauled stone, but just never did do very well at farming. His wife had passed away, so he was ready to sell.

So, I bought it. In less than 30 days after we had started to farm it in the fall, the former owner's daughter, a member of the Old Dunkard Brethren Church, phoned me one day. "Victor, I heard you bought my dad's farm, and I've been waiting for 20 years for that farm," she said almost accusingly.

"Oh, my goodness!" I said, quite surprised. "What happened? I was told no family members were interested."

"Well, yeah, but I *was!*" she continued.

"I don't want to take it away from the family," I replied, suggesting, "why don't I *sell* it to you?"

By the time they decided they wanted it, I had already spent almost $175,000 in starting to fix it up. I had put 1,200 tons of lime on the ground, and spent $80,000 in tile lines to drain all the wet spots. (Tile lines are 4- to 6-inch perforated underground pipe that will siphon the water out of a wet spot in a field and take it down to the creek without making a mud hole in the middle of the field. I knew this technique worked so I decided to install it and had spent a lot of money in doing it.)

Early in the spring they came around and told me, "We want it now." I told them I would be willing to sell it to them for the cost plus what I had put into it, and they agreed to that.

That evening at home, I got out all my bills and added them together and determined that I would charge them $590,000.

When I informed her of this, she responded, "Oh, I didn't think we'd have to pay that much!"

"You don't *have to*; I can continue farming it," I countered.

They didn't want to consider that option, but were determined to buy it, so they gave me a check for $59,000 as their down payment. We agreed we would have final settlement on May 1 the following spring.

I didn't hear a word from them until the next April 28th. When driving past their place, I stopped and said, "You *are remembering* that in two days we'll be getting together for the settlement?"

"Oh, that's right! We have to go to the bank and see if we can get some money," they replied.

I thought, "In two days?" And then I knew I was in big trouble.

He never did show up for settlement, and he never told me he wouldn't be coming. I called him and said, "You might as well cancel the settlement." I had already checked with some of his neighbors and was told he hadn't been able to get any money.

So, we started making hay and planting corn. While we were doing those things, he stopped by one day and declared he really was serious about wanting to get the farm.

"That's okay with me," I told him. "If you get the money, I don't want to take the farm away from you."

He started harvesting a few crops, but all his promises fell through. The bank told me they would let the money in the farm for me, but not for him, because they knew it was beyond his farming abilities. He practically begged me to leave the money in it, but I told him, "If I had a half million dollars *to waste*, I might consider it. Right now, I just can't do that."

They were really disappointed and felt bad. It seemed they couldn't accept the fact mentally that they couldn't have it. One day I had to go to the farm and actually tell him to leave.

"Aren't you going to let me make the hay?" he pleaded.

"No. You didn't buy the farm!" I declared. He was just dumbfounded and *very* shook up.

We farmed it all that summer. The interest rates continued to rise from 20%, to 21%, and finally as high as 22%. In the meantime, I had bought another farm at Prescott for $500,000, and I decided I am *not* going to pay all this interest. With both farms, I would have been paying 22% interest on a million dollars!

One day I got an idea and approached this man again and suggested, "I know your brother who lives in York County owns three or four farms. Why don't you get your brother to help you?"

"He won't," was his terse response.

I said maybe the two of us could go over and visit him, and we did. The brother responded, "Aw, Victor, *you* finance it for him."

"I can't," I declared honestly. "I'm using the bank's money. You finance things with *your own* money, but I can't."

Finally, his brother said that if I would drop the price $50,000, he would take over the payments, so I lowered the price. When I got home, Grace said, "Why would you lose that much money on that big farm?"

"Well, interest rates at 22% eat you up in a short time. If the interest stays at that rate, in just two years it would have cost us over $50,000 in interest alone," I explained. I added, "We'd be spinning our wheels, working hard, and this way I'll just be losing a lot of work I put into that place. It's not like we are losing a lot of cash."

So, I sold it, and we finally got out of that transaction. Everybody called me and said, "You must have made $200,000 on that farm!" (They remembered that I had bought it for $400,000 and sold it for almost $600,000. They didn't know that I had come down $50,000 and *gave* them all those expenses free, so to speak.)

"You can think what you want to, but that's the way it is," I would say. People who were never caught in circumstances like that just didn't comprehend it or "get it." They just see the glitter as it shines on the surface.

The most interesting aspect of that whole situation was that after this guy's wife died, he hired a 38-year-old housekeeper. Although she was a good housekeeper, all the neighbors said, "We guess you are aware that she has a few marbles missing." Although she was clean as a pin, you didn't have to talk to her long to realize that she was slow mentally.

Within two weeks after she found out that he had finally been able to get the $400,000, she married him! Now *she* owned half the farm, as she was entitled to $200,000 bucks the very day she married him, so she was pretty smart after all.

Another interesting episode occurred when I went down to northern Berks County and bought a farm from a bank. That one was a beautiful 138 acre dairy farm owned by a 65-year-old man whose bank was foreclosing on him. The realtor said that the farmer could not approve or refuse any offers, and I was to deal only with him and the bank. When they stated the amount they wanted, I made an offer. Soon the realtor called and said that the bank accepted it.

Then I discovered that the owner had been born and raised on that farm and was presently living in a mobile home on the farm property. I thought to myself: "How do I put an old man out like that without upsetting him and the neighborhood?"

I told him, "You can keep your mobile home. I'll move it to a one-acre tract across the road, hook up water and sewage for you, and it'll be yours as long as you live. When you or your wife leave the grounds, either by moving or by death, it'll revert back to the farm." So, that's what we did.

The interesting thing was that this was the very same guy who 35 years earlier had driven past our home farm and remarked, "That Ziegler boy isn't going to make it in farming!"

He was a real stubborn guy. He used to come to me and complain, "Hey, Ziegler, that new guy you sold the farm to ain't treatin' me right."

I finally had to tell him, "I told you to stay on *your* side of the road. If you don't, I'm gonna come down and *put* you over there! Those new buyers are a good young couple and they want to help you, so don't abuse them!"

After that, he didn't cause any more trouble for them, and they actually became best friends. They both have died since, but that was quite an interesting experience.

About 20 years ago, I decided to take a day off and jumped in my car and drove around New York State just sightseeing, looking at land, talking to people, farmers, or businessmen, just loving life and learning. I stopped at a realtor's office, and he invited me in. He was a very friendly guy, about 50 years old, and I introduced myself. Then he said, "Well, Victor, what can I do for you?"

"I don't know," was my honest answer. "I'm just sort of on a hunting mission, looking for a 'learning experience' and trying to find out what is available around here. I don't have a thing in mind *at the moment*, but I always know there are people who are looking for help, encouragement or direction."

We spent a whole day together. When I left him about 9:00 p.m., he said, "Well, I hope you return sometime. We could use a few Pennsylvania farmers and businessmen up here."

Approximately a year and a half later, I got a call from a stranger, Jim Keiper. Apparently, Jim and his wife had been traveling in New York state in approximately the same area where I had been sightseeing, looking at farms, lands, and opportunities. They found a farm which was owned by the FHA (Federal Housing Authority), a government agency. Although it had failed and been repossessed, they thought it seemed like a nice farm, especially since it had over 250 acres and its selling price was only $67,000. To a Pennsylvania farmer, that sounded cheap, and they got my full attention.

However, in New York State, the taxes are double and there are other differences also. Since they had enough money for the down payment, this couple had paid it, making a commitment to the FHA.

Ten days later, after they were back home, they received a letter from the FHA stating that they couldn't accept the down payment because they had changed their position and now had to have the full $67,000 before the buyer could take possession. They were discouraged.

If they hadn't happened to meet the same realtor . . . not "happened," it must have been *God-ordained,* in fact, the way it all ended I KNOW it was *no coincidence.* This realtor was on the phone with them one night and said, "Do you know what? About two years ago there was a guy here from near Lebanon, Pennsylvania, and I spent almost a day with him. Did we ever have interesting conversations! I think it might be helpful for you to talk with him." From his filing cabinet, he got my phone number and gave it to them.

It turned out that this couple lived in Middletown, Pennsylvania, and their situation was that their father's farm was being sold for a golf course at a price of $600,000 which they couldn't begin to touch. They had been driving around searching, found this farm in New York State, located this realtor who gave them my name, and as a result, I got this interesting phone call. Jim told me that the realtor had suggested to them that I might be able to give them some ideas of how they might be able to buy this farm.

"Is this farm in New York *really* what you want?" I asked. "Are you *sure?*"

"Yeah, we think so," he assured me.

"Okay, why don't you bring all the soil maps, the tax records, and everything related to the property to my house some night and we'll look it over together. Maybe we can come up with a creative idea that will work for you." (Soil maps tell you the type of soil on various parts of the property–low grade, medium grade, high grade–or around here in Pennsylvania, it might say Hagerstown limestone, which is the #1 grade, a deep, rich limestone soil. In New York State it was various kinds of loam, but I could never memorize them all.)

About 7:00 that same evening, they arrived at my house with all the information and stayed until 11:30 p.m. I examined it and concluded, "It looks like you couldn't possibly go wrong. If I were your age, (they were about 28 years old), I'd go by my own philosophy: *"If you have everything to gain and not much to lose, DO IT!"*

Still slightly doubtful, they hesitated and said, "But we're not quite in a position financially to get any bank to make it happen."

In my own case, I didn't have the cash either, but I *did* have the credit.

"I'll tell you what," I said. "I will go along with you to New York and we'll physically look at everything. However, from what I see on these papers and the little bit of knowledge that I *do* have, it *should work* and not harm either of us. I don't want to be a part of any deal where I'd say 'Yeah, it looks good,' and then I'd go home and later you guys are left there struggling or in a 'sink or swim' situation."

So, one morning they picked me up at 3:00, and we headed for New York. I had told them to inform the real estate office that if everything seems in order, by 3:00 p.m. we'd be ready to settle 100% for the $67,000, paid in full. In looking over the place with the realtor, we discovered the old barn was not in the best shape. The old three-story house had a New York flat roof, intentionally built that way so the snow would pile on top and serve as insulation to keep them warm. On seeing it, I said, "If I were doing it, I'd take a chainsaw and knock off the whole third floor and put a nice peaked roof on the house. It would be very economical, and with the amount of insulation today, it is no longer necessary to insulate with snow." We did a few more calculations and everything seemed set to go, so that afternoon we settled for the farm.

I had told them that in order to borrow $67,000 from my bank, I had to show an asset worth that amount. This is a bank requirement to keep things fair and balanced, no matter with whom one is doing business, even if it is with one's own brother. I explained the process to them by saying, "I'll tell you what I am going to do. I will buy the farm, and I'll pay it cash. Then, if they demand a cashier's check, I'll get one. We'll turn right around and pay this attorney $25 and he will write up an agreement that you will pay so much per month. After two years, we will look at it again, and perhaps I can be free of it, but we won't mandate it. Since two years might be a little short to get things turned around, it may go as long as four years."

Some unpaid taxes of several thousand dollars surfaced during the final process, and I simply paid that out of my pocket. So the settlement was agreed upon and signed, the attorney had shaken hands with us, and we were heading toward the door.

Sitting in the office with us and observing this whole

process was the attorney's secretary, a woman who looked to be about 55 years old. When we were about to leave, she followed me to the door and tapped me on the shoulder saying, "May I ask you a personal question?"

"Sure," I answered, smiling, adding "if I can answer it, I will."

"You know," she said, "I've been working in this office since I was twenty-two years old. In all those years, I have never had anyone come in and help to purchase a property to this extent for a person who wasn't a family member, and you just met him *last week*?"

"I really believe it wasn't a coincidence, but it was *an act of God*," I explained.

With tears filling her eyes, she continued, "I just never experienced this–that someone would help another young couple get started–and the way you set it up . . . for two years . . . or four years . . . and if it is not working, it is settled and everyone would get paid!"

I was touched, seeing her tears and her amazement.

And she went on, "Why would you do that? You even *lost* money! It cost you a couple days of your time and several thousand dollars in those extra taxes for which you didn't even charge them!"

"Well," I answered, "it's as simple as this. The Lord has blessed me, and I thought I would like to pass it on."

She just could hardly talk. It was extremely moving to me to see her response. I'm sure she must have been a Christian, but we didn't have time to talk further.

As we drove home from New York, this young couple was really elated. Shortly thereafter, they, along with their three-year-old daughter, moved to their new farm about sixty miles west of Albany.

About two years later, one morning I said to Grace, "Let's go up to New York and see how Jim Keiper and his family are doing." We had heard they had a little baby boy in the meantime.

When we drove in their lane, he was in the old barn shop repairing something. They had some livestock, but the old barn still looked pretty rough. However, he was a cabinetmaker and was doing all his own work. The house had already been remodeled, and what was finished looked great. They greeted us warmly and we had a most pleasant visit. Because we had come impromptu and they weren't expecting us, we didn't stay overnight with them but told them we had just wanted to stop by and wish them well.

It was fifteen years before we got in that area again, and their "little" boy was now seventeen! When we met their family, they just looked at each other and smiled. The father turned to his son and said, "You don't know this guy, do you?"

The son just shrugged his shoulders and laughed, and the father continued, "No, you wouldn't, as you were only two years old when he was here last. If it wouldn't have been for *this man, Victor, and his wife, Grace,* we wouldn't be living here on this farm at all. They were the *only ones* who would go out of their way to help us."

Then the boy understood.

This was a Christian couple who had attended the Brethren In Christ Church. However, in New York they joined a Bible Church and were very active members, with their children attending a Christian school sponsored by their church. Helping them get started and seeing their appreciation was a very heart-warming experience.

Two years after the settlement, they notified me that they thought they could carry the loan between their bank and themselves and they could pay me back. However, at that time the interest rate was 2% or 3% higher in their bank than in mine. On realizing that, they asked me, "Victor, would you think that we are being too selfish if we would ask you to hang in there a year or two longer so that we can save that extra interest?"

By that time, they had their debt down to $40,000, so I replied, "Look, you are doing so well, and you are improving things there, that I have nothing to lose. If you just want to continue sending the monthly payments, I'll just take them to my bank."

After about two more years of payments, they only owed $15,000, so one day he called me to say, "Do you know what? Our principal is now so low, I think we'd better pay you off."

"That would be great–to get one thing more off the books . . . in case something would happen to me," I replied.

The two most soul-satisfying aspects of this story were to see their response of appreciation and to see the impact on the secretary at never having witnessed anything like this in 30 years! However, it was nothing that WE did, but they were happenings that we could just see the glory of God shining through.

From 1959 to 1969 we were blessed–not four-fold, but *ten-fold!* It was unbelievable, just miraculous. Everything just doubled and quadrupled. In the meantime, we had added a second farm of 60 acres to the home farm just a month before I got hit with the disease in my herd. To buy it, I had to go in debt an additional $25,000, and in 1971 we added a third farm to it. Now we farmed an L-shaped area and incorporated it all together. This made my burden a little heavier and I had more payments to make with less income.

It was so amazing how it all worked out. Over the years, we purchased 17 farms and 32 houses. At one time, I had seven farms in my name. However, the banks had half the money in them, and I was just a 50% owner.

To be perfectly honest, I guess I must admit I was a high-risk guy!

Chapter Six

Financial Trouble-Shooting and Betrayals

"The time to act is when someone wants to help you . . . Seventy-five percent of success is positive thinking . . . Plan ahead . . . To get ahead you often must be willing to go into debt . . . When an opportunity comes along, don't be afraid to stick your neck out."
—Victor K. Ziegler

Some years ago, I was chosen as one of several businessmen from Lancaster and Lebanon Counties who were asked to mentor persons struggling in business, to give them tips and show them how to utilize good business practices. Much of that counseling was done one on one, through phone calls, and working behind the scenes. One principle I emphasized was: *"Little things can make a big difference."*

In addition, the New Zealand milking machine company, whose equipment I had been using for years, had suggested that I try to convince other dairymen to try their product, so I visited a few farms doing demonstrations.

In one situation, I stopped by to see four brothers, Tom, Dick, Harry and Larry, (not their real names) who were farming together. These brothers confided in me saying, "We don't know what we are going to do. We can't get along with our dad, and he's threatening to sell out and put us all out of business."

After listening to their complaints for about an hour, I began thinking, "It's really not *this* bad; there must be a missing link here." I asked the boys, "What would you *really* like to do?"

They answered, "We'd like to keep on farming, but our dad is just too hard to get along with."

Having known the family for a number of years prior to this, I knew that these boys had lost their mother through an accident and that their dad had done ten times more for them than most dads do for their sons. He had literally bent over backwards for them, so I was sure there were some psychological or emotional undercurrents at work here.

One thing I *did* know: Regardless of the events in our lives, none of us can look back, blame our parents, and make excuses for ourselves by saying, "If *they* hadn't done this or that, I would have turned out well." Everytime I heard stories like that, I would say, "Do you know what? That's true. You may have had a good-for-nothing father and mother, but are you and I going to be any better? Let's forgive them for the things they did in the past and assume they did the best they knew. How can anybody do better than he or she knows how to do? You *can't* share something that you never experienced."

I continued to listen to their sour grapes stories for over an hour and then said, "You boys really have an opportunity here, if you look at it right. I am going to visit your dad and see how *he* is feeling."

When I met with their dad, I discovered he was a likeable guy, a little quick-tempered, and at that stage of his life, he may have been worth about $2 million considering all his assets, including real estate. I had always felt that if a guy was quick-tempered, he was someone I could work with. I just had to keep remembering that as long as he was treating me well, I had to overlook some things.

However, this dad, being quite discouraged, was considering selling out, throwing in the towel. He *really* shocked me by saying, "There *is* one more option. You and your sons and son-in-law seem to 'click' in your operating of a large farm, but my sons and I can't seem to make it happen. I'll do one thing more. I'll sign all my buildings, equipment, and real estate over to you for one dollar, and you can take it and do with it what you deem to be best!"

"Man, that is *scary!*" I exclaimed. "I don't know if I want *that* responsibility."

I pondered upon all the anguish, hard feelings, disappointments and brokenness of this family and then went back to talk to the boys again.

"Your dad suggested something that I admit I'm scared to try. He said, 'If you'd give my boys a second or third chance to make this 800 acre farm operation work, I'd sign everything over to you, and let *you* decide what is right and what is wrong here. Just let me out of it.'"

So I asked the boys, "What do you fellows think about that idea?"

After a little discussion, they concluded, "That would be a whole lot better than working with our dad."

"Well," I warned them, "I am here to warn you it could be *worse!* I may be a little rougher and harder to get along with, and I don't bend as easily as your dad does. If I would have treated my sons financially the way your dad has treated you, as I've seen in going through his account books, my sons would be visiting me every day to say 'thank you.' That obviously hasn't happened here."

"You just don't understand it at all," they concluded, adding, "but we will go along with this plan."

Cautioning them again, I said, "Remember, the agreement is that 'the buck stops here.' I'm going to treat you as I would a member of my own family. What's right will be right, and what's wrong will be wrong. All my decisions will be based on that—not on anybody's feelings or personalities or who did what for anybody."

And so we did it, farming together for two years. By that time, I noticed Tom and Dick were sticking together this way, and Harry and Larry were going the other way. They had made *slow* progress, although I met with them and advised them every two weeks. One day I said to them, "This isn't working. Did you ever see four horses hooked together to plow with two hooked facing east and the other two facing west? With that arrangement, they couldn't get anything done except spinning their wheels. That's what's happening here. Nothing is working, so this is it. I'm going to go home. I will have these 800 acres surveyed and divided into two tracts. Everything will be as equitable as we can do it. Two of you are going to get these 400 acres at this price; you other two guys are also going to get those 400 acres at this price. Tom and Dick, you are always hanging together and blaming the other two, and Harry and Larry are always blaming you two. So, you will stay on this side of the road and farm, and they will farm on the other side."

So, I hired a surveyor and spent a couple thousand bucks. When that was done, I wrote out a contract and said, "Here you are, now you can buy it." In this case, I had also said to the boys, "Do you know what? I *could* sell this land tomorrow for $3,000 an acre, but I am charging you only $1,600, which is almost half price! As your legal trustee and guardian, I can't do what is illegal in the eyes of the federal government. I must be fair, and also you have some sisters, and we want to have something left for them."

"Ah, but you are overcharging us," they complained.

"It's okay if you don't want to buy it. You can just go home, and I'll sell your portion. You'll make it easy for me if you say 'No.' I'll just cash that million dollars and invest it for your dad somewhere, and we won't have to discuss it any further."

After they realized I wasn't going to bend, they decided to go for it. Tom and Dick were married and had families, and they did pretty well. Every month for thirteen years I received a regular payment that sometimes included a thank-you note from the one guy's wife who took care of the account books. She'd write, "We appreciate your effort," and "We made it this far," and things like that. That was heartwarming.

Harry and Larry were both single, and I had a strong feeling that something was wrong in their lives–either involving drugs, alcohol, or women. I just wasn't close enough to really nail it down and I didn't want to make any false accusations. I did sneak in to their farm sometimes, even at midnight, to see what was going on.

One morning at 5:00 I went there, and the cows hadn't been milked for two days, the water pipes were frozen, and nobody was around. They were out carousing somewhere. A seventeen-year-old boy, who was supposed to be doing all the work, told me, "I didn't know what to do; they never came home. The water pipes froze, and the cows had no water. This wasn't working, and that wasn't working." So this poor kid gave up.

When I saw the cows were being so neglected, that was "the straw that broke the camel's back." I couldn't be there myself seven days a week, and I felt strongly that I shouldn't have to be. I told these two guys that things *had to* change.

During this same time, they were behind in their payments, so I finally issued them a legal document that in ninety days everything would be sold. However, the law required 180 days. On the day when the foreclosure was scheduled, I got a call from their attorney saying, "These guys raked together enough money to bring everything up to date, but they need two more days. You wouldn't be so cruel as to not give them a two-day extension, would you?"

"No, I guess I wouldn't be," I admitted reluctantly. The amount was $30,000 or $40,000, I just don't remember exactly. They never came up with the money, even though I heard later that the one guy had borrowed $5,000 from a girlfriend in Florida and let her stick. They would "sweet-talk" their way into borrowing, robbing, or stealing things or selling something behind one's back.

This went on for about a year, and finally, one day I said, "You know, fellows, I'm not going to get ugly about it. I know that if you give a guy enough rope, he'll hang himself with it, and you guys are fast getting to that point."

A year later, I met with a neighbor who was interested in buying land and had the cash in hand to pay for it. So, on a Saturday afternoon on a yellow tablet I wrote up a sales agreement for one million and two hundred thousand dollars ($3,000 per acre for 400 acres). Never before in my life had I walked away with a check for $200,000 based on a handwritten agreement and without involving any attorneys. As we parted, I promised him, "I'll get this written in legal language and get back to you."

"Naw," he said, "I know you, Victor. Take the check and feel free to cash it. I *know* you'll be back."

So, I went to Harry and Larry and said, "Hey, I got the place sold."

"You can't do that, Victor," they exclaimed.

"Yeah, I have spent how many years here, and the result is that you are just spinning your wheels. I told you long ago that this is the way it was going to be," I reminded them.

"Well, we'll stop you from doing this," they declared.

"I can't keep you from trying to stop me, but remember, anything you do to fight against me is coming out of your own inheritance. *I am not* going to pay for it! All expenses are coming out of the farm income. If the place goes broke, I might go home empty-handed, but I'm not going home paying everybody else's bills in this case. You have one choice today. If you don't sign this, I'll go back to the buyer and tell him you refused, and I'll keep all the money and give it to your dad and stepmother, and you will lose it all. If you do sign it and do it voluntarily, your dad and I will only keep the balance due. The rest we will give to you, so each of you should have a profit of between $300,000 and $400,000."

At that point, they allowed the sale to go through, and they both signed the agreement.

Later, I warned them saying, "I don't want to falsely accuse you guys, but there's definitely something wrong here. Whether it is some kind of Satanic intervention, or alcohol, drugs, women, or cults, I don't know, but I *know* it's something serious. If you don't change your course, it's going to kill you physically and spiritually. At this pace, five years from now, you fellows will be missing!"

Larry took his inheritance, went to another state and bought a 200 acre farm, paying for it in cash. Sure enough, in less than two years, he had disappeared! When he left home, he had told his dad, "I'll let you know what I'm doing."

"Good!" his dad responded.

A year went by, and no one heard a thing from him. One day his dad said to me, "We're getting homesick for our prodigal son. I'd love to know what happened to him."

Understanding how he must be feeling, I said to him, "Do you know what? I'll take a couple days off and go with you, and we'll look for him."

I drove the parents (the stepmother and Grace also went along) to that area of the country where we thought we might get a few leads. We were so fortunate. Stopping at a lumber company, we went to the front desk and asked if they'd seen a young fellow by the name of Larry, and I described him.

"Was he ever in here buying building materials?" they asked.

We told them that we'd understood that he had bought a farm nearby and might have wanted to remodel an old log house that was on the property. However, the personnel there just looked dubious and shook their heads denying ever having met or heard of such a person.

"He was a very likeable young man, handsome, and a real charmer," I added. Then I got an idea. "Could I talk to the girls in the back office?" I asked.

"Sure, go back and talk to them," I was told.

When I went back there and described him, one of the girls immediately exclaimed, "Yeah, I know him! I've seen him several times, and he comes in here now and then." So she told me exactly where he lived and gave me detailed instructions how to get there.

Getting there was so weird. We went under a real old underpass with a stone driveway at the entrance. After going a little further, we came to a driveway that was all grown up with weeds and looked like it might have been a month since a car or truck had used it. Moving ahead slowly, we then came to an old wooden gate that was chained and locked shut and had on it a "No Trespassing" sign. We drove right up to it and stopped. "Wow, this looks like this is it," I exclaimed, adding, "but I am not going to break the lock."

The father pondered that for a moment and then declared, "If we are within five hundred feet of the house, I can't go home without seeing my son." Upon saying that, he got out of the car, jumped the board fence's wooden gate and started walking through the tall weeds and grasses toward the house in the distance.

Turning to the women in the car, I said, "I can't let him go in there alone. He might meet up with a police dog or something. There's something funny going on here." So I jumped over the fence and soon caught up with him, and we hiked up together.

When we got to within 300 feet of the house, I spoke to the father in a low voice, "Here comes Larry from around the back of the house. At least, it walks like him." From this distance, I could see it was a man who was built like he was and sure looked like him.

At that, the father stepped up his pace. When Larry saw his dad, he stepped up *his* pace—*toward* him! What really got my heart beating was that the closer the father got to him, the son would literally fall down in front of him with his hands outstretched. It brought back to me so vividly the vision of the return of the Prodigal Son as Jesus told it in Luke, chapter 15. The father and son hugged each other. The father cried, and the son cried, and I did, too—at seeing it happen.

We never got closer than about 250 feet to the house. Although we practically begged Larry to allow us to come in and visit, he kept saying, "No, everything is torn up. Wait until I get everything fixed up and have it completely remodeled. *Then* I'll invite you and Mom down here for a weekend, and we'll have Sunday dinner here."

I used all kinds of tactics to try to get into the house. I said I wanted to bring in my wife, Grace, along with his stepmother. His response was, "No, I wouldn't want them to see all the junk that's in there from the construction. I don't want my stepmother to see the mess I live in." We knew it was a cop-out, but we honored his request.

Suddenly, he said, "My car isn't working and I need to go to town yet tonight to get some groceries. Victor, would you drive us all back into town (about 8 to 10 miles), and I'll get my groceries and take you all out for dinner before you leave?"

We all agreed that would be nice, so we went to town and Larry bought enough food for an army of people! He came out with 20 loaves of bread, 20 pounds of cheese, and 20 pounds of bologna and other lunchmeats. I started suspecting that his home might be a cult headquarters or something. Not wanting to upset him, we allowed him to bring all this stuff into our car. I wanted to hear his story and didn't want to throw a wrench in it that might spoil his enthusiasm.

He then directed us to a beautiful place for dinner and said, "Now you order anything you want, and I'm going to pay for it." And he did! When the waitress came out with our platters, I said something like, "Who wants to bless us and our food before we eat?"

Before anyone could answer, Larry began praying out loud. He prayed on and on for five minutes! The waitress came back with another armful of platters and just stood there waiting and listening to him praying. Finally, I whispered to her, "Just set them down," and she did.

During the course of his prayer, I could sense strongly the tug-of-war that this man was experiencing between the Lord and Satan. Larry said he wanted to bless his parents, but he felt caught, like someone in a trap that couldn't be released. I was sure he was definitely involved in a Satanic cult of some kind, something I didn't understand at the time, and still don't. His prayer went on and on. It went *so long* that I felt compelled to do something. Since I was sitting next to him, I put my arm on his shoulder and said out loud, "Thank you, Lord. Amen." After that, he wound down. What an experience! What an experience!

The rest of our meal was uneventful, and on the surface, we had a nice visit with him. However, all of us had to be careful what kind of questions we would ask. If we got into a sensitive area, we could feel a bit of a stand-off. He'd respond with something like, "Aw, Mom, I can't talk about that now." He kept promising, "When the remodeling is done, I'll invite you down, and we'll have a great weekend."

When we took him home, Larry opened the gate, and I said, "Hey, we'll drive you right up to the house."

Surprisingly, he did allow us to do that, but he made us stop 50 feet from the front porch. It was a log house that was sort of built into the hill. From below, there were steps up to the porch, but if you walked up the hill and around the back, you were on the level. (I never did get back there.) I suggested, "Why don't you visit with your dad and mother, and I will carry the groceries in and set them inside the door, or better yet, just set them on the front porch?"

"Oh, no, no, no," he said emphatically. "You just let

everything set here. We'll visit here a few minutes and then I will take them in after you go."

Of course, that made me even more suspicious.

Before we left, we stood there huddled together among the weeds and tall grasses and one of us, I forget who it was, offered another prayer. We got in our car, turned around in the grass, and as we left, he waved, saying, "I'll be in touch."

As we drove out through the old underpass, I said aloud, "I wonder if we'll ever meet again." This happened in the month of August.

That following November, there was an article in the newspaper that the local police in his area had found a dead body in an abandoned farmhouse. Larry must have been killed within a week or so after we had been there as they had to call to Pennsylvania to get dental records to identify him.

In retrospect, we were so thankful that we had made the effort to go to see him and had spent that time with him. However, we had many unanswered questions. When we had left him, we had very heavy hearts for we were deeply concerned about him, about what was going on in his life, and about what his future would hold.

Several weeks later, Larry's parents received a phone call stating that the laboratory tests had confirmed that this man was definitely their son. He had been killed by "a violent act." According to the condition of his skull, he had been hit with a blunt pipe or hammer and killed while he was asleep in bed. A man, who had helped out on the home farm and whom I had met on frequent occasions through the years while working with this family, was blamed for the murder and is serving time in jail. I don't know if he is the one who *really* did it or not.

According to the laws of that state, if a man dies who is single and has no heirs, no will, and no one designated to receive his assets, everything would go back to his parents. So, Larry's dad got the farm and all the nice equipment he had there including several tractors. I believe it was at least $100,000 worth. I went along with him to load it and bring it back to be sold around here.

After we got all the proper documents, we were supposed to go into the house and clean it out, doing with the things whatever we wanted, sell the farm and give all the money to his parents. Nobody had a key, so we had to break in. With the permission of the authorities, we did that. We had a crew of about a dozen who worked at this. We left early one morning, worked all day, slept there overnight on the floor on blankets we had brought with us, and arrived back home about midnight on the second day. Were those ever tiring and heart-wrenching days! Having to go through all this was so tough on those parents! What makes a sad story even sadder is the thought of how Larry wasted the wonderful opportunity he had, just threw it down the drain. He paid a terrible price. Things could have been so different.

We sold his farm after I was able to get a neighbor interested in it. When we closed that deal, we were glad when that was all behind us.

Months later, they did have a memorial service. After everything had wound down, the things that gave me peace of mind were that first of all, *I tried*! And secondly, the father and stepmother came to me and said, "Victor, how can we ever pay you for putting you through all the pain of getting slapped in the face, told to go home, and ordered to keep out of this?"

Two of their boys, Harry and Larry, *had been* very rude to me. At times, their two brothers, Tom and Dick, who kept their four hundred acres and *still* have them, stood up for me. I told these two, "You are in good shape. I would suggest that you go to the bank now and get the $50,000 that you still owe me, and then we'll close the books, and I'll go home." That's what happened, so after thirteen years of working with this family, I finally went home.

Ironically enough, about two years later, I met the dad somewhere and he told me, "I miss associating with you, Victor, and the little pep talks you used to give me every two weeks or so."

So on a moment's whim, I suggested, "Grace and I are leaving for a trip next week. Why don't you and your wife go along with us?"

They *did* go with us and we made stops with friends all over the place, visiting everybody. Sometimes we stopped at motels here and there, and one time we even stayed with an Amish family overnight. All of us had a wonderful time. His wife still talks about it. We actually traveled with them *twice*, on ten-day trips each time. "That was a highlight for us," she says today. It is wonderful that she has those pleasant memories because he died about five years after the financial difficulties were resolved.

One day when I was still occasionally helping those boys with the work there, Jim, (not his real name), a neighboring farmer, came to me and said he was in trouble with his bank and asked if I would consider helping him. We looked at all his documents and bills, and I said, "You know, this *could* work. However, your farm and everything will have to be sold."

We sat up together until midnight and laid everything out, dollar for dollar, and determined the value of everything. I said to him, "You are 100% financed, but it *could* work because there is enough here in your favor."

So, I bought Jim's farm with my line of credit at my home bank and paid off his bank. Lo and behold, after I thought I had everything under control, his well went dry. I drilled a couple wells there, and we finally got water.

One day, I was working in a ditch there putting in a new water line. A fellow walked over to me and said he is looking for the guy who farms here. I told him Jim is out in his field getting ready to bale hay that afternoon. Then I asked, "Can I help you with anything?"

Hesitating, the man said, "Well, I guess I really ought to talk to *him*." However, he went on to say he wanted to talk to Jim about a couple of his bills that are over six months delinquent.

"I hope they aren't big ones, because we just went over all his figures last week. If it is $500 or so, we can handle it, but . . ."

"Oh, no," he interrupted, "it's about $20,000!"

That just messed us up! Finally, I called all the creditors together and said, "We might as well sell out, and I'll take my licking and get whatever I can out of it, and I got to tell you guys, there won't be anything left!"

A feed company owner, who was the one with the biggest bill, said, "Victor, I really appreciate the way you have handled everything. We're willing to lose it all if we have to if *you* think you can keep the farm and make it work."

"It will take us at least five years to pull out of this," I explained. "In the meantime, I'll give each of you a written statement that I will work to the best of my ability to help Jim get out of this mess, but if, in a given period of two, three, or four years, I can see we're not making progress, I will pull out of here before I get in *too* deep, and I'll go home."

They all agreed saying, "Look, we won't push him." (And *legally* they couldn't, because by now the farm was in *my* name.) They added, "Victor, if you can make it work, we are willing to wait."

"If it works, you all stand a chance of getting a little bit out of it. If not, we'll all lose anyhow, so what route do we want to go?" I asked. "If I go home now, I don't lose a penny, but if I spend all my time here for the next three or four years and *then* go home, I'm going to really be hurting also."

Since I laid everything on the table and told them the way things were, they assured me that they would work with me and suggested that I report to them every six months as to what progress was being made. And that's what I did. However, *I didn't know* that Jim also had a veterinarian bill for $9,000!

Within the next four months or so, I began thinking, "This really *might* work!"

Didn't I get a phone call one Sunday morning about 4:00 from Jim who told me excitedly, "I just came out to the barn and discovered that my veterinarian came during the night and took nine cows! He left a note on the milk tank saying, 'You never paid my bill, so I'm taking nine cows in payment for my bill.'"

Well, they were cows that I had paid for at the bank. I knew that what the vet did wasn't right, in fact, it was illegal, but when a person has something in his possession, it is very hard to get it back. Having it in your possession is 90% of ownership, and the other guy has to *prove* that *he* is the rightful owner. Even though the man stole the cows, we would have to spend a lot of money to fight that.

Jim added, "I thought I heard something driving out the lane during the night, but didn't check it out."

Earlier Jim had told the veterinarian that he would pay him his $9,000 after we had gone over all the figures, settled things up, and had everything squared away, but he had never told ME that he had this bill. He was smart enough to know that if he could pull me in so deep financially, he had a good chance of convincing me to pay *another* $9,000, because by that time it would be too late for me to back out.

I called the veterinarian and reminded him, "You know that what you did wasn't right."

The Dr. replied, "Well, Jim had promised to pay me for a couple years now and never did. When I get a check for $9,000, I'll bring the cows back, or you can come and fetch them, whatever you say." I never paid him, and we never got the cows back.

When all was said and done, although he never admitted it, this young farmer, Jim, who was so nice to work with and claimed to be a Christian, was living two lives. One night at midnight, with tears in his eyes, he wrote me a note saying,

"You'll never know on this side of heaven how much my wife and I appreciate how much you've helped us."

I remember one night sitting around the kitchen table with them and praying for health, success in our efforts, and that God would guide us to do the right thing.

Imagine my disappointment when I later learned that Jim and the veterinarian were in cahoots! They had agreed together that the vet would "take" the cows because "that would force Victor to pay for them."

From then on, I knew I was being used and *really* in trouble. With deception that great, using his tears, prayers, and the name of God to convince me that he was sincere, and really a "nice guy," I knew I had to tread lightly. But I was already in so deep I didn't know how to get out.

The next step I took was that I sold the farm. In the meantime, I had bought another one in Berks County, so I offered Jim the chance to continue farming at that site. One of his gifts was that he was very good with dairy cows as far as feeding, nutrition and production were concerned. I told the neighbors there that he was a good dairy farm boy, and I helped him get started. However, after a whole year I could tell we weren't getting out of the (financial) hole as we had too much overhead, too much hanging over us. About that time, I had an opportunity to sell *that* farm.

My son-in-law, Ron Myer, had been helping my two sons and me do the work on our home farm. He had been feeling a call to the ministry for a long time, and finally decided to answer it and change his life's work. So, when Ron left our farm team, and I sold the Berks County farm, I told Jim that I'd do one more thing: I moved him *here* to work for me, and he lived in our farmhouse for a year. During that time, he cooperated very well and we never had an argument. Although his wife was a hard worker, he was a wily operator, a smooth talker, and he would lead her on and convince her of this and that.

One thing bothered me. We weren't really making money as I was used to doing because we were kept busy paying back his bad debts. After we had priced the cattle and the equipment, we had made a written agreement that in 10 to 13 years, Jim would pay so much a month toward buying them. Having itemized everything, after so many years, he would have owned all 300 of the cattle plus the equipment here. The boys and I farmed the land, and we sold him the crops. However, I would often say to him, "If you can ever get a better opportunity than I have given you from *anybody,* take it! I will never stand in your way."

One day he called me and said, "Two businessmen (and he named them) just bought a dairy farm up in Bradford County. They are looking for 300 cows to put there and a farmer to run the whole operation."

"Well, we have 300 cows here that they could have," I offered, adding, "but they *must* be paid for before they leave (since the amount was almost $350,000)."

A few days later, Jim came back and said, "I think I'm gonna take them up on their deal, and they will buy these cows and I'll run their farm for them."

"That sounds good to me," I answered. "If you're happy, I'm happy." I wasn't sure if this was good or bad, but I thought it can't hurt me *too* much. However, I reminded him, "You tell those guys that no trucks are coming in here for any cows and that I have to hold a bank cashier's check in my hand for $347,000 before you load anything up."

During a visit with one of the businessmen, I told him the same thing. He responded, "Oh, we can settle up any time."

"No," I insisted, "we can't. I've tried it that way before and a settling date never came. I've done that too many times, but I can't do it now. You are capable of paying me and doing a lot more than I ever could."

So, they *did* come up with the money. When I got the check, I took it to the bank. The bank said the check was good, and everything was squared away.

In my conversations with Jim and the businessmen, I had warned them, "Don't plan to move the cows on the hottest day of the year, or you will upset their production. The minute after they have been milked here, you should be ready to load them. You won't hurt them as much as they travel, bouncing them around on the road, as you would if you'd do it while they are each holding 40 pounds of milk."

But do you know what? They did everything *wrong*! They came in one day with the trucks, loaded them, and they were gone. I had warned them, and I had my money, so I wasn't going to argue with them.

Before all this took place, the one businessman had asked me about Jim. I told him honestly that he's not a bad guy, but when you question him, you do have to be sure he tells you everything. He *does* work well with cows and takes good care of them, and that's what you are looking for. I reminded him that while Jim worked for me, I was with him every morning and evening.

I also remember telling him, "Milking cows is different than pumping oil! There is a great difference in climate and land quality between Lebanon County and Bradford County, and if the milk price drops 20 cents to 50 cents per hundred pounds, you could be bankrupt in less than a year."

"Naw," he said unbelievingly, sure that he had everything under control, but he had never farmed!

He would fly up to the farm in his helicopter, bringing along an Amish shoo fly pie to share with Jim, who was now his young farm manager. Sometimes he would bring along his wife and various visitors. They would land and walk around for 20 minutes, and he would ask, "How's it going?"

Farmer Jim was such an optimist that even if everything had died, he would have answered, "Just great, we're in good shape."

Within eleven months, they were bankrupt!

However, the businessmen were clever enough to have put everything in Jim's name so they got their money. Since the other assets were registered in the courthouse against Jim, and he had nothing, no one could make any claims. These businessmen had planned it carefully, so that if it didn't work, they couldn't lose.

One of them, I'll call him "Fred," though that is not his real name, was angry and started to bad-mouth me saying that I had given him a "bum steer." In other words, I had given him a hired man who was no good just to get rid of him.

When I heard that, I went to him and said, "Fred, do you want to know what made the difference? When I employed Jim, I *worked with him* every day. It's like this: If you put a train on a track at Harrisburg and head it towards Philadelphia, it will end up there. This Jim was a guy that you had to get started right every morning, and you had nobody to do that. If you would have hired me as your farm manager, I'd accept the blame. But you never asked me, and I'm glad you didn't, because I would have said, 'No.'" I knew how ruthless Fred could be.

That incident, plus several others, ended our friendship. We had attended the same church, and he left, saying it was because of me. At least that's the reason he gave to people. He started to say to anyone who would listen, "That Ziegler, you know, he is a *skunk*! He gave me a bum farmer, and everything went wrong. I'm going to sue Victor."

When I heard that, I reminded him again, "I warned you and spent a whole evening telling you his strong points and his weak points. You didn't bat an eye. You're the one who made the decision to hire him, not me."

But he continued to blame me for his failure.

A few months before Jim left my employment, I had the milk checks put in my name in a separate account so that I could teach him to pay his bills. However, the checks were no good unless I signed them. One day I said to him, "Get all your bills together and we'll pay them."

We discovered that the last month Jim worked here, he had bills totaling $44,000 and just $40,000 worth of income. That meant we lost $4,000 that month. That also meant that it was taking the whole milk check to pay the bills!

Fred said, "The cows are mine now. I want that money because that $40,000 check belongs to me!"

"Now wait a minute, Fred," I cautioned. "I'm not that dumb! You are going to learn something. The milk produced on *my farm* is what pays the bills made on my farm. The milk produced on *your farm* is going to pay the bills on your farm. You can sue me all you want, but you won't succeed."

Then Fred left me alone because he saw he couldn't scare me. He was so used to threatening people until they'd give in, but he found out that I wouldn't budge. One woman who had worked for him for several years told me that he had propositioned her and she had turned him down. Three days later she was fired. She empathized with me and observed, "You don't say 'No' to Fred!"

After attending a service at the Midway Church of the Brethren, a deacon approached Grace and me and said, "A group of us have decided we're going to boycott the chain of stores that Fred owns because they are selling pornography."

"You can't do that," I objected. "Fred says he is a Christian, and the Bible says that when you have a difference with a brother, you should go and talk with him. Why don't two or three of your deacons go and visit him and tell him what you are planning to do?"

As far as I know, nobody did, but that very night on the way home, I stopped at one of his stores. As I was getting what I needed, I got an idea and suggested to Grace, "Walk through the store and nose around and look if you can actually see any pornographic materials."

When I went to pay my bill, I made eye contact with Grace. She just rolled her eyes and shook her head and said, "Such filth!"

I said to the girl at the cash register, "What about this? Isn't this pornography?"

"You know, sometimes I am so ashamed to work here," she admitted in a low voice. "I'm a Christian, but I need a job. I don't want to quit without having another job to go to. My mother and dad were coming to visit me not long ago, and I wanted to get one or two videos for them to look at, and we didn't have *any* here that were decent! They were too filthy, so I just gave up that idea."

Then I had the evidence. I made an appointment to meet with Fred to talk about it, but I didn't tell him it was his own employee who had told me.

We met on a Monday morning, and he was very cordial and receptive. After I shared with him my concern, he said, "You know, Victor, the store manager is in charge of that, and I have nothing to do with it."

On hearing that, I could hardly contain myself and blurted out, "Fred! I'm not *that* stupid! The buck stops *here!* I know where it stops, and you do too. *You* are the owner and *you're* the one in charge. If it wouldn't be bringing in any money for you, you'd soon put an end to it."

I found out that the following week they cleaned those materials out of the local store, but they appeared again in another store farther away. Some of his employees told me later, "When you came and spoke to him about the pornography in his stores, he felt you were interfering in his business, and he really got mad. We heard him say, 'That so-and-so Ziegler! It's none of his business what I sell in my stores!'"

But it *was* my business to warn him about the influence he is having on my children, my grandchildren and my community! It *was* my business as a loving Christian brother to bring to his attention something that he was doing that was wrong!

Several months before he died, one Sunday morning Grace and I arrived at church early. I said, "I think I will go into town and get a cup of coffee before I go into church." I'm not a big coffee drinker, but something motivated me to do that.

Just as I was entering the store, Fred came out, all dressed up and on his way to church in another town. We almost ran into each other, and I held out my hand and said, "Good morning, Fred, how are you?"

He smiled and shook my hand and said, "Good morning, Victor." Then we both went on our way.

That was the last time I spoke with him. I might have seen him drive by after that, but I purposely kept my distance from him. I didn't go out of my way to walk in front of him or away from him. When I was sixty-four and he was seventy-four, he got very sick. We were only ten years apart, almost to the day. At least, that's how I remember it.

Some of his employees came to me and asked, "Did Fred ever meet with you to apologize and make things right?"

"Nooooo, what should he make right?" I inquired.

"Well, he sometimes said he 'has to get back to Victor,'" they responded, implying that he must have had a guilty conscience. However, he never tried to call me or make an appointment.

During his last years, Fred had one tragedy after another. When he got cancer, he told his doctor, I'll give you a million dollars if you can turn this disease around." But this time his money didn't speak, didn't work, didn't buy him health. Next, his wife died, and he had all kinds of turmoil within his family.

About a year later, two of the top men in his company were killed in a helicopter crash at the edge of the farm I owned near Prescott. One of these men was the one next to Fred in power in his company. This man was having a problem with a store manager in middle Pennsylvania. That morning he had called that store and asked the fellow who answered the phone, "Did you give the news to the manager that he is fired as of tomorrow?"

"No, I didn't, but I'll talk to him today," the fellow promised.

"Well," said the top boss, "don't bother. I am coming up myself. I want to have the *fun* of firing him!" He had worked for Fred since he was 16 years old and every day was becoming more ruthless like Fred was.

This top boss, two other company officials, and the pilot flew by helicopter to middle Pennsylvania. While they were there, the top boss had the "fun" of firing the store manager there. Then, as they were homeward bound and flying over his hometown, the one official, whom I know personally, asked to be dropped down there as he wanted to check on a store there before he went home. He told me later, "I can still see the helicopter taking off, and ten minutes later, it was reported on the radio that it had come down over at Prescott and all on board were killed." Apparently, the pilot got disoriented somehow and the helicopter fell upside down. The impact of the propeller made a hole in the ground that was four foot deep.

While driving his tractor-trailer home from Lebanon that day, my son, Lynn, saw it happen. Upon seeing a fireball and a flume of smoke, he called me on his cell phone. "Hey, dad, we didn't leave a pile of tree stumps or brush or anything in the fence row over at the Prescott farm, did we? We did clean it all up, didn't we?" he asked.

"Yeah, we cleaned everything away," I answered, puzzled as to why he was asking this.

"Well, there is an immense fire going on over there," Lynn explained. It turned out that what he was seeing was the helicopter burning because of the fuel it had aboard. What a sad story! The events in the last year of Fred's life were so terrible that I wouldn't wish that on anybody, but you know, God's grace only lasts so long. This sometimes becomes evident even in our daily lives.

One day a young couple, whom I'll call Don and Doris (not their real names), who were members of a neighboring church, came to see me about going into a store business. Don asked me to go along with him to look at it so I could help him make a decision. The more he talked, the more he was dragging me in, so to speak.

When he asked me to meet him at Pine Grove for breakfast, I really got drawn into his scheme. He bought me a nice little breakfast and offered up a prayer for me, that the Lord would bless me and help me make the right decision. Finally, I went in with him to the tune of $240,000 to buy, renovate and stock the building that would become his store. It was to be a type of discount grocery store commonly known as a "dent and bent" store. (You know, where you can buy cans that are dented or boxes that are punctured, but everything inside is wrapped in plastic. Although there is nothing wrong with the contents, they can't be sold in regular stores. These items can often be bought at ten cents on the dollar. So, if a guy gets it for ten cents and sells it for 40 or 50 cents, he makes a nice profit. Some of these types of stores really thrive.)

In this case, I made several BIG mistakes. First of all, I put the property in *Don's* name. He was a man with terrific gifts, business-wise and people-wise. Having the ability to design and engineer buildings, he had built a couple houses on his own, sold them, and made a little income. He sure was no dummy in financing—with other people's money! For the first six or eight months, I began to trust him as much and maybe even more than my own son! That was my second big mistake! I got so relaxed that instead of stopping in once or twice a week, at one time a whole month went by between my visits. I was so busy and kept thinking, "The Lord is going to bless him."

While going through the area one day, I stopped at the store and Doris and their 16-year-old son were running it. "Where's Don?" I asked.

"He went on a hunting trip to Alaska," they explained.

Discovering that he had spent $14,000 on that trip, all I could think about was the fact that he owed me all this money and hadn't even been able to make his payment that month. Their explanations were giving me the wrong signals.

I didn't want to upset his wife, so I just asked, "When is he coming back?"

"Well, he is going to be gone another week."

Although I knew he was getting behind in his payments, he had been keeping current and had a good track record for the first six or so months. What *really* triggered my concern was that when I walked through the store, I saw shelves empty here and there. I knew that was not right. I had made it plain to him that we had to keep over $100,000 in inventory. Since selling involves just "cash and run," inventory can walk off in a hurry. The building will stay—you can ruin it, but it will stay. I had warned him, "Now, remember, when you get $100,000 income in sales from your inventory, that money *has* to be used to restock the shelves. If you get $100,000 income, and it only costs you $80,000 to restock, that extra $20,000 is your profit toward paying off the mortgage and you and your wife's labor."

"I know that," he had affirmed.

But when I came in that day, what I discovered was that he had done just the opposite. He took $14,000 that month to take the hunting trip and then had no money left to pay me. (We had it all amortized, and he owed me about $1,000 per week.) His business *could* have worked. The need was there; the market was there, but when I saw the empty shelves, I saw warning signs.

"If you have a check for me today, I'll just take it along, and it will save you the cost of mailing it," I suggested to Doris hopefully.

"No, he didn't leave me nothing," she replied. (He kept her in the dark about his finances as much as he could.)

When Don returned, we got together and he said, "Victor, I am short another $20,000."

"I already have too much money invested in this place; I can't give you another $20,000," I declared. "You need to restock your store. We should have talked about this before you went on your hunting trip. That would have saved three-fourth of the amount you need."

"Well, I had to get away," he said, using that old excuse. (I thought to myself: "Don't you ever think that *I* might have to get away?")

"What am I going to do?" Don asked, finally seeming a bit worried.

"I know one thing," I replied firmly. "We popped enough in here. If you're not going to make it now, I have no choice but to lock the doors and go home."

"If you do that, I am out of business."

"Well, if I do anything else, I'll just be in another $20,000 to $40,000. Then, instead of being in this for $240,000, I'd be in it for almost $300,000. A lot of this is the bank's money, and I helped you by faith." When Don had asked for the loan originally, I had told him this up front, reminding him that money doesn't flow by the millions, it is just by the grace of God. If we are honest before God and our fellow men, it always works out. He had seemed to understand it, but I was caught this time by a trick of the devil.

Finally, everything was sold out, but he was still around $200,000 short. I still have the property, but I lost the interest on that $200,000 for ten years and was paying 8% for it at the bank all that time.

Another couple is using that building now as a clothing exchange place, catering to low income families. So far, they have been faithful in giving me their rental check once a month. Eventually, it will all work out.

Just last week I told Grace, "I have to live until I am eighty to make my last payment on that mortgage."

She quickly responded, "Victor, that's outright *stupid!*"

And I couldn't help but chuckle because it always works out. I could sue him, but "you can't get blood out of a turnip," they always say. There's just nothing there. Don was so shrewd and clever that all I could do was take the place back, pick up the pieces, and go on from there. That hurt us for ten years and tied up our giving. That would have been $200,000 "extra" for us, and all that time I was paying for it at the bank, interest and principle, on a debt that should have been his. *When you do something with the bank's money, you pay double. When you do it with your own money, you only pay for it once.*

Although that *really* set us back, I never lost any sleep over it, but it troubled Grace a good bit. Not to the extent that it made her nervous, but I'd give her a friendly reminder once in a while. I'd say, "I can't believe it. I always thought you had a smart husband, but this 'learning experience' proved otherwise!"

One interesting aspect of this story is that this was the only deal about which Grace told me she did not have peace of mind. That should have been a warning signal to me, but I ignored it. I had visited Don's pastor and a deacon in his church, and both of them assured me, "Boy, that guy is really going to be something. We feel he is going to be a strong leader in our church." I believed them.

However, Satan got hold of him. Now he is in the Midwest doing the same thing to another guy. A relative of his told me that he went to Alaska again and while he was there, he met a farmer who had a ranch in one of the Dakotas. Don *claims* that he talked this guy into signing his farm over to him, and he is paying him $1,000 a month for life. I predict that he'll do the same thing to him that he did to me—you know—walk away from it some day. He knows how to prey on people, to win their hearts.

I told Grace some time ago, "One of these days we are going to jump in the car and take a little trip and look up Don. If I get enough leads, I'm sure I can find him. We'll drive into his place, smile, greet him, walk in and visit him as though nothing ever happened. Then we'll say, 'Hey, come on, we'll take you out for dinner, and you can tell us all about life in the Big Sky Country.'"

During the meal I will be inwardly and silently praying, "Lord, help him to say something that will give Grace peace of mind."

One of the last times we spoke together I asked him, "How are we going to settle this?"

His response was, "All I can say to you, Victor, is that it is your tough luck for helping me!"

Aaaaah! That was like sticking a knife in me!

"Don, don't ever say that! Do you know what?" I said. "If you would come to our house once a month and ring the doorbell and give us a one dollar bill and say 'Victor and Grace, this is all we can afford to give you in repayment right now,' we would smile, and the next month would be better. When you talk like this, it is just like sticking a double-edged bayonet or sword right through a guy's heart. Don't *ever* say that again to anybody!"

I felt he *really* betrayed me. He never backed down, said anything different, or apologized. That was a hard pill for me to swallow. I had to tell Grace about this, and that was tough too. That was really tough. You know, it is easier to forgive those that just touch you. Those who really try to take the life out of you, *well, it just takes more forgiving!*

Chapter Seven

Committing My Finances to Christ

"God is seldom early, but He is never late!"
—Victor K. Ziegler

One day, while alone in the field planting corn in the early 1970's, the thought came to me: "You know, Victor, you're spending $15,000 per year simply for insurance to protect livestock and equipment that ain't even yours! You know good and well that you read just this morning that 'the cattle on a thousand hills are the Lord's'(Psalms 50:10). He's the Owner, and you're the steward. Why are you insuring the Owner's property?"

When Grace and I were eating lunch that day, I said to her, "Do you know what? If we would cancel our insurance, we would have $15,000 a year *more* to give to charitable ministries. Although we're already giving generously, by doing this, we'd have $15,000 *more* to give. In twenty years, that would be $300,000 and at 7% interest–it doubles every ten years–it would be $600,000!"

"Are you *sure* you want to do that?" she asked cautiously.

"Yeah," I replied. "I'd really be ready to do it. Let's just insure what the bank owns, keeping the liability insurance on our vehicles so other people are protected, and let the Lord take care of our interests."

So I did. I called the insurance company, and they weren't too happy. They suggested, "Let's just lower your level. That would reduce your premium."

I said, "No, the coverage that I don't need I am just going to forget about."

We put the amount that we had been paying for insurance into missions through our local church, a prison ministry (I spent twenty-five years promoting that), and Teen Challenge. I especially loved ministries that related to young people because "*if you can change young people, you can change the world.*"

That October, we had a terrific electrical storm in our area. After a storm like that, we usually would go out and check things to see if any trees had blown down or fences broken. After all, you don't want your cattle running on your neighbor's property!

So, that evening I went out checking and found nine of my best dairy cows had been killed by lightning under a tree. Immediately, I had a flashback: "The cattle on a thousand hills are the Lord's," and then I realized *I* didn't lose any livestock after all! My second thought was, "How would I be able to go back to the house and tell Grace?" At that time, cows were worth almost $1,000 apiece.

"What are we going to do now?" Grace asked after I broke the news to her.

"Well, *we'll just go on in faith, believing,*" I assured her.

Within the next six months, at least a dozen people asked me how my insurance company had treated me. Before I'd answer, I'd think, "They're not going to believe me."

Then I would answer them aloud, saying, "Well, I had *no earthly insurance*; they were insured from above."

In dairying, the most valuable animals were those that produced milk from August to April, over the winter months. Nature promotes a lot of milk in the spring of the year, during what we called the "spring flush," a result of the green pastures.

Most healthy cows produce a good amount of milk from April until you get the excessive heat and droughts during August. During the *winter* following the storm, the remaining herd produced beyond our expectations and the total volume of milk was *greater* than the year before. My income and production were even *up* a little. The milk price was up 10 cents a hundred, so within six months my total income was much better than a year earlier. I never even *missed* those cows that had been struck by lightning. In fact, I fed nine less cows and had more money! I call that a miracle because I can't explain it. In the end I had less cows, less expense, less work and had over $1,000 *more* for ministries and missions because I was diverting the equivalent of my former insurance costs to Christian causes. I concluded that everybody was blessed.

On another occasion, I bought a brand new tractor, and it was automatically insured for 30 days. *Forty days* later, while a new fellow who was helping me was driving, he hit a sinkhole and split the brand new tractor in half! When I checked my papers, I discovered it hadn't been insured for the last 10 days. Even though I hadn't called in to register the purchase, they fixed it for $2,000. Nobody was hurt, and by the following year, it was working so well you would never have known it had been repaired.

Through experiences like this, I learned and shared with many others that *God is seldom early, but He is never late!* I've had so many "Red Sea experiences," where I waited, stepped into the water, and when I thought I was about to drown, all of a sudden a miracle happens. You know, it's beyond our control. There were things I'd wish I could do, but I couldn't. All I could do was pray and wait. More than once, at the last minute, I was rescued and came out smelling like a rose and clean as a pin. When you have experiences like that, three, four, or a half dozen times, you just can't quit! You just *can't* quit.

I would have to admit that some of my most fun was with the Internal Revenue Service. Although I was really blessed a couple years, the only times I was ever challenged were in 1975 and 1976. During those years, we might have had a $70,000 to $80,000 profit, which wasn't much for what we were doing, but we were happy.

When the IRS called, they said they'd be setting aside a whole day and coming here to see me. Because I was giving as high as 50% of my income to charity, they wanted me to produce all my checks and receipts.

When most people who have become used to living on $20,000 to $30,000 a year experience a sudden increase, shooting their income up to $70,000 and $80,000, they will spend more money on themselves, getting bigger cars, renovating their homes, and buying luxuries they couldn't afford before. When that happened to us, our lifestyle just never changed. I was the kind of person who didn't care whether I drove a 20-year-old car or a new one, as long as it took me where I wanted to go. I felt the same.

The first IRS man who came was about twenty-eight years old and was an interesting guy. We spent a whole day together, with more time talking about miracles, missions and charities than we did about the internal revenue!

My opening statement to him was: "I love the country I was born in. I would rather give Uncle Sam $10 too much than being an outright thief or cheat. So, if you find a mistake, and I can't show you the difference, we'll be happy to just write you a check, and we'll go on from there. You won't have to spend any time here arguing with anybody."

Well, at the end of that day he gave me $27 back! He couldn't find one thing wrong, and he shook my hand and went home smiling.

The next year I had another good year and the IRS sent out a man who was in his early sixties to see me. When he called me ahead of time, I could tell he would be a hard-liner because he said, "We want to see *all* the checks *and* receipts, not just checks."

After I met him face to face, I realized he was "all business," the type you could hardly get to smile. I gave him a similar opening statement: "I appreciate the country we live in and want to be fair to it. I know that somebody has to pay for the roads and education, and I want to do my part."

We kept on digging and digging through my records, and at the end of the day, he just gave up on me and gave me a check for $740. I couldn't let him leave without harassing him a little bit and I told him, "I wish you could come back *every day!* I *never* make $700 a day farming. If you keep coming back, and we do this every day, we're going to find some more!"

But he was ready to quit while he was ahead. He then wished me well and went home.

Those were fun times for me. Not that I looked forward to those visits, but I knew–however the chips may fall, God's hand was in it, either way. And you know, 1976 was the last time I ever got a call from the IRS, and that was about twenty-eight years ago!

When I was out driving, I often stopped along the road to pray for a minute and then I'd take off and suddenly a new idea would pop into my mind. I must confess I was never a person that prayed for three or four hours at a time, but many times when I was alone, my thoughts were focused on meditation, the Lord, and praying for others. And you know, when you are thinking about blessing other people–that's all the Lord came for and did with his life–it just opens doors to service. There are other examples, but if I'd tell you all of them, we'd be talking here for *days!*

At one time, we had renters, an older couple, and he was handicapped, in a wheelchair, and we helped them buy a house for $12,000 to $15,000. His wife told me later that when I broke the news to them that I had purchased a home for them and they would be moving there, he got really mad at me and swore.

So, when I saw him again, I explained, "Mr. Smith (not his real name), I've found a house for you that is much nicer than the one I am renting to you. It will cost you just $10 more each month, but after a period of time, you'll *own* it! I'll never find a deal like that again."

After I took him over to the new house and showed it to him, he was happy. Then he asked me a question I would never forget: "Now, Victor, my own brother wouldn't do something nice like this for me. *Why* did you get this place for us?"

"The Lord's been so good to me that I want to pass it on, whenever possible," was how I answered him.

One day his wife came home from getting groceries and found that their gas stove was turned on and her husband was dead. He had committed suicide.

The day after the funeral his wife called and said, "Victor, you might as well take the house. I don't want to continue making the payments here, and I won't need this place anymore. Since I don't want to live alone, I'm going to go and live with my daughter in her mobile home."

"Well," I responded, "if you say so."

Because the deed was still in my name with a sales contract to them, I sold the house and had $1,200 left over after I subtracted my expenses. So I wrote out a check to her, the widow, for that amount but she wouldn't take it. I urged her again saying, "I did this for you."

Finally, after I visited with her for about an hour and explained everything to her, she accepted it. Then she added, "All the running around you did and the gas you bought . . . would you at least let me give you 20 dollars to cover some of the gas?"

"If that would make you feel better, I'll do that," I agreed, and that was the end of that story. Of course, those people never forgot it.

Every year it seemed there was something unusual, some special situation or blessing happening that I could never have orchestrated myself. I was too busy!

My neighbors always accused me of making money by the millions. I would never argue with them, because they wouldn't believe it anyhow. I used to say, "If you would understand that *I, Victor Ziegler, never owned a thing,*" you know. Then I would start quoting scripture to them like, "The cattle on a thousand hills are mine.' The Lord owns everything!"

That used to shut them up. I discovered that when I quoted scripture, they quit asking questions. That was funny. Then they'd just smile.

But I *would* always tell the bank what I am doing. That's why I had no problems with them. I would call them and say, "I want $100,000 on Monday morning at 9:00 because I have a commitment."

"What are you doing?" they'd ask.

Then I'd say, "Well, I bought something (a piece of equipment or some land) . . ."

"Yeah," they'd say, "come in on Monday morning and sign the papers and you can take the check along with you."

Sometimes I would buy a house trailer or a home for some family, hoping that by doing that, they could get on their own feet in two to four years. In doing this, I discovered that God has many ways of compensating us. For example, this year (2004) I had $2,000 of extra expense that, in all honesty, won't cost me a penny, but it will cost Uncle Sam! Instead of my paying $5,000 to $7,000 income tax, I will get a credit of $2,000 for that loss or direct expense. The end result for my year would have been the same—whether I gave it to them or paid an extra $2,000 in taxes. So, it is almost a Biblical principle that *when you give in the name of the Lord, you receive all kinds of blessings, but they are not always in dollars and cents!* In this case, it *is* reflected in my balance sheet in dollars and cents. I'm thankful to God for that, and I'm also grateful that my government allows me to do that.

Around 1975, I was involved with the Lehigh Valley Milk Producers when they filed for chapter 11 or bankruptcy of some sort, and every farmer lost a whole bunch of milk checks. They had drawn off so much per month for years from our checks, and they had taken approximately $28,000 or more from me and put it in their stock. We were supposed to get this back in cash if we'd ever retire or sell the farm. As long as you were a producing member, you *had to* participate financially.

Well, everything went wrong there. People were really upset as the word got around that Lehigh Valley was bankrupt and their stocks were no longer good. The stocks for which I had paid $28,000 were now only worth a penny or two on the dollar! The law stated that if I sold them for $25, it had to be an 'arms-length transaction,' as determined by the Department of Revenue. This meant I was not allowed to sell them to a relative because since I had paid $28,000 and was selling them for $25, they were suspicious that a relative would refund them to me, and I would keep a couple thousand dollars for returning the favor. The sale had to be a transaction where there were no strings attached, where I couldn't force or coerce the buyer to give them back to me.

So, I mentioned this to a friend, John Kreider, a Christian man, who had a dairy farm and a farm equipment business in Lancaster County under the name of Show-ee Stall Company. I made him this offer: "John, would you be interested in making a good investment? I have $28,000 worth of stocks that I will sell you for $25."

"Yeah, I would do that," he agreed.

"Remember, they are not worth more than $25 today," I warned him.

"Yes, I know," he affirmed. "I have some of my own like that." (He was in the Lehigh Milk Producers Co-Op also. He was a very likeable fellow, a Spirit-filled man, about five years younger than I was.)

I added, "You know, John, if these ever become worth anything, I want that money in the hands of a believer who I know, if he doesn't need it for himself, will use it for missions or some organization that helps to alleviate suffering and pain."

"Boy, Victor, I'd be happy to do that," he agreed heartily. "In fact, if these stocks ever become worth anything, I will call and ask you to designate a charity, and we'll give it whatever comes back."

About seven years later, I was part of an ecumenical group called Lighthouse Ministries who bought a house in Richland, Pennsylvania, to serve as a home for unwed mothers and abused women and children. I had put in the initial investment, and although money was tight, we were blessed. We served as an in-house committee, with the pastor of the United Church of Christ as our treasurer. We were still in the beginning stages of this ministry and only had a couple hundred dollars in the checking account. When we went to settle for the house, we discovered that one of us had miscalculated, and we still owed an extra $1,800 (in extra expenses, settlement fees, taxes, and what have you), that we hadn't counted on. Pastor Lengle, our treasurer, said, "Victor, I can't write a check for $1,800. We don't have it!"

"Well, Pastor," I assured him in faith, "go ahead and write the check and give it to the attorney. We'll find the money by tomorrow somehow." That settlement occurred about 3:00 in the afternoon.

Wouldn't you know, when I got home, there was a note on the kitchen table that said, "Victor, call John Kreider as soon as possible. He wants to talk to you about something." (You remember John was the guy who had bought those Lehigh Valley stocks years ago.)

So I called John and said, "John, what's good happening?"

"Well," he said excitedly, "I have received a check for $4,000 for those old stocks, and I have designated $2,000 of that to our Mennonite Mission. Now I'm writing the other check for $2,000 and whose name shall I put on it?" (The Lighthouse Ministries needed $1,800 to cover our overdrawn check–and *within an hour's time,* this all happened: the settlement and the phone call!)

I told John the story, and he exclaimed, "If that isn't a *clear act of God!* Oh!" he added, "that makes it really exciting!"

So, the next thing I knew, I had a check coming for $2,000.

After supper, about 7:00 p.m., I called the Pastor/treasurer and said, "Hey, remember I told you this afternoon that I'll go to bed, and you can stay up and pray all night and pray that money in? I just want to give you some good news. You can go to bed early and cut your prayers short, because I have a check coming in the mail for $2,000 designated to Lighthouse Ministries."

He almost fell off his chair!

Later on, I gave him a little of the history. Those kinds of things happened over and over again.

On another occasion, Ray Brubaker used to have a Florida-based radio and television ministry. Because he was a good-natured, godly man, a Pentecostal who was full of fire, I promised him $1,000 toward his work. It was due before Christmas, but I was running short at the end of that year.

One day I said to Grace, "I am going to send Ray a $1,000 check. Be sure to remind me on Monday morning to go to the bank to make it good, because I don't have anything coming in for the next week or two."

Lo and behold, I stopped at the mailbox to pick up my mail before going to the bank, and there was a check from someone paying me $1,000 that had been due five or ten years earlier. I had written it off in my mind and had never kept track of it. I had been living well without it, never missed it, and it never crossed my mind that this guy still owed me money. So, here I had a check for $1,000 and I never had to borrow it from the bank! I just had to deposit the check I got.

Along with the check was a note that said, "Since we've been blessed the last year and have a little extra money, we've decided to pay you what we owe from years back. We'll feel a lot more comfortable having it paid than continuing to let it slide."

You know, when things like this happen, time after time, you get so excited about seeing the miracle-working power of God at work, financially, physically, mentally, and emotionally, that it is like going to a ball game that is so interesting you want to see them play another inning! It's like, "Lord, what is going to happen to me today? What is going to happen in the ninth inning? The first seven were *really good*. Let's go with a nine-inning game!"

I really lived with that on my mind seven days a week. Especially now. When things would go wrong, I would say things like, "Get thee behind me, Satan," and "Tomorrow will be a better day."

Fasting was not something I did very often, but sometimes I would skip a meal and pray a bit more earnestly saying, "Lord, I'm not really hungry, but I just want to meditate on the good things that are happening." Or I would spend that time thinking about the miracles of God and how blessed I was and ask, "Lord, what's going to happen next?"

Then I'd begin to anticipate things and they'd happen! But it never happened when *I* thought it should. That's why I'd often say, (and I don't remember where I first heard this), *"God is seldom early, but he is never late!"*

Grace and I had the privilege of traveling to Hawaii twice. On our second trip, we went with Richard Canfield's group of about 75 persons because we thought it might be fun to go with a Christian group. Every morning we would meet from 7:00 to 7:15 for inspiration and devotions.

One morning Dr. Canfield asked, "Did anybody call home? What's new back in the States and around Pennsylvania?"

A few people commented, and then I said, "I just talked with our dairy herdsman, and he said everything is going fine, but three cows died since I left."

When the people seemed sympathetic, I added, "Well, we might as well take a positive view of this. The only thing I can figure out is that I am missed so much that the cows are dying to see me!"

I had earlier assured my employee: "Just keep on keeping on, because they probably would have died if I had been there. Something unusual must have happened. Perhaps something got in their feed. Don't get discouraged, and don't give up! Just do what you know is the right thing to do, and we'll see you next week."

You know, I *could* have jumped all over the guy who was in charge and say, "What in the world are you doing? Don't you realize it is costing me a thousand dollars a day every day that I am away from home?" But I was always convinced that in any unfortunate circumstance, things could always be worse! And if you think about it, *it could be,* in most cases. Why cry over spilled milk, as I said earlier, when you can't do a thing about it? But you *can* change the future!

Sometimes misfortunes add up to the point that you feel everything is working against you. However, in time, things turn around and eventually you see a blessing in the end. You never could have foretold or predicted it. I am convinced that God has many ways of bringing out the best in you and testing you, and each person will be different, depending on your educational background, work environment, and whatever you are involved in. We just have to be objective and positive and willing to sit back and think, "*What does God want me to learn through this?*"

When we were faced with the doubling costs of health insurance around 1978, I remember asking Grace, "What would you say about saving that money and, as we are able, contributing that amount also toward charitable ministries? We've both been blessed with such good health, and I believe, by faith, that it's going to continue."

I'd known so many people who immediately ran to their doctor whenever they had an ache or a pain because they had a five-dollar co-insurance. They'd take a day off work, play sick, and it cost them five bucks, but they got their day paid because of "sick leave," or whatever they called it.

I feel our system really encourages lack of faith and self-discipline. I've been telling various ministries that I don't want to label it as a "sin," but it is not right, and it *is* a misuse of God's money when we spend $40,000 or $50,000 a year for health insurance for ministry employees. I do agree that we should protect them and work with them, and I don't want them to do what I do exactly, but what I'm saying is: "There would be a lot less people running to the doctor if they had to pay $50 per visit instead of $5. We are promoting a system that encourages absenteeism, playing hooky, and pretending to be sick, because the workers are guaranteed their $100 per day for "sick leave."

Being self-employed most of my life, if I didn't feel well at night, I went home, drank a glass of water, went to bed an hour early, and I was ready to go the next morning. Sometimes I didn't quite feel like working, but I did it anyhow, because I had nobody to take my place. I actually know many people who admitted, "Oh, I'm going to go on partying here until midnight, and if I don't show up at school to teach tomorrow or can't be at the shop, factory, or office, I'll just call in sick. I may even go to the doctor, and it'll cost me $5, but if I am getting paid $100 per day for sick leave, I'll still have $95, you know." I think that mindset is degenerating our country, but on the other hand, I don't want to take anything away from people who *need* help. (I wouldn't want to be *that* radical!)

What *really* bothers me is to sit in groups of Christians who say, "We pray, we are committed, we believe God can move, God is working." In fact, I attended a meeting one time of a ministry that was really on fire and doing many wonderful things. They brought in a man who spoke so well that by the time he finished, I had a strong sensation that he would be an ideal person to work in this organization. He finally came out and said, "You know, I could work for you guys, but you'd have to cover my $8,000 a year medical insurance."

That was a little more than I could swallow, especially after he had given such a fired-up speech about trusting in God, having faith in His timing, taking care of the needs of our ministry, and things like that. When I had heard my fill, I got up enough courage to say, "Brother, you don't believe what you preach, do you? You just got done saying that God takes care of everything, yet your very first demand, the one at the top of your list, was that we must put up $8,000 to cover your health insurance before you'd be willing to work part-time or do anything for this organization to enhance its ministry. What happened to God? Where is your faith?"

That ended that exchange.

I wouldn't have said that, but I was put to the test several years ago. I gave that money to ministries and trusted God, and I've been blessed for it.

When we were going out the door that night, another guy whispered to me, "Boy, I was sure glad to hear that. It made *me* think, and it really stopped *him* in his tracks."

At that meeting, I had also said, "Not everybody is called to be a radical, like some of you may label me, and that's all right, but let's think about it. My nature is somewhat Pentecostal, and it sure works my blood up to hear a guy preaching and talking like that and the minute he blows his nose, he runs to the doctor. He's afraid he's going to die or something. It just doesn't make sense!"

Whether it was good or not, the fact is that I never went to a doctor for forty-seven years! However, Grace did have a few physical problems through the years, and did consult with doctors, but her bills were small and never hurt us too much. The biggest one she had was when she was over sixty-five, and the doctor asked, "What kind of health insurance do you have?"

When she answered, "Nothing," he said, "well, we'll operate for 80% medicare," and of course, that makes it different.

With my current illness, (about four months ago I was diagnosed with lymphoma), I am just amazed at the bills I am starting to get. They are *so reasonable!* For instance, what started out as a $400 charge for an extraction (to be tapped of fluid—and it was *worth it* to get the relief!) was reduced to $200 because of medicare. Then it was further reduced because of an in-house deduction, so that all I had to pay was $56, and the doctor had spent an hour with me!

When I had first gone into that doctor's office, he and his secretary called in a social worker and asked, "What are we going to do with this guy who has no insurance? He could end up with a bill of $50,000!"

First of all, the social worker explained to me that 80% is covered by medicare. Well, 80% of $50,000 is $40,000, so I said, "Do you know what? I do have an extra car I could sell for about $5,000, so if I would still owe you $10,000, I have half of it paid already. If worse comes to worst, I could sell my second car and ride a bicycle and pay it all!" I just kept going on and on.

But, you know, that never happened. Ever since I started giving sacrificially, something good always happened and I got my bills paid either before the due date or before the grace periods had expired. And it's happening again!

The other night the social worker called and gave us all these options and said, "You might be eligible for all this aid . . ."

(I had never told her my history. Grace remarked, "If you would have told her you go to the bank board every other Tuesday and tell all them people how to spend their money . . .")

I *did* tell her I have a small investment in bank stocks, and she said, "You might have to liquidate that to pay your bill."

"That's okay," I affirmed. "I don't own any farms anymore. The only things we own are a car, a truck, and the telephone! And I have nothing in my name. Our only expenses are the car, the truck, the telephone and the electric bill. And it's kinda fun that way."

People say, "Now, that's ridiculous that you don't even own the house you live in!"

You see, it belongs to the farm, and in 1990 I sold the farm to my son, Leon. We agreed at the time that the house was worth $150,000 to $180,000. We added half the price of the house to the cost of the farm with the stipulation that I will rent it with a life right at $1 per year, but he never collected it! We never see the dollar; we just smile!

What most people don't understand is that success is not *owning* something, it is *controlling* it. I control my own house, but don't own it. I can live here as long as I want. In our agreement, we stated that if I don't show up for one year (because of illness or because I decided to move to Florida, etc.), I would lose all my controlling rights and privileges. I'm in better shape now than I was when I owned it. The guy who owns the house must pay the taxes and put on a new roof when needed.

We could have gotten an outside family to rent here, but that could have created a lot of grief for my son, the current owner, and I have too good a family to do that to them. The buyer, my son, understood that and they are happy with this arrangement. I am so happy with it also and feel so blessed. *I never knew you could have it so good without owning anything!*

Living a life of total financial commitment to God creates many opportunities to open people's eyes and to be a witness. The funniest thing that I've encountered, and I try not to tell too many people is that I never had a cash savings account until I was sixty-five years old! At that time, I finally put $1,000 into a cash savings account. Grace had mentioned one time, "What would you *do* if you needed $1,000 tomorrow?"

"Well," I answered, "we would need to sell something or go to the bank and get it."

That got me to thinking, and since she had mentioned it, I did it as a token gesture. I saw the statement the other day, and it is still only a little over $1,000. You know, it only gives you ¼ % interest, so it is a poor investment.

Of course, I have no life insurance either, except that three years ago, the bank where I serve on the board, went out on a limb and bought life insurance for the board members. As long as I am on the board, it is in effect. If I quit and go home, the insurance stops. However, I enjoy serving too much to quit, and I get paid for attending the meetings. I very seldom miss one because, first of all, I enjoy them, and secondly, because they pay me to talk!

God's blessings sometimes work in reverse. An example is that 25 years ago I bought a new tractor, and because I always trusted people, I gave the salesman a check. A day later I returned to pick up a part and he said, "You know, I made a mistake yesterday. I didn't charge you $1,000 enough!"

Although I was surprised, I replied, "If you made an honest mistake, then I should make it right."

"Well," he conceded, "I'll let you go this time."

I responded, "To be honest with you, I'm going to set you straight. That money wasn't 'lost;' I have it."

Smiling, he agreed, "Yeah, but I don't."

"Yes, but *you will.*" I predicted.

Would you believe—two days later I needed some new equipment. New wagons at that time cost $1,500 apiece. Because of that, we kept using an old one that was so deteriorated it finally broke down and had to be replaced. *Within two days* that man got his $1,000 back, because I returned and bought several more new pieces of equipment and he recovered it all. I pointed out to him, "Do you see how God works? I came back and you got all your money back within two days!"

He smiled. We've been friends for a long time since, and now the old man has passed on, but the son and his brother are operating the business, and we are still friends.

I used to tell people–"Never worry about money. Money is never lost unless somebody lights up a cigar or cigarette. Then it always ends up in smoke! If you sell me something, and I pay a dollar too much, that money is not lost. That dollar is in your possession and *you* are responsible before God what you do with it. Therefore, don't fret over a dollar or two or even a hundred. It is not lost! Whether it was a mistake or mis-calculation or whatever it was, God had a *reason* for allowing it to happen. When you look at it that way, it is altogether different. God knows where it is. It is never hidden from the eyes of God."

All through the years, if there was a mistake against me, I never brought it to people's attention, but if there was a mistake in my favor, I would go back and tell them, "You overpaid me." In nine times out of ten, they never allowed me to make it right but would say, "You'll give it to charity anyhow." To hear that was a good feeling, a verbal testimony.

People often asked me, "What are you going to do if you get struck with something?"

I would answer, "Well, the same as you do. You are either going to live or you're going to die! If you are *ready* to die, it is not too serious, but you *want* to enjoy life, and I'm going to do my part."

When you are covered by the world's system, you generally follow the guidelines of the world. By that I mean you accept every drug and prescription that is written up for you although many of them are hurting rather than helping you.

When you are spending $1,000 of your own money, it makes you think twice before you will buy something that could poison your system. It puts a whole new perspective on living.

My commitment to Christ was also evident in what I chose to eat! When we'd stop at a restaurant, Grace frequently told the waitress, "He probably wants soup and salad," and she was right!

It's always the cheapest thing on the menu . . . and it's the healthiest! In addition, sometimes I'd add a little jello, a cookie or a small piece of pie, always in a limited amount. Then I'd feel good. But boy, if I'd eat a big steak, I got a bloated, stuffed, sluggish feeling. If I know eating a big dinner will make me feel bad, I don't want to do it. I've learned that my body tells me what works and what don't work, plus eating healthy saves money.

The *greatest* rewards of giving, whether it be of yourself, your time, finances, or anything would be the joy, the satisfaction, the warm feeling you get when people come years later and tap you on the shoulder or put their arm around you and say, "Boy, you sure made a difference in our family! We would never have made it." Or they might say, "You got us going when we were about at the end of the road."

Those emotions and feelings are just immeasurable. You just *can't* measure it. That is *really IT!* That's a far *greater reward* than getting a monetary return.

The amazing thing was that in some instances, you *do* get a financial benefit. People *want* to bless you, you know. Over the years when talking to groups, I would often raise this question: "All you people sitting here in this circle, if you had the choice— to have a million friends or a million dollars, which would you take?"

Many of them would answer quickly, "Give me the million dollars!"

Then I'd say, "Do you know what? I'd rather have a million friends, and let me tell you why. If I get in trouble and have a million friends, and each one gives me one dollar, then I'll have a million dollars AND a million friends! Then I'd have a *double* blessing."

Hopefully, you'll never need to rely on other people to that extent. However, there may come a time, I believe, in everybody's life when we gotta accept a little help. If we have been self-sufficient for years, that is hard to do. You might call it "swallowing your pride," but even though you've been so used to moving on your own, sometimes you have to ask others for help.

At times like this it is so rewarding to know you've made a difference in the lives of others, that they remember your deeds of kindness, and above all, come to you and ask, "What can I ever do to repay you?"

When that happened to me, I said, "It's impossible for you to repay me." Then I would suggest, "I can sum up what you *can* do in just three words: *pass it on*! If you were blessed, remember that I am not going to be here forever, but you can go on and bless someone else."

If you help to pull somebody out of the snow and they offer you $5 and you accept it, that kinda pays their way, gets put on the back burner and it don't have a long-lasting effect. However, if they offer you $5 and you tell them to keep it, they'll often insist, "Wait, what do I owe you?" Then you should smile and say, *"Pass it on and do a favor for somebody else."* They'll never forget that, and everyone *will* receive a blessing!

Chapter Eight

Miracles in Cuba

MIRACLE: *"An extraordinary event manifesting divine intervention in human affairs."*
(Merriam-Webster's Collegiate Dictionary)

It was our last Sunday night in Cuba and we were scheduled to take an island tour and visit a small country church. About 100 to 150 people were expected to attend the service that evening, and the pastor was supposed to preach.

Enroute there, I was sitting near the back of the bus. The Cuban girl who was serving as our interpreter, came back to me, hit me on my knee, pointed to the pastor who couldn't speak English, and said, "He wants to tell you something." That morning he had preached a non-stop two-hour sermon and his voice had become hoarse and raspy. Now, several hours later, he had no voice left at all and could barely whisper. With difficulty he communicated to the interpreter, and she turned to me and said, "He wants you to preach for him tonight. The congregation will be waiting for you at that church." I was stunned and simply exclaimed, "Oh, my!"

After riding in our bus over rough, pot-holed roads for about thirty miles, we arrived at a little farmhouse. It was evident everywhere that they were experiencing a severe drought as the crops looked terrible and the people's truck gardens were just drying up and dying. When the bus pulled off the stone road into the dirt lane, the dust was so deep that it rolled up under the tires.

In our party were 16 students from Manchester College, Indiana, their advisor, Yvonne Dilling, Elgin, Illinois, Faye Kreiner, Manheim, Pennsylvania, and Grace and I. While our Cuban hosts took us into this farmhouse, they pointed out a little concrete church building about 1,000 feet away. It had a tin roof and just one single light bulb hanging from the ceiling.

Our dinner that night consisted of a very tasty chicken broth. It was thin and would have been even better if we could have added a little toast or crackers, but it was good and we were thankful and the fellowship was wonderful. The conversation kept coming back to the fact that they just didn't see how they would survive this terrible drought. I could tell these people were really anxious and hurting.

About 6:30 p.m., our leader suggested that we'd better get ready to go over to the church so we wouldn't be late for the service. The pastor again approached me and speaking through the female interpreter said, "You're going to have to preach for me tonight because I have no voice, and we can't disappoint these people because they came to worship God."

I said, "Well, I'm not a practiced, ordained preacher, but the Bible does say that 'You are to be ready always to give an answer to every man that asks you a reason of the hope that is in you,' (1 Peter 3:15). I'll just give the best testimony I can to the glory of God."

As others were preparing for church, I opened my Bible and paged through a few Scriptures and in about three minutes decided, "Okay, this is what I'll do." So I was committed to speak.

When we were all ready to go to the church, I felt a tremendous burden on my heart because of the desperation of these people. They were so concerned that they wouldn't have enough food for the coming fall and winter. So I asked, "Could we all stop for a minute, join our hands, and pray for rain? Let's ask the Lord to send rain, real showers of blessing to water the earth, because these people need help. Whoever has an urge to pray, please feel free to offer a prayer, verbally or silently." One fellow did, and he prayed "that there would be showers of blessing from heaven, even tonight yet, and we won't get done saying 'thank you.'" I closed with a prayer and added, "Lord, demonstrate Your power one more time like You did when Elijah called for rain from heaven. These people are hurting, but let Your will be done. We want You to get all the glory!"

Then I told the people, "Let's go. Something good is going to happen!"

As we started down the walk and through the gate headed toward the church, one guy said, "Look at that," and pointed toward the sky. Black clouds were circling and swirling above us and coming in closer and closer. Within minutes, it became dark. Before we were halfway to the church it started to rain. Then it poured! By the time we got into the church, we were all soaked. It rained and rained. All through the service, the tin roof was rattling, and it was music to our ears. What a manifestation of an answer to prayer! (I hate to admit that I didn't expect it would happen, but it sure was a lesson in answered prayer.)

Of course, as far as the "sermon" went, I didn't have any time to read or think much about what I would say. I opened my Bible and thought, "Where is it in the Old Testament (or is it in the New Testament?) that it talks about 'we are just pilgrims and sojourners here traveling through a strange world?' Heaven is our home and we're just traveling through."

I was so moved by these verses due to my being a foreigner here, an American sharing with these Cubans in their country, as well as all of us who are Christians living in this wicked world (1 Peter 2:11), that I began talking and building on this theme. After I would say a phrase or two, the translator would share it. Occasionally, some persons in the audience would stand up and clap or shout, "Hallelujah!" The longer I spoke, the more verbal they got! I was really being motivated and could hardly stop!

After I had spoken about a half hour, I realized that right after I said something, they clapped and shouted, "Glory, Hallelujah, Praise the Lord!" I was trying to think, "What did I say that triggered so much enthusiasm?" I stopped and said to the translator, "Aren't you going to tell them what I just said?"

She said, "No, I don't have to. You said the last two sentences in full and perfectly understandable Spanish!" (At that time, I only knew and understood one Spanish word —"Gracias.") I forgot what I said, because I didn't even know what I had said! But they understood it. From then on, it was all English again. The only explanation that I can make is that evidently, there was something that I was supposed to say to "clinch it" or "to hit them over the head," and for that reason, God gave me the words in Spanish. I never spoke in another language before or since that one time. I had said it in English, I thought, and my wife, Grace, heard it in English, she thought, but they heard it in Spanish. I guess this is how "speaking in tongues" sometimes works (Acts 2:5-11). It was amazing, an absolute miracle! In fact, I was dumbfounded! I was so excited that I went on talking for another fifteen minutes!

Meanwhile, the rain continued to pitter-patter on the tin roof audibly reminding us of the miracle happening outdoors. Inside, the people sat on wooden benches under the single light bulb. It was so heart-warming. By the time the service was over, the rain had ended.

Earlier, when we arrived, the dirt road was like a dusty playground where one would walk bare-footed and the dust would roll around your feet like water and get between your toes. I commented to the bus driver, "You know, if it would happen to rain, we will never get out of here. This will be like grease or ice. Perhaps you should park the bus closer to the stone road."

He moved it ahead slightly, but it was still 50 feet or so from the stones, and after the service and the heavy rain-shower, when we wanted to leave, we did get stuck! Twenty-eight of us took off our shoes and stockings and got out to push the bus. After all our efforts, we got it to move a bit, but not far enough. We finally found an old tractor and a log chain. With the tractor pulling and us pushing, we finally got the bus out on the stony road.

Because we were flying back to the United States the next day, we planned on going to Havana that night. However, the last couple nights we had been sleeping in a little old church in that small town, so we stopped there first to pick up our luggage. When we arrived, the church members there said, "Sit down. We're gonna wash your feet!" Imagine that! They wouldn't let us wash our own muddy feet! They insisted on washing our feet. Boy, that was a tear jerker. The world says Americans and Cubans are enemies, but here they were, washing our feet! And in this instance, we weren't reenacting a ritual or an act of remembrance, but it was a necessity! What a lesson this was to the American college students in our group! Whew! What a night!

You may be wondering how in the world Grace and I ever got to Cuba in the first place. That in itself was another miracle.

In 1987, Grace and I volunteered to go to Nicaragua with a group of youth in an exchange program. One day we were up on a mountain picking coffee beans for the Communist government there. (That was the first and only time I ever worked for the Communists.) Anyhow, we were working along side fifteen young people from the Pentecostal Church of Cuba and a couple of their pastors who were there also as part of this exchange program. Carlos, a Cuban pastor who spoke English fluently, was their group leader. On this trip, I had taken along one hundred soft-cover Spanish/English (side by side) Gideon

New Testaments and literally had to keep them hidden because everybody wanted them. I had one hidden in a pocket under my jacket, and when we were up in the mountains alone, I gave one to Carlos. When he saw what it was, he said, "Oh, Victor, we need a thousand of these in Cuba! These are so wonderful because they have both Spanish and English. Our Spanish children could read the Spanish side of it, and when they are learning English, they could read the English side and at the same time, be reading the Word of God."

"Well, Brother Carlos," I said, "if I could come into Cuba, I'd bring you a thousand New Testaments at no charge, but I can't get in. I am simply not eligible to come into your country. As a lay person, there's no way I can get into Cuba because of the embargo and all of the regulations, unless I'd have a government invitation." (What I didn't know was that the National Council of Churches was communicating and getting along fairly well with the Communist Party there at that time.)

Right then and there, we both stopped working and knelt beside the coffee bushes and prayed. I remember that with tears running down his cheeks, Pastor Carlos had a most fervent prayer saying, "Lord, there's got to be a way! We don't know it, but You do!"

About four years later, in the late fall of 1991, the national office of the Church of the Brethren in Elgin, Illinois, received a letter of invitation from Cuba for a group of students to come there for ten days. Included was this statement: "If we can have this student exchange and if they can come, be sure to send Victor and Grace Ziegler along." Nobody knew why.

Someone in Elgin knew Faye Kreiner who lives in Manheim, about fifteen miles from our home. They asked her if she knew us and she replied, "Yeah, sure!" The caller said, "Well, we have a note here that they are to come along to Cuba with a group of exchange students, but we have no idea why."

Faye said, "I wouldn't know why either . . ." Then they asked, "Would you give us the Ziegler's phone number? We need to make reservations for them, because the time for this trip is coming in just a few weeks."

So, one day I got a phone call from Faye and she said, "What's all this fuss about you going to Cuba?"

"Tea for Two"

I said, "What do you mean?"

"Well, you're going to get a phone call. The people at Elgin called me and wondered who this Ziegler guy is. They got a letter from Cuba requesting that a group of college students come for a ten-day visit, and a pastor there requested that they should be sure Victor and Grace Ziegler come along."

Then it dawned on me that I had promised Carlos that if I get an invitation, I would bring one thousand New Testaments. (I had never told Elgin about the prayers Carlos and I had shared. I never told them about my promise to bring a thousand New Testaments.)

Now Faye wanted some answers. "Victor, what is going on?" she asked. When I told her, she said, "Oh, that sounds exciting. I'm signing up for this trip also but I promise I won't tell anyone the background story, the real purpose for your trip."

When Elgin called, we didn't say a word but just graciously accepted the invitation. We agreed to pay for our own tickets and meet the group at the Miami airport.

During the next few weeks, Grace went shopping at every thrift shop in the county and found twenty little briefcases or travel bags, just big enough to hold 50 Spanish/English New Testaments in them. Some of my friends helped to cover our costs. After we packed 50 books in each bag, we took them all to the Miami airport.

There I was surprised to discover that there was a $4.00 per pound penalty embargo on anything that an American citizen took into Cuba. I wasn't prepared for that! I hadn't planned on spending anything at the airport and since we planned to eat and sleep at various churches, I didn't think I needed much money. In my pocket I had only a credit card and $100 cash. I didn't even have a checkbook with me.

The official weighed all the bags and matter-of-factly stated, "That will be $400.00." I asked if there was a MAC machine nearby where I could withdraw money from my bank, and he gave me directions, putting my bags to one side, and said, "See what you can do." After I found it, I couldn't get it to work and was keenly aware that the time for our flight was approaching fast, so I returned once again to the official. I explained my predicament and said, "I just don't know what to do. My friends have all gone through the line and I'm here alone."

"What are you sending?" he asked.

"Well, I have 1,000 books here," I explained. "They are actually English/Spanish New Testaments, and I sure hate to leave 'em here, because I promised a friend in Cuba that I'd bring them."

After staring into space a moment considering what he'd do, he suddenly said, "Why don't I just mark it paid in full and throw all your bags on?" I broke into a big smile and before I could answer, he just marked them and tossed them one by one on the conveyor belt.

"How can I thank you?" I asked.

He just gestured that I should move on. The New Testaments and I had passed the first hurdle.

To board our plane, we had to walk outside across the tarmac. I couldn't possibly carry all these bags and I wondered, "How are we going to get them on the plane?" Suddenly, it occurred to me that there were close to twenty in our group, none had boarded yet, and we were each allowed a carry-on. So, I went to Yvonne Dilling, who was from the Elgin, Illinois, headquarters of the Church of the Brethren and in charge of Hispanic Ministries. She was accompanying the student group as their advisor, so I asked her if it would be possible for the youth to help me out. Would that be okay?

She agreed, so I went to the college students and asked, "Would you do me a favor? I have twenty travel bags here and I need some help. I promised to take them to Cuba, and I can't take all of them by myself. Would each of you be so gracious as to carry one, take it on the plane and put it under your seat or in the compartment above, however they instruct you? Nobody will really question you, and I would really appreciate it."

Slowly, and rather reluctantly, they each picked up a bag, headed to the stairs, and climbed into the plane. I was the last one to board and discovered that several students had been questioned but were allowed to keep the bags with them. During the flight to Havana, several disgruntled students made remarks to Yvonne Dilling, asking "Why is this guy bringing all these books?" Yvonne came and sat with me and asked, "What is going on? There is some uneasiness in the group about this."

So, I told her the whole story of how Grace and I had met Pastor Carlos in Nicaragua four years earlier, the prayers we shared among the coffee bushes, and the promise I had made to bring him 1,000 Bibles. Her response was, "Oh, my goodness! That's exciting!" We both felt that once the students understood how they were helping fulfill this promise, their attitude would quickly change.

However, it wasn't easy. Some of the youth acted like spoiled kids, as though they weren't even from Christian backgrounds. They seemed like "highfalutin" college kids who thought they owned the world. These attitudes on their part bothered me a little bit, but I began joking with them, sharing some interesting stories, and soon felt them warming up and realized I was starting to win them over, one at a time.

The flight from Miami to Havana was very short. It took about fifteen minutes to get up in the air and about fifteen minutes to land, and there we were! When we got off the airplane, I was again the last person. Somebody had tipped off the guards that there is a guy coming with a whole bunch of flight bags. After the inspection officer at customs looked into several of the bags and pulled out a couple of the New Testaments, he shook his head and said, "No, No, No!" Of course, he meant "We can't let these come into our country." (I was aware that bringing any Scriptures into the country was illegal.) He couldn't speak English and I couldn't speak Spanish, except for the one word, "Gracias."

He was wearing a very attractive and sharp-looking uniform. I had a Gideon New Testament in Spanish in my pocket, and on the cover it said, "Nuevo Testamento." As he kept saying, "No," I made eye contact with him and smiled and said, "Gracias, Gracias." Then I pulled the shiny New Testament out of my pocket and grabbing the chest pocket on his uniform, I inserted the New Testament into it and gestured saying, "Sir, a gift–from me to you–something that is good for your country!" While I pointed from myself to him, I kept saying, "Gracias," and he finally returned my smile and said, "Nuevo Testamento?" Feeling he was understanding, I quickly replied, "Yeah, Nuevo Testamento." Then, still smiling, he said "OK, OK, OK," as he pulled the zippers shut on the first few bags, pushed them along and said to me, "Go, Go, Go," waving me on. With a silent prayer of gratitude to the Lord, I gathered up the bags and headed toward the group waiting outside. Against all odds, Grace and I and the thousand New Testaments had actually arrived in Cuba!

An old school bus was waiting to transport us to the church where we would be sleeping overnight. As I approached them, some of the students said, "Here comes Victor, the Bible Man." And that was all right. I thought, "Boy, there are a lot worse names they could call me!"

As soon as Pastor Carlos saw me, his eyes lit up with tears and he came quickly and gave me a big bear hug. He never asked me a question and never said a word about our previous agreement. Later, I took him aside and showed him all our travel bags and opened one and pulled out a New Testament. I said, "Brother Carlos, you may have to help me and give me a sense of direction as to how to distribute these. I don't know if you and your church want to do it or if you want me to help."

"No, you keep them together, and we'll do it one at a time," Pastor Carlos replied. "However, if you are moved to share one, feel free to sneak it out and give it to that person."

I'll never forget giving away the first New Testament. One of our first activities was taking a city walking tour in Havana and we ended at a local market. Sitting on a big stone on the street corner, on some kind of road marker, was a boy who appeared to be about twelve years old. I always had some Spanish New Testaments hidden in my pockets, so I looked around and when I felt nobody was looking, I gave one to the boy. His eyes lit up and he smiled, looked at me, and quickly said, "Gracias." I smiled and said "Gracias" back to him (for taking it)! Two hours later, we came back to that same spot to meet our bus, and the boy was still sitting there reading his New Testament. He looked up, recognized me, and gave me a big smile and I waved to him. I thought, "Wow! This is exciting!" And that excitement hasn't worn off yet!

We had to be very discreet in passing out the New Testaments. If we gave out one, and someone saw it, in no time there would be twenty people gathered around holding out their hands wanting one. We wanted to make our supply last for the ten days and we also wanted to distribute them over the whole island. Some were given to pastors and to Sunday School teachers who could use them for teaching others. So, we were very careful as to who got them and where we gave them. We decided that if we had some remaining, we would just leave them with Carlos and ask him to hand them out.

On our last morning, I had only one English/Spanish New Testament left, and I hid it under my pillow. As we were preparing to go to the airport, a nineteen-year-old Cuban girl approached me and asked, "Sir, are you the man who was handing out Bibles?" I said, "Yeah."

"I am a public school teacher," she explained, "and President Castro said that I can use any book that I can get my hands on to teach my students English. That one with the Spanish and English side by side would be a wonderful tool to use in teaching my students English and at the same time they would be learning about Jesus and the truth of the Scripture."

"Can you wait here a minute?" I asked. "I believe the Lord told me to save this last one until now." Hurrying back to my room, I got the New Testament I had hidden under my pillow and brought it to her.

She just cried, hugged me, and said, "Gracias, Gracias, Gracias." I'll never forget that moment. I said to Grace, "I just wish I had 1,000 more!"

Other memories of our 10 days in Cuba include a visit I made to a dairy farm. One day while driving through the country, our bus went by a dairy farm. I said, "Up here's a dairy farm, and I've been a dairy farmer all my life. We gotta stop and visit with them."

The Cubans traveling with us said, "Aw, there's nothing to see here. They won't even talk to you." I said, "Yeah, they will talk to me!"

While the bus and students parked beside the road, I walked in the lane alone about a quarter of a mile. Soon six or so of the farm workers had gathered around me. I noticed that everything was very antiquated, looking much like a farm in Pennsylvania would have looked 50 years ago. They were milking cows by hand and doing everything the hard and old way. A few of the people could handle English fairly well, and they were eager to share with somebody who had gone out of his way to talk to them.

When I returned, the group of American youth who had been waiting for me in that hot bus called out, "It's about time. We just told the driver to leave without you." They were kidding me, but I responded, "Well, then I'd just have to apply for citizenship here." A person needs to make the best of any circumstance in which he finds himself. I shared on the bus what I had seen, and they seemed very interested.

During our time in Cuba, we often felt that we were being observed and followed. One Hispanic man, calling himself "Martinez," spoke excellent English and said that he worked for the government but appeared to be a television reporter. He pumped me with questions such as "What do I think of their country?" I was always determined to give him a positive answer. He said he was planning to visit the United States that following May and I told him, "You let me know. You are welcome to come to our house and stay a couple nights." (But that never happened.)

Before we came to Cuba, a friend called me to say good-bye to me because he was sure I'd "say the wrong thing and Castro will have you locked up!" I replied, "If they put me in prison, they'll only keep me there one night. Once they discover that I can cut sugar cane, I'll be the work crew leader the next day."

So, when this Cuban reporter questioned me, I always talked about the good things that I was seeing here. For example, I told him I met so many lovely people and saw such beautiful countryside. I said, "You don't have quite all the things we have in the States, but that Castro, is so enthusiastic, so positive, that he gets your attention. If he'd ever become a preacher of the Gospel, he'd be a second Saul turned into the Apostle Paul, the world's greatest missionary."

When I thought of that reporter appearing on television every night, I thought to myself, "Man, if you could only share the gospel! That would captivate your audience."

Visiting Cuba was a real experience. We discovered that everybody in Cuba has a TV, a refrigerator, and a chicken. They didn't have anything else, you know, but they weren't starving. They were living on cheap food, but it was nourishing. Most of the Christian people that we met were from a Pentecostal background. They were sincere, but they had to be very careful what they said or did as they could lose their job or face persecution.

The whole goal of the student exchange was to promote better mutual understanding, to build a relationship and to improve communication between our culture and theirs. In this way, they could learn that Americans are not bad people, the world's enemies. In addition, as Christians, we wanted to reach out in friendship and share the love of Christ.

At the end of our trip, Yvonne Dilling came to me and said, "Victor, these students keep telling me that you made their trip wonderful because they were able to experience and to witness all this." So it was worth it all. I keep telling people—"Never get discouraged if someone turns a cold shoulder to you, even if it is your own son or daughter. Never give up. Just keep on believing, keep on praying, keep on loving them. You can't lose!"

I would never exchange that trip to Cuba for anything in the world. I would never have planned to go there at all if we had not met Carlos in Nicaragua and his expressing the need for New Testaments. Even so, humanly speaking, I wouldn't have thought it physically possible to get through all the restrictions and red tape to get there, and much less, to take 1,000 New Testaments along! However, never underestimate our God. NOTHING is impossible for Him! He truly is a God of miracles. Praise His Name!

Chapter Nine

Traveling Around God's World

"When you travel and you don't know what to expect next, it can be a little heart-throbbing, but it usually turns out to be a great experience." —Victor K. Ziegler

"I can listen to my brother preach at home. I don't have to listen to him here tomorrow. I'm going to explore the island and meet the natives as I want a 'new' experience."

It was a Saturday night and Grace and I were on the beautiful South Pacific island of Tahiti. My brother, Earl, who was directing our tour group, had just announced that the next morning our group would have its own worship service at a grove of trees by the ocean. That's when I made that "smart" remark.

The next morning I got up early and started out alone, rented a bicycle, and rode about an hour until I came to a village with a little stone and mud church which could seat about 150 people. Outside the church was a sign which said: "Hora 9:00 a.m., Worship and Sunday School."

Since I was about an hour early, I sat on the stone steps and read my Bible a little bit. Soon a woman came walking toward me and started talking to me in English. She introduced herself as the pastor's wife and told me she lived in a little house about 150 feet away. Then she asked who I was and how I got there, and I told her I was part of a group who were visiting the island, staying at this hotel, and planning to fly home to the United States that afternoon. I explained that we were a Christian group and that the others were going to have a worship service at the hotel, but I had decided to come and attend her church that morning.

"Oh, I'm so glad you did," she exclaimed, adding, "you are a God-send. My husband is deathly sick and can't get out of bed. Everything falls on me when that happens. Would you come in and pray for him?"

"I'd be glad to," I assured her.

So, we went into the house and I met her husband, the pastor. He was hurting and feeling kinda feverish. We talked a little bit, and I discovered they were missionaries from England living here to help these people. Then I prayed for him.

"Brother, when I don't feel up to it, my wife has to do everything–teach Sunday School, preach, lead the singing, and getting everything done in the worship service," he explained. He added, "The Lord sent you here for a reason. I just *can't* get out of bed and preach a sermon this morning. There will soon be 100 to 150 people in the church *waiting* to hear a message. Would you be willing to take my place?"

"I can't take your place, but I'm willing to do the best I can and share some good news from the Bible, and that's all that matters," I told him, adding, *"pray for me."*

First, they had a Sunday School discussion. I could get the gist of it by listening to them reading their scripture texts. I always get a little nervous in situations like that until I calm down and silently pray, "Lord, I don't know what to say." Then I spoke to them about a half hour non-stop, using similar ideas to what I had preached when I had been in Cuba. The main subject was that although we may be discouraged and lack many "things," none of that matters, as we are just passing through this world on our way to heaven. As Christians, we are all strangers here looking forward to our heavenly home.

They clapped, and even shouted "Glory, Hallelujah" and "Amen" at times, and were so excited, though not quite as lively as the Cubans had been. With the pastor's wife serving as my interpreter, it was a good and unforgettable experience.

After the service, I told them, "I'd better go. My group might leave without me." Then I rode the bicycle back to the hotel and fortunately arrived on time. I remember sharing my exciting morning activities with the tour group. Although I would have liked to have stayed and worshiped at the hotel with them, I felt the Lord had led me to a true cultural and inspirational experience.

When I recall being in Tahiti, I remember not only a beautiful island with graceful palm trees and gorgeous sunsets, its quietness and serenity, and the blue colors of the Pacific Ocean, but also the fellowship I enjoyed with the Christians there.

On our first visit to Hawaii, a farm trip with ten or twelve people, we met Glenn Miller, a group member, who was a real joker. He had respect for Christianity, but wouldn't call himself a Christian. On our trip, he did the dumbest thing, something that would be illegal today. On the airplane, he went into the restroom and came out wearing a bear suit that looked very real. He walked down the aisle and put his arm around the stewardess, and she screamed.

When we got to our hotel, he pretended that he had his hand stuck in the elevator door and it looked like real blood was dripping from it! He sure got everybody's attention. We were shook up momentarily, and then had the biggest laugh when we discovered it was fake blood. He was the limit. It just never stopped! Of course, we kinda fed him a little bit and urged him on. At that time, one could get away with jokes like that without offending anybody. Unfortunately, he died some years later in a tragic accident.

Before our first overseas trip in 1979, I contacted the Menno Travel Agency in Ephrata, Pennsylvania, and told them I have fourteen people who want to travel to Germany, Holland, and Switzerland and see the countryside there and visit a few farms. They helped me put a tour together and I even took my mother and her friends, Hilda Balmer and Hilda Leffler, along. (Later, she visited Nigeria along with my sister, Ada and her husband, Monroe Good, who were missionaries there.)

When we were riding in the bus in Germany, we spotted a man digging potatoes, so I asked the driver to stop so we could chat with him briefly. "That guy won't talk to you. You're just wasting your time," was his response.

However, although he was reluctant, he *did* stop, and four of us went out to speak with the man. Since my knowledge of the Pennsylvania Dutch language is limited, I listened as those who knew it better were able to communicate with him. Our conversation with this guy was about the differences between the way they farm and the way we do it in America. We informed him that we also have a lot of small crop farmers who do a lot of intensive things on 10 or 20 acres. He seemed to be as interested as we were, and all of us had to laugh at our broken language and the way we had to gesture and repeat things, but that made it all the more fun.

Afterwards, our driver told us that in all his years of driving bus nobody had ever done that before. He concluded, "That was great."

Grace and I also went to Honduras on a mission trip with a medical and dental team. The dentist was Dr. Mark Weaver from Strasburg, and I was the "go-for" or "labor" man, helping to carry the many cases, boxes and supplies. In the refugee camp there, as we treated and/or pulled teeth from more than 300 people, I had several real learning experiences.

I'll never forget one 16-year-old girl who was having severe pain in her tooth and wanted it pulled. Her tooth had such deep roots that as the dentist attempted to clamp on it with his pliers-type tool, she was lifted out of her chair! He then instructed me, "Victor, put your hands on her shoulders, and when I am pulling, put all your weight on her to hold her down."

So I did, and he almost lifted me up! He had to rock it right and left, back and forth, until finally it let loose. When that happened, this girl jumped up, gave out a shriek, and with tears running down her cheeks, hugged the dentist saying over and over, "Gracias, gracias, gracias."

Then she turned to me and did the same thing! She just couldn't get done expressing her appreciation.

One particular man told me his toothache had been so severe that he took the tip of a bayonet and worked at his tooth for a week until he finally was able to loosen his infected tooth and push it out, getting relief. In other words, the suffering was harder on him than the pain of trying to remove it.

People would wait patiently to be treated. Arriving at the break of dawn, they waited in line until dusk, and at that time there were still often 50 people waiting. They would go home and return the next day and wait again. When we left, there were still some unattended, but we had treated a lot of them.

Since Grace and I went with several dental and medical teams on short-term mission trips to Central American countries, such as Honduras, Guatemala, and Nicaragua, my memories of those experiences sort of flow together, so it is hard to remember exactly *where* in Central America they occurred.

One example is that we would travel up the rivers in a wooden canoe. At times the natives paddling the canoe would almost upset us as they'd turn out for something in the river that we hadn't even seen! It was amazing to see how they had the location of every rock in the river memorized.

One time we had to cross a river by walking over fallen tree logs, and it was pretty dangerous. To make sure no one would fall in, we formed a human chain, and all were able to cross successfully without getting hurt.

If anyone has an opportunity to go on a short mission trip like this, they should never turn it down. Along with the medical and dental assistance, we shared the gospel with the people there. It was a wonderful experience.

Another Central American happening occurred when we were flying in a small old airplane. When we took off, it started raining a little bit. As we got farther up in the air, it began raining faster. Then I noticed the pilot opening up an umbrella! He was flying this plane and holding up the umbrella at the same time because he didn't want his instrument panel to get wet. About the time I noticed all of this happening, a beeper went off sounding like a warning signal, and the engines cut out. I shouted, "We're going down!"

And we *were* descending, but for a different reason than what I thought. We landed on a dirt road that went by a sawmill. There we saw two guys busy sawing. Imagine this: As one man stood down below in the dirt and the other guy up above, they were sawing boards that were 16 foot long and one inch thick with a 2-man saw.

We picked up two men there, and then I understood that we had dropped down because we had arrived at our destination. *When you travel and you don't know what to expect next, it can be a little heart-throbbing, but it usually turns out to be a great experience.*

In 1982 seven of us went on a three-week agricultural tour to South America set up for us by the Menno Travel Agency. While traveling all over the continent, we visited farms, factories and agricultural experiment stations in the different countries to see what projects they were working on and how they were trying to improve their farming practices.

One day we rode twenty-two hours on the back of a pickup truck on a dusty road. We almost ran out of water and were sure we were going to choke on the dirt! They had numerous military checkpoints and every now and then we'd be stopped, and guys would come up and shine flashlights in our faces while holding a rifle. Then they'd let us go on.

At the end, when we had to go to the airport, for some reason the driver stopped when we were still 50 miles away and ordered us to get off.

"No," I objected, "we go to the airportee."

He just stood there shaking his head "no".

I looked him straight in the eyes and said firmly, "Yes! We go to the airportee *today!*"

Then he shrugged his shoulders and conceded, "Oh? Okay."

He closed the door and started driving down the road again. We finally arrived at the airport, but we weren't too early, if at all! This had been quite a learning experience.

Sponsored by Heifer Project International, our next trip to South America was also a three-week trip and we had a group of 12 persons. All of us were asked to pay our own way and write a follow-up or summary report of our impressions. Three times I had invited my brother-in-law, Norman Kline, who was another Lebanon County farmer, to go along, but every time he said emphatically, "No way!"

On the day before we were to leave, Norman came to me and said he wishes he wouldn't have said, "No." So, that same day he drove directly to Philadelphia and was fortunate to be able to get a passport, and then, at the last minute, was able to join us. Our group included a real cross-section of people: a medical doctor and his wife from the Chicago area, a veterinarian, and farmers from Pennsylvania.

One morning our goal was to visit several families who had received goats and dairy cows from the United States through Heifer Project International. To get there, we boarded an old gray bus, something like a Greyhound bus, with tires that I noticed weren't too great.

As we rode down a steep gravel mountain road, I noticed that the bus driver was pumping the brakes. Being used to driving tractor-trailers and straight trucks, I knew exactly what could happen. When the brakes get too hot in heavy equipment, you either burn them out or blow a tire out from the excessive heat. I was sitting in the middle of the bus and I called the fellow who was supposed to be our interpreter and guide and told him, "Hey, you'd better warn the driver that he had better shift gears because he is going to wear out the brakes and blow out a tire or something. I can already smell the heat coming up through the floorboards."

The guide went up and told him, but the driver just smiled and said, "Don't worry; I know what I'm doing." He said it in Spanish, and the guide told me that, adding, "There's nothing to worry about."

The doctor and his wife were sitting above what we would call the wheel well. Less than two minutes later, a blast exploded like a shotgun. The doctor's wife screamed, as she thought somebody had gotten shot. I knew exactly what had happened. The bus driver pulled over to the side of the road and we sat there about four hours until they found a tire and tube and had it changed and replaced. After that, he drove like I had suggested earlier, but we had lost four hours, and it cost him a tire and a tube.

We drove until the road came to an end, piled into a 4-wheel drive jeep and drove into the jungle until we couldn't go any farther. Although it was a hot, muggy day, we walked the last mile and one-half through the thick jungle until we came to a clearing. There a native and his family lived on the second deck of a little hut with a few chickens running below and a dairy cow tied to a nearby tree with a rope around her neck.

They had received this cow through Heifer Project, and they were so happy because now they had fresh milk. The man's wife milked the cow while we were there. One interesting thing I noticed was that the dairy cows that were fed one or two bananas each day along with their native grass got much more production. Because of the nutritional balance between the native grass, which they called "star grass," and the potassium in the bananas and other trace minerals, their production was almost doubled. While we were there, the owner's wife picked a couple bananas right off the tree and chopped them and fed them to the cow! That was interesting.

They couldn't get done expressing appreciation. In some rare instances, we were told, somebody would come and steal or slaughter an animal, destroying a family's income and a valuable source of milk, so they always had to be on their guard.

We told them we understood that things like that may happen occasionally, but we want to continue the project because in each case, somebody is getting blessed. Then we went on to visit another place.

In Peru, we went up in the mountains to see all the goats. The animals sent out by Heifer Project International are always selected according to the climate, so we found rabbits, sheep and goats in those cool, mountainous areas. It was heartwarming to see how well the concept was working.

Until I learned it through Heifer International, I didn't know that a pair of rabbits will exceed an angus cow in a year's production of meat! Rabbits multiply so fast, that if you take the total pounds from their offspring at the end of a year, you will have more meat for a family than you would by giving them an angus cow or a beef animal for slaughter. Rabbits can multiply every thirty or forty days and have six or eight in a litter. In another thirty or forty days, those six or eight will start multiplying. They grow so fast, especially if they have access to nice clover, grass or other natural vegetation. It is amazing how God created things, putting the right animals in the right climates. If we would live according to the plan that God had at creation, there would be no need for anyone to be hungry.

In Lima, Peru, while staying at the Mennonite Guest House, we met a farmer who had dairy animals to sell. We had been seeing how well the Heifer Project animal recipient families were doing, so our group decided to collect money among ourselves to purchase a cow to become a part of the program. (The whole goal of Heifer Project is to adapt livestock, poultry, and/or plant life to the various climates so that the people living there can become self-sustaining and self-supporting.)

The farmer who had the cow for sale told us that because of the 300% inflation in their country, if we would buy his cow in the morning, it would cost about ten dollars less than if we would buy it that evening or the next day. It was hard for me to understand that inflation could be *so wild*, that the value of money could change that much in one day! But that was the fact.

Because their money was practically worthless, they had to carry it in small bundles and put rubber bands around it. I remember carrying it in a little briefcase. To buy a hamburger would take a whole pack! When we got our American money changed, we received a whole bundle.

It was so strange. It reminded me of my cousin, Carl Bross' wife, a German native, who told me the story that after World War II, she needed 50 cents to ride the bus to school. By the next day, the money had changed in value so drastically that she needed five dollars——ten times more! She said the money exchange went wild overnight due to inflation, and suddenly, their money was worthless. People would actually have a wheelbarrow full of money just to go to the grocery store. In America, we think 10% inflation is a lot, but they were experiencing far greater inflation in Germany that long ago.

Many of the Peruvian natives couldn't afford to buy and sell. They just had to barter and hope they could live off the land and whatever they could scrape together.

At one point on our trip, Norman Kline and I left the group for three days to visit Isaac Martin, a fellow we had known in Pennsylvania. We heard he had bought 400 acres in Paraguay, brought in a new backhoe and bulldozer, and had built a church, a school, and started a Mennonite settlement. I had met him when he was nineteen years old and single, and in 1970 he helped to build my house, so he knew me. When I was planning to come to South America, I contacted some of his relatives and they told me he lived in Paraguay, about four hours out of the capital city of Asuncion.

At the bus station, Norman and I were informed that no buses ran during the day because it was just too hot and they would overheat. When we bought our tickets, we asked about where we would get off, and the ticket agent just said, "Oh, the bus driver knows. He will drop you off when you get there."

So, at 11:00 p.m., we boarded an old bus, all beat up, with smooth tires, door hinges that didn't work, and half the windows unable to be shut! We sat near the back bouncing all night with our suitcases between our legs. In spite of that, we fell asleep and hung forward over our suitcases so we wouldn't have so much dust flying in our faces.

About 2:00 a.m., the Spanish driver's assistant came back and hit me on my knee. Norman asked sleepily, "What's going on?"

"I think they are tired of us," I answered.

There were about fifteen or twenty passengers on the bus and people got off and on as we drove along. Suddenly, in the middle of nowhere, the driver just stopped and ordered us to get out. I wasn't quite sure if we were at the right place, and since I didn't know Spanish, I tried in every way I could to make him understand that we were looking for the "Mennonite Colony" or Settlement. The driver just kept motioning and saying, "Go! Go! Go!"

I said to Norman, "This must be the place," but we felt sure he didn't understand anything we had said. As I look back on it now, I believe he did.

Anyhow, we got off, and the bus left, and it was 2:30 in the morning. It was pitch dark and we just stood there for about 20 minutes, not knowing where to go or what to do. Finally, I observed to Norman, "You know, the longer we stand here, the prettier the sky gets! Look at those stars. Those are probably the same stars we see at home. The moon's coming out." And we had absolutely no idea which way to go. Just no idea!

We knew we were on a dirt road, but couldn't see a thing. After a while, I suggested to Norman, "Well, we have one thing left to do—we can shout, we can sing, we can praise the Lord for the beautiful sky that we have never seen before."

Just about that time our eyes started getting adjusted to the darkness, and as the moon came out further, we could see a little bit more and more. Suddenly, across the road I recognized the shape of a school bus shanty. Isaac Martin had told me that he had built one out of slab wood at the entrance to their settlement and had put on it a wooden shingle where he burned in the words, "Mennonito Colony." I walked over to it, spied the sign and joyfully informed Norman, "We must be at the right place. It says, 'Mennonito Colony.'" A narrow gravel driveway seemed to branch off to the right.

Just then, we heard a sound coming down the road like a herd of wild pigs running, with their teeth grinding, and squealing "Oink, oink, oink!"

I was alarmed and alerted Norman, "Hey, we are being attacked by wild boars!"

"What are we going to do?" he asked in a panicky voice.

I started stepping it off across the road and stood inside the school bus shanty holding my suitcase in front of me for my defense. Then I noticed that there was a sawed off telephone pole standing next to the shanty. I didn't know if it was there to tie horses to or what, but I said to Norman, "Do you know what? If we could get up that pole, we could get up on the roof of this shanty and sit up there and wait until daylight."

Now the pole was about six feet high, and Norman was a very obese man, about nine years older than I was. I never would have thought Norman could get up on a 6-foot pole, but HE DID! He grabbed that pole and I gave him a push, and he ended up on top of the pole.

Then I asked, "Now *you* are safe, but what about *me?*"

So, he stood up on the pole, which was a little risky, but it was a good-sized one. He leaned over on the roof and crawled on top of it. I climbed up the same way, and we decided to just lay down on the roof so we wouldn't damage anything.

When the pigs ran by, we watched them from our perch on the roof. We stayed up there until it was daylight and then climbed down and walked to the middle of the road and continued to wonder where we would go from there. (We found out the next day that the pigs weren't wild, but were a bunch of tame ones that had gotten out of their pen and were just having a ball running around the community.)

Some man came by, but we couldn't communicate with him. We both agreed that we would tell him, "If you are going to eat anybody, eat my brother-in-law!"

At the break of dawn, we heard someone cough a couple hundred feet away, and it looked like a young lady walking alone. I whispered to Norman, "We are going to scare the wits out of her; what will we do?"

When she was still a long distance away, we started calling out to her, "Manana, Manana," (thinking we were saying "Good Morning." We found out since it means "tomorrow!")

She stopped abruptly and looked confused, and of course, we were too!

I said to her as I gestured, "Ma'am, ah . . . we . . . Americans . . . visit a friend, Isaac Martin."

Then she started walking toward us. Eventually, we were about five feet from each other, and I kept saying "Isaac Martin."

Suddenly, she said, in broken English, "Oh, you want E-zak Mar-tee-nez!"

"Yeah, Yeah, E-zak Mar-tee-nez!" I exclaimed excitedly, smiling. "My friend, my amigo."

She motioned and pointed in the gravel driveway, "He lives in here."

Isaac had brought a subsorter along equipped with a steel bar which went two feet into the ground, and he buried two miles of telephone wire between all these houses. It came to the very last house which was only about one hundred feet from the shanty where we stood talking.

The young girl continued, "You might know the family who lives in this first house. They are from Pen-sill-vain-ee-uh and their name is Showalter."

She took us to the house and rang the bell and rapped on the door. They were just getting ready for breakfast.

When the woman came to the door, I recognized her immediately as the sister of a friend of mine in Myerstown, Richard Weaver, who had built me two silos. I exclaimed, "You are Martin Weaver's daughter, Richard's sister!"

"Yeah, and I remember you too," she acknowledged with a big smile.

They invited us in and of course, we had a wonderful time. After eating their delicious ham and egg breakfast, we weren't even tired! It was so exciting, so much fun!

These people, the Showalters, were hooked up to the telephone, so they called Isaac Martin and told him we were here. We hadn't told them we were coming, so our arrival was a complete surprise. "You tell Victor to wait right there, and I'll come over with my tractor, and we can throw his suitcases right on it," he responded.

Within 20 minutes he was there and we slept in his house for two nights. His wife's name was Lena, and since I have a sister named Lena, that was an easy name for me to remember.

We had a great time. They kept a barrel of water on the roof. If the sun was shining, you had a warm bath, but if it was a cloudy day, your bath was cold! That's the way it was.

At their Wednesday evening Bible study and prayer service, a generator was running outside to keep their one electric light bulb burning so the preacher could read while he spoke.

While we were there, they took us over to an area between Paraguay and their neighboring country, Brazil, where they were building the world's largest turbine hydroelectric plant. Reagan was the U.S. President at that time, and we spent millions and millions of dollars there helping them develop that plant. It looked like a 6-8-10 lane highway. They already had three turbines in operation and said they have enough water power here to generate current for the majority of South America. Now there is a bridge going over the top of it connecting the two countries.

Because we wanted to buy a water pump and some plastic pipes, we traveled across the bridge. We asked Isaac how he gets over and back so easily. "Well," he answered with a wide grin, "I wear my black Mennonite hat and my straight-laced blue or black Mennonite coat with the buttons up to the top, and they think I am a Catholic priest, and they would never question a priest!"

When he'd jump into a taxicab, the driver often said, "How are you doing today, Father?"

So he would drive him to the border, and when they got there, Isaac would jump out and say, "Ah yes, I have some friends visiting from the U.S.A., and we brought some supplies back."

Then they'd step aside and let us all in. His mode of dress gave him entrance.

Paraguay had had a dictator for many years who was sympathetic to the Mennonites and had ordered his military to look after them because they were good farmers. He welcomed them because he saw they were helping to build up his country. A dictator who is committed to the ways of the Lord can be a wonderful thing.

However, when a new dictator took over, they lost the protection of their president and government. I understand that 50% came home to the United States having lost their farms there and everything. In fact, Isaac Martin, himself, came back and told me that I could have his 400 acre farm for $40,000, which was what he had paid for it. All the improvements he made there and the years doing it were lost. Although the Mennonites were widely known to be caring and industrious people, toward the end some of the women and girls had their bicycles stolen, were beaten and even raped, so many decided instead of fighting it, they would leave. I believe there is a small settlement there yet, but not like it once was or like it could have become.

On our trip to the Holy Land, we were part of a tour group directed by my brother, Earl. Visiting the sites mentioned in the Bible was such a thrilling and moving experience. However, one could feel that the tension there was very high. When we went through one of their checkpoints, possibly when we went from Jordan into Israel, they took me in and made me just about totally undress. I never learned what they were hunting for or what I had said that raised their suspicions. I do know that the rest of the group were telling Grace, "They'll keep *him*!" But it always worked out.

Another time, I had bought a crate of tree-ripened oranges to share with the group from time to time. We came to another checkpoint, and were told "You can't take those along."

"Would it be okay if we take them along in our stomachs?" I asked.

The guy just smiled, so for the next ten minutes, we all ate oranges and we ate every one of them! We took them along with us that way. It was funny.

One of the places I *really* wanted to see was the Dead Sea. After reading about it in the Bible and hearing about its high salt and mineral content from other travelers, I was eager to see it for myself. However, the local guides discouraged us from trying to see it because of the tense political situation in that area.

Since my brother was the tour director, I decided to heckle him a bit, so I declared loudly on the tour bus so that the whole group heard me, "I'm not going home until I get to see the Dead Sea!"

Some of the others expressed the same thing, and if we had persisted, we could have gotten a little insurrection started. However, the local guides came to us and explained the danger and it was also getting late in the day, so we reluctantly said that was okay. It didn't ruin the trip for me.

On another trip with my brother, this time to Alaska, he had such a large group that he needed two buses. We flew up to Anchorage, rode by bus to various points, boarded a train, and then came back to Seattle by cruising down the Inner Passage. On our first day Earl got on the bus and announced, "I'm going to go on the other bus, and Victor can stay on this bus, because there is not enough room here for the two of us. Furthermore, I don't want to be responsible."

I couldn't let him get away with that, so I jumped up and said, "I am here to tell you that my older brother *never* was responsible!"

Of course, they all got a charge out of that, considering where it came from. Doreen Creighton, my niece and Earl and Vivian's daughter, was on my bus also and we shared the duties of helping out as tour leaders. We had a lot of interesting conversations on the bus and the friendships that were built are just . . . forever!

We toured Alaska in July which turned out to be a beautiful time of year to see the abundant and unusual plants and wildlife. Until you're there, it is hard to imagine how long the daylight lasts, and how hard it is to go to sleep while it is still so bright outside. Some people could still take photographs outdoors as late as 11:00 at night! I guess what interested me most was seeing the dogsled demonstrations. When we saw how aggressive and yet well-trained those dogs were, it was obvious that they just wanted to "up and go." Their eagerness to run was hard to believe before one actually witnessed it.

When we were in New Zealand, again as part of another of Earl's tour groups, Grace and I digressed from the scheduled route for a day or two and went out on our own to visit several dairy farms. Since I had been using the New Zealand made milking equipment for many years, I was eager to compare my progress with that of the dairy farmers there and see if there were other and newer techniques that I could be learning.

One big difference I discovered was that many times they will milk a whole herd of dairy cows for ten months at a time and then take a two month's break. (In the United States, we keep our production close to level all year 'round, as our dairies count on and want a more uniform milk production.) In New Zealand, more emphasis is put on cheese-making and dry milk products, so they balance it out that way. We discovered that we had a lot of things in common, but a lot of variations also.

When we were in Australia, we ate supper one night in an elegant restaurant. Although I am not especially fond of seafood, we were told that fish was a specialty in this area, so I reluctantly ordered it along with the others. When the waitress brought out my platter and set it in front of me, the eyes of the fish were staring at me! Some in the group said I turned pale. I don't know if that happened or not, but I sure didn't like the idea of eating something that was watching me while I did it! I know I decided quickly that I wasn't very hungry that night after all.

One time we went with other farmers to Kitchener, Canada, on a tour organized by the A.O. Smith Company, who sold blue silos, glass-lined water heaters, and water tanks for municipalities all over the United States. For years they had been begging me to buy one of their units—their glass-lined silo. It was the "Cadillac" of all of them.

Their salesman stopped at my farm one day and said, "We have 34 farm couples going to Kitchener and we need one more couple to fill the plane. Would you be willing to go along?"

"I'd feel bad going, because all these other guys bought something from you," I explained, adding, "I don't want to take advantage of you. I'll tell you what: If you can assure me that we'll still be friends when we get back, whether I buy from you or not, Grace and I will go along."

"Okay, that's a deal!" he quickly agreed.

So we went along to Canada, visiting farms in several counties there, and it was a good experience.

On the flight back, there were a group of passengers on our plane who wanted to get off at Buffalo, New York. We headed that direction, but the plane didn't land. After they announced that we were arriving in Buffalo, we noticed that we kept seeing the same lights. We were in the midst of a snowstorm, and after the plane was circling the city for a good hour, some of the people became upset.

You know how they serve you beverages, ginger ale and coke and sometimes even alcoholic drinks (but I don't think the majority of that group drank any). Anyhow, after this one stewardess served everyone something to drink, some of them needed a plastic bag to bring it back up! She was so busy and so upset and running back and forth in the aisle trying to keep everyone happy.

The pilot told her, "Do something just to shut them up and keep them content."

"I don't know what to do," she answered, almost in tears.

So I said, "Give me the loudspeaker, and we'll try to change their attitude."

The mike was only two seats away from me, so she grabbed it and handed me the cord. I stepped up to it and announced, "Good evening, ladies and gentlemen, I am just helping our Captain out tonight. I don't know anything about flying, but *I do know* that if we are going 600 miles per hour and we already have flown in circles for an hour, we all got a 600 mile free trip! Maybe we ought to give our pilot a hand for the extra free mileage. If that isn't enough, they tell us that there is a heavy snowfall and they are busy deciding what is the right approach. So now, we are all going to sing for a few minutes. Because most of us are from the United States, let's start off singing 'God Bless America.' After all, we need His blessing, we *all* need it, and we need it NOW!"

So, we started singing and I got half of them to join in. In a muffled airplane, it didn't go so good, but *they could hear ME* because I was on the loudspeaker! We got through it twice, and I said, "Do you know what? You guys didn't do your BEST. Although you tried, I'm a little disappointed. If I were the pilot, flying you back to the United States, and you couldn't sing 'God Bless America' any better than that, I'd take you back to Canada!"

I had just got done saying that when the pilot came on the loudspeaker saying, "This is the Captain speaking. Due to inclement weather conditions, we are returning to Kitchener, Canada."

Boy, did I have trouble convincing them that I wasn't in cahoots with the pilot! And I really didn't know a thing about what was going on. He went on to say, "Those who *must* go to Buffalo tonight may want to travel by bus. You can get there on the road—by bus. To those of you who will layover, we'll see that you get home as soon as it clears."

So, we were given hotel accommodations overnight and they took us back the next day. For years afterwards, whenever I would meet one of those guys who were on that trip, even if I hadn't seen them for a long time, they would talk and laugh about that experience.

Every time I went traveling around God's world I was more informed and better educated. I guess I have to admit that the more I traveled, the more aggressive I got in doing things and asking questions. I probably stepped out a little bit farther each time. On different occasions some group member would say, "Aw, Victor, that isn't going to work!"

"Why do you say that?" I asked. "I read in *my* Bible that 'With God, *all things* are possible!'" (Matthew 19:26)

"That's true, but *you're not God*."

"I know that, but I am *a child of the King!*"

Chapter Ten

Managing a Nursing Home
at Villa Pine Farm

"Whatever I can do for them, I do."
– T. Grace Ziegler

Grace always had a heart for people and got much joy out of helping them, whether they were foster children, refugees, mentally handicapped children, or senior citizens. During the ten years after our initial financial losses, God really blessed us. Job talked about being blessed four-fold. Well, I was blessed ten or twenty-fold! I was buying and selling farms and building up our herd, and although we had the five children and Grace helped with the milking and caring for the chickens, she still felt she wanted to do more with her life–for people! But she wanted to do it from her home base.

At that time, there was a shortage of nursing home space in Lebanon County. After we thought about and discussed this, Grace called the County Office for the Aging and offered to care for one or two older folks in our home. We thought we could handle up to three, but we ended up doing it for eleven years with a maximum of eleven people at one time between the ages of 65 and 88, nine women and two men!

After we had the first two or so, the County Office would call us and say, "Hey, we have an eighty-year-old woman and we don't know where to put her. Would you take her?"

That's how our "nursing home family" grew. Every time Grace would get a call, I'd say, "Where are we going to put them? Must we enclose the back porch and make a bedroom?"

Grace cooked for all these people, gave them their medications, and did all their laundry and cleaning. For doing this, she was paid $125 per person each month, which was well-earned. (When we closed our facility and they were moved to another one, their maintenance fee doubled and they had to pay $250 per month.)

They also needed personal attention, and she had to be careful that she didn't favor one over another. There was one lady, Sarah Frank (not her real name), who was a professor's mother. Every time Grace came in the door, Sarah was right there and wanted to talk to her. And there were others also who demanded a lot of attention. Grace began to realize that she not only had to cook, clean, feed, and do laundry for them but also keep them entertained. Having the children here helped somewhat with that, as the senior citizens enjoyed watching them play and talking with them.

We also ran into some human relations problems that we didn't expect. One old man, Sam, (not his real name), fell in love with Sadie, (not her real name), one of the older women. They were both in their 80's and would sit on the front porch and talk and visit all day long. One day Grace found them in the front hallway of the house, and he was hugging, kissing and caressing her.

At that time, I was busy remodeling the basement, making an apartment down there. Sam would come down and watch my progress and one day I told him, "You and Paul are going to be living in this new basement apartment when we get it finished."

He looked belligerent and declared loudly, "I don't wanna!"

"You're gonna get the nicest bedroom and bathroom in the house," I continued, trying to "sell" him on the idea. I had put in all new carpet, all new paneling, and a picture window so he'd have a lot of sunlight. It was beautiful! I really was making it so we could use it later as a mini-apartment for a young married couple. It had a kitchen, bathroom, living room, bedroom, and a little laundry enclosed on the back porch. It was really neat. I could have lived there!

But boy, he gave me a hard time about it, and even called the police! He was a nice old guy, but he turned on me like a mad dog.

"I called the police on you," he declared, glaring at me.

"Good!" I responded. "We want to do this right."

I knew who the township policeman was, but I didn't really know him personally. When he arrived, I invited him in and said, "Talk to the old man and listen to his story, and then I'll chat with you a little bit."

So he did. The cop was very congenial.

Sam's chief complaint to him was that "Victor is trying to get me away from my girlfriend, Sadie, and that's why he wants to put me down in that basement apartment."

On hearing that, the policeman, Sam and I sat down for a ten-minute chat. I explained to him, "Now, Sam, you misunderstood me. We *want* you and Sadie to sit on the front porch all day and eat dinner together and all that. We're not here to make it difficult for anybody. Relationships are important, and we know your wife died ten years ago and that all of us get lonely at times. Sadie is a wonderful woman," and I built up her case a bit.

Sam started smiling, and the cop said, "Why, Sam, Victor is giving you a good deal here. You'll never get treated like this someplace else!"

And that was the end of that.

After that, Sam and Sadie would continue to sit on the porch, or carry the lawn chairs out under a tree. It was amusing to see the two of them together like that, but there was something very nice about it too, seeing that they enjoyed each other's companionship.

At that time there were not as many rules and regulations for nursing homes as there are today. Someone came out and checked our house to see if it was safe in case of fire–you know, that we had enough doors and exits, and that was about it. We didn't even *have to* have fire alarms.

For Grace, it never seemed to matter if she cooked for 3 people or 33. It seemed like the work was the same for her. I was a little the same way: if I milked 50 cows or 500, I didn't think much about it. We just did it. We learned to encourage our helpers, and we taught them all the good short-cuts.

We learned early that there are right ways, hard ways, and easy ways to do things. Some people will never take advice or learn an easier approach to something because they think, "My way is *the only way* that works, and I'm not changing it." All they are doing is "cutting their own throats," so to speak, and missing a blessing.

Of course, Grace was always pretty open to new ideas. Although she was a lot more reserved than I was, if I had an idea, it didn't take more than a day to sell it to her. I always told her, "If it doesn't work, we'll just go back to what we were doing before this." I would also repeat to her my philosophy, *"Remember, when you have everything to gain and nothing to lose, always do it!"* By trying something new, if you didn't gain anything physically, mentally, time-wise, or monetarily, you've at least gained a new experience and you'll have a better idea of what works and what doesn't work!

There are some things you just can't learn from a book. You may get your basic education there, but when you get in the field of hard knocks, you learn in other ways. I understood that, but many people (to their downfall) fight change and the thought of trying something new.

As our daughters grew up, they helped with the old people, entertaining them, feeding them, and doing things for and with them. As they cared for these people, they learned what it means to be a nurse's aide. Even though once in a while there were a few challenges that would make you wish you wouldn't be in it, the whole adventure of having a mini-nursing home here turned out to be a learning experience and a blessing for the whole family. It taught our children to respect older people and to better understand their problems.

It reached the point that I told Grace if she takes in one more person, we are going to have to sleep out on the roof! That stimulated my thinking, and I said, "Do you know what? We are really being blessed. Why don't I build my wife a new house?"

We were beginning to feel it wasn't fair to our children to have to be quiet because of the older people, and they weren't having the home life that we wanted them to have. The children were between junior high age and grade eleven at the time, and we felt we wanted to give them a home of their own.

So, in 1970, we built a new, nice, four-bedroom home at the cost of $28,500, just up the road from the farmhouse. About the same time, we hired a young, recently married farmhand and his wife, and they moved into the farmhouse with the old people. The husband helped with the farm work, and his wife loved people and also wanted a job. So, we hired her to help Grace in managing the old people. Grace would go down every day to help her and together they prepared the menus and cooked the meals. She told Grace later, "You made me do all this cooking and I didn't even know how to cook!"

Sometimes when Grace got there, this young woman would say, "I have no idea what we're gonna have for dinner today." So Grace would show her the possibilities and they would prepare and serve it together.

However, the nicest parts of having the couple living with the old people were that we could spend more time with our own children, Grace could get away from the stress there, and it just gave us more peace and freedom.

I remember telling Grace in 1970, after we had built the house, "You know, Grace, the Lord willing, and if we continue to be blessed, I would really like to see you spend the rest of your life helping charitable purposes, children, senior citizens and others. The way it looks now, it will never again be necessary for me to ask you to help on the farm.

And you know, that is exactly what happened. After the girls all graduated from high school and went out on their own, the young couple also moved on and bought their own farm in New York. Lebanon County built more facilities for the elderly, so we gave up serving as a nursing home and used that house for some of our farm employees.

Having the nursing home here was a valuable learning experience for our whole family, but neither Grace nor I feel we would want to do it again.

The new home we built in 1970 along Weavertown Road, Myerstown. Ten of the 15 refugee families we sponsored lived in our basement for different intervals of time.

Chapter Eleven

Sponsoring Refugees

"The reason I have money left over to buy you a good used coat is because I wouldn't buy a new one for myself while you are cold."
—Victor K. Ziegler

We started sponsoring refugees in 1972 after I got a letter from Church World Service stating that there was a real need for sponsors for refugee families. That next week I attended a council meeting at the Heidelberg Church of the Brethren and I brought up the possibility of the church being a sponsor. "As a congregation, we have been so blessed," I reminded them, "and it would be nice if we could help some poverty-stricken or hurting people, whether they be local or foreign refugees. It could be an especially interesting learning, growing and cultural experience if we would help a family from overseas."

However, I could soon tell that nobody was getting excited about it. They seemed tired of discussing it, so I pushed a little harder. "Do you know what? We are so blessed that we've just *got* to do something!"

Then, to shut me up, an old brother said, "I make a motion that if a refugee family comes into our community, we will help to sponsor them," and it passed. I had that statement on record and the secretary wrote it down.

The next morning I got on the phone and called the Brethren Service Center at New Windsor, MD, and within three days, we had a refugee family here. They were the Pabani family, an Indian family who had moved into Uganda and were driven out by the dictator, Idi Amin. The father had owned a big store in Uganda, but was chased out of the country, along with his wife and their two children, with only the clothing they had on their backs and about $100. The youngest son, Samsudin, whom we called "Sam," a tall boy of 17, became the family spokesman because he handled the English language very well. He also had a younger sister, Zebunnisa, in ninth grade.

I met the family at the Harrisburg airport, and as soon as Sam and I saw each other, we each felt a bond, as though we had known each other all our lives. God brought us together as though we were family, and he became a real pleasure to both Grace and me.

For the first couple weeks, they lived in the basement of our house while Grace and I were looking around for a house to rent for them. When a house in Schaefferstown came up for sale, I bought it, put in a new furnace and got it set up for them, but Sam and his family didn't *want* to move out of our basement! "Sam," I questioned, "I thought you'd be happy for your family to have a place of your own. What is it that's hurting?"

Tearfully, he explained, "I'm afraid you won't come to see me every day. Here I can always call on you." Obviously, he felt a real sense of security here.

"No, we won't abandon you, and we'll get you a telephone so you can talk to us anytime you want," I assured him.

Since his parents were too old to work away from home, Sam realized he had to work to keep the family going. Consequently, he wasn't able to graduate from high school here, although he did finish later by taking a GED test. However, eventually he *did* get a college education at Millersville University.

His first job here was at the shoe factory in Richland. On only the second day that he was employed, we got a phone call from them. Our first thought was, "Uh-oh! What's going on now? Did Sam do something he shouldn't have?"

Instead, they simply called to say, "If you can find ten more guys like him, we want them!" That's how he was.

Later, he worked for the Suchard Chocolate factory in Lititz. They really loved him also. Grace remembers that he carried a bag lunch to work every day. One day while he was eating it, some guy came up to him, grabbed his apple and took it, sorta making a fool of him. He told her later, "I remembered what you said, 'If somebody comes and wants to hurt you, just sit back and walk away from it,' so I didn't allow myself to get angry or fight back."

Before Sam got his first car, he said he didn't want one because he knew we wouldn't be picking him up at work, taking him home or stopping off here at our house. Although it was a great feeling knowing he cared so much for us, we had to explain to him, "Sam, when you get a car, you can still come and visit us."

Around Christmas that first year, Sam called and said it is so cold in their house. Because I had just put in a new furnace and storm windows, I went to their home to check on what was happening. When I got there, the door was wide open, and the screen door was shut. I said, "Sam! You are no longer living in Africa or India. It's *cold* out there." Because he was raised in another culture, he had never even thought about shutting the door. The change in climate was a difficult adjustment for them.

One time while they were still living in Schaefferstown, Sam got sick, and Grace went over to see if she could help in any way. She noticed he had a little necklace lying on his nightstand, and she asked, "Sam, what is this thing for?"

Immediately, he protested, "No, no, no, no, don't touch! That's my God!"

Grace was shocked. "Oh, no, Samsudin," she exclaimed. "You don't believe in things like this, do you?" She felt she could talk straight out to him about almost any subject.

Without answering directly, Sam just pleaded, "Please don't touch."

Another of God's miracles was that Sam, who grew to be about six feet tall, actually became like a son to us even though he was of another nationality and race. When Sam attended Millersville University, he got an apartment there, so we didn't see him as much anymore.

Now he is married to a lovely Indian woman, Pervez, whom he met at the Indian Moslem Church that met in Akron, Pennsylvania. Before they moved to Canada to live near other relatives there, Pervez worked at the Ephrata Hospital as a nurse's aide. Sam is active in the Moslem faith and is one of the head guys in their mosque in Canada.

Today the Pabani family are still very dear to our hearts and we still have close contact with them 33 years later. We get a phone call from Sam in Toronto about four to six times a year, whenever any of us has a birthday, on Mother's Day, Father's Day and at Christmas, giving us an update on his family and just keeping in touch. Over the years, in spite of the distance, we have also visited back and forth a few times.

Samsudin Pabani and his wife Pervez with their children, Alim and Farah.

Of course, in sponsoring refugee families there were always a few frustrations, but the joys far outweighed them. We had many learning experiences and they were good.

Through the People In Crisis organization, we got a Cuban couple who lived for almost a year in our farmhouse and misled us by pretending to be man and wife. She had worked for us here on the farm, helping in the milking parlor, and she was pretty good. He worked for some greenhouses over near the Teen Challenge headquarters, and one day he pulled a knife on one of the other workers there. Of course, they called us right away and reported it to us.

We told him very frankly, "If this is the way you are going to be, we will not continue being your sponsors. We won't allow our reputation to be ruined just because of your attitude." He settled down, and when they left, we had no idea where they went or what became of them.

A couple years later, we received a letter from New Jersey from the Cuban woman. In it she wrote, "Victor, I want to make something right. In Cuba, we were told that only husband/wife teams and families got first preference in coming to the United States. This guy invited me to go along, and this looked like a way for both of us to escape from Cuba, so I went along with it. I just lied and told everybody I was his wife."

She continued, "When I left your farm, I ended up in New Jersey and started attending a little Pentecostal Church. Then I got saved and felt so convicted about how I had lied to you folks when you had treated us so nice. Now I am married to a Pentecostal pastor of a little church and am living a good life. I just wanted to write this letter to tell you that I know the Lord forgave me, and I know you will too. I just had to tell you."

That was amazing and heartwarming!

Along with a doctor, we co-sponsored a Vietnamese family who lived in our basement for a while. In escaping from Vietnam, the husband and wife were separated, and he got on a boat, but his wife and children had no idea where he was. Later, she and their two young daughters got on another boat. Somehow, at sea, they were able to communicate from boat to boat and discovered that he was on one boat and she on another. Eventually, they got together, and ended up in the United States and lived in our basement for about three months. Every day

Grace took the children to school, and they were very bright. In fact, their one daughter is studying to be an eye doctor now.

They had a son, David, who was born here. The father, Quang, had been a commander in the navy, and that's the way he ruled his family. One evening Grace heard the father scolding his son, David. She went to check into it and asked, "Quang, what in the world is wrong?"

"Well, David came home with a 'B' in penmanship, and he should have had an 'A,'" he replied.

She admonished him by saying, "Oh, Quang, come on now. Not everybody can write nice. Just give him credit for what he *is doing right.*"

In all they had three children of their own, but when they came, they brought another boy with them who we thought was his nephew, but later we found out he wasn't. We discovered that many times when Vietnamese families came to the U.S., if there was somebody who wanted to come along, they would put them in their name just to help to get them over here.

The co-sponsoring doctor was able to buy them a house in Myerstown and rented it to them until they were gradually able to buy it. The mother worked at the Evangelical Congregational Home in Myerstown, and everybody liked her. She was a special lady. We kept in touch with them. Last year she died of cancer, and that was really hard on her husband and children. When she was sick, even though the hospice lady was there, Grace went over several times just to sit with her and let her know she cared.

Each of the families had heart-wrenching stories. Hai Ngoc Vu and his two sons, then 8 and 10 years old, escaped from Vietnam by boat in 1981. Sharing the boat with 35 others, they traveled for three days and four nights before reaching Thailand. Five times along the way, they were attacked by pirates who boarded their boat, stole everything of value and even struck some of the other passengers with logs and hammers but no one was fatally injured.

When they first arrived in Thailand, they slept on the sand, were often wet and cold, and had only rice and sauce to eat. During their time there, they lived in three camps under very unsanitary conditions. Sleeping in vermin-infested tents, two to a bed, they only had enough water for baths once a week.

From Thailand, they were sent to the Philippines for a year to learn English. Here Hai, the father, worked as a cook in the mess hall, and their living conditions improved considerably.

In September, 1982, they arrived in the United States through the efforts of various sponsor groups, and ended up living just up the road from us in a house we were able to rent for them. Although he was a railroad worker in Vietnam, Hai became employed by Plain 'N' Fancy Kitchens in Richland, and the boys entered the ELCO (Eastern Lebanon County) schools.

Many months later, when arrangements were finally made for his wife to arrive and the pastor from the sponsoring church, the Midway Church of the Brethren in Lebanon, was about to pick her up at the airport, he said to Grace, "Did you ever say anything to Hai about contraception or the use of condoms?"

She laughed and quickly responded, "No, that is your job–you can tell him about that on the way to the airport."

Hai's wife, Vu Thi Lanh, had another story. Five times she and her two very young daughters had tried to escape from Vietnam. On her fourth attempt, the communists caught her and put her in jail. After being held for three months, a friend bribed the local officials and she was released. On their fifth try, the trio succeeded in boarding a boat for Thailand, but they, too, encountered pirates who not only took all their belongings, but also the engine of their boat, so that the boat drifted on the seas for 13 days before the wind carried it onto the Thailand shore. They arrived there in January, 1982, and were there almost a year until December 18, 1983. Through the efforts of the sponsor groups and her husband, the family was finally reunited in Pennsylvania on Monday, December 19, 1983. At that time, their four children's ages were: Hung, 12; Minh, 10; Ha, 5; and Hoa, 4. The father and two sons had learned to speak English, but Lanh and their daughters spoke only Vietnamese. When he was asked why they left their native country, Hai said simply, "We were looking for freedom." Hai also added, "Everything was new to me, but everybody helped me."

A year later Lanh became pregnant and Hai was afraid an additional family member would be a heavy financial burden. When he consulted a doctor by himself, the advice he received was that his wife should have an abortion. Feeling somewhat uneasy about that prospect, he came to talk to Grace about this issue.

"No," she advised. "We as a church are sponsoring both of you, and we are willing to help you through this difficult time."

Then he asked what she thought about the option of giving their baby up for adoption, and again, she talked him out of that idea.

When Lanh found out the advice the doctor had given and the various alternate plans her husband was considering, she was very upset. She confided in Grace, "No way would I have had an abortion or given up my baby. I *wanted* this child."

When it was born, she named her baby girl, Linda Grace, after my wife, Grace. When Grace heard about it, she kidded the mother, "You are *really* in trouble now!" But, in fact, she felt honored and humbled. Today that daughter is through college and doing quite well.

Since then, of course, the family has grown up, but like all families everywhere, they did encounter some problems. Grace remembers one time when Hai came to her and confided, "Grace, I am really upset. I don't know what direction to go."

She asked, "What's on your mind?"

Then he explained, "My daughter is not married but she is pregnant, and we don't believe in that. We don't like those things to happen."

Grace advised him, "Hai, you are just going to have to love her at where she is. If you don't, you are just going to have more problems."

In time, it all worked out beautifully. She kept the baby and got married, and her husband's family accepted and treated her well. She is now in college, and the whole family came through it all, but it was tough for them for a while.

Only one of the refugee families that we sponsored turned out to be a disappointment. They were a couple from Hungary who arrived with an attitude.

It seemed that their goal was not as much to experience freedom as it was to make a lot of money and become rich. Expecting us to hand feed them and buy them everything, they weren't willing to wear secondhand clothing; they wanted *new* clothes! I finally told them, "I don't know what your background is, but if you would *really* get hungry, you might appreciate the blessings you have. You might be from the country of Hungary, but you never got hungry enough to be willing to wear a good used overcoat, and that's what I've been wearing all my life. In fact, that's the only reason I can help *you. The reason I have money left over to buy you a good used coat is because I wouldn't buy a new one for myself while you are cold.*"

The Nguyen Family. Seated left to right: LyLy, Kim (mother), and Cathy. Standing: David and Quang.

Sponsoring refugees was challenging, but interesting, and it was very time consuming, especially for Grace. She worked with them more than I did, driving them here and there, seeing that they got groceries, taking them to job interviews and to their English classes at night. Balancing all that with managing our own household and not having our own children feel deprived of her attention was a real job.

In all, we sponsored fifteen different families, but ten of them lived right here in our basement for different intervals of time. We felt that our children learned a lot about other nationalities, customs, and simple human relations through these experiences. We were so fortunate in that there were several businesses nearby, such as the Richland shoe factory and the Plain 'N' Fancy Kitchens, who were willing to hire refugees, and that helped us so much in getting these people jobs.

Some of the families moved to other areas to make a living for themselves and be closer to other members of their families, and we didn't feel bad about that. If the situation were reversed, and we would have moved to another country and learned of other Americans there, we would want to be with those who looked like us, spoke our language, ate the same foods, understood our jokes, had our same religion and a similar heritage. We would want to be with *our people*.

Not all sponsors understood that.

People would ask us why we expended so much of our time, money, and effort in resettling these people. When Grace was in high school, she had a strong desire to go to the mission field. As a start, she got an application for Brethren Volunteer Service and filled it out, but her foster parents wouldn't allow her to send it in. With the refugee program, she has felt that the Lord brought the missions to her doorstep, and she could help, serve, and witness to these people right here.

And it wasn't just refugees who lived here. One local couple whose house burned down needed a place to live for six weeks while their house got repaired and redecorated, so they made our basement their home. Another family nearby discovered that their house had lead paint that chipped off and could have been poisonous to their children, so they had to move out. They moved in here, and were with us at least three months. They appreciated it so much that we still receive birthday cards from her and once in a while, she sets a pot of flowers at our door.

Even today, our basement is still open to emergencies.

Just a couple weeks ago we had one of the Vietnamese families insist we come to their father's birthday party. They had a big supper prepared, and we had a nice time. They still keep in touch with phone calls and Christmas cards.

Recently, we were invited by a family we had sponsored to one of their delicious Vietnamese meals. One of their sons also came, and it was funny. He was heavy and all the rest of the family were thin. His explanation: "That's because I like the American food." And he laughed.

Our resettling of refugee families has kind of wound down the last few years because of our activities with all our grandchildren and our involvement in church activities. However, in looking back, we feel it was very worthwhile.

With all our experiences with the refugees, there were very few disappointments. Of course, our definition of a disappointment is different from that of the world. We look at it as an oversight, a misunderstanding, or a lesson we needed to learn–in short, a

The Vu Family. Below left to right: Lanh and Hai. Above: Ha, Taria, Linda Grace, and Minh. Not pictured: Their son, Hung.

"learning experience." I know sharing with all these different people and cultures made us a better family and hopefully helped them and others as well.

Chapter Twelve

Endorsing Natural Healing Concepts

"I still don't understand all that I DO know."
—Victor K. Ziegler

About 15 years ago, in 1989, Grace and I traveled to Juarez, Mexico, south of El Paso, Texas, to visit the clinic of a Central American medical doctor who was practicing alternative medicine there. I was especially interested in learning what he was doing to assist persons from all over the United States and Canada who came to him with heart conditions, cancer and other debilitating diseases.

Among the interesting procedures he used was the "colon cleanse." It was there that I experienced my first "coffee enema." I had to smile when I heard its name and told the nurses there that I like coffee, although I am not a big coffee drinker, but "I never drank it in reverse before!" I suggested to them that if they'd run a tube through me from the top to the bottom, it would give me the same effect, but they did not agree.

One of my main reasons for going there was to learn about treating the human body through natural means rather than using drugs. Also, since I never went to the doctor, I figured that I could learn some preventive things to do to keep on feeling healthy.

In my interview with the doctor I challenged him, "Now I want you to tell me what's wrong with me."

"What do *you* think?" he asked.

"I noticed my feet and lower legs get a little cold in wintertime, and once in a while, they tingle," I admitted.

"Well, that would be a symptom of a little hardening of the arteries or a lack of circulation," he decided.

After some tests, they suggested opening up my arteries through a chelation process. Dr. Soto wanted me to undergo a treatment each day for twelve days. However, I had promised to be home the following week, so I only had the treatment daily for six days. Grace went through it also.

"What will happen if I quit in the middle of the treatments?" I questioned Dr. Soto.

"Well, if your furnace is clogged up and you call the plumber and he opens the pipes and washes them out with acid and really gets them clean, but only gets half finished, you will have a job half done but it *will* work," he explained. "However, it will clog up again much quicker."

Nevertheless, I did come home. Eventually, I started taking artery care capsules and got great results with those, and never did go back to Mexico. During the week we were there, Grace and I spent $5,000, but I got $10,000 worth of education and didn't regret a minute of it.

Along with emphasizing diet and lifestyle, another technique they used that was new to me was that they put me in an ozone tube where they forced oxygen through the cells in my system. That was *really* invigorating and I enjoyed it!

We met an engineer there from Alaska who had a tumor in the back of his eye. When his Alaskan doctor wanted to take his eye out, remove the tumor, radiate the cavity and then insert a glass eye, he refused. Then he heard of this center, flew to Mexico, and they took care of it and he never lost his vision. In his case, it only took three weeks to shrink that tumor.

A 37-year-old farmer from Lubbock, Texas, was there with throat cancer. He told me that he had five friends in his same age bracket who also had throat cancer. They had gone to the big cancer hospital in Houston, and they all died within 18 months! He was here at this center ten years later and enjoying good health. To get treated here, he had spent big money, perhaps $10,000 or more, but his friends had spent over $100,000 each—and had died!

Although Dr. Soto was obviously doing something right, something that was working, he wasn't allowed to practice in the United States.

The way Grace and I heard about him was interesting. A former Amish boy helped me when he was 27 years old to build a bottom silo loader (an invention which he got patented years later). A doctor at the Lancaster (PA) General Hospital told him he was going to die because he needed a 4-way bypass operation. Instead, he checked himself out and went to Cottonwood, Alabama, where Dr. Soto was learning and practicing under a senior doctor who was getting up in years. When he came home, after 30 days there, he said, "I could walk 15 miles, wasn't short of breath anymore, and I could do anything."

Because he never overemphasized things or stretched the truth, when he said something, to me it was the "gospel." He became a personal friend and explained to me that this Dr. Soto had used a chelation process to open up his blood vessels. That is what really triggered my thinking and sent me to Mexico to see what I could learn and experience firsthand.

The first morning these two Pennsylvania Dutch skeptics were there, we were taken from our motel to the medical offices in a van along with 12 other people. A 50-year-old woman, sitting on the back seat with Grace and me, started questioning us as to what brought us here and how we learned about it. She prophesied, "You won't be sorry you came. This is only my third day here and I am noticing results already. The biggest thing I've noticed is that my vision isn't as blurred as it was."

I remember bumping Grace with my knee and whispering, "In only three days? Boy, she's a dreamer! He really has her brainwashed!"

And you know, by the end of that week, Grace said the same thing! Although she didn't have a serious eye problem, she found it easier to read. She didn't have her "morning blur" any longer. He also discovered Grace had a blockage in her neck that was restricting her blood flow. The less blood you get to the eyes and to the brain, the more it affects your total well-being.

We both testified that the chelation process really made a difference. I couldn't do more than praise him. In a local hospital, with expenses at $1,000 a day, you could spend $5,000 very fast. At this clinic, *both of us* spent a whole week there, got all these treatments, and also had our room and board—all for $5,000.

And the treatment was so simple. We'd sit in a lounge chair as we were fed intravenously, and we could feel our bodies warm up as it flowed through us. It wasn't nauseating or painful. Everybody just sat in big chairs, read a book, took a nap or visited, enjoying meeting the people there from many states and all walks of life.

That experience really stimulated my interest and enthusiasm for alternative healing and for looking beyond the Western cultural methods of medicine and drugs. Every year my interest grew keener. As I got older, I saw many of my friends being all drugged up with prescriptions, while I was enjoying health, and I thought, "There's a reason."

My years of working with livestock had taught me that I needed four things to maintain good health: good nutrition, pure water, moderate exercise, and fresh air.

Historically, in the northeast, we pitied the animals when it got cold. We would shut the barn doors, and even stuff a paper bag in any broken windows, with the result that the livestock weren't getting any fresh air. Because they were breathing foul air, they developed health problems and even pneumonia.

I soon learned that was wrong, so I started opening the barn doors and keeping it as cold inside the barn as outside. The result was that the animals were *much* healthier. If they have

The Ziegler family including in-laws. Seated, left to right: Glen, Rhoda, Abraham, Earl, Victor. Standing: Reba (Copenhaver) Ziegler, Monroe and Ada Z. Good, Wayne and Mae Z. Patches, Verna Z. and Norman Kline, Lena Z. Kreider, Vivian (Snyder) Ziegler, Irvin Kreider, Grace (Cox) Ziegler. Photo date: May 28, 1984.

the freedom, an animal will never lay in a draft. If they are able, and not chained or tied, they will *always* reposition themselves. They're not as dumb as people. People stay there and get sick!

Nature has given them an inborn gift of taking care of themselves, of self-preservation. That has always been fascinating to me: that people learn things the hard way, but animals have that knowledge as a natural instinct.

I remember one Saturday night when we had a snowstorm and the temperature was down to zero. I had a bunch of dairy heifers, about a year or so old, and because of the cold, I pitied those animals. That evening I said to Grace, "I'm going to go over about 9 o'clock and throw 20 bales of straw among those animals so they have a nice warm place."

On Sunday morning I stopped to feed and check on them. Those animals had come in, kicked up their heels in the straw, and run out on the silage side of the hill and soon had fallen asleep in a foot of snow—and enjoyed it! In the morning, they each had two inches of snow on their backs and were lying there chewing their cud and smiling at me when I came! If you took a clippers and checked an animal that was kept in a warm building and one that was continually kept out in the cold, you would discover that the latter had developed a fine mat of thick hair under the upper coat that insulated them to almost all degrees of coldness. In fact, the only way you can kill an animal by keeping it outdoors in sub-zero weather is by not giving it enough to eat. They all have a built-in furnace. We always noticed that during zero weather, they ate a little bit more, and the reason was so that they could generate heat and energy. That always fascinated me.

When I came indoors that Sunday morning, I declared to Grace, "Those heifers are really something. They didn't even appreciate what I did for them!"

About that time I began to think that if I would just observe the animal kingdom more, I could learn a lot about my own self-preservation. Animals seldom get sick, however we shock ourselves with heat and cold. We take a hot shower and then walk outside with a wet head! Animals aren't that stupid. We'd learn a lot if we would just observe them more carefully.

About 20 or more years ago, the Avian Flu was prevalent among chickens in Pennsylvania, and that's when I learned about the many healing qualities of hydrogen peroxide. The flu didn't really hurt the value of the chicken meat, but because of the phlegm in their windpipes, they'd stand around coughing and choking.

Although I didn't have any chickens at that time, our neighboring farmers had them by the thousands. I visited one guy who had 30,000 broilers ready to go to market in three days when the inspectors from the State Department arrived and couldn't find a thing wrong with them. However, they said, "Well, look, all your neighbors have the chicken flu, so your chickens *must* have it also!"

So, they made him shut the doors and they came in and gassed them, killing his 30,000 market-ready birds! Of course, at that time, the poultrymen were compensated, but at varying rates–some overpaid, some at a fair market price, and some were underpaid.

I asked this guy, "To what would you attribute the fact that all your neighbors' chickens had the symptoms of the flu, but no signs of the disease could be detected in your flock?"

"Well," he answered, "I never told anybody this, but I've been putting 30 to 40 parts per million of 35% hydrogen peroxide in their drinking water through an automatic medicator." Because he did that, the disease never got hold of his chickens.

One other thing I noted was that where the hydrogen peroxide-treated water was used, all his little water fountains were shiny and sparkling clean. On the neighboring farms, where the chickens had the disease, the water fountains were always a little dusty and dirty and didn't have that sparkle. You know how moss soon builds up in a little dish settin' out in the rain. There was none of that in the disease-free chicken barns, so I concluded that the peroxide kept the bacteria down and served as a natural purifier.

I told this chicken farmer, "If I drink a half glass of milk or eat a plate of ice cream before I go to bed, I feel wonderful the next morning. However, when I get up, I could spit phlegm five or ten times! If it works for a chicken to eliminate phlegm, it will work for me! The only difference between a chicken and me is that God created man and gave him the breath of life, and the chicken he didn't."

That night I asked Grace, "Where is our bottle of 3% hydrogen peroxide?" (We kept it on hand as an antiseptic.)

"What do you want with it?" she questioned curiously.

"I want to put five drops into a glass of water and drink it," I replied.

"Well, it's poison," she informed me.

When I read the label, it said, "If children use it for a gargle, dilute it one to one or three to one." I said to Grace, "It can't be *that* deadly if children are allowed to use it to gargle. The reason they dilute it is so that in case they swallow it, it wouldn't really hurt them."

So, I started with five drops that first night. The next night Grace asked with concern, "What if that would knock you out?"

"It's very simple," I answered, "I would have passed out of this world from 'natural causes.'" So, on the second night, I tried ten drops.

After taking it a third night, even after drinking milk and eating ice cream, I couldn't spit phlegm at all the next morning!

That was many years ago, and I don't drink it regularly anymore, but every time I did, it worked. I told so many people about this "home remedy," and of course, they laughed at me and called me "Mr. Peroxide."

One time at a meeting I said, "There are 101 uses for hydrogen peroxide if only we would know them!" My sister, Ada Good, was skeptical and just smiled. Three months later, Ada brought me a book titled *101 Uses For Hydrogen Peroxide* written by a Dr. Dornsburg from San Diego, California, who practices across the border in Tijuana, Mexico. Ada admitted, "I guess I have to quit laughing, because here is a doctor documenting all these uses." It was amazing!

I kept on experimenting and learned another use from a mother who told me her young (less than a year old) child had frequent earaches, causing him to cry and fuss. Every time, if she would put three to five drops of hydrogen peroxide in each ear, lean him over and rub it in a bit, within five or ten minutes the fussing would be over. Although she had several children since then, she said, "I never went to the doctor again for a child's earache."

Years later, Donna, my daughter-in-law, the wife of my son, Leon, expressed her exasperation to me saying, "I just spent two hours in the doctor's office and spent 40 bucks for this little year-old girl because of an earache."

Immediately, I remembered the old remedy and I apologized to her and said, "You know, I could've told you how to relieve it using just three cents worth of hydrogen peroxide!"

I understand that after that she never took her children to the doctor for an earache. Many people told me how it worked for them, and I just passed it on.

One time I was at a meeting and having fun talking about the fact that the simplest things in life are often the cheapest, but we don't use them because they don't cost big bucks and we're afraid of them. I questioned, "Do you know that hydrogen peroxide will cure or help anything from headaches to hemorrhoids?"

Of course, everybody laughed and said, "You'd better go home!"

But I persisted, "Look, if any of you have hemorrhoids that are so out of control that your doctor is suggesting an operation, try this first. Take a tissue every day and soak it in 3% hydrogen peroxide and after a bowel movement, dab it on the area for one minute. After anywhere from three to 10 days, you should notice a marked improvement."

Within a year, five different people came to me and said, "Some thought you were kidding, but we took you seriously," or "We knew you weren't joking, but we thought it was a big joke, and now we found out it works!" One guy came and said he had

had headaches for years, and when he drank five drops in a glass of water, that cleared it all up for him.

I also suggested to people that if they wanted to energize themselves, they should dump a whole cupful of hydrogen peroxide in the bathtub and fill it with water and sit in it up to their neck. I didn't want to recommend something that I hadn't done, so I *had to* do it myself! When I tried it, it felt so good that I laid down in the tub, sliding down until the back of my head was in the water. When I came out and dried off, the back of my head looked like a brown pony tail. It actually changed colors! Grace said, "It looks like the rust is coming out of your head!" I heard jokes about that for a number of years afterwards.

Another thing people often talked about was a "spring tonic," and what they used for that was dandelion. We never sprayed the lawn with 2-4-D. My dad and mother would send us kids out in the spring of the year and tell us to dig up every dandelion plant we could find in our yard or meadow. Mother would then make dandelion salad or soup with it, by enhancing the dandelion with hot bacon dressing, a few chopped tomatoes or slices of hard-boiled eggs. I used to think it tasted a little bitter, but perhaps that was the tonic part. I've often thought, "What a shame! We spray the dandelion in our front yards and then go down to the health food store and buy dandelion root, dandelion leaves, and dandelion tea. While we spray the dandelion in our yard, the chemical poison actually seeps down through the soil and gets into the water table and some of it leeches into our wells and we are actually drinking the poison. Now we have lost the tonic, lost the dandelion, and we're poisoning our water!"

We do everything wrong because it makes big dollars for somebody! If you want to make a good decision, just watch the money trail. If there is big money flowing, people work hard to shut you up, saying the natural methods are myths, old wive's tales, and they won't work. They don't *want* the public to use the simple methods because that would cut off the money they are making. This is especially true with the drug companies.

My dad always advocated using black strap molasses and I have used it also. It is a good stomach and intestinal cleanser, and I sometimes liked to call it a "lubricant for the digestive system," making everything a little bit "smoother and sweeter."

Vinegar and honey are useful in treating arthritis. My Uncle Levi Ziegler told me personally that when he was 27 years old, he had crippling arthritis and was working for a carpenter building and remodeling houses and farm buildings. He was so crippled that he could hardly work and his doctor said, "You'll never work again."

A friend approached him and said, "Levi, you're only 27! Don't believe that doctor. You go home and drink a mixture of one tablespoon of vinegar and one or two tablespoons of honey in a little water, and you drink that every day." Uncle Levi said that his joints started limbering up, the pain left him, and within 30 days he was back working full time on house roofs until he was 72! If he quit taking that mixture for three or four days in a row, or for a week, he could hardly put on his shirt or his sweater because his shoulders would hurt. My mother said the same thing. I never saw my mom pour pickle juice away; she would just drink it. She felt that by doing that she stayed in good condition.

Recently, a friend told me that if you put vinegar in an empty glass cleaner bottle and go around your lawn in the daytime and spray your ugly weeds with it, the weeds will dry up, the grass will get "rain," you won't poison anything or hurt anyone, and you don't need to worry about a child stepping into it or anything.

When I hit 50 years old, I stepped on the scales and weighed 199 lbs. People could hardly believe it. The children had all left home, and I remember telling Grace that I felt I was getting short of breath. Because Grace was baking all this good rich food and I was eating it, I was getting heavy. I would say, "She's cooking me to death and I love it."

However, I could tell I was headed for trouble. I got convicted about "being temperate in ALL things" (1 Corinthians 9:25) not just in what suited me. I had to cut out all that good stuff and just eat it now and then or on special occasions like a

Entertaining my brother, Earl, and his son, Mike. December, 1997.

birthday party. After that it wasn't too long until I got down to 175 pounds and I stayed there until the present time.

When I was still somewhat heavy, a salesman, whom I knew to be a Christian, stopped by at our farm and lit up a cigarette in front of me as we were finishing our conversation. I observed, "Hey, I can see you are really a committed Christian. You are 'on fire' for the Lord; I can see the smoke flying!"

He just laughed and said, "You're being a little rough on me, aren't you?"

I retorted, "You know, when I was a boy, I actually thought that people who smoked would go to hell. Now I know that's not true. Smoking will never take you to hell . . . it just smells like you've been there!"

Of course he laughed again, and we had a little fun.

Then I shared with him that "I am convinced that the Bible talks more about gluttony than it does about smoking. Just last night I got awake about 2:00 a.m. and thought, 'Victor, you are good at giving a guy a lecture on smoking but what about your own gluttony?' "

That's when I told Grace I have to change my eating habits because this gluttony is going to shorten my life. I could feel it. After I ate less and lost twenty pounds, I could walk more easily and work an extra hour or two a day without getting as tired.

One of the times when I was roughest on anybody was when five of us were in a huddle. I knew the one guy was a Mennonite preacher, and I had always heard he had a good, heart-warming Bible-based, gospel-believing message that wasn't watered down. He was big and heavy-set, some of which may have been genetic, but I suspected most of it was self-inflicted. I knew the other three guys were his friends.

In building a case to have a little fun, I said to these three, "Hey, brothers, tell me something. Why is it so difficult to get a fat preacher to preach on gluttony?" (And he was standing just three feet away from me!)

He looked at me and laughed. "Boy, you don't spare any words, Victor. Do you?"

He wasn't angry, but he had a good answer. Just then I was prompted, as I had never had a chance to be close to this guy before, to put my arm around him, and I said, "Hey, brother, do you know what? *You're* the one who taught me this. Your friends tell me that you have good, gospel-based sermons that are convicting people of their sins and helping them to understand the love of God. They lead people to repent and surrender to the Lord and become His followers. I learned it *from you! You* don't spare any words in the pulpit, and I praise God for that because your preaching is making *a difference* in the lives of people. Now, as my pop used to say, 'If the shoe fits, wear it.'"

He laughed again. Then we dropped that subject.

I did tell him of my own struggle. If I wouldn't have taken control of myself, I could easily have gone up to 250 pounds because I *love* to eat. Especially when I have a cook who makes everything so delicious! Whew!

Often at a moment's notice, when I was with people like that, something would come up that would spark a healthy discussion, and I'd mix a little fun in it, and out of the humor, we'd all learn a lesson about making better health choices.

A devout Christian friend, whom I had known for more than 30 years, invited me to help him in his health business. This man, Ivan Martin, started out as a farm boy, but he didn't enjoy farming. With God-given mechanical abilities, he was always putting things together, inventing and experimenting. In fact, he built an automatic knotter for the Case Equipment Company. They had built a baler that a man had to stay on and trigger something so it would tie the bale. He figured how to put a little gadget on it, so that when the bale got 36 inches long, it stopped and quickly made a knot in the string, tied it up, and pushed out the bale. Eventually, he got a patent on it. He was the kind of person who would get something patented and then, without really finishing it, go on to the next project.

He was a little like that in the health business also, but he was self-taught and *very* knowledgeable. He had studied many medical books, and his advice and diagnoses were so well respected, that many people called him before they would call a medical doctor.

One day he called me and said, "You know, Victor, I am so busy. Knowing you, I feel you would really complement me a lot. Would you help me out?"

I quickly responded, "Yeah, we were just talking about the fact that I am not really needed on the farm anymore with the grandsons coming along. In fact, I've been saying I want to get out of the way so I am not a hindrance to their learning experience."

Then, he actually offered me a salary. He said, "Hey, I could use you 40 hours a week." He was that busy.

As I grew closer to Ivan, I learned his doorbell and phone were ringing from 8:00 a.m. until 8:00 p.m., with someone always coming or going, questioning him, or picking up a health product. Many had consulted a doctor and nothing was working, so they came to Ivan. He would give advice or recommend a health product, and had a very good success rate. Because people had confidence in him, they kept coming back.

His own story was a miracle in itself. When he was 60, he had a heart attack. When his doctor said to him, "Tomorrow morning we are going to do a 3-way bypass on you," Ivan, being a feisty guy said, "No, doctor, I am going home today."

"Mr. Martin, you *aren't* going home today," the doctor declared, warning, "you won't make it home!"

"Well," Ivan responded, "I guess that is *my* problem. Yesterday you told me I needed $30,000 cash for this operation. I have no insurance and I have no money. I got awake last night and I really believe there is a better way."

So, against the doctor's wishes, he checked himself out and went home. Eleven months later, he had invented the formula for an organic capsule called "artery care," which has helped hundreds, well, literally there are thousands of people using it from here to California and Florida. It is just amazing how God used this tragedy of a near-death experience to stimulate him to do this.

After I joined him, we doubled and tripled his sales, because I spent more time in talking to people and getting them to try it. They would call back and say it is working for them according to our recommendations. Most of his products were sold by word of mouth, although he did do a little bit of advertising also.

I kept on looking for good, reputable and effective products to add to our line. In our search, we met Dr. Santillo from North Dakota, who was helping people overcome heart disease and cancer 15 or more years ago with juicing machines. He would give them the right combination of fruit and vegetable juices, correct their diet, and suggest moderate exercise. However, he realized that juicing was a lot of work and these patients needed a large supply of fresh fruits and vegetables every day.

With the help of an engineer, they figured out a way to get the water and salt out of fresh fruits and vegetables and then put that substance into a juice or capsule without destroying the enzymes. That way, it was so much easier for patients to simply take a fruit capsule in the morning and a vegetable capsule in the afternoon. People could get a day's supply of required nutrients even if they never ate any fresh fruits or vegetables.

However, he would always add, "I would never tell anybody *not* to eat fresh fruits and vegetables, because I think that is the RIGHT way."

The vegetables and fruits he used in making his products were all organically grown with no chemicals or additives, whereas many of the fresh fruits and vegetables that people commonly ate were from fields and orchards that had been sprayed. The growers *claimed* that they'd been run through a washing process, but that only destroyed about 50% of the poisons. We ate and absorbed the rest.

After Dr. Santillo perfected and got his preparation process patented, he joined the NSA Company and they now prepare and sell it as "Juice Plus." We began selling it and still do, as everybody seemed to benefit from it. In fact, I take it myself regularly. I think that's what kept me going for so long.

Another new product we are handling is Colostrum, sometimes called a Transfer Factor. For the last hundred years we knew that a mother cow's first milk was *so* important in building up her baby calf's immune system. This is true of any mammal.

If a calf skipped this, you could be sure it wouldn't get the growth, it would have more trouble with pneumonia, and it would always be a little slow.

On the farm, we would always check every newborn calf. If that calf wasn't nursing within ten minutes, we would hand milk the mother and put that milk called colostrum in a plastic bottle. We'd put a nipple on it, placing it in the newborn's mouth, and when that calf tasted the warm milk, within seconds it would almost go wild drinking the bottle empty in one or two minutes! If you'd then walk away, after the mother licked it dry, that newborn would jump up and run! If it didn't get that milk just after birth, it would be sluggish.

For years, we never threw colostrum away. I remember that even my dad kept an old fifty gallon wooden barrel (because metal was more corrosive), and we would save all the colostrum in it. That is all the milk that the cow gives during the first two days after birth. We would feed that to the chickens and pigs and those animals would grow and be so healthy. We knew the value, but we never considered it for human consumption.

Now, 50 years later, it is being packaged and sold to people. With the new technology, they are able to dry it down and protect all the enzymes and value, and it has been a terrific blessing to people. What most people don't understand is that every hour the colostrum has less and less antibodies, and this is called "transitional milk" as it changes from colostrum to milk. One company calls colostrum the "6-hour miracle." They will not use colostrum that is over six hours old in their products, keeping the transitional milk for animal feed. The results have been amazing!

In reading an article on this, I discovered that the biggest decline in health in the United States was during World War II when women began working in the defense plants and factories and the food companies started making baby formulas, such as Similac and the like. The health of many babies was ruined, and we are paying for it years later because they never got that basic start. It's like a contractor cheating on the foundation and 20 years later cracks appear in all the rooms of the house. And someone asks, "What went wrong?"

Well, what they don't know is that 20 years ago the contractor cheated on the foundation. We're finding out years later that the same is true of nutrition.

Another thing I learned from history was that during World War II, meat, sugar and other things were rationed and families were encouraged to plant "victory gardens," raise their own vegetables, and even have one or two fruit trees. Consequently, we were all eating more fresh fruits and vegetables and less cheap, imported sugar. I remember my mother never allowed us to add sugar to anything, even cereal, but she would allow us to use honey or take a cookie and break it up in our cereal to sweeten it.

Now we live in this modern and sophisticated age of technology where if it tastes good, we eat it, and pay for the consequences later. The late Larry Burkett used to say, "The simplest way to know if your diet is good—if it tastes good, spit it out, and if it doesn't, eat it!" Everybody spits out the celery, cabbage, broccoli, spinach and cauliflower, but they eat the cake, ice cream, soft drinks, and doughnuts. That's why we are raising a generation of sick, overweight people who are ruining their health.

Mr. Martin imported an exercise machine from Taiwan, and although it sold well and people got good results from it, he said, "I can build one even better than that," and he did, and got it patented. However, his model actually cost $100 more, and the average person couldn't tell the difference. His model was bigger, better, and should last longer, but the cheap models ran for several years. The American people preferred to buy the cheaper one, use it for five or seven years, then throw it away and get a new one rather than pay double for one that would last longer.

Because it was his "baby," Ivan wanted to keep on making it, but I said to him, "Ivan, you have to remember, more American people go to Sunday School and church in Fords and

Chevrolets than they do in Cadillacs, Jaguars, and Mercedes Benz. We have to do what the market will allow."

We have sold several thousand of these machines and people have given us some terrific testimonies. People who can't go out and walk every day and don't get proper exercise find that five minutes on the machine is almost the equivalent of walking a mile. If you lie on a rug and put your feet on the machine, it stimulates your blood so much you can feel it tingle in your head.

The lymph system doesn't have a pump like your heart so it is motivated and activated by muscular action, activity and exercise. The action of this machine is a great stimulator for the lymph system, which is the defense system of your whole body, and using this machine makes a *big* difference.

Because he had a neighbor who bought one of our machines and liked it so much, an 82-year-old guy from Michigan bought one. However, he called me and said, "I'm sending back your machine. I was on that thing for 15 minutes and got nauseated and a headache."

"Did you go on it for 15 minutes the first time?" I questioned him on the phone.

"Yeah!"

"Well, the instructions say you shouldn't do more than three to five minutes the first time—unless you are a very active person." I went on to ask, "Did you do a lot of exercising or walking or jogging before?"

"No," he admitted.

"Well, you shook everything loose in your system, and you are detoxifying and getting too much of an overload," I explained. "I would suggest that you back off and start out slow, doing it a little longer each day. If it doesn't help you, call me back, and I'll return your money and you can send the machine back to me."

That was three years ago. He kept it.

Ten or 15 years ago Grace and I spent a week in Florida visiting an Amish couple helping them to tear down their old house and hire a contractor to build them a new one. During our time there, we arranged for financing for them, got things going, and several months later they were living in their new house.

While we were there, I saw a paper lying on the table with the story in it of Caisse, a Canadian woman who was taking all the patients that the medical doctors were sending home to die. She would get permissions from the doctors to prescribe her Indian herbal tea recipe, which she called "Essiac tea," (the spelling of her name Caisse backwards). She gave it to these patients, and had a 98% success rate, with her own mother being one of them. When her mother was 72 and dying, she drank this Essiac herbal tea, recovered and lived until she was 90.

It is so ironic that because Caisse was so successful, they tried to put her in jail for practicing medicine without a license. Although she died in poverty, there were so many heart-warming stories of people who were blessed by her. What a testimony and legacy!

However, it is still true today. If you get a good product, somebody will try to squash it! When I was in high school, there was a fellow who put a special carburetor on his car and drove it all around town. While others were getting just 15 to 18 miles per gallon, he was getting 40+ miles per gallon of gasoline. Someone from a car factory visited him and said they would give him a new car each year for ten years if he would give them his old car. Before he knew what was going on, they took it from him. The reason they wanted his old car was to squash that carburetor, because if that would be installed in many cars, the gas companies wouldn't make enough money selling oil and gas! Their sales would have been cut by 50%.

The sad thing is that this same attitude has affected the health business, and you would think that would be the last place that people would be interested in attacking.

For example, acupuncture was scoffed at and condemned for years. I was even afraid to try it because people would smile and say "You're stupid" if you tried it. Now, I've been listening to doctors like Dr. Sam West who say your whole system is nothing but an intricate, God-made, wonderfully-crafted and created electrical system. That's why acupuncture works. It opens and connects the electrical contact points and makes your body become a conductor that heals itself. *Drugs and doctors don't heal you! They just treat the symptoms, not the causes!*

In our society, it is tough breaking into the market place. To sell our health supplies, we use the technique called multi-marketing, which is really "word of mouth." We invite six to 12 people into our living room and simply talk together about what *works!* Four people say a certain product works 90% of the time, and one or two others then are willing to try it. Another person in the group has a meeting at *his* house and a few more buy it. The ones who promote it get a small commission on their sales as a little remuneration for their effort, a reward of the free enterprise system.

Along with everything that we give or sell to people, we say, "This is NOT approved by the Food and Drug Administration," but we also add, "it has worked for a number of our friends, so you might want to try it." Nobody can put us in jail for simply stating that something works! We can't guarantee healing or even use the word, "cure."

What motivates me is seeing people really hurting and spending, as the scripture describes it in Luke 8:43 (KJV), "a woman having an issue of blood twelve years, which had *spent all her living upon physicians*, neither could be healed of any," and when she touched the hem of Jesus' garment, she was made whole. When I see persons, who had been spending $400 a month for drugs that didn't work, come and buy a health product for $39 and come back after six weeks saying they feel so much better and are back at work–let it be!

But let me back up a bit. When I picked up that article on the table in the Amish home in Florida, I read it while they were making breakfast. The story of Caisse was so heartwarming that I took it to the photocopy machine in the post office and copied all ten pages of it. I brought it home to Pennsylvania, put it in my filing cabinet and it stayed there for ten years.

In 2002, I re-read this story and thought, "What if this stuff has some value and I never told anybody?" It's almost like having thrown your Bible on the shelf, and you'd be the only one who knew about the saving power of the Lord Jesus *and you had never told anybody!* I got to thinking, "Whew! That would be terrible!"

Every day I would get lots of phone calls and I would interview people. One call was from an Amish woman from Indiana who wanted to order a health care product. During our conversation I said to her, "Before you hang up, I have a question for you. Have you ever heard of Essiac tea?"

"Oh, yes," she affirmed enthusiastically, "that saved my little girl's life!" She added, "My two-year-old daughter had leukemia, and the doctor said there was nothing he could do anymore to help her. We went home that day, very discouraged, thinking we were going to lose our little girl. Then, it had to be an act of God, somebody called and asked if we had considered giving her Essiac tea. I had never heard of it, but at that time we were introduced to it and gave it to our daughter. Today she's ten years old and every year I take her back to the doctor to be checked, and so far, he's found her to be cancer-free. She's doing well in school and has no health problems."

Another testimony was that of a Dunkard-Brethren farmer-preacher, 74 years old, who called for a case of artery care. On a hunch, I asked him, "Have you ever heard of Essiac tea?"

"Ah, yes, that saved my life ten years ago," he responded enthusiastically. He went on to explain that when he was 64, his doctor had told him he had only nine months to a year to live at the most. Somebody told him he should try Essiac tea, and he did. In three to four months, he could feel the biggest difference. He also had a brain tumor, and someone suggested that he add shark cartilage to what he was taking, and he did that, too. Whether it would have worked alone or if it was the combination of the Essiac tea *plus* the shark cartilage, *something* succeeded.

With joy he reported, "Now I'm 74, I work all day, and just came back from a mission trip to Arizona. We had a three-week preaching tour where I visited every day and preached every night. I get tired, but I'm blessed with good health and have *no* signs of cancer."

Another interesting story was that of a 62-year-old guy who belonged to an old order Mennonite group. He lived in Missouri and was scheduled to have bypass surgery. He told me, "We had struggled all our life, just got our mortgage paid, and had no insurance. My doctor told me to have $40,000 with me when I came back for the surgery. The next day when we were ready to leave to go to the bank intending to mortgage our home again, my wife had tears in her eyes. Before we went out the door, the phone rang, and a friend said, 'Don't do that! Instead, call Victor Ziegler in Lebanon, Pennsylvania, and get a case of artery care and put everything on hold.'"

He did that, and started getting into activities slowly. Within 30 days he was back at work and 90 days later, when his doctor checked him, he asked, "What are you doing? You don't need a bypass."

He was so happy. Instead of spending $40,000, he paid $160 and never mortgaged his house. He told me, "Boy, is my wife happy!"

A 57-year-old woman in Mt. Joy, Pennsylvania, just 30 miles from my home, had cancer and was sent home to die. She had already sent farewell letters to her friends and family. Her doctor had told her she had about 12 weeks to share with her family and then her time would be up.

My wife, Grace, participated in a yard sale in Schaefferstown, Pennsylvania, and had a table set up displaying various health products, including a paper describing Essiac tea and what it could do. A couple stopped by and said, "That looks interesting. Tell us about this. We are from Florida."

"Well," she explained, "many people are saying Essiac tea helps cancer patients who are really hurting, especially those whose doctors have given up on them."

"We have a friend who was sent home to die," they shared. "How much does it cost?"

"The first pack costs $14.95, and that will make six quarts which will last for a month or so," she informed them.

They decided to buy it for their friend, and Grace thought they were taking it to Florida. What she didn't know was that their friend lived in Mt. Joy, and they gave it to her.

About 12 weeks later, they were back home in Florida and he called me one Saturday night. When I answered the phone, he said, "You don't know me, but we met your wife, Grace, at a yard sale and bought that Essiac tea. We gave it to a friend of ours in Mt. Joy and we just got a call from her and she said she is feeling so good. She went back to her cancer doctor and he can't find anything wrong with her! She wants to go back to work and is so happy. All her friends had received her farewell letter that as much as said, 'You are welcome to attend my funeral in a couple months.' I just thought you and Grace would appreciate knowing she is doing so well."

"Do you think she'd mind if you would give me her name and phone number?" I asked, adding, "I would LOVE to talk to her personally and hear her story."

"No," he said, "I'm sure she wouldn't mind."

It was a month or two later when I called her, and she said she was still feeling great. Her doctor wanted to check her again in 90 days to see if she was still doing well. In the meantime, she bought more of the Essiac tea so she could keep drinking it. She ended up going to Florida and speaking to a women's prayer and Bible study group in a church in Lakeland. Through her experience and testimony, we received well over 20 phone call orders from Lakeland, Florida. Many called back to reorder saying, "Hey, something's happening. Send us another pack!"

We've heard of so many unusual healing miracles, and it seems that Essiac tea is one of the simplest remedies. It reminds me of the story of Naaman in the Bible (2 Kings 5:1-19) who had leprosy and was told by the prophet Elisha to go and dip himself seven times in the dirty Jordan River. Because it was so easy and simple, he didn't want to do it. What good would that do? His servants said to him, "If the prophet had told you to do some great thing, would you not have done it? How much more, then, when he tells you, 'Wash and be cleansed!'"

That's *exactly* the way it is with Essiac tea. In our society, we don't believe in *simple* things. If one health product costs $100 and another costs $1,000, people tend to believe that the higher cost product *must surely* be better! And sometimes it *is* true: "You get what you pay for." However, people should not reject this remedy without giving it a fair try.

Of course, all my life I have had the philosophy: *"If you have everything to gain and nothing to lose, for goodness sake, for your sake, for God's sake, TRY IT!"* Somebody *is* going to get blessed. People miss so much because they want to be in control, are just plain stubborn, or are simply afraid to risk. I would rather attempt things and watch people laugh at me, (because I kinda get a kick out of watching them laugh), and in due time, about 90% of it works, and boy, they forget quickly about that 10% failure. Then "he who laughs last, laughs best." You don't find that saying in the Bible, but it does say that if we bite our tongue and "bless those that curse us," (Luke 6:28) we *will* be blessed. At times, you just can't listen to all the "world" says, and even your own family may ridicule you, but you must just keep "truckin" away and working at it.

The Amish have been more open to trying new simple products than most other groups. Often, I would give them a bottle of a new product and say, "Just try this for 30 to 90 days, and if you don't see good results, you'll never get a bill." I always liked to deal with people who "put their money where their mouth is." When someone makes an offer like this, it tells me that he has confidence in his product.

It is difficult to convince people. If you get 100 people together, 90 will say, "That looks like a really good product," but they won't buy it or try it. The other 10% will. Later, when they realize they've been missing a blessing, they come around. Then you just have to smile and go on, knowing somebody got blessed because you shared.

Although I sell health products, I firmly believe that a positive outlook accounts for 70% to 90% of healing. In fact, when I give little lectures at our marketing meetings, I say, "Always remember the Bible says, 'As a man (or woman) thinketh in his/her heart, so is he' (Proverbs 23:7, KJV). The next part of the verse that isn't found in scripture is: '*Whatever you think and whatever you eat, is what you become.*' If all you think about is soda, cake, and ice cream, and that is all you eat, you *will* ruin your health. But if you think of your body as the temple of God and you want to preserve it and use it to the glory of God, then you will eat differently."

When I was around 66 years old, I went with about 40 guys who were in their 30's and 40's on a bus to attend a Promise Keepers meeting in Washington, D.C. On the way home, we stopped in Maryland to eat at a beautiful restaurant that had a huge buffet. I chose to have the soup and salad bar that cost around $6, and when I left, I felt wonderful. The other guys got big steak dinners for $10 and more. As they boarded the bus, they were groaning and saying, "Oh, my gosh, I ate so much my stomach hurts!"

I thought to myself, "I'm going to have some fun!"

After the bus started rolling, I got up and gave them a "free lecture." I began, "I always thought the younger fellows were the smartest, but now I have second thoughts. Think about it. I went in that restaurant and had that beautiful salad bar and soup for $6, and I'm feeling great. You guys went in there and had immense dinners for $10 and more, and now you're complaining. Something doesn't add up. From a stewardship point of view, your body is the temple of God and you shouldn't kill it or weaken it by smoking, drinking or gluttony. Also, I have an extra $4 or more than you do for the offering on Sunday morning because you spent yours here tonight making yourself sick!"

A few of the guys who knew me said, "Boo, Victor. That's enough of that!"

I pretended to protest, "But I'm only halfway through!" Then we'd all laugh and have fun, you know. However, all that I had said *was true*! I tried to say it with humor but at the same time "hit the nail on the head while I had the hammer."

When I worked at the Manheim (PA) Auto Auction, there was one day when about 50 guys were sitting around and I knew a small percentage of them were "beer bellies" and the rest were "food bellies." As I approached, someone would say, "Here comes 'Preacher Victor,' so we'll have to shut up."

So I said to these men, "Hey, fellas, take a look at yourselves!" (At that time, I was so thin that if I took a deep breath, my belly button would touch my backbone! So I felt I had room to talk.) I came on strong but softened it with a little bit of humor.

"Each one of you will determine your own destiny. Each day you are choosing if you want to die healthy and happy or if you want to die because you ruined your health by being a glutton or a drunk. I believe God designed us to live our life to the fullest to the last day and THEN, just give up the ghost and go to be with the Lord."

The guys would kid me, "Why are you always worried about health, Victor, and always trying to sell health stuff?" Some guys would add, "I'm not gonna live like you do, Victor. I'm gonna enjoy life, and keep on enjoying eating this and that."

I'd point out to them that once food gets past the taste buds and the middle of your mouth, you don't taste it anymore. The enjoyment is temporary. God gave you those taste buds, first of all, so you could enjoy food, and secondly, so you can detect poisons or something that doesn't taste right and spit it out rather than get sick. How can you argue with the fact that 'we are fearfully and wonderfully made?' (Psalms 139:14 –KJV) The Scripture says it; I believe it!"

To live life to *the fullest*, we need to conform to Biblical principles, the guidance of the One who designed us. It's all in the Book, the Instruction Book, but many of us neglect reading it, saying disdainfully, "Aw, we don't need that. We can do it on our own!"

However, we are all paying a big price physically, spiritually, and even financially. All of us can name people who have spent $100,000 on their health. In many cases, if you look at what they've done the last 20 years, their poor health is self-inflicted. They have kept doing the same things over and over again, but keep expecting better results. I call that "stupidity." They are paying a high price.

One night I got awake thinking about some of the meetings and seminars that we would soon be having. When I invited people to attend, they often asked, "What are we going to talk about?"

I answered, "We're going to talk about living GRACEfully! Living with grace, dying with grace, being blessed by God's abundant grace, and it all involves grace."

What really triggered me was my wife, Grace. Her name was just . . . was God's unmerited favor. I think that's the definition. We can *all* have that and enjoy it. That led me to say our lectures will be on "Gracious Living." Then I thought of the slogan for our business: "GRACious Living—The Way to a VICTORious Life."

I can't say that I was a big winner or victor in anything except when I was with my family and friends, I always felt like I was in the winner's circle because I enjoyed such good fellowship with them. In our business, we always tried to remember that in whatever we did, we tried to never focus on the monetary returns but on what we could do to bring glory to God and to bless others. When we ourselves are a good healthy living testimony, others will listen.

When I sat in meetings and listened to a 400 pound woman talk about health and welfare, I turned to the fellow beside me and said, "I'd like to go up and put my arm around that speaker and say, 'When do you plan to begin *practicing what you are preaching?*'"

On the way out, people commented, "She was very good at what she was good at–talking, but what she said surely wasn't working for her!"

In our meetings, we discovered that people responded more positively when one or two shared testimonies of how they had suffered and how their lives changed. We would say, "Look, you don't have to necessarily believe everything, but if you are hurting anyhow, try it. You'll save money, and if you get the improvement that others have experienced, you, too, will want to tell somebody else."

Because there was a certain credibility in having medical or professional people, we would occasionally get persons from the fields of nutrition or medicine, those who believed in living a balanced life without chemicals and drugs, to come and share with us. If some were too expensive to come in person, we tried to get their permission to use them on a video tape.

One who was very effective was Dr. Lorraine Day from California, a tremendous medical doctor who was caught up in the drug industry until she got cancer herself. She expresses it, "I was so caught up in taking people's money, and all we did was cut, poison and burn." That was her language. "If some organ wasn't working, use a surgical procedure and *cut* it out. If that doesn't work, give the patient a drug, a chemical, *poison* and try to kill the disease that way. If that doesn't work, try radiation and *burn* it out of them."

Dr. Day testified, "After I was stricken myself, one night I fell flat on my face and asked the Lord to turn me around because I knew I was being carried away by the terrific income that money had generated. I knew it was so wrong. It was wrong for me, and it was wrong because of what I was doing to other people."

When she gave up her practice, she was threatened multiple times because she was so outspoken against the procedures that were being used and weren't working. She realized that by adhering to all she had been taught, all she was doing was giving a multi-billion dollar business to the drug companies. By following the way the money flows, one can soon figure out what is behind it. Many good and sincere doctors know only what they were taught in medical school and what the drug salesmen tell them. As more and more people get impressive results from less harsh procedures and products, the practices of many doctors are slowly changing.

About ten years ago, when we were traveling home from Florida, we stopped in Georgia to get some gas. Often, when we did that, I would sit down with people and drum up a conversation with them. They were just sitting there smoking and complaining about their health problems, so while my gas was pumping and I was paying for it, I sold them ten bottles of artery care! That really *was* funny! The one guy bought a bottle saying, "If it's good enough for you, I want one!" I went out to the car six or seven times to get more bottles! Even the cashier bought one. She wanted it for her mother.

I kinda led them on and got them to have a little fun. I told them they had "never met a man like me, because I am the best blest man in the world. God has given me health, strength, and excitement about life, and do you know what? If you think this life is exciting, you ought to know what I know: *The best is yet to come!* The Bible says we can have an abundant life here and now, but eternal life is going to be sooooo much greater."

Sometimes I would come in the back door and give them a soft lecture.

We all are at different levels of spiritual understanding. *I still don't understand all that I DO know!* But I do know that God's grace is a real gift. Once you accept it, you start getting really blessed. Some people just can't understand that. I'd say, "It's like driving a car. Your headlights only shine so you can see 500 feet ahead. If you are stubborn, you might say, 'I am not going to drive farther than the light shines.' So you only drive 500 feet and you stop. But, no, you must take the next step, keeping the wheels turning slowly, and now you go 1000 feet. After a while, you are home, and that's the way life is. If you keep following the light, after a while you are 'home.'"

Very few people walked away. Once in a while I'd hear someone whisper, "Where's that guy from?" or "Is that guy crazy, or does he know what he's talking about?" And I'd just smile.

"Don't you think you made a couple of them guys angry?" Grace asked.

Then I admitted, "For a while, I could feel something stirring up in them. But then, as they came closer and listened, I could tell they were warming up." After all, while I tend to "say it like it is," only the Spirit of God can move people–not me! I hope and pray that *something registered* with them.

Chapter Thirteen

Helping Others Through Christian Organizations

"Ye have not because ye ask not." —James 4:2b (KJV)
"Plan for the worst and hope for the best." —Victor K. Ziegler

Because of her love of children, Grace volunteered a half-day each week for nine years serving as a teacher's aide in the class of educable mentally retarded children of the Eastern Lebanon County Middle School. One of the highlights of the school year for those children, and for Grace, was in May when they had a field trip to our farm. All sorts of activities were planned for them including a tour of the farm and animals, relay races, volleyball, other outdoor games, and a scavenger hunt, a picnic lunch, and several hours in our swimming pool. The children looked forward to this day so much that one teacher told us that "since the second day of school in September, the children have been asking when this outing would take place."

One year the children had an extra special experience on their field day here. We had a cow that I had put in a box containing fresh straw. She had just delivered one calf, and I sensed that something didn't seem right. It had been a breech birth, meaning that the calf had come out backwards. When that happens, it usually means either that there will be twins or that some kind of trouble is looming.

On this occasion, I rolled up my sleeves, put a long plastic glove over my arm and inserted it in the cow only to discover that I felt TWO MORE baby calves in there, waiting to be delivered. At that moment, all these little students came walking in!

"You are just in time for the grand performance," I said, inviting them in to watch.

While they were there, they witnessed the birth of these other two baby calves. Generally, in multiple births, the calves are apt to have a little mucous in their lungs and my practice was to hang them up on the gate and pop their lungs. This would release that mucous and get them started breathing. If you would lay them down, they wouldn't drain properly. You've got to hold them up and spank them a little to get them started. This encourages them. So I did this to these three calves, and these little kids saw it all. Their teacher was as much in awe as they were, as she had never witnessed it before either–and then these were triplets. She kept saying, "This is *amazing*! I am *so glad* we got here at this moment!"

"Yeah," I agreed. "I'm glad you were here also."

When I got all the calves to be breathing well, I laid them around in a circle in the straw and the mother went around and licked them all, especially working on their noses and their eyes, to stimulate them. It's just amazing how nature has taught them to clean out those special areas. Of course, then she went down over each of their backbones, massaging them and stimulating them some more so that in about five minutes, they'd jump up on their feet!

Those children just couldn't go home that day. They were so fascinated! They talked about that for a couple years. This outing on the farm had turned into a real learning experience–to see life come into being. Then they could equate the facts—"My gosh, my mom had *me* as a baby! Was I all wet when I was born? Was I so messed up and dirty-looking before they gave me a bath?" You know, that kind of conversation. That was rewarding. That was *really* rewarding!

You know, these special needs children are sometimes pretty intelligent. They just need a little extra help in certain areas. When they get it, it is always exciting to see the best come out of them. Yes, that was a memorable experience. They were brought in at *exactly* the right time. If they had come ten minutes later, they would have missed everything.

One Sunday morning a young man and his wife from West Virginia were invited to come and speak at the Heidelberg Church of the Brethren. They both had a deep love for children but never had any of their own. Consequently, they started helping delinquent teenagers and underprivileged children and incorporated many of their experiences in their message.

When they arrived in our area, their old car blew up, and they had no way to go back home to West Virginia. Just several days before that, I had been at a used car place and junk yard. There I saw two '55 Chevys that still ran pretty nice and weren't all beat-up looking. I wanted to buy one for the young fellow who worked for me so that he could drive to work himself and I wouldn't have to pick him up each day. Since the seller had two vehicles, he was asking $300 apiece and I could take my pick. On a whim, I asked, "What if I take both of them?"

"Ah," he replied, "take them both for $500."

So I had bought both of them, and this happened just a few days before I met this couple who needed a car to get back home. I then donated my second car to them, signing the title over to them and doing what we had to do legally so he could drive it back.

That began a period of two years that I supported them and their Home for Delinquent Children in West Virginia. I visited them occasionally and helped them get things going. They began on a small scale with five or ten children. Then I began to realize that because of the distance involved, I needed to back out. With all my other responsibilities, I kinda lost track of what they were doing. Later, I discovered that things went wrong there. He deserted his wife, somebody else took over the work and eventually their facility closed down.

During the time I was involved with them, they planned a special meeting and I wanted to attend. My neighbor's 21-year-old son, Jesse, and his friend had just gotten a 3-seater airplane. Jesse had a pilot's license, but hadn't flown across too many states yet. One day I said to him, "Jesse, if I pay you, would you want to fly me to West Virginia?"

"Yeah," was his immediate answer. "That would be fun!"

"Grace don't wanna go along," I informed him.

"There will still be three of us going," he replied. "I'm sure my friend, Bruce, will want to go along."

We had a great trip flying across the Appalachian Mountains in Pennsylvania. At one point, while we were above the mountains, we hit a downdraft and the little plane started dropping like we were going to hit the treetops. When we got to a certain level, I asked, "Jesse, are we running out of power?"

"I have it on full throttle," he replied. "That's all I can do."

We kept going down so far and then, all of a sudden, whoosh! We lifted up! We thought we were done for!

The pastor of the local church where this couple attended also served on their board and had informed us that he would meet us at a little country airport. To help us identify him, he said he would be standing outside of his 1965 white Ford station wagon. He added, "I am six feet tall and weigh 300 lbs. and I'll be waving a flag or something."

Well, we got within what I thought should be our destination, and I said, "Jesse, I believe we passed it by about five miles!"

In disbelief, Jesse protested, "But I didn't see *anything* that looked like an airport."

"'Way back there," I explained, "there was a little gravel country road with a shed at the end. I wonder if that could have been it."

So I got him to turn around and sure enough, when he lowered the plane, there was the white Ford station wagon and the man standing waving.

"There's our guy!" I exclaimed.

Jesse looked over the situation and remarked, "I never landed on a dirt road before, but it looks like I'm gonna do it here."

So, he did it, and we had a nice landing.

After the meeting, when it was time to return, all three of us were a bit shaken up from our scare in the mountains coming down, and we debated if we wanted to rent a car to drive home or take a chance at flying back.

"Well," I said, "we came this far. Let's pray and get in and go."

And we did. We got at least to the Pennsylvania line, and I don't know the exact geographical location, but all of a sudden, the plane flipped sideways like we were going up and around. I was in the middle behind him, and I said, "Jesse, did you do a lot of practice flying upside down?"

In a terrified voice, he shouted back, "No! I never did!"

He had never flown any somersaults or acrobatic maneuvers. Being curious, I persisted, "Really? Don't you know what to do when you are upside down?"

"No," he quickly responded.

Well, we flipped the whole way over. Then all of a sudden, we flipped right back. Oh, it scared us terrible! It happened so fast. All three of us had wet hands and were sweating.

After that we had a nice trip home and ended up at the Harrisburg airport at sunset. Before we drove in our car onto the highway, we stopped and thanked the Lord for bringing us home safely.

About 12 or 15 years ago, we started the "On Fire" Youth Ministry in Richland, Pennsylvania. Because we began by meeting on the second floor of the Fire Company building, that's how the ministry got its name. They had a little basketball floor there, and each Wednesday evening we had food, recreation, and discussion groups with the youth of the community. A couple of boys who came one night said, "Oh, we thought we were coming to a fire training school!"

Eventually, we outgrew that facility and then the Myerstown Church of the Brethren gave the ministry the use of their gymnasium one night a week, which was a nice gesture. Although my sister, Verna Kline, Grace and I used to help part-time, I wasn't a key leader in the On Fire program.

One night I drove to the meeting in my car, a '96 Jetta. My usual practice was to just stick the keys in my pocket but very seldom locking the car. That night I was going to go home a little bit early, so I came out, jumped in my car and started driving away. Suddenly it hit me, "Wow! I smell cigarettes. Somebody has been smoking in my car!"

I pulled to the end of the church's parking lot and turned the light on, only to discover that the whole radio had been ripped out of the dash! We had a "gentleman's agreement" with the Myerstown Community Police Department that if anything ever got out of hand at our youth ministry, we were to promptly let them know and keep them informed about any unusual activity. So, I gave them a call.

The woman police officer who showed up that night asked, "Do you have any idea who it could have been?"

The young people were not allowed to smoke on the property, but there were several boys who were trying to sneak away that night and I saw them. I smelled a rat, called them back, and after talking to them briefly, I could identify the culprit. I told the officer, "I believe I know who did it because the car smells right like he does!" (It was the same cigarette smell. Some cigarettes are rank, and others are sweet, and I am especially sensitive to certain odors.)

The officer laughed and asked, "What do you mean?"

"Because the cigarette smell in my car is identical to the smell of that boy," I explained. "That boy's clothing smells like it is from the same type of cigarette."

Sure enough, the next day they picked him up and he had the radio. The officer brought my radio back. It was funny. Within 48 hours, I got it back, and it was all because I smelled the same cigarette in my car! Later I told people, "I think I smelled him out!"

The officer stated, "We can't prosecute him without you pressing charges against him."

Hesitating to do that, I said, "Let me think about it. Let me try another approach first, and if he don't respond, we'll have to go the second step."

"That's okay," she agreed. "It's up to you."

Although I knew now who it was, I didn't let him know that I knew.

One night when we were both there at an On Fire meeting, I said to him, "Hey, something tells me that you are a master mechanic at electrical wiring, and I am trying to put a radio in my car, and I am too dumb to do it. Would you help me?"

His expression brightened, and he said eagerly, "Yeah, I would."

He had no idea I was leading him on. I asked, "When can you do it?"

"I'll give you a call," he replied.

That was funny. We came home from church one Sunday noon and the phone rang. It was this boy, and he said, "Hey, I can come over this afternoon and put that radio in for you." He added, "But do you know something–my dad is better at it than I am. I'll bring my dad along."

Sunday or no Sunday, I wasn't going to miss this opportunity, so I told him I'd be looking for him.

So, on that sunny Sunday afternoon they were here aside of my house–putting this radio back in. I soon realized he *did* know more than I did! Some of them guys are pretty smart. In order to finish hooking up the radio, his dad had to go to Walmart to get a few electrical clips. When he returned, we were having fun talking. I was mostly observing, and they were doing all the work.

After awhile I said to the son, "Do you know why I *really* wanted *you* to install this radio?"

He shook his head; he had no idea.

I went on to explain, "Whenever I had a piece of machinery, I always wanted the same man to rebuild it as tore it apart. I figured that if you tore the radio out, you might know *best* how to put it back in!"

That was the first inkling he got that I knew it. Of course, he was just caught cold, you might say. He never denied it.

Then I assured him, "I am not going to press charges or do anything, but I want you to know there's nothing that you do that goes unnoticed, either by your fellow men or by God. Always worry more about the eyes of God than those of your fellow men. *When you want to do something, always look up!*"

He stopped in to visit me several times after that. I haven't seen him for a couple years and have lost track of him now.

When the Church of the Brethren Youth Services (COBYS) was first organized about 25 years ago, I served on their first board for eight or more years. Their goal was to help underprivileged and abused children, establishing them in foster homes where they would be loved and taught Christian values. Prior to that, I had begun serving on the Lebanon County Children's and Youth Services Board as a volunteer board member in an advisory capacity for the Lebanon County Commissioners, and met with them once a month for almost 20 years. Seeing children get a second chance and feeling that I had a small part in it was tremendously satisfying. Anything that affected the lives of young people was exciting, because a lot of good things were happening. *If you change young people, you can change the world.* Of course, COBYS' ministries have multiplied many times since I was a part of their organization, and today they continue to have a wonderful program, fulfilling a great need in our society.

In 1980 a small group of us began Lighthouse Ministries, a home for unwed mothers, located three miles from our home in Richland, Pennsylvania. This ministry functioned for ten years and during that time I served as their president. In 1990, we decided to join forces with the Susquehanna Valley Pregnancy Services program that had a full staff. We realized we could support *them* and get the *same job done* more effectively than working independently. So, we sold the property, paid all the bills and had about $25,000 remaining. We divided this amount equally between the "On Fire" Youth Ministry (discussed earlier), and the Susquehanna Valley Pregnancy Services, benefiting both local ministries.

When we first organized the Lighthouse Ministries, I told the committee, "The most important thing in setting up any organization is deciding how to dissolve it in case the need isn't there any longer or if something changes." Deciding these procedures up front saves a lot of headache and heartache later on. So, in this case, we had planned that *if* this would ever happen, and *if* there were any remaining monies, they would go to like charitable ministries that helped local men, women, and children, and eventually, that's how it all worked out.

In a Christian organization and in the business world, it is so important that you *plan for the worst and hope for the best.* When you go into things, everybody is gung-ho, but when you lose $100,000, you have some enemies. People really don't want to stick with you through thick or thin. If you always plan *for the worst* scenario, and always work and pray *for the best* to happen, it usually happens to the good. In the event you have some setbacks, you are never disappointed, because you knew this could or could not happen before you started.

In fact, I think a lot of young couples make that mistake. They get married and think from now on, it's all glory. And it's not. Marriage isn't a guarantee of heaven on earth. It *can* be! But the two persons involved must work at it daily. It's all based on how strong their commitment is. People are enthused about being a part of something as long as they *feel* good about it, but when they lose their *feeling,* then their commitment goes too and everything, including the marriage, falls apart. That's why it don't work! As long as you both have that commitment, you can always rebuild. Anything good can happen *again!*

When I think of the most important qualities of leadership, I am reminded of when I was a boy and a neighbor had a pair of headstrong, ambitious horses that would just bust up all of his equipment. He just couldn't handle them. Then my dad bought them for half price because he knew how to harness young horses to get full advantage of their potential horsepower. Instead of beating them up and whipping them, he talked to them gently and let them know he was in command. With that same team of horses that had been so unruly for our neighbor, my dad could plow two acres of land before others could finish plowing one because he knew how to harness their energy and get the best out of them.

That's also true with people. That's the difference between a good leader, somebody who knows how to make everything fall in line, and a mediocre one. For a good leader to lead, sometimes he needs sideline coaches like board members. Whether you are a chairperson or a pastor, those people on the sideline can see some of the weaknesses more clearly than you can when you are in the lead position. A good leader needs to keep his ear tuned to their input. Then he or she can be tremendously successful and God gets the praise and glory. When the sidelines are ignored, I've seen good people self-destruct.

I always felt strongly that if you are a leader, you should always have your door open to those working with you, aside of you, or under you, so that they can share any input for the benefit of the business, organization or church. Sometimes the person that you might suppose has the least ideas can come up with the greatest thoughts to enhance the business or group of people working together for a common good. Any leader who loses that input will eventually fail, because no one person has all the answers or all the wisdom of God. *There is wisdom in the counsel of many.* If you have ten employees or 110, these people can generate some real constructive ideas. A good leader will work alongside his employees. As he allows and encourages them to bring out their best, he will look good. Their ideas just reflect to the top and vice versa. A good leader can either reject some good thoughts and self-destruct or take the good and thank that person for contributing and even give them a blessing or a reward of some sort, so that it brings out the best from them next time. Many leaders are afraid that one of their employees might have a better idea and eventually take their job! I've always said, "The greatest thing is building people that *are capable of taking your job* because if you do it the right way, the Lord will always make a better place for you in the end. You always end up being better."

My interest in the work of the Gideons dates back to the beginning of World War II. I remember so vividly the grip of fear I felt when I heard on December 7, 1941, that the United States had been attacked in Pearl Harbor by the Japanese and 1,500 men had been killed and numerous ships destroyed. Although I didn't really understand it all, I thought, "Oh MY!" My fears increased whenever we heard the air raid siren and we practiced the black-outs, pulling all the shades, turning off all the lights, and living, waiting and praying as communities in silent and pitch-black darkness. As a child I thought, "This *could be* the end of the world."

I'll never forget when some of the boys I had known left for the war and never returned. While it never changed my peace position, it gave me a love and respect for persons who are willing to lay down their lives to protect the American system of democratic government and what we all hope, value and believe. After all, Jesus taught there is no greater love than this. (John 15:13)

One of the most striking events when I was still a student was when a young fellow came back from World War II and spoke in a school assembly program. I remember so well that he said, "While I was serving in the military, the Gideons gave me a shiny New Testament. I thought to myself, 'I don't have time for that,' but I stuck it in my vest pocket over my heart. I was serving in the Pacific, and in the heat of one of our battles, when a friend and I were hiding in a foxhole, an enemy bullet hit me right in the chest. I cried out to my friend, 'I've been hit. Help me get my jacket off. I'm dying.' As he held me and pulled off my vest, this skinny New Testament fell out with a bullet hole punctured ¾ through it. The bullet pointed to a verse that led me to a saving knowledge of my Lord and Savior."

When I heard that, I was awestruck, and thought, "Boy, what a testimony!"

About forty years later, I joined the Gideons myself and started sharing New Testaments. The mission of the Gideons to distribute Bibles by placing them in hotel rooms, giving them to military personnel, college students, school children, etc. is well known. They believe strongly in Isa. 55:1 where it says, "My word . . . will not return to me empty, but will accomplish what I desire and achieve the purpose for which I sent it." (NIV) By simply reading God's Word, many people from all over the world have accepted Christ as their Savior and changed their lives.

One of the most tear-jerking events occurred when I was with a group of Gideons making a presentation to about

30 or 40 fifth grade students in the Fredericksburg-Jonestown School District. I told these children the story of how I had first heard of the Gideons through that young soldier from World War II and how his New Testament had prevented the bullet from penetrating his heart. I no sooner got done, when an 11 or 12-year-old girl jumped up and excitedly exclaimed, "That was my Grandpa!"

I was just stunned. This happened fifty years after I had first heard him tell the story. What a testimony! How amazing it is to see how God works in people's lives! It just motivated me to keep on doing more.

Although I always appreciated the Gideons, I wasn't too involved with them until two older gentlemen approached me and asked me if I would consider playing a more active part. When I explained that I thought I was too busy, they countered back. "Everybody has to start at some level. Could you give us an hour a month or a day a month, or could you help distribute Bibles or tracts? We would like you to make a commitment, no matter how small."

So, I did. Every year, as we kept having rewarding experiences, I got more heavily involved. We used to be able to distribute little red New Testaments to fifth graders in public schools, but only a few schools allow that anymore. To see the children light up because they had something they could call their own made it so rewarding and worthwhile. The testimonies we'd get back from children and adults were so moving that we just didn't want to quit.

One of my favorites was one I read of a ten-year-old boy in Brazil, who had been given a New Testament in school by a Gideon member. His dad was an atheist. For three nights in a row, this boy would beg his dad to read it to him, but his dad said, "Throw that book away. It's just junk. You don't want to read that!" But the boy never gave up, and kept this little red New Testament in his pocket.

Usually his dad went to work about an hour after the boy had left for school. One morning as he approached an intersection on his way to his job, the father noticed an ambulance and a truck, and realizing there had been an accident, he stopped. To his shock, he discovered that his son was lying in the street having been hit by the truck. His shirt was blood-stained, and as his dad knelt beside him, the boy pulled his blood-covered New Testament out of his pocket and said, "Give this to my father as I see Jesus now." Moments later, he went home to be with the Lord. The father was so touched that he *did* read it, and in a matter of months, the whole extended family had become believers.

When I tell that story, I say, "That boy accomplished more in the ten short years of his life than most people do in 50 or 80 years."

He didn't die in vain. He already is enjoying the promise of living with his Heavenly Father and has the blessing, I believe, of looking down from heaven and witnessing the good things happening in his parent's family. I always had the feeling that God will allow us to see some of the good things, but I also believe we couldn't enjoy heaven if we saw the murders and the ungodliness on earth, people forsaking what is good.

Another story I enjoy so much is about a Gideon who gave a New Testament to an older guy. The man took it and grumbled a little bit and walked farther down the sidewalk. Moments later, the Gideon looked back and saw this man throw the New Testament into a garbage can. Feeling discouraged, the Gideon said, "I think I'll quit handing out Bibles. It just isn't working."

Two months later, when his Gideon camp got together, someone stood up and said, "Never give up in what you are doing. A couple months ago I was emptying a garbage can and a shiny New Testament slipped out of the can and into my truck. I retrieved it, and stuck it in my pocket. Later, for the first time in my life, I started reading the Scripture and came to know the Lord as my personal Savior. So, *never give up*! I was one who went from the guttermost to the uttermost."

When you are handing them out, you feel bad when you see them being thrown into a garbage can, but look how God used that one. That truck driver picked it up and got the message in a hurry. Every month I love to read the testimonies of men and women, young and old, who came to know the Lord through the printed scriptures. It's so rewarding.

I keep telling new and prospective Gideon members, "You might not be as verbal and vocal as I am, but if you are faithful in just handing out a little printed message, the Holy Spirit will multiply that over and over. However, we have to do our own acts of kindness and put a little effort into it."

God's multiplication table is so different from ours that we can't figure it out. The Gideons are *always* short of help, but it was true already in the Scriptures, "The harvest is great, and the laborers are few." (Matt. 9:37) I served as president or chairperson of the local camp of Gideons, but I never served in a statewide or national position.

They *do* have a wonderful program. For many years, they only distributed the King James Version, but now they also are promoting the New English Version. As with any group, there are a few things that could be changed, but some of the old guys always say, "Hey, it's worked this way for 100 years. We don't want to mess it up!" And there is some truth to that. *If you change too much, you lose too much of what is good.*

One thing I really like about the Gideons is that they don't want us discussing denominational beliefs, but they always tell us to share just the basics, the plan of salvation. I think that is the secret of their success. I am convinced that if we emphasize Jesus Christ as Lord and Savior, that God sent His only Son whom we can accept or reject, that's so basic that all the other things fall into place. That doesn't create a spirit of bitterness among people. Instead, they have that one bond, that Christ is Lord of all. Without His sacrifice on the cross, we are all doomed. That's the basic bottom line.

Between 1970 and 1986, I was active on the board for the Pennsylvania Teen Challenge Organization. When I first came on the board, our budget was $300,000 per year, and when I left, it was $3 million! I was the "acting-treasurer" for about eight years and watched this thing grow. I refer to my role in that way because we had a woman who was a tremendous treasurer and bookkeeper. Since I was treasurer in name only, I met with her once every couple weeks and didn't have to sign many of the checks. I'd read the treasurer reports and then meet with the in-house treasurer, because I said I wanted her to point out anything that I might have missed. Occasionally, she'd draw my attention to something and say, "Here's something that doesn't seem right, and you might want to work on."

Then I'd bring it up at the meetings and we'd try to get it resolved.

The main goal of Teen Challenge was and still is to help free young men with addictions to drugs, alcohol, sex, or whatever and lead them to a saving knowledge of Jesus Christ. Through their new-found faith, many of them were able to experience the freedom, forgiveness, joy, peace, and God-given love enabling them to overcome their addictive habits and find a purpose for their lives. I think there were about 50 boys enrolled in their program when I joined, and when I retired, there were 250 or so. It just kept on growing. Of course, there were a few failures along the way, but the success rate was so great that it would be a waste of time to talk about the failures.

For a couple years, I served as chairman. However, I was the kind of person—I never liked being chairman. I wanted to be able to think on my feet and express myself instead of following all the parliamentary procedures. By simply being a board member, I felt I could accomplish more than by being chairman. Because he doesn't want to influence people the wrong way, the one in charge has to be more diplomatic and tactful.

In one instance, the government had given Teen Challenge a nice amount of money, something like $100,000. They sent a government psychiatrist who was supposed to live on the premises for two years, have an office there, and make observations, summarizing the ministry from the present back to its beginnings.

When this psychiatrist attended her first board meeting, we felt she might be an atheist. She was about 50 years old, and it was very obvious that she wasn't too excited about what we were doing, but was simply completing an assignment. At the end of the meeting, she just said, "Well, we'll see."

After two years of gathering statistics and following up on various cases, she met with our board again, and I'll never forget that meeting. She admitted, "You know, I came here two years ago as an unbeliever, but you have made a believer out of me!"

I think her findings were that we had an 85% success rate while the government's programs were just 2% successful. What she also found to be most amazing was that "Teen Challenge is having this success on interest money, when the government is funded with millions of dollars of principal sums. Yet you have this high success rate with so little money spent!"

I'll never forget Prange Reynolds, our director at that time, who was a full-fledged Pentecostal preacher and an associate of Dave Wilkerson, the founder of Teen Challenge. Although he was ten years older than me, Prange was a wonderful, down-to-earth guy who could farm, milk a cow, pray for and counsel with a guy. There was just nothing he couldn't do! When he was asked how the Teen Challenge program worked so well, he replied, "It is so simple. There's only one way I know to explain it. These young men come here and we give them God in the morning, Jesus Christ for lunch, and the Holy Spirit at night. And," he continued, "it works! We get them to concentrate on their being a gift from God. It doesn't matter who their family or parents were, even if they are in prison. Each one is still here by an act of God and created for a special reason or purpose. Once they learn that one's circumstances are not controlled by where you are or who you are, but by the fact that you are a child of the King, they view life differently. By accepting Christ, every boy was convinced that 'I am God's son, through adoption' . . . and it works!'"

And it *still* works. Since the ministry has grown, some things have changed and things may be done a little differently, but they still hold to that basic belief and practice. Without the Spirit of God possessing a person, he is doomed and will never change, no matter how many drug programs he may go through. If it is just a surface training program, that's all it is. He may temporarily feel good and do well, but after awhile he will sink back into the old lifestyle.

For quite a few years I went to Saturday and Sunday night services as part of a team from Teen Challenge who would present a program and give their testimonies. I'll never forget one Sunday night when we were at a little church with about 150 persons present. A group of 12 to 15 boys were getting carried away singing, giving testimonies and having a wonderful time. When I looked at my watch, I discovered it was a quarter to ten, and I couldn't get these guys stopped! It was my responsibility to kinda moderate or slow things down and bring the meeting to a close.

Finally, I walked over and put my arm around one of the boys and said, "It's a quarter to ten and a lot of these people got to get up early tomorrow morning to go to work." Turning to the audience, I continued, "You know, these guys are so full of all the good things God has blessed them with that they could easily talk until midnight, but we can't do that tonight. We'll have to continue that at a later time."

"Furthermore, we have been listening as they talked about all the things that they were delivered from. Here you and I are, sitting in this congregation, and we have been spared from all that. Their testimonies should remind us that we have *even more* to be thankful for than they do. They have come from the pits of hell, and can't get done talking about their deliverance from the evil one, the devil himself. Having been spared from those experiences, isn't it strange that you and I are so quiet about our salvation, about God's loving gifts to us? With that, we are going to have to close tonight, and we thank you all for your presence. Let's go away being more verbal and vocal witnesses so that people might not only *see* the difference in *our* lives, but will also hear *why*." With that little speech, I finally was able to close the meeting.

Let me tell you how I got to be on the Teen Challenge Board in the first place. It was funny. I was facing seven ordained Pentecostal preachers who were pretty well-versed. And you can imagine, since Pentecostal guys are all pretty excitable and say what they think, we had a great exchange.

In this situation, I again thought I would get myself in the door by using a little humor. I said, "You know, I come from the old Brethren church, and basically, we believe the same as you brothers do. Salvation only comes through Jesus Christ shedding His blood on the cross for us and giving us the abundant life, the promise of eternal life, and heaven's our home. However, we, the Brethren, are so much more reserved in expressing it. That's the only thing I would like to see our church doing a bit more of—becoming more vocal in sharing our personal faith publicly. We were that quiet and that dead that one Sunday morning one of our deacons had a heart attack. Someone called 9-1-1. The doctor rushed in and had to check all seven deacons to discover which one was dead!"

Oh, they liked that. They just laughed. Then I told them, "You are all old enough to take that for what it's worth, but it's just a story anyhow. The Brethren are changing a little bit, and I am happy to be starting to hear some personal stories occasionally. As people are starting to share what the presence of the Spirit of God coming into their lives has meant, it has made such a difference. The more we do of it, the more it rubs off, and the more young people see something that's real. I don't see that I would have any conflict with anything that your church believes. You might baptize backwards or forwards, but it's all in the name of the Lord Jesus, and that's what really matters to me. *What's important is the mode of the heart and not necessarily the mode of the outward action.*"

We continued on for a while, and then they said, "Boy, we can't find any fault with you. We think we are going to ask you to serve on our board."

And I did for almost 17 years. When I first joined, there were seven on the board, and by the time I left, there were 12. All were Pentecostal except for a Mennonite insurance man and myself from the Church of the Brethren. We had a great time serving together.

One time a guy asked me, "Victor, what do you believe about speaking in tongues?"

"Well," I replied, "I'm like this. Until everybody understands me speaking in English, I want to accomplish that task first, *then* I'm ready for the next step."

And they laughed.

Then I continued, "But if somebody has a special gift of speaking in tongues that I don't understand, I'm not the kind of person who will condemn it. However, I *am* the kind of person who will get concerned if that is the *only* thing he can do or talk about and puts down all other aspects of a Christian's faith. I do believe that God works in mysterious ways, so I have no real trouble with it. After all, hey, one day even I might experience something different and as the world would say, 'I might have to eat my own words!'"

I only ever spoke in a foreign language one time, and that was in Cuba. That was funny. I can still feel my blood circulating when I remember how they got so excited and I couldn't figure out why. I had said the last two phrases in Spanish! And I couldn't repeat it! I know I was emphasizing the fact that they were experiencing persecution and hard times, physically and financially. Nobody was starving there, but they were hurting. Then I convinced them that we are only strangers and pilgrims here, just traveling through the world, and they jumped up, clapped and shouted. That was fun! It makes me want to do it again! I never even gave it a thought or practiced trying to speak in *any* language, because I *knew* I couldn't master it. You know, when you try something and put on an artificial act, it doesn't work anyhow. When I was speaking in a foreign country, I would just tell them, "You've got to translate what I say, because I just *can't.*" The Spirit of God translated for me that night in Cuba, and the Spanish-speaking translator knew it.

For 25 years I was also on the board for Jubilee Ministries, a prison ministry associated with the Lebanon County Prison, and for seven of those years I served as president. Back in the beginning another guy helped to organize it and then I took his place. Later I got another guy to replace me, because in this organization also, I preferred being an active board member doing more things behind the scene rather than being president, one who often has to "play politics" and avoid stepping on people's toes.

When I came on the board with Jubilee, we had a $7,000 a year budget and a young man serving as part-time chaplain. When I left, the budget was $1 million and today it is $3 million because they now have a gift shop, a furniture store and a re-use it store, and they just opened up another building in Palmyra. The general public has been so generous with gifts and donations, and the proceeds help poor people get things that are still very usable for 50 cents and $1.

It works two ways: We are generating cash for the ministry and at the same time helping low income families have low-cost but decent clothing and furniture. People are constantly bringing in tons of good meat or fresh and frozen turkeys and we are selling or even giving them away. It is really rewarding to see things like that.

I found the *most* rewarding to be when we had a couple fellows out of prison come and stay with us in our home and work here on the farm. One, in particular, had left us and about six months or so later had a fight or some disagreement with his girlfriend, and she turned him in.

He called me and seemed frantic as he told me, "I'm going to jail again. My girlfriend is putting me in jail."

Surprised, I asked, "What did you do?"

"Aw," he admitted, disgusted with himself, "I was drinking and did the wrong thing."

"Now, Charles (not his real name), you know better than that," I reminded him, as he really was an awful nice guy.

"What can you do for me?" he questioned.

"What do you think I should do?"

"I don't want to go to jail," he stated.

"No, nobody wants to, but you have to pay the price, you know." Then I said, "I'll tell you what, I'll go along with you to the hearing and depending on how things go, at the last minute, I'll decide. I can't tell you now what I might do, because first I want to hear what the attorney who is throwing the book at you says and what the judge says."

When I went into the courthouse that morning at 9 o'clock, I discovered that Charles' case was the first one on the agenda. I also discovered that the prosecuting attorney was Bill Sheaffer, who was in my sister Verna's high school class back in Richland.

When he looked around and saw I had come in, he was so shocked and said, "Victor, what the h--- are you doing here?"

"Well, I just want to see what this situation is here with Charles," I explained smiling.

"To be honest with you, I am going to throw the whole book at him," he confided, adding the prediction, "And he isn't going to walk out!"

During the hearing, his attorney called on me and asked, "Are you here as a reference or what?"

In addressing the court, I said, "Your honor, Charles is really a good kid. He did do something awful stupid, and I'm not going to defend him for that stupidity. What he did was done under the influence of alcohol, and he messed up his life and admits it. However, he has so much talent and I believe if this kid had a second chance, he'd make it." (I knew that was putting my own integrity on the line!)

"Okay," the judge said, "do you have anything further to say?"

"Only that if anything changes, rather than sending him to jail for the next several years, I'd be willing to follow up on him a little bit to help make it happen."

So, when the prosecuting attorney was called up, he simply said, "Your Honor, if Victor Ziegler says this kid'll make it, he'll make it! We'll drop the case!"

Oh, my mouth dropped open, and I spoke silently within my heart, "Thank You, Lord, but now You have to help me. If this boy betrays me, I have my whole life and reputation at stake here in the county."

Afterwards, I talked firmly to Charles saying, "You break up with that girlfriend and stay away from her. Don't you *ever* talk to her again! Don't you *ever* get involved with drinking or drugs or anything again. Honor your father and mother, and do what you are told to do."

He was only about eighteen at the time and lived with us here in our basement apartment for about a year. He was a nice guy, a good worker, and he ate dinner with us each day, but had his own bedroom downstairs. I sort of forget the course of events, but he ended up in New Hampshire as an electrician's assistant and later became a licensed electrician.

For several years, we lost track of him. However, about eight years later, one Thanksgiving Day, he came driving in here with a woman and two boys. He jumped out of his car, he just grabbed Grace and hugged her and said, "I want you to meet my wife and my two stepsons."

Then he turned to his wife and said, "If it wouldn't be for this couple, I would *still* be sitting in jail."

He repeated it again to me, adding that the only reason he wasn't there was because "somebody had given him a second chance."

Today he is a probation officer and works in and out of a prison for the state of New Hampshire. One recent experience he had was with a 17-year-old boy who was acting smart and doing all kinds of dumb tricks. Charles grabbed him by the collar and shook him up, saying "Let me tell you something, kid. There's not a thing in the book that you're going to do here that I don't know what you're going to do before you do it."

This kid just looked at him and asked, "Officer, how would you know?"

He answered, "Fifteen or twenty years ago, some guy grabbed me and got my attention. I sat up and took notice as I knew I was headed for jail. I was into everything. I got into drugs, alcohol, and stealing, and I did *everything* that *you* are doing now, but I thought nobody knew it. But this man, Victor, knew it all the time, except he didn't know the details."

When he told me this story, he remembered that I often would tell the Jubilee guys, "Now remember, you can fool a lot of people, but if you give a guy enough rope, he'll hang himself. The truth will be made known, and there won't be an argument about it."

Continuing his story, he added, "You know, that kid started to listen when I told him I was one like him. It really made a difference when he realized I had stooped as low as he had!"

Those were some of the rewarding things from serving with Jubilee Ministries, and their good work continues to this day.

One idea I had—to use a farmhouse I had bought as a halfway house—was not too well received by some of the neighbors. One complained, "I moved here from Philadelphia to get away from that trash, and now you're bringing it into my backyard."

Then I explained to him, "The only difference between Philadelphia and here is 60 miles and 20 years. We're giving time and money *now* to help offenders *before* they become hard-core criminals."

Every ministry that I felt good about, that I could conscientiously support, whether I could give one hour a year or one dollar a year, I would do for them whatever I could. I've always been a firm believer in giving pledges to ministries as I feel it takes real faith to pledge money without knowing how you're going to get it. Of course, there are limits to everything, but it was so spiritually rewarding. The most frequent question that I got asked was: "Why do you *do* all this?"

After I had entered the prison ministry as a volunteer, I took a friend along to a Dairy Cooperative meeting one time and mentioned that I had been in the prison the night before. He was aghast and asked, "Why in the world would you waste your time doing that?"

"I'll quit if you will answer this one question," I replied. "You have three teenage boys: 15, 18, and 19. If you get a phone call at 3:00 in the morning saying your 18-year-old son did something stupid and he ends up in jail, should we do what you just said—throw him in jail, lock him up, throw the key away and let him rot? If you tell me to, I will quit tomorrow."

"Victor, keep up the good work," he responded.

"It makes a difference if it is *your* son, doesn't it?"

End of conversation. I'll never forget that. He never challenged me again!

There is nothing that gives more pleasure than being able to rescue a child, pick him up out of the gutter, giving a second chance to someone who is down, or even helping an elderly person who did something that everyone should have enough sense not to do. You know that he just wasn't thinking of the consequences and something went wrong, either emotionally or Satan had a foothold. I am so thankful that I can be the one helping instead of being the one *needing the help*!

Chapter Fourteen

Witnessing in Words and Deeds!

"My dad always believed that a person was not ready to live until he was ready to die."
—Leon Ziegler, son of Victor and Grace Ziegler

One Sunday night in December while we were still living in the farmhouse, all five children were in the back of the car ready to leave for church. Grace and I had been held up a little and it was getting to the point that we needed every minute to get to the church by 7:30 p.m. when the Christmas program was scheduled to begin. It had snowed during the day and was beginning to drift a little when we finally started the short drive to the Heidelberg Church of the Brethren.

When we were less than a quarter mile from the church, we came upon a vehicle that was stuck in a snowbank. The 25-year-old driver had a ponytail and looked a little gruff and rough. Although I *could have* swung around him and passed him in the tracks that had been made by others, I went past him and stopped. Walking back to him in my tire tracks, I said, "Can I help you?"

"Yes," he replied, "I need somebody to pull me out. I am really stuck in a bad spot."

"I'll tell you what. I got my wife and five children in the car and we are going to the Christmas program at the church where you see the lights across the field here," I said, pointing in that direction. "I'll take them over, and I'll come back and help you get out."

I started to walk back toward my car and then stopped and said, "Better yet, you look cold. Why don't you jump in our car and   go along with us and warm up in the church? As soon as   the   service is dismissed, we'll take my wife and children h o m e   and I'll get the tractor and a log chain and come and p u l l   you out."

He agreed to that and went with us to church. By the time we arrived at the Heidelberg Church, we were five minutes late. Most everyone was already there when Grace and I came parading in with our five children and this rough-looking guy with the ponytail. Because the seated section in the middle of the church was mostly filled, we had to sit on the raised seats at the side where everybody could see and watch us.

The funny part was after the service. The people were friendly, coming to talk with this young gentleman and thanking him for attending our service.

"Well," he would explain, "I got here because this guy stopped and promised to come and pull me out of the snow."

It turned out that *five people* who were in church that night had seen him and passed by him and never offered to help him. They came to me with such a sheepish look and said, "Do you know what? We drove by that guy. We thought we didn't have time to stop. Now here he came along to church with you, and he is such a friendly fellow. This might have been the first time he ever heard the true message of Christmas!"

Everybody was so friendly, talking to him and including him, and you could tell he was takin' this all in. (None of them told *him* that they passed him by on the other side, but they told *me!*)

On the way to my home I told him, "Hey, you can go along with me inside and we'll both get a cookie and a cup of hot chocolate to warm up, and then we'll come up here on the tractor and pull out your car."

So we did that. He was so appreciative and wanted to pay me and this and that.

In declining, I said, "No, I was just so glad that we were there and able to help you out."

And we've never heard from him since! However, sometimes you wonder if at times like that you might be "serving angels unawares." (Hebrews 13:2, KJV) I can't believe that he would ever forget that . . . especially when the couple who stopped to help him had five little kids in the back of the car.

Although my friends and family often warned me not to do it, when I was driving alone, I used to love picking up hitchhikers. "You don't do that; you don't do that!" they'd tell me, and I knew, in a sense, they were right and had my best interest at heart. But when I'd see somebody in need, I usually . . . well, a few times I saw them and was going too fast, so I'd start praying. Then I'd put on my brakes and back up, sometimes as far as 300 feet! Every time I was so blessed!

On one occasion I was going down route 83 in my '78 Volkswagon Rabbit to Baltimore and saw this young fellow about 25 years old. It was around the fourth of July and it was a hot day. Although this guy looked pretty rough and weather-beaten, I stopped and said, "Jump in. I'll take you along as far as I am going."

"That would be a great lift," he said.

He got in my car and looked at me and said, "Sir, where the h--- are you going?"

"Well," I answered, "I'm on my way to heaven, but I'm going to Baltimore today."

That started a conversation that didn't end! I told him all that I believed and how I got to this point. His whole attitude changed. When he got out of the car, I thought, "He'll sure be glad to be rid of *me*!"

But you know, he wound the window down and hung onto the door for another five minutes and talked to me and then wished me well, and I've never seen him since. I'll never forget that.

One day one of the chaplains from the Lebanon County prison and I were on our way to Harrisburg to attend a prison ministries meeting. We met regularly with prison ministry personnel from other counties, such as Dauphin, Lancaster, and Berks Counties, to keep up with what was going on around us and exchange ideas to enhance our respective ministries.

It was raining hard, and I saw a guy standing under a bridge in a futile attempt to keep dry. I turned to the chaplain and said, "I'm going to stop and take this guy along."

When I pulled over, the minute I got stopped, another guy jumped out from behind the bridge, and both men jumped into the back of the car.

"Good afternoon, fellows," I greeted them. "How are you doing?"

"Well, we are all wet!" they answered

"We're going to Harrisburg," I informed them. "How far do you want to go?"

"That'll help us," they agreed. "That'll be great to get to the Harrisburg area."

So we started driving awhile, and then I said, "Hey, fellows, let me tell you something. I *love* to pick up hitchhikers, but the average person in the world in which we live is a little bit fearful of doing that."

"Yeah, we understand," they affirmed. "There is so much going on and there is a risk."

"From now on," I advised them, "do yourselves and people like me a favor. When you are hitchhiking, *both* of you should stand out and display yourselves. The average person probably would have said to you, 'Would you mind stepping out a second?' And then took off in his car. He would have done that because he got scared when the second person appeared. You probably didn't think about that from where you are coming from, but . . . I never had a bad experience, so I tend to risk more than some do. My friends always tell me their horror stories and try to stop me from doing it."

They agreed and admitted, "Yeah, we understand that many people realize we need a ride, but they won't stop because they are afraid. They heard about some guy being held up or something."

So, we continued to have a nice conversation with no tense moments and had a nice ride together. They thought it was wonderful that we were using some of our spare time in Prison Ministries, helping young men and women who got their lives messed up and giving them a fresh start. We made it clear to them, "We wouldn't be doing this, but as Christians, we feel that one of Jesus' commandments was, 'If you are blessed, share your blessing and pass it on.'"

I never felt that any of my witnessing efforts were in vain, because I feel sure that some way, somehow, they struck a chord and we won't know the results until we reach eternity. I believe that some day I'm going to meet some of those people face to face in heaven, and that will be *really* exciting! We'll have a thousand years to talk about it!

Sometimes I was called to be a peacemaker. Less than a half mile from our home, we had a neighbor couple who had been married thirty years. The husband, Roy, (not his real name), was an alcoholic, and when he was sober, he was a nice man, but when he was "under the influence," he could be wild.

One year, on the Wednesday before Thanksgiving, the wife, Millie, (not her real name), called us at about 9:30 p.m. We had just been at a Thanksgiving eve service at church. Ironically enough, that night the congregation had decided that instead of having a full sermon or lecture, we would have a time of sharing testimonies of thanksgiving. After several had spoken, I stood up and said, "I want to thank the Lord for my godly neighbors. They challenge me in one way and my ungodly neighbors challenge me in a different way, but having both kinds gives me an opportunity to see God at work."

We had just gotten home from this service and walked in the door when the phone rang. Millie was crying and all upset. She quickly explained, "Victor, can you come over? My husband is threatening to shoot me, and he is stronger than I am and is running around in the house with a gun."

Without hesitating, I assured her, "Okay, I'll be up."

Before I left, I did call the state police and told them what was happening and what I was about to do.

"All right, we will send a man over," they promised, adding, "you can go there awhile."

Expecting the prompt arrival of an officer, I went, but it took 45 minutes until the policeman arrived! (I found out later that he really didn't want to come, because he knew it wouldn't be a good situation and could become messy. So, he admitted to me, he had stopped at a restaurant on the way and got a cup of coffee!)

When he finally got there, I came out of the house to meet him and tell him what I had found. "Roy is in there, dead drunk," I explained. "He fell asleep on the sofa with the rifle yet in his hand. I told Millie to just go to bed and don't try to talk to him, touch him, or irritate him in any way, because when a person is 'under the influence,' you can't deal with him. He's not in his right mind. He's just not thinking clear. When he sobers up, he'll probably be altogether different."

The next morning Roy called me and apologized. "I hear you were up here last night," he said.

I thought he was going to be angry with me. Instead, he added, "Thanks for stopping in."

From then on, I tried to help him overcome his drinking habit. He had a good job and worked every day until about 4:00 p.m. Then he'd go and sit in a bar until about 8:00 every night, spending almost four hours there every evening and about half his money. I finally got him to make a commitment that every day he would come down and see me right after he got home from work, either so we could talk together a little bit, or–I said, "Do you know what? You could help *me* get some of *my work* done."

"Yeah," he quickly agreed. "I'd like to work for you any day."

So Roy did that, and I'd pay him as long as we had something productive to do. And as long as he did that, that really worked! Later on, I guess he drifted a little bit, and finally, after thirty-five years, he died.

The best part is that during the last six months of his life, he asked the Lord to save him. He was in the hospital at that time, and we visited him there a couple times. He said, "Victor, I can't go on like this." (He was five to seven years younger than I was, but his drinking all those years had taken its toll on him.)

"Well, Roy, you don't have to," I reminded him.

"Yes, but I am so messed up!" he confessed.

"Christ died for *all* of us. It doesn't matter how much we have messed up our lives. You just have to ask the Lord to save you and take possession of your life and be in control of everything, and He will do it," I explained.

He did it and from then on, he was a different guy. He was baptized, but he died shortly afterwards.

During the Korean War, we were farming and I was eligible for the draft. At one point, they were going to take me as I was classified as a farm deferment. They finally deferred me on the basis of being self-employed and the difficulty of being replaced. Being married and having a six-month-old child created more liability for the government, and they gave some of those guys a deferment if they could prove that they were involved in food production and agriculture. This was a high priority because they recognized that if a country doesn't have a good food supply, everything stops. At the end, though, I would have been classified as a C-O, a conscientious objector, but before they would allow that, I was to appear before an attorney at a hearing to determine if I am faking my position or not.

Unknown to me, before the hearing took place, an FBI agent had visited four local places of business to inquire about me. Among them was a teacher at an Amish school, the hardware store, and a local feed mill. He questioned them about my reliability and such things as whether I paid my bills, kept my promises, and was truly sincere in my beliefs. I know that all four of them gave positive answers because they showed me the full report after the fact.

At the 30-minute hearing held in Harrisburg, the attorney questioned me, and I soon realized he knew more about the church's position on peace than I ever did. He really put me on the spot! One of the toughest questions he asked was, "Now, you have a six-month-old baby girl, and you say you don't believe in resistance. Suppose that tonight at midnight someone breaks into your house. At gunpoint, he threatens to drag off your wife and daughter with him, or even to kill them. Are you going to just stand there and smile? You aren't going to put up any resistance?"

My response was, "Well, first of all, I have an old rifle out in the garage on the second floor. I've never kept it handy, because I believe that many people who respond quickly do the wrong thing. Whereas, if they are forced to think something through or go to an effort to do an act, they will usually do it differently. That's why I never kept anything handy that could be used to destroy someone. I'd rather talk to the guy, trying to talk him out of it, to change his mind, and I would pray. If worse came to worst, I'd never kill him, but I probably *would* attempt to restrain him at the risk of my own life versus having him hurting or kidnapping my wife and/or daughter."

I finished by saying it is only by the grace of God that anybody knows what they would do in the final moments of a crisis like that. I also mentioned that I would rather die at the hand of somebody else than to kill anybody, because I would have to live with that the rest of my life and that would be tough. I know when I die I am guaranteed to go to heaven, but if I murder somebody, it would raise a lot of questions in my mind, such as "Did I do the right thing?"

In looking back, this was a good experience. I enjoyed being drilled, going through the questioning and having people check up on me, because it made me more aware and conscious of my own position on these issues. It also made me wonder— could I measure up, in the final analysis? I believe I could, but it would only be by the grace of God. No one ever quite knows until he or she is *really* put to the test.

I believe that the very fact that *you set your goal* according to the Scripture and in what you believe, God will honor that in your response when you are under pressure, even when you are incapable of thinking clearly. I think this has been true from the beginning of time until today. Many people would *like* to go back and respond differently, but at the time, they had the wrong motive and vengeance took over. We can't guarantee *anything* except by the grace of God because we're still human. You hate to think that you'd do the wrong thing, yet I believe that God honors the very fact that you *believe* and this is what you *want* to do. In our moment of weakness, He will give us the ability to overcome and will see us through so that He will get the glory instead of involving us in a destructive situation that we must live with for the next 50 years.

After he questioned me for a while, the attorney said, "Well, your answers are so convincing and satisfactory, we will reclassify you as a conscientious objector."

Between that and my agricultural responsibilities, I was never called to serve, even as part of the alternative service program in which many of my friends, who had no obligations, served. Those in that program did have many good learning and social experiences. In looking back, I felt that maybe I should have taken a year or two to go away and do something different, but through it all, it worked out real good.

When I was still a teenager, my brother, Earl, had already been licensed and ordained as a minister. One night I decided to attend a revival meeting at the Midway Church of the Brethren. The custom among Brethren ministers at that time was that if the one in charge on the platform noticed a minister in the audience, he would feel free to ask the congregation to "kneel as Brother _____ leads us in prayer." That was the only warning the visiting minister got. On this night, the minister in charge announced that "the congregation would be led in prayer by Brother Earl Ziegler."

I had not seen Earl come in. In fact, I was 95% sure that he was definitely at another location that evening. As the congregation knelt, I gave a quick look around and didn't see him so I was *positive* Earl was not there. To avoid an awkward and possibly lengthy pause, I just began praying out loud. To this day, I'm not sure if that minister ever realized that the person who prayed was NOT Brother Earl Ziegler but it was *Earl's blood brother*, Victor!

In 1983 I was invited to be a lay speaker for a 4-night series of Lenten services at the Black Rock Church of the Brethren near Hanover in York County. My brother, Earl, had been pastor there from 1960 to 1970, but their pastor at this time was Rev. Eugene Bucher. At the beginning of this service, just as Eugene and I had walked up to the pulpit area and sat down, I noticed Earl, and his wife, Vivian, walking in. When I saw them, I thought, "Oh my! I'm going to faint!" (Earl had just received his Doctor of Ministry degree a few months earlier in 1982 from the Lancaster Theological Seminary.)

Suddenly I got a thought I never had before, and it hit me so funny that I felt I just *must* tell it. When it was time for me to speak, I remember getting up and telling the congregation,

"I'm a little bit nervous tonight. I notice that my brother, the Rev. Dr. Earl Ziegler, just walked in. If I ever needed a doctor, it is now, because I think I am fainting!"

After the laughter subsided, I added, "But do you know what saves me? When I was ten or twelve years old, there were seven children in our family, and I overheard a conversation that my dad was having with my mother. He was confiding in her and saying, 'Five of our children, we believe, are going to do all right in life, but the other two we are going to have to send off to college!'" (Those two were my brother, Earl, and my sister, Ada Good.)

Of course, the congregation laughed again, and Earl got such a kick out of that. Earl knew me well enough, so I knew I could get away with saying just about anything. The congregation never forgot that.

However, I continued by saying, "You know, I am convinced, that if the Lord gives you ten talents, he expects you to use ten, and if he gives you one talent, he expects you to use that one. If you give that one your best, you can equal the guy who has ten! That's the way God works. He'll make something come through to people, to really reach their level of understanding. Sometimes a rough speaker can reach people where they are, while a more sophisticated speaker's message might go totally over their heads." So, we had a lot of fun.

Actually, until I got my current illness, I was invited to speak at quite a few churches, especially for the Gideons. Grace and I spent about eight years or so participating in Lay Witness Missions, going out several times a year. That was a rewarding and heart-warming experience because it involved different denominations such as Methodists, Presbyterians, and Church of the Brethren and we got to meet people who were committed to sharing the gospel in many different ways. We traveled to churches as far away as New York, Maryland, Virginia, and western Pennsylvania sharing the story of our spiritual journeys and what our faith means to us. It was a good learning experience and I wouldn't regret any of those moments.

Of course, Grace and I were always actively involved in our local church and served as deacons for almost twenty years. For seven years, I taught the youth at the Heidelberg Church of the Brethren as Rev. Alton Bucher's assistant. I felt very incapable, but we got along really well. Although I wasn't too knowledgeable about the Bible, we did get a lot of discussion going. It seemed to make them want to dig in all the more. It was a joy.

At the Richland Church of the Brethren, where we currently attend, I served for nine years as the moderator of the church board when we grew from having just 35 people attending Sunday worship to almost 200. Our peak was 207, but we would average about 180. That was quite rewarding, to get people motivated.

When I quit working at the Manheim Auto Auction, they said, "We have to find another Victor Ziegler to work here." That's because I was always giving them a hard time, and we had so much fun and laughter. Sometimes I would tell a story and get ready to really slam them with the punch line, and then I would stop. Expectantly, they'd say, "Well, you brought us this far, you might as well say the rest."

Then I'd promise, "I will if you let me stand right at the exit door," and I would start edging closer to the door. That would just increase the fun, you might say.

To egg them on, I would say, "Do you know what? I don't know much, but the little bit I do know, I learned from guys like you who told and showed me what works or what don't work. So I thought to myself, 'Why don't I, being a slow learner, just do one thing different every day until I get a little bit nearer to perfection, whether it is in the area of my health, my work, my habits, or anything, whatever my nature is?'"

Then I'd let them hang with that, and they had to go home thinking about it. Some weeks or months later, when I met some of their wives, they would come up to me and say, "Oh, *you* were the troublemaker?" Then they'd laugh. It was a great experience.

For one year, I worked at High Steel in Lancaster driving an escort truck that had a two-way radio. Occasionally, on the radio I would get a guy who would use God's name in vain or other improper language. That gave me the opportunity to say something like, "Do you know what? The airwaves are so polluted, let's not mess them up more!" Or I might say, "Let's keep it constructive, because if you or I don't—a lot of us have children or grandchildren—can you imagine what it will be like for the next generations? It will be nothing but deterioration, degradation, physical and mind pollution. You and I will be a part of costing the next generation a great price!"

I'd give them a little lecture like that, but I'd keep it short, because we were supposed to keep the airwaves clear for emergencies up ahead. Somebody could holler at you or wave and flag you down.

After I chimed in with a little insert like that, more often than not, some guy would come on and say, "That must have been Ziegler. Thank You." Very seldom did somebody get on and say, "That's so and so—Goody Buddy!" Very seldom did that happen.

One Saturday noon I went to the Richland restaurant and a funny thing happened. Just as I was finishing paying my bill at the cash register and almost ready to go out the door, a whole bunch of dishes crashed. I don't really think they broke, but they were kinda sliding across in a metal trough, and it rattled throughout the whole restaurant where about 20 people were sitting. It was so funny, and I just shouted, "GLORY, HALLELUJAH! IT'S RESURRECTION DAY TOMORROW!"

They all laughed, and a few of them even clapped a little. Then I added, "We hope there isn't too much damage, but folks, always remember, it *could* have been worse! It could have happened to *me*!"

Then I left.

The woman who owns the Richland restaurant knows me because I go in there so often. Six weeks ago, she thought she would never see me again (because of my current illness). When I came in, she hugged me and said, "We never fail to pray for you."

Three weeks ago, she confided in me and said, "My son is having marital problems. He's back there working in the kitchen. Would you sneak back there and pray for him?"

So, I went back and he was standing at the door and had a couple minutes. After we talked a bit, I advised him, "Always remember, Satan is trying to destroy you, but God is greater than he is."

I put my arm around him and he asked, "Victor, would you pray for me?" (I didn't tell him his mom had just asked me to do that.)

He never knew that. After our prayer, with my arm still around him, I said, "Don't give up the faith. Even though you may think your wife is a miserable skunk, God can perform a miracle in her. Kinda take the blame yourself, and keep on paddling and struggling, and God will reward you."

Around five days later, I stopped in. I didn't eat anything, but I got a cup of coffee just for an excuse. He noticed I was there and came out and said, "Victor, it's working. It's starting to work for the good," and he smiled.

I'm not sure what that meant, because I didn't ask for any details. I did warn him, "Remember, when it starts working, then the devil is going to attack you again. This ain't the end. I am 71 years old and have been fighting him for 71 years! But 'greater is He that is in you than he that is in the world.' (1 John

4:4, KJV) Believe that, and you can never go wrong and . . . never give up."

Whenever I advise someone to keep believing what is right, to never give up, I am reminded of the little story of the two frogs that fell into a bucket of milk. They were kicking away, and the one said, "This is too much work," and he quit and drowned.

The other one paddled away constantly all night, and the next morning he was sitting on a mound of butter! He was rewarded–in two ways. He saved his life, and he had something to share with others.

That's the way the Lord works, but He'll take you to the nth degree to test you. I don't understand what the Bible means about "refining you with fire" and "putting you through the furnace," but I've had a little bit of a glimpse. If I understand just the tip of it, that's all that matters. God will reveal the rest in due time. It's awesome! Terrific!

When I would go for a chemo treatment, and the nurse was done hooking me up, all those receiving chemo were sitting in a circle in lounge chairs. I would always turn to the person on my right, and if he or she wasn't reading a book or taking a nap, I would ask, "And how are *you* doing today?"

They always lit up and wanted to talk and would tell me what their background was, where they lived, and all that, and we'd get a nice conversation going. When we'd wind down, I'd turn to the person on my left and sometimes discover that several other persons had been listening in with some interest.

A few people were simply bored as we sat there. I think discouragement had set in for some of them. So, I would talk to them and say something like, "You know, most of us have had about 70 good years, and the Bible talks about a life span being three score years and ten. Maybe some of us will be granted a lot more, and maybe not, God only knows. All of us are going to leave this world anyhow on short notice. It really don't matter if we live to be 100 or if we live to be 75 or 80."

Then I'd try to build a little case for *being ready,* pointing out that it is the secret of success in anything. Whether it is being ready to help a friend or neighbor, being ready to act in case of an emergency, or being ready to go on a trip, I'd eventually get around to being ready to meet our Creator. He is the one who has promised us an abundant life here and now, but his greatest promise is still to come when we reach our final destination of heaven and experiencing eternal life.

I conceded with them that some people just don't understand it, but when you do, it sure makes a difference. I shared that I wouldn't want to run the risk of all that discouragement and the horror of that uncertainty when the Bible makes it so plain that our destination is *guaranteed* at the cross.

As we got close to Easter Sunday, 2004, I cried out to the group, "Hey, ladies and gentlemen, remember that today is Friday, and things look dark. But Sunday's coming, and that's Resurrection morning. I might be the first one to go up!"

After that statement, all I had to do was look at their eyes and they'd smile. You can easily identify all the believers, you know, because they all share that hope.

Then there are some that *say* they believe, but they're not quite sure. Occasionally, I will meet someone who will come back and slowly say, "Yeah, Victor, I'm ready, but I'm not quite *sure.* I don't know if you *really can* know."

Then I'd say, "Wait a minute. I think it was John, the Apostle, who said, 'These things I write unto you that you may KNOW.' (1 John 5:13, KJV) Those disciples, who witnessed Jesus' perfect life on earth and His resurrection, were *eyewitnesses.* They experienced something that we won't experience until we get to heaven. If you're not quite sure, you must be like I was—from the old Brethren or Mennonite background—but you just gotta hang in there."

We had a little fun discussing that. Then I would confess that I had wondered about these things myself, but not anymore.

The more I read the Scripture, the more I can understand the guarantee is plainly there. The beauty of it is that when I do stupid things, if I confess and make it right with my neighbor, it is all erased.

Then somebody would say, "Well, but I did some terrible things."

My answer would be, "You are misreading the Bible. Now let me quote it and you listen. The Bible says, 'the blood of Jesus Christ cleanses you from all (A-L-L) sin.' (1 John 1:7, KJV) That's all sin . . . not some, but all. Not just from some stupid thing you did or got carried away with or got trapped in. It is ALL, and it don't matter if you murdered a person, committed adultery, stole something, or whatever you did, if you confess it and make it right, you can come back and discover *it is all washed* in the blood. We should never forget that."

I have friends who say, "Well, I believe, but . . ." Then I tell them that that little word, B-U-T, is keeping them from experiencing a blessing! When you are saying "but," it is just like throwing mud in the face of God. It's like saying, "My God isn't big enough," or "He don't do what He says." Whenever you feel discouraged, just pray, "Lord, I believe. Help Thou mine unbelief." (Mark 9:24, KJV) We are all human. We *can't* understand every circumstance. More than once, I experienced miracles in my life but I was nervous, and really had to slow down and take time out to think and to pray, before I could recognize the miracle. I had to admit that I know it is true, I believe it is true, and I am never going to give up on that belief, but my human mind can't understand it. Then we just have to tell God that we can't understand. That's who God is! God is a God that *nobody* can understand!

I couldn't believe that an iceberg could weigh 10 million tons because I had just seen the TIP of the iceberg. That's the way it is with my faith. I just got a glimpse of the Savior from a friend who helped me out or did something special when I was down and out, and I KNOW He was there in that situation. You can't explain how it feels until you say, "Lord, I believe. Help me take the next step in living it out." Then go on by faith each day, one step at a time.

I think I may have shared earlier the illustration of going home. If you get in your car and refuse to go any further than where the headlights shine, you'd only get about five hundred feet. That registers with people. We're not that dumb or that stubborn, I hope. To say, because I can't see all the way home, I'm not going . . . or I'm afraid to take even the first step!

I love to draw little verbal pictures, and I've been blessed with a little bit of spur-of-the-moment insight to match the circumstance of that individual's hurt, pain and suffering. It's the best way I've found to get people turned around.

That's what I find so interesting in people. No two are alike. You can come in and encourage somebody, and I'll take another approach in encouraging him, and although it's altogether different, it's something else he needed to hear. We all have different talents so we share what we have. You never get done being blessed as a result, because God's multiplication is so different.

When we pour out our lives, our time, our tithes, whatever it is, it just "don't get all." We think it's gonna, but if it's done with the right motive, it'll always come back in some form of blessing.

I have always opposed going around and preaching a "prosperity gospel" where you would be able to tell on Monday morning in your bank account that the Lord was with you. I would *never* tell anybody anything like that, because I don't believe it.

When you're hurting and you have a lot of friends surrounding you, supporting you with encouragement, prayers and physical help, it is impossible to measure the amount of blessing you receive. It is indescribable! You *know* God is working, and I feel I've been privileged to have been blessed both ways—as the giver *and* as the receiver.

Chapter Fifteen

Being a Community Leader

"If it is right, I will defend it, and if it is wrong, I will go against it."
—Victor K. Ziegler

The little village of Reistville, Pennsylvania, located along route 501 between Scheafferstown and Myerstown, is close to my home. In the center of Reistville was a very dangerous intersection. What made it so dangerous was that there was a house built at the edge of the road during the "horse and buggy days" that was used originally as a roadside stop. Although it was never called a tavern or an inn, it was some sort of guest house, and later became used as a farmhouse. As Route 501 became more heavily traveled by cars and trucks, the road was widened, the dirt road became gravel, and finally a blacktopped highway. The speeds traveled past that house went from 15 miles per hour to 50, 60, and even 70. Pulling onto the highway from the intersecting roads was difficult because the house obstructed the driver's view.

Although I knew this intersection was hazardous, sometimes the real danger of a situation doesn't register until it affects your own family. What really got my attention was when I parked my pickup truck in the back of that house one afternoon and stood at that intersection for 20 minutes just observing the traffic and listening to the brakes screeching. Then the local school bus approached carrying three of my little grandsons on it. They recognized me and waved to me. The very cautious woman school bus driver tried three times to pull onto the road and the third time a tractor trailer came barreling through at about 45 miles per hour. If she wouldn't have drifted back, he could have hit her broadside and killed many of those children. It was that bad, you know. You had to pull out halfway on the road to see if anything was coming.

In 1985, the township tried negotiating to buy this house and relocating it or at least changing this section of highway, but they couldn't agree on what plan was best. They brought in highway engineers who devised a plan costing $440,000 to totally redo the intersection. Their plan resembled a "dog leg," in that you entered the highway and then drove up the road 500 feet where you made another turn to get around all this garbage. That plan would have created more havoc, giving the village an appearance that wasn't very "homey-lookin'," plus costing almost a half million dollars!

I said to a few of the concerned people, "There's *got* to be a better way to do this."

The township guys explained, "We were trying to buy that house to tear it down, but the owner wouldn't negotiate. Now we've been told that it's a 'historical house,' and we can't tear it down without going through a lot of red tape."

"It would be simpler if I'd just buy it myself and tear it down," I answered. "Nobody can stop me from buying an old farmhouse and destroying it."

The next township meeting was interesting. They had been working at this problem for over ten years and nothing had happened. When I came into the meeting, I asked if it would be all right if I would do it on my own. They let me know they didn't believe it would happen, but they said, "Good luck!" Of course, that just lit my fire!

When I called our state representative inquiring about doing it myself, he replied, "I don't believe it can happen, but it is nice that you are making an effort. The township wouldn't be allowed to do that, but if you purchase it outright, we can't stop you. God bless you for trying."

With that in mind, I got busy and went to see the owner. He was mad at the township and wanted $300,000 for his property. I pointed out to him that if it were auctioned, it would probably bring $95,000 to $100,000. In addition, I said I would give him $50,000 to move, so the total I would be willing to give was $150,000. He balked a little bit at that and said, "Oh, I don't know about this."

As I continued talking to him, I explained that in dealing with me, he would do a lot better financially than any of the other alternatives. He would be very fortunate if he got any more than $100,000 from anyone else.

When he still hesitated, I made this proposal. I said, "I'll tell you what I'm gonna do. I'll give you a check for $500 today as a 'good faith deposit,' and I'll be back in a week's time with a check for $149,500. I can honestly tell you I don't have the money, but by God's grace, I'm gonna find it. If I don't come back in a week with the money, you can just keep this check for $500."

I was able to say this by faith, believing that *I was going to find the money.*

So, he accepted the check and was probably thinking, "Well, he surely won't be back in a week, and I'll get to keep this $500."

That week I went visiting a number of friends and neighbors who were long-time residents of the township. One was a Church of the Brethren guy, one Amish, and two others were Mennonites. I told them I am looking for five guys who will give $30,000 each to invest in our community so we can buy this property for $150,000 and sell it for $100,000. In doing so, we must all decide to lose $50,000, with that loss to be shared among the five of us. They all objected somewhat at that, but I reminded them, "You know, we have a choice to make. Each of us and our families use this intersection every day. Within the next five years, one of the families in this community is going to spend $250,000 for hospital expenses or have a funeral because a loved one was severely injured or killed here. Today we can correct this problem for $30,000 each and not suffer those losses or at least move with the best intentions to make this road as peaceful and safe as possible. The Lord will bless us all for that. Also, I'll tell you upfront that we will each probably lose about $10,000, as we would be *most* fortunate if we could sell it for more than $100,000."

After hearing my little speech, one guy hesitated, saying, "Well, see what the others say."

So I talked to three others and the last one questioned, "Victor, what are *you* going to do?"

"I have no money, but tomorrow morning I am going to the bank and pick up $30,000 for my share," I told him.

"If you are putting in $30,000, I will put in $30,000," he agreed, and the others also joined us with their shares. Within three days I had $150,000 worth of checks in my pocket.

When I went to the owner with the money, he agreed to accept it. We shook hands on it and were friends. That was in August, 1995, and I told him we would wait until after the Christmas holidays, probably beginning the demolition work shortly after January 1. Although he felt it was short notice, he agreed to it, and he moved out December 31.

The next day about 75 men arrived, including many local Amish and Mennonites, and a demolition contractor came with about $200,000 worth of equipment that could reach in to the top of a house and tear the whole thing down. I said, "Let's save everything we can," and we laid aside every piece of attic flooring, the bricks, important logs, anything that still had some value. Everything was sorted and put on piles.

As the demolishing was happening, some men would say, "I want this," or "I'd like that," so I suggested having a little sale among the neighbors in this area. That way, if I would have said I wanted something, someone could have complained, "Aw, Victor, is chair of this project, so he took whatever *he* wanted!" I didn't want to be accused of that. Thirty days later we had a leftover sale that netted $4,000. They were all happy and agreeable and it worked out great.

On the demolition day, some men were up in the attic working while others were still helping the former owner move out of the kitchen and the basement and helping him clean up. We had a great time. Television crews were there photographing the Amish up on the roof. It was exciting to see the volunteers and other interested persons coming with their dump trucks to help to haul away the debris. People stopped by with cameras and said, "We were waiting for 20 years for this to happen!" Other passing drivers stopped just to thank us for eliminating this dangerous spot.

We started at 8 o'clock in the morning and by the time we finished at 8 o'clock at night, we had everything bulldozed and leveled and ready to spread on topsoil and sow grass seed on it. Just as we finished, it started to snow, and by the next morning, two feet of snow had fallen on that spot. The timing had just been perfect!

An interesting twist to this project was that in 1957 when my parents, Abraham and Rhoda Ziegler, moved from the farm, they bought the grocery store located right across the street from this site and moved into Reistville. My dad quickly recognized that with the traffic building up year after year, this was going to be a real hazardous point. He went to see the owner at that time, and offered him $12,000 to buy that house. (Of course, about 40 years later we paid him $150,000.) My dad told him he only had $1,000 to put toward it himself, and he was trying to find eleven other men to each contribute $1,000, but he never got it done. Dad and Mother tried hard to achieve it, but they never were too financially strong, and that's why it didn't happen. But he had made an offer. If the owner had accepted it, my dad's intent was, "I would like to tear down that whole house personally, brick by brick, if it takes me a year!" He was so dedicated to seeing it happen in the interest of his children, his grandchildren, and the neighborhood.

So, almost 40 years later, we completed Dad's dream. I told the other volunteers, "My father must be looking down from heaven smiling seeing that we fulfilled his dream and eliminated the danger spot here." That in itself was worth it all.

After it was all completed, graded and leveled, I called the state representative and said, "I want to thank you for your help in getting this project done so quickly."

On hearing that, he was kinda stunned, but I continued, "I remember that some of the last words you said to me were, 'Well, it probably won't happen, but God bless you.' *You're* the key to our success. You asked God to bless us, *and He did*! So, I want to thank you for God's blessing on us!"

That set him back a little, but he took it graciously, and he knew me well enough to accept it. That was heartwarming, and the local people talked about it for almost 10 years.

Approximately three months later, I was eating in a local restaurant and a girl came to me and asked, "Are you Victor Ziegler?"

I said, "That's what I'm called."

She continued, "My mother was almost killed at that intersection four years ago, and she is still going to the doctor for her back pain. My mom said to me, 'If you ever see anybody named Victor, please say a big thank you to him for getting that done.'"

We just had so many compliments. One of the greatest satisfactions was seeing the whole community work together with no one turning in a bill or worrying about how much they did. We did offer to pay the local demolition contractor for the use of his equipment and he refused it saying, "No, the Lord blessed me too good. I'm glad I could help."

It took almost 5 years to get the property sold. A young Amish couple who were in the crafts business, working out of the basement of their home, seemed interested in that spot. I suggested to them that this might be an ideal spot for an Amish craft center, and when they asked about the price, I told them we were asking for just what we had paid for it, $150,000. They couldn't see paying that amount, so I suggested that they go to their bank and see what they *could* do and come back and make an offer. Between their own resources and the bank, they offered $125,000. Instead of all 5 of us losing $50,000, we just lost $25,000, so we were happy about that. Till we all paid our equivalent of 7% interest, our loss was soon close to $50,000 anyway. So, the place was sold, and that couple built a nice crafts store there and made it a beautiful spot. Their business is still going but is not as profitable as they had hoped it would be.

That intersection is still not as safe as it could and should be, as there are some trees there that still obstruct a driver's vision. We had offered to buy a new tree for one owner—to cut the old one down and plant a new one 15 or 20 feet back, but we didn't get that done yet. We're still working on all of this.

The biggest problem there now is that the speed limit should be about 40 miles per hour, and vehicles come speeding through there at 55 miles per hour. A truck or bus going through there at 55 and 60 miles per hour is going entirely too fast. I said that for $100 we could put rumble strips in there. That wakes everybody up! Drivers hate them. They hate going over them too fast. When I suggested it, the township authorities said, "Welllll, we can't do that . . ." for one reason or another.

I said I could do it for nothing if they'd just let me cross the highway with our heavy disk and drop it. That would leave natural "rumble strips" that would slow them down! But that would be illegal, and I couldn't really do that. I don't know how hard I'll have to work on this yet, but I think a rumble strip is the cheapest, simplest and safest solution. Anybody who is not paying attention wakes right up as it's more attention-getting than a blinking light. By the time a driver hits the third and roughest one, if he hasn't slowed down, that one will really vibrate him enough to make him more alert. It doesn't ruin any vehicles but is just like crossing railroad tracks. If we could get drivers to slow down to 25 or 30 miles per hour by doing that, we'd be in good shape. I hope we can really get that done for the safety of everyone.

Around 1989 I got a phone call from Senator Manbeck, a multimillionaire owning a number of chicken processing plants. He was also chairman of the Pennsylvania Department of Transporation, having served as a senator for years, and was involved in many other organizations and quite an influential guy. Through the years I had had a number of contacts with him and he knew me fairly well. When I answered the phone, he said, "Hey, Victor, our little bank at Fredericksburg (Pennsylvania) is thinking of expanding into Lebanon County. We are looking for someone to represent us and would like somebody who thinks like you do."

"Well, Mr. Manbeck," I confessed, "I was never in your bank, and I never had a checking account or a savings account there or anything."

"That doesn't matter," he assured me. "We need guys at the bank who will help us to make the right decisions."

"Could I attend one of your board meetings first, and then give you my answer?" I questioned.

"Okay, we're meeting on Tuesday from 9:00 a.m. until noon," he informed me. "You plan on coming in and meeting with us."

At that time the popular thing in banking was the mergers. They were big stuff. I remember at that first meeting I told the board frankly, "If you are interested in being a community bank that will really provide personal services for the local people, I'm interested. But if you are just interested in counting numbers and eventually selling out for another $10 million and making big money and everybody going home, I'd rather not serve here."

"Oh, no," they assured me. "We want to keep this a community bank. We want to build a few more branches and offices, but we don't want to sell out."

By April, 2004, I will have served on that board for 14 years, meeting with them every two weeks, and enjoying it. We have an office in Iona, near the Lebanon fairgrounds and just built our eighth one in Schuylkill Haven.

From time to time our bank gives back to the communities it serves. For example, we just gave $5,000 to the community library to update their computers. Some time ago, we put $50,000 in a public school program to help children with special needs. Giving to the community in these ways promotes good public relations and the bank profits through a federal tax credit. We try to do as much of those kinds of things as we can. It feels good to be part of a group that wants to do something to help others.

One morning in the 1970's, John Yingst stopped in to see me and said, "You know, Victor, this school system is going to pot. They need a new school board member and you're gonna be the guy."

"John," I protested, "I don't have time to go out drumming up support and talking to people . . ."

"You don't have to do that," he interrupted. "I've already talked to Martin Bennetch, a friend of mine, and all you have to do is say 'Yes,' and we're getting you elected, and you *are gonna serve,* representing us."

And you know, he did!

When I saw the strong support for my candidacy, I would attend the school board meetings when possible. Often they'd have an "open forum," or ask for comments from the audience. If it was a heated discussion, they'd only hear from two or three.

One night the school board president asked, "Does anyone here have any comments?" (I forget what the issue was that time.)

At that invitation, I stood up and raised a few concerns. I pointed out several things that I felt were not quite right in the name of education, in the way money was spent, and above all, in the morality standards set before our children. In suggesting there was room for improvement, I also predicted the cost of change would not be excessive and the important thing was for the board, administrators and faculty to have different attitudes and approaches.

Do you know what? I got a letter the following week that the school board president had dictated to his secretary saying in essence, "Tell Victor to stay at home. We don't need his comments!"

That was four weeks before the spring election. Four weeks later, the very same president was reelected with 400 votes, but I got 800! The following week his secretary called to say, "The school board requests your presence at every meeting possible so you can be kept informed on current happenings because we know you are already elected for November."

After the fall election, they just had to bite their tongues. It was a blessing. All the other guys on the board were college graduates. Some were school teachers, some were in industry, and they were all high-priced fellows. I had to laugh as I was always challenging them about something. We had a good working relationship, and I hung in and served on the board eight years. Then I found I was interested in so many other projects, and I realized there were some really good persons in the community who could also serve. With a sense of finality, I quipped, "Hey, take my place." So, I bowed out but it had been a great opportunity to serve.

While I was a school board member, a boy in the senior class used some terribly vulgar language toward one of the administrators. A special hearing was called at one of our school board meetings that also included the parents and an attorney to decide whether to expel him or give him a leave of absence without penalty.

Just a few weeks prior to this incident, I heard there were books that contained some unacceptable language in the school library and also in the English department as required reading. To me it was all hearsay. Whenever I would hear something like that, I would always try to check into it in order to find out if it was true. If so, I'd look for a way to make it right or see what could be done to correct it.

The principal at the time called himself a Christian but wasn't too verbal about his faith and was the kind of guy who wouldn't make any waves. When I spoke to him about this problem, he agreed to help saying, "Yeah, Victor, I'll get you a half dozen books. I know there are a few that shouldn't be there, in my opinion."

So he gave me six books or so, but I didn't have time to read them. Instead, I gave them to my dad because he was a good reader. He read 10 or 15 pages in each one and one morning reported to me, "I'm not going to read anymore of these. The language is so foul and disgusting."

He handed the books back to me, but he had marked many of the objectionable words and passages with yellow strips of paper and notes. When I saw the enormity of the problem, I prayed, "Lord, what am I going to do with this? I'd like to challenge this in a Christ-like way, but I don't want to hurt anybody either. I can't let it go because it is warping the minds of our youth."

So, I just kept the books for another week or ten days and didn't return them.

When I was called to the special hearing on a Monday night to talk about expelling this boy, I brought the books along in a paper bag and placed the bag under my chair. As we went through the process of the hearing, the attorney asked the parents and the principals to leave. Then he turned to the superintendent and the school board members, and the president of the board asked, "Where do we go from here?"

Everything got as quiet as a pin. Nobody wanted to talk.

I reached for my bag of books and stood up and began talking non-stop for at least three minutes, reading all the yellow-slip marked passages of vulgar language. You should have seen their mouths drop open because of the language that was coming out of my mouth. One of them said, "Victor, I never thought you'd say words like that."

"They're not *my* words," I quickly explained. "They are words that you paid for out of tax dollars and printed in the books you purchased to be used in our school. This is a very simple choice. Tonight you are going to throw these books out of the school or you'll throw me off the school board. One of the two are gonna fly!"

And I continued, "You *can't* throw me out because I was elected by the constituents. That means we are down to one option: what are you going to do?"

The president turned to the superintendent, addressed him by his name, and ordered him to "take action immediately!"

Then we all went home. Just like that.

Three days later, the school's maintenance director flagged me down on the road and said, "Victor, what happened at your school board meeting the other night? There were special staff meetings in every building. The principal and the superintendent issued a mandate that all teachers should check the materials they were using, and if any contained unacceptable language, they are to be reported to the superintendent. Changes are going to be made immediately."

And they did clean house! I haven't followed up on it to this day, and I know things like that can easily creep back in. It was to that principal's credit that he followed through like that. Although he was a Christian himself, as I mentioned earlier, he wouldn't take a stand until somebody pushed him. The word quickly got around that one school board member, that Ziegler guy, was making all these people extra work.

By the way, the final decision about the senior boy was that I said I was in favor of disciplining him. He had an out-of-school study course for three weeks, and then they reinstated him. About a month afterwards, the parents came to me and thanked me.

I never had any trouble getting anybody's attention after that if I wanted to get something done, because they knew *if it is right, I will defend it, and if it is wrong, I will go against it.* So, those were eight interesting years. That was good.

Chapter Sixteen

Living With My "Amazing" Grace

*Grace was very talented and truly 'amazing.' I didn't realize what
I had at the time, and I still don't, even after being married to
her for 52 years!" – Victor K. Ziegler*

After our wedding, Grace and I came out of the church
and heard someone calling us. At the same time, we saw an
old deacon, affectionately known as Uncle Elmer Gibble, who
owned the farm across the road from the church, sitting in a
little three-seater airplane that he owned. "Jump in, Victor and
Grace," he shouted, "I want to give you a flying start."

He flew us over the farm and probably because of
"wedding day anxiety," when I looked down, I was sure I saw
that our cows were out. When we landed, I asked Irvin Kreider,
(who was to become my brother-in-law in the future when he
married my sister, Lena), to drive to the farm to check on the
cows, but all of them were safe within their fences.

Through the years, we kept in contact with Uncle Elmer
Gibble and his wife, and he never forgot us. Thirty or more
years later, they lived in Florida in Leisure Acre Park. On one of
our trips to Florida, we decided to pay them a visit. As soon as
Elmer saw me, he said, "Victor, how are ya doing?"

With a big smile, I answered, "Well, Uncle Elmer, you
gave me a flying start and I didn't land yet."

For the first night of our honeymoon, we didn't get any
further than Kline's motel in Reading, Pennsylvania. We didn't
tell anyone where we were going, but I had gone there the week

before and made a reservation. I kidded everyone by saying that, "We don't have much money, but we will travel north, so that when our money gets all, the law of gravity will turn us around, and we will come coasting home."

The farthest point north that we got was to Mount Washington, New Hampshire. Riding up the 14,000 foot mountain on the cogwheel railway was a wonderful experience seeing how the scenery changed when you got above the timber line and went up a big old Jacob's Ladder while you were about laying on your seat and wondering, "Ooooh, are we going to make it?"

Interestingly enough, three days after we got home we saw in the newspaper that something released on the safety latch of the cogwheel railway and one man was killed. According to the newspaper, that was the first accident in many years, and it was not determined if the cause was human error or a malfunction.

We did enjoy seeing the beauty God created in the White Mountains of New Hampshire and in Vermont, and have wonderful memories of our honeymoon.

We're still newlyweds here in April, 1953.

When we got back from our trip, we lived with my mom and dad for a couple weeks. The farmhouse was a double house, and the couple that lived on the other side worked for my dad. However, they were moving out shortly. When they did, we moved in and for a couple years, my parents lived in the main part of the house and we lived in the tenant part. We had a nice living room, two bedrooms, a kitchen and a bathroom.

Within the next ten years, we had five children, all born at home. Our family doctor was Dr. Franklin Zimmerman, and

Our Wedding Party—Aug. 24, 1952. Left to right: Owen Ziegler, Winona Cox, Grace Cox Ziegler, Victor Ziegler, Harold Keller, Stanford Cox.

he said to me after the fourth birth, "No more home deliveries, Victor. When the next baby comes (and Grace was expecting within a few weeks), you are going to take her into the maternity ward at the hospital."

"Ah, that sounds good," I said. "I'd like to see what it looks like in there anyhow." Then I added, kidding him, "I understand you are getting pretty independent like the U.S. Postal Service: No more home deliveries."

Then he laughed.

However, we never did get to the hospital. At ten minutes before midnight, Grace said to me, "Get dressed; we are going to the hospital. The baby's coming."

By the time I got dressed, she had crawled back into bed, and at 10 minutes past midnight, Leon was born! My mother came, and in about an hour or so after the baby was born, we finally were able to get hold of a doctor. It so happened that Dr. Zimmerman was out of town, so I asked the telephone operator if she knew of a local doctor we could call.

"I'll try to get this new young doctor who has just come to Myerstown," she said.

So, about 1:30 a.m. Dr. Carl Miller, who was about 38

years old, arrived at our house. We had just washed the baby with my mom's help and wrapped him up. Neither my mom nor I wanted to sever the umbilical cord, so he tied the cord, cut it, and signed the birth certificate. Then I looked at him and asked, "Whom do I pay – our family doctor or you? Do you have any kind of a working agreement?"

"The guy that is here when the baby is born gets the $50, and the other guy has to do the follow up work free," was his answer.

I paid him the $50 and said, "I don't know how you write this up for a delivery charge when my mom and I did all the work!"

He just laughed, and I laughed with him.

Grace had fast deliveries every time. When our second child, Sharon, was born, my brother, Glen, who was a teenager, was in the kitchen with Grace. She told him, "I am going upstairs to have the baby. You go and tell Victor to come in."

Although I ran in right away, by the time I got there, the baby had already popped out!

We wondered why Grace had such an easy time with labor and delivery. The doctor explained to me that the difference lies in each woman's muscle tone. My working with dairy animals correlated with this observation. He explained further, "Your wife was out there feeding chickens until the day the babies were born. She was carrying two 5-gallon buckets of feed weighing 25 pounds each, stooping over, and walking up and down the three stories of steps to the chicken house. Because of this, her muscle tone was strong, and she was in perfect shape to have her baby without any help."

And do you know what's interesting? Remember when old King Pharaoh in Egypt had the Hebrew people mixing mortar, carrying straw, and forcing them to work so hard making bricks? Then Pharaoh ordered the Egyptian midwives who assisted the Hebrew women in giving birth to kill their boy babies and allow girl babies to live. However, they feared God and didn't obey that order, so Pharaoh called them to his court and asked them why they are allowing the boys to live. To put their response in my language, the midwives answered, "What are we to do? These Hebrew women pop their babies out so quick and then hide them that we can't get there in time." (Exodus 1:11-19) Their hard work and physical exercise had made their muscles strong.

The doctor explained to me that a woman will not hurt herself by exercise or hard work before the baby is born. But afterwards, it is important that she slow down for a couple weeks. After giving birth, her organs and muscles contract and reposition themselves, and if she picks up fifty pounds, she can tear or damage something.

After our fifth and last child, Leon, was born, Grace wasn't doing too well, so I figured, "Why don't I bring the bed down in the living room so she wouldn't have to climb any steps, and I'll put a bathroom on the first floor?"

That project turned out so well that we started to do a little creative thinking and ended up with three bedrooms, a kitchen and a bathroom on the first floor. The boys' room was just 8'x12'. They slept on bunk beds and never complained and lived like that until we moved into our new home in 1970.

Several weeks after we got married, I got really ticked off inside when my so-called mother-in-law, the foster mother, gave Grace and me a bill for $30 for flowers that *she* ordered and wanted to decorate the tables at our wedding reception. Now, $30 at that time was like $300 today, and I was just, well, I had no money! I even said, "Why didn't that cotton-pickin' woman keep her flowers? We would have been good and happy without 'em!"

My first inclination was to send the bill back to her and say, "Since we didn't order them, it's not our obligation to pay for them." However, we had a pretty good working relationship, and because we didn't want to get off to a bad start, we reluctantly paid it. At least, I *thought* it was a good relationship – and it was, as long as everything was in *their* favor.

During our courtship and early marriage, I was aware that Grace had lived in several foster homes and that there had been difficulties in the last one. I was about to discover that I never knew half of what she was going through. She was very quiet about some things and very open about others.

By the time she reached puberty, she was a victim of physical and sexual abuse. However, she just smothered everything and never talked or complained about it. She told me she didn't complain because "I always wanted to prove to my friends at school that I had a mother and dad the same as everybody else. I defended them even when they were hurting me."

Being young and dumb, so to speak, my only concern was that I was afraid her foster parents were not going to allow her to get married. An adult signature was required and they kept saying they were not going to sign for her. Although we wanted to get married in August (and we did), they put us under tremendous pressure by threatening not to allow it to happen until Christmas when *they* wanted it. Little did I know that in the meantime, they would go away for weekends and Grace would have to do all the farm work -- and they had 20,000 to 30,000 chickens. She'd feed them, clean up, gather the eggs and do everything including throwing around 100 pound bags of feed, and she only weighed 98 pounds herself! I found out later that she had some back problems as a result.

When I heard her story, it made me feel like we were living in the days of slavery. It took her quite a few years to really open up. After we got married, I found out a little bit, but I learned the worst part after we had been married 12 years and had all five of our children.

The family of Victor and Grace Ziegler. Children left to right: Bonnie, Sharon, Theresa, Lynn, Leon. Photo date: About 1963.

After our fifth child was born, I remember thinking, "Boy, I am living on the top of the world. I have *the best* family! I have been *really blessed!*"

As time went on, Grace was in and out of the hospital during 1959 and 1960, and she started to share some things about the physical, financial and sexual abuse. That was pretty tough but the hardest part for me to accept was that the financial and sexual abuse didn't stop when we got married. During our first 12 years together, I lived in ignorance and Grace lived in fear. I thought I had such a wonderful family and couldn't begin to comprehend or imagine what was *really* happening. I never even thought to ask or suggest, "Let's talk about how things *really* are."

Until one day, my world exploded!

I'll *never* forget it. It was a Saturday night in September, 1964, and we were getting ready for bed. I don't remember exactly what comment was made – something like, "If you only knew …" or "I never told you the whole story of all I went through, but …" At the time, I didn't know what she meant, and because I was blinded by love and ignorance, I didn't know how to ask the right questions. Instead, I was fearful of saying the wrong thing.

Her tearful confession was, "Victor, I don't know how to get away from the guy. Since I was 12 years old, he's made me feel like he owns me. He tried to make me feel that nothing was wrong with what he was doing to me, and I was so, so afraid. Until now, I never had any one to go to, to tell what was going on."

Then she started crying. After spending all night talking, hugging, and praying until 4:00 in the morning, we got about an hour's sleep, and then had to get up at 5:00 a.m. to get the farm work done.

We were scheduled to be at the Skippack Church of the Brethren near Collegeville, PA., at 10:00 that morning for worship followed by a family reunion. Some of my Ziegler ancestors, including my dad, had migrated from there, and we had promised to attend. We made it, and went through the whole day smiling, visiting with everybody and acting like nothing had happened.

But something really *did* happen, and it was a big relief to have it out in the open. When we could talk again, my first question was: "*Why* didn't you tell me? I thought to myself, that if she *had* told me, we could have stopped this years ago.

"I was so afraid," she responded. "Who was going to believe me?"

She was afraid that if I learned of it, I would no longer want her or would consider leaving her and she would lose the only security and love she had ever felt. Many times Grace would say to me that she was not good enough for me because her life had been ruined. I gradually started to recognize how fearful, helpless, shameful and guilty she had been feeling and the more I realized the weight of her burden, the more highly I thought of her and loved her. In looking back on that night, *which I will never forget*, I was really blessed when I thought, "Oh, my gosh! She lived in torture from the time she was 12 years old until she was 32 years old!"

As I thought later about all the difficulties and abuses Grace endured and the years it took to uncover and talk about it, I realized why I wasn't aware of this situation earlier. If I had known when I was 18 or 20 years old what I learned 14 years later, I wouldn't have been able to handle it. This knowledge would have destroyed me! I've shared with people that it was like getting a six-year-old boy to carry a 100 pound bag of feed. He'd break his back. You have to wait until he builds muscle, and then he can handle it. When I was younger, I didn't have the spiritual, physical or emotional muscle to handle this, and God knew it, so He kept everything quiet. *In due time*, what I thought was a curse ended up as, well, I don't want to call it a blessing, but He blessed a number of people because of it.

Remarkably, shortly after that Grace sat down with our children and told them the whole story. She wanted to tell her children before someone else did. At the time, I didn't know how fast she should move on that, but then it hadn't been my burden and experience all those years. Also, we never consulted with professional counselors as to the right or wrong approach; however, I did agree that if they are to be told, it would be better that she do it than me. She also shared early on with her brothers and sisters and some members of my family. Together we shared her story with my brother, Earl, who had officiated at our wedding and was now serving as a pastor. He helped us cope with, handle, face and accept this dramatic turn of events,

After weeks of discussion, I finally got up enough nerve to call the perpetrator and say "I got to talk to you."

I went directly and met him alone and said bluntly, "This has gotta stop."

At first, he acted dumb, you know. Then I continued, "I'm here to tell you today I don't want you to ever set foot on my property again, and don't even invite us for dinner again." We used to go there for Sunday dinners about once a month, and this was all "glory and roses." Even three or four years after we were married, when we would visit them Grace would end up having to wash all the dishes and being their slave again – while I was watching! They made it up by buying "things" for our five children, since they had the money. The foster mother-in-law would throw toys at our children and that would make me angry. I used to say to Grace, "That makes me sick. They're just buying these little kids off! Buying them off!" (And I even had those thoughts before I knew the half of it. In looking back, I could see it all clearly.)

The foster mother-in-law always tried to deny that she was aware that the sexual abuse was happening. Yet, when she was confronted with the evidence, she would say, "It was Grace's fault. She should have stayed out of his way."

By blaming it on Grace, she tried to take herself off the hook. Grace has told me she suspects that one reason the foster-mother was so mean to her was because *she did know*. At times the foster-father promised Grace the whole world, but of course, those promises were never kept, and she continued being the "slave" of the household.

Ironically enough, while all this was going on, he was putting on a "front" by being an active churchman and an excellent Sunday School teacher. Because of that, when I

Grace and Victor, May 3, 2003

confronted him, he finally agreed with me and said, "You're right. This has gotta stop. I'm sorry. I was wrong."

However, I did not relent. I just declared, "Well, this is just the way it is. There will be no association with you any more. I am not going to ignore you in public. I won't be mean, but she'll never be in your path again, and you'll never use her again, *as long as I live. Never!*"

I felt strongly about that because now, I was *really* determined to protect her.

About a week after that, I had a meeting with the foster-mother-in-law, and her husband was with her. Of course, she passed the buck, but I told her, "I just wanted you to know *exactly* what I told him and also to tell you not to bother phoning Grace or me or bribing the children any more. (She used to call us once a week). She was upset, but that was the end of it. For years, if we would meet them, passing them in church or in a store or something, we'd say "Hello" and "Good-bye," and that was it. We never crossed their path, and they never crossed ours. Some years later we did get an invitation to his funeral, and we went to the viewing out of respect.

In the meantime, it took years to become public knowledge. I talked to a few of the elders of his church and their response was what I expected: "Victor, we can't believe you are bad-mouthing this guy."

"Well," I answered, "You can accept it or deny it, but I am telling you *the truth*."

He had been so clever at deceiving people and so convincing in his Christian activities that even Anna, (not her real name), one of the highly respected older ladies in his church, said to my mom one day, "Why does Victor say such bad things about this man? He is a Sunday School teacher, leads the singing in church, takes the young people to youth camp, and gives sizeable contributions to worthy causes." But she didn't realize *then yet* that those activities were just a cover-up.

The minute we got married, they hired another teenage girl, a Mennonite, coincidentally also named Grace. Lo and behold, it was the same thing all over again. He went from one Grace to another Grace. She also was trapped and felt afraid, so I understand that she just clammed up and wouldn't talk. Without an explanation, one day she left.

Then he hired Anna's daughter, Helen (not her real name), to work for them. Before Grace's experiences "hit the fan," I heard him say, "Helen is such a good worker. She is feeding the chickens and helping in the house."

About a year later, Anna's husband came home late at night and thought he saw a car parked in his field. He turned his car and drove across the field and saw this church leader with his own teenage daughter, Helen, going through the same thing that Grace and the other young girls had experienced. Of course, after that Anna became my best supporter.

Finally, the elders of the church opened their eyes a little, but they still hesitated, and he got involved with even more young girls. What they didn't know was that he would love to take a group of teenagers to camp. One weekend they had a mountainside retreat and he slept over on the girl's side of the hill. Grace told me later that his motive in going was that he had one of the counselors, a 30 year old woman, sleeping with him up on the mountainside. So it just went on and on.

Today he would be labeled a true pedophile. It was sad, but he never changed. I don't know how much it went on after I threw in the wrench, but I know it slowed down. He and his wife never had any children of their own, but they had a daughter they adopted in 1950.

Nothing seems to stop people who are sick like this. If I didn't have this firsthand experience, I probably wouldn't have believed such things could happen. Now *I hope I am never guilty of calling anybody a liar when they say they are trapped in an abusive situation.* In fact, I warn people, "Such stories are just the tip of the iceberg. Take those stories as a warning. Something's wrong. People are crying out for help and are not being heard. These are not made-up stories. These young girls aren't in dreamland, but are experiencing something, nightmares that are *real*. I really developed sympathy for people who are living in abusive situations.

Now I'm going to ask Grace to share about her many interests and activities.

Grace is speaking.

If I were to describe a typical day in the 1960's when our children were small, it would begin about 6:00 in the morning. That's when I usually got up and went out to feed the chickens and pack the eggs so that I could be back in the house again before the children would leave for school. My days were filled preparing meals, getting the washing done, keeping the place neat and clean, and taking care of the lawn. I was just busy from morning until night. There were some nights when I'd think, "Ahhhhhh, I just can't make it."

I especially felt that way often on Saturday nights and I'd think, "Do I really have to fold all this wash tonight, because, man, I'm soooo tired."

But then I'd tell myself, "Yeah, you gotta get it done because tomorrow is Sunday, you know."

Although we had five children, I can say one thing: Our children were always well behaved, even when they were quite young. I didn't have a lot of "fussin' 'n' mussin' " with them to get them to do things.

Although I sewed most of their clothing then – and mine, today I think, "How in the world did I ever do it?" I wouldn't want to sew now. In fact, I can hardly sit at a sewing machine any more unless I am hemming or sewing things for Victor.

It was really a busy life, no doubt about it. In the beginning, I helped in the barn a little bit, but after we had children, Victor got hired men to help him. I worked with the chickens and can't remember what year we got rid of them. In the summer, I had a big garden and often canned 60 or more quarts of fruits and vegetables and also froze large quantities of them. In addition, I was always baking and cooking for all our hired help, our foster children and our whole family.

Making crafts, door wreaths, and floral arrangements used to be hobbies of mine. If a craft needs to be done for a special event, or if I want to give a gift to someone, I can still put something together. I just don't sit down and work at it like I used to.

A couple years ago one of Victor's cousins taught me how to make roses out of plastic spoons.

Now I only do it when I need them. For example, a family in South Carolina wants me to make a number of them to decorate at her daughter's wedding.

Although I always enjoyed making things with my hands, as I got involved in other things, I sort of put that to the side. The sewing went by the wayside also. People ask me, "Why don't you like to quilt?"

I tell them, "I do, but I just don't have the patience to sit still!"

I'm so used to being on the go and helping other people, you know. I do enjoy writing poetry and have collected all my poems and keep them together in a drawer.

For nine years I enjoyed giving one day a week helping out with Special Ed children at the local school. I'd be there from 9:00 in the morning 'til 3:00 in the afternoon working with those children who were slow. Their teacher was an amazing person. Because she had polio when she was young, she always walked with an obvious limp. She and I really got along well together. By volunteering there, I fell in love with those children with special needs. Even today, whenever I meet children that are slow or have Downs' syndrome, I just reach out to them.

The community group that I have been most active with is the Susquehanna Valley Pregnancy Center. In fact, they have a "Walk for Life" coming up soon, and I have to get busy. Last year I raised $2,000 for them. Usually I don't have the time to walk with them, but they say you can walk whenever you want to, so I walk around the stadium at the high school. On the "Walk for Life" day, I'm usually tending their stand, giving out T-shirts, checking the books and things, and I'm currently serving on their board

I've also been very active in helping with the Church of the Brethren's Atlantic Northeast Disaster Relief Auction held annually on the fourth weekend of September at the fairground in Lebanon, Pennsylvania. From 1985 until 2001, I was chair of their food committee, and after a year of planning, during the auction I would put in two full days of HARD WORK. My responsibility was to get people to make and serve the Friday night meal and see to it that things were running smoothly.

On Saturday I had to oversee the preparation of the breakfast and lunch, see that there were enough of all the foods, enough paperware to serve the meals, and that everybody was tending their stands. We literally served thousands of people. It was always a long and busy day, but I enjoyed it because I was seeing people and working around them.

We started the Lighthouse ministry in Richland to aid and provide a home for young girls who were pregnant. Along with their board of directors, we encountered a few personnel problems such as persons who didn't want to handle the responsibility or didn't have the tact to work with these girls. Sometimes we brought some of the girls here to our house.

I remember one, an especially beautiful 14-year-old, of another nationality. They called me from school one day and asked me to come. I had no idea why, but it was because of this girl. The health teacher had talked to her and sympathetically remarked, "You are carrying a heavy load, aren't you, carrying this baby?"

"Yes," she agreed with a sigh adding, "But I was raped by my pastor." Can you imagine? But her parents really stuck by her and when the baby was born, they raised the child as their own.

I think I was able to reach out to those kinds of girls because of my own background. Most of them were basically nice kids. Because we had such difficulties in getting qualified people to run the Lighthouse Ministry, we became more involved with the Susquehanna Valley Pregnancy Center. Now I do all their mailing every other Friday, help with the Walk for Life, and if they have any other needs, I will reach out for them. I debated being a counselor for them, but didn't feel quite capable, although some had encouraged me to try it. Whatever I can do for them, I do.

At church, I was a Sunday School teacher for years, teaching from third and fourth graders up to the teenagers and high school seniors. Then I thought, "It's time for me to step out of this. These boys need a man, too, as a teacher, not just a woman." So I went back to teaching third grade again for quite a few years and just resigned from that last year saying, "We need to give some younger people opportunities to teach, too." It seems funny to not be teaching anymore, but yet, I must say it is relaxing to not have to prepare a lesson every week.

Now I am helping at my church with what we call "Rejoice Club" programs every Wednesday night for children from all walks of life, from kindergarten to sixth grade.

A few of my other involvements have been with the JOY bookstore near Sheafferstown where I volunteered two days a week for about a half year, the Atlantic Northeast Church of the Brethren Women's Fellowship where I served as president one year, and serving on the board for the Alpha and Omega Church of the Brethren, a Hispanic congregation located in Lancaster.

Although Victor and I went together on a lot of interesting and enjoyable trips, I think the most meaningful trip was one I took by myself to Juarez, Mexico, two years ago to visit our granddaughter, Melanie Martin, who was teaching at a Christian camp for youth. There I helped to cook for 148 kids, and we all seemed to grow close. Even though I was busy cooking, when they came through the food line, I would always mingle and talk with them since they could all speak English. I am still getting letters from some of them and just got one recently saying I was "the best grandma from the United States." There was just a bond formed there.

Although I was unaware of it before I came, when I arrived they informed me that they usually asked people who were helping them to give their testimony. So, when I gave mine, I shared some of my background with them. Melanie was sitting there hearing this and she hadn't known about my abusive experiences at all. However, she was really pleased that I was able to rise above what I went through. I called my little talk "From the Pits of Hell to a Child of the King." That's the way I felt my life was. I remember how hopeless I felt. I often thought of writing a book about my experiences and I would title it, "Joy Beyond the Tears."

During my years at the last foster home, I never felt love at all. If I ever wanted to buy something, they would say I didn't need it, and yet they were always buying good stuff for themselves.

I really think my foster-mother knew that I was being sexually abused by her husband but didn't know how to handle it. I was never told a thing about the facts of life and I never dreamed that because of what my foster-father was doing to me, I could get pregnant! But, you know, I think that God must have worked a miracle there, protecting me from becoming pregnant. I also strongly believe that God was always in my life, working out His plans for me, walking right with me, protecting me and giving me strength.

In hindsight, I can now reach out to girls who have been hurt, raped or abused because I have had all these experiences too. As a result, God has given me a compassion for them. I'm not afraid to talk about it and to share ... and that's another miracle! Many women with a past like mine can't do that. However, I was able to share my story with my closest relatives and even with my children. I feel that God has forgiven me for all that took place.

After we were married, and the abuse was still continuing, I would wonder, "Why is God allowing these things to happen? Why did God ever put me in that home?" Even now, I sometimes need to have a good cry and ask, "Why?" Then I tell myself, "Stop it! Don't let the past destroy you. You can't change it. It doesn't help anyone to look back or even think about that. Think about all the blessings you have now and just go on!"

And I do.

My life has certainly not been smooth and easy, but I guess I've just been able to see the stumbling blocks as stepping stones. Victor, and all the Ziegler family, have given me so much love. It seems when one door in life closes, the good Lord just opens up another.

Every chance I get, I want to tell young people they must each make something of their own individual lives. We can't make excuses about the past. I know a door was opened for me, giving me a second chance, so I want to keep reaching out to others. After all, that's what life is all about, isn't it? Love is the open door.

Now I'll let Victor continue his story.

Perhaps now you can understand a little bit why Grace caught my eye, and I decided that she's the woman I wanted for my wife. *Grace was very talented and truly "amazing." I didn't realize what I had at the time, and I still don't, even after being married to her for 52 years!*

She has the terrific gift of loving little kids and working with senior citizens, enjoying her associations with all ages. In ten minutes she can wrap them all around her finger. They'll eat out of her hand and . . . I can't win people like that!

Because of her own history as a foster child, she can take in and love underprivileged kids and make them respond better than anyone I have ever seen. It doesn't matter how badly messed up they are mentally or emotionally, she can still love them, hug them, tuck them into bed and bless them.

When my brother Earl's adopted Korean daughter, Konnae, was going through a rebellious stage as a teenager and was very difficult for them to handle, Grace even "mothered" her for several weeks one summer. I don't know what made the difference. Perhaps it was simply the change of environment, but there was something that Grace did that clicked, and Konnae did better after that.

In addition to our own five children, Grace *always* had two or three foster children living here with us. I enjoyed watching it, although I was usually the silent partner. It never seemed to make a difference to her if she did laundry for five or for ten. Her attitude was always the same. She just went through it like a breeze and smiled. In between, she would often say, "I'll feed the chickens tonight. You don't need to come in from the fields to do that." What a blessing!

She also has the gift of housekeeping, and she can cook as easily for 12, or 20 as for six people. Sometimes I would call her at ten minutes before noon and say, "Hey, I have two extra guys helping me today, and I hate to make them go home for lunch. What do you think?"

"Just bring them in," she'd always say. "I'll have something extra."

My mom was also like that. Even though unexpected guests appeared, she could always cover it up and make it appear that it was all planned to be that way.

Grace is also very artistic and an excellent seamstress. She is *good!* She just has so many gifts. I used to tell her, and still do, "Grace, you work so hard at being a perfectionist." (At least that's what I would call it). "Don't worry about a little dirt on the floor. With five kids running around, don't get excited if somebody happens to let their jacket lie on the floor." She wasn't a radical, but the children soon learned she liked to keep things in order. She was so good at that.

In addition to all these qualities, she always had a wonderful working relationship of mutual respect and caring with the neighborhood women. She has always been so pleasant, with a great sense of humor, a delightful laugh, and has been a real partner to me in every way.

In looking back at those difficult times, I only can say as Joseph said to his brothers, "You meant it for evil, but God meant it for good." (Genesis 50:20, KJV) Boy, it was a blessing in reverse, or a blessing in disguise. I don't even bat an eye thinking about it any more, except occasionally for the thought: *"How dumb could I be?"*

Chapter Seventeen

Being a Father and Grandfather

"I think all my children are doing a lot better than I did, but they should. What I learned from my dad, I passed on to them. Now they have the wealth and wisdom of TWO generations in their lives!"
—Victor K. Ziegler

How did I learn about the facts of life? In our family there were not many deep discussions about reproduction or sex, but we observed puppies being born, the births of baby calves, and saw chicken eggs hatch. We got "on-the-job training" which created a reverence for the propagation of life, and we never felt anything was evil or bad about it.

At one point, I remember my dad asking me if I wanted to go along because they were going to get this cow bred tonight. Although I knew there had to be a contact between the male and female, I wasn't quite sure how this would happen. It was interesting to watch, and after you witness something like that, most of your questions about baby-making are answered instantly. It is better than having somebody simply explain it to you or reading about it in a book. Even with that, there is a certain level that isn't understood until you grow up, get married and experience it yourself. Then you *really* understand the details. However, sometimes it takes a few years of adjustment to really figure everything out.

I used to have a standing joke with our family doctor that we had five children, and if he hadn't told me what caused them, we would have had six . . . but we couldn't afford to have more.

In preparing us for marriage, my parents did the best they knew how. We were never told to shut up, go away, not ask questions, or that sex was a "hush-hush" subject, and of course, stories that were degenerating or off-color were never tolerated. We had the advantage of being exposed to all this in observing life on the farm, and I just wish every child could be raised in the country with animals and poultry, because that atmosphere gives a reverence for life that you don't get any other way.

Most urban children learn their sex education through street language which is always slanted the wrong way, and doesn't emphasize the Master Plan, the beauty, and the miracles of God's creation. Man has turned something beautiful into a terrible nightmare, and it is difficult for our city cousins and their families to understand the beautiful things as God intended for them to be used.

Grace and I had five children, three girls and two boys. Bonnie was the oldest daughter, and it is a miracle that she survived. At that time, babies were given a shot to prevent whooping cough, and she was scheduled to receive hers on her next visit to the doctor. However, before that happened, she caught whooping cough, and for almost two weeks, from 10 p.m. until about 3 a.m., she would cough and cough for dear life. I'll never forget holding her upside down at 2 o'clock in the morning, patting her on her back as she was gasping for breath, struggling to drain the mucous out of her lungs. I said to Grace, "I believe she is taking her last breath," and then she'd gasp again.

Watching her struggle like that was a tough two weeks for us. She was just six months old and was our first child. We thought we were going to lose her, especially that one particular night. She was blue in the face and had started changing colors. My mom was with us, and Grace frantically said, "Mama, I don't think Bonnie's living anymore." But we kept massaging and patting her, and just that quick, she snapped out of it.

Her body was always the smallest and thinnest one in the family, and we often wondered if that was a result of her whooping cough experience. On the other hand, even though she was so tiny, she was also the one with the least colds and health problems.

Bonnie married Ron Myer who farmed with us for about 10 years and then felt the call to the ministry. Now he heads up the Dove Fellowship Church and is one of their top guys in the nation. Ron and Bonnie have been married 30 years, live on our same street, and have five boys and one girl.

Sharon, our second daughter, has also been married for 30 years, to Dennis Martin, a dairy farmer in the Ephrata area and they have two daughters and one son.

Theresa, our third daughter, a medical assistant in the office of an eye, nose, and throat specialist, married Randy Hower who is the father of her one son, Nick, and one daughter, Janelle, our oldest granddaughter. After she and Randy divorced, she married Mark Wickert, a schoolteacher in Lebanon.

So, our youngest daughter, Theresa, had our oldest granddaughter, Janelle, and she, in turn, has two little girls, our first two *great*-grandchildren. In all, we have 20 grandchildren, but when I tell people that, I add that we also have 20 great-grandchildren. If they give me a puzzled look, I quickly explain that our 20 grandchildren are all so *great*!

Lynn, our oldest son, was next, and he's spent 17 years on the road driving a tractor trailer as an independent trucker. Although he enjoyed his work, he wanted to be home at night more with his family, so he sold that. Now he's a truck salesman for the company that sold him his truck. He admits that he's making a little less money, but he's at his home near Buffalo Springs every night now, and enjoys it more. Because he had a health problem with diabetes, this schedule allows him to be more regular with his meals and eat more healthy foods. He married Kathleen Peifer and they have two boys and two girls.

Our youngest child is Leon, now 44 and farming on what had been our home farm, the Villa Pine Farm. Married to Donna Peifer, Kathleen's sister, they have three boys and two girls.

Those little girls feed anywhere from 25 to 50 baby calves just like they know what they are doing professionally. They have a good teacher and model in their mother, Donna, who is a terrific partner for Leon. She can do *anything* on the farm, even running the equipment so nothing stops if Leon is not there. He is really blessed, and he knows it.

What a joy to be surrounded by ten of our grandchildren. Seated left to right: Mark Meyer, Emily Ziegler (hidden), Ryan Ziegler, David Ziegler and their grandpa Victor. Standing: Melanie Martin, Craig Ziegler, Laura Ziegler, Jordan Martin, Charity Martin, Blake Ziegler.

The Peifer girls, Donna and Kathleen, grew up in the Cornwall area and graduated from Cedar Crest High School. Leon still tells his friends that the main reason he married Donna was that his dad never gave him enough money to buy gas, so if he wanted to go anywhere, he had to go with his older brother. Even when Lynn was dating, Leon would tag along. By doing this, Leon says he saved gas, time, money, and everything, and got a good deal! Both claim that he has the best sister!

When I was growing up, we literally had one trip of a lifetime! My parents took us to the Philadelphia Zoo. That was a big deal for us, and was a whole day event. In those days, not many people had cars, and those that did, didn't have much gas because it was rationed. Even with those restrictions, we still had lots of fun things to do right in our own neighborhood. Our city cousins would visit us on the farm, and they'd help us with the chores, and then we would play together. It was different then. Nobody had any money, but we had a lot of fun.

On the first big trip Grace and I took with our children, we repeated our wedding trip and toured the New England states, stopping to sightsee at the usual tourist towns. It was about 1967 and Bonnie was 13 years old.

Late in one day, we drove to the base of Mt. Washington in New Hampshire and saw a sign that said the gates close at 8:00 p.m. I said, "Do you know what? We should be able to get to the top and down before that."

So, we drove to the top, and enjoyed the view from the mountaintop. Then we headed down, but while descending the mountain, the brakes gave out! Well, there we were facing a 14,000 foot decline ahead of us and this was all curves. Instead of guard rails, they had big rocks that each weighed a couple ton, parked between the edge of the road and a steep drop-off. A car *couldn't* slip between 'em. You would have had to *try* to drive down over the cliff, you know. So, we were debating what to do. We could have sat in the car and slept until morning and then tried to get a wrecker from the forestry service to come and tow us down, or we could continue down and see what happens.

Since our old Chevy station wagon had an automatic transmission, and this was the first time in my life that I ever did this, we came down those eight miles of curvy mountain roads with the transmission *in reverse*! When we'd get to a curve, the car would want to run away, so I would touch the throttle lightly and it would shift into reverse and slow us down.

But I will never forget that experience. The girls were lying on the floor, crying and praying. They were so afraid that the whole car, with their whole family, was going to go down over the cliff. It *was* a little heartstopping! Yeah, *I wouldn't advise anybody to do it!* But by the grace of God, we did get down. Just as we drove away from there, we saw the guard swing the big gate shut. If we had been five minutes later, we might have been parked inside the gate for the night. The next day I got new brakes put in the car.

A couple years later, we drove to Florida on a one-week trip with the children, visiting some friends and relatives and doing some sightseeing. Grace said the boys thought it was boring because I would wait until dark to get to a swimming pool. They always wanted us to choose a motel that had a swimming pool, and would say, "Let's stop at 3:00 this afternoon. We don't want to see anymore!"

Then I'd counter with, "Yeah, but we have to see the beauty of the country during the *day.*"

We got a bird's eye view of key points such as the Everglades, Cypress Gardens, and the glass-bottomed boats, but we never took them to Disney World. Grace and I did get there many years later.

Other than that, we took a few shorter day trips including going to Ocean City, Maryland, to the beach. After our family had experienced hardships such as losing cows because of disease and because of being struck by lightning, I was afraid to borrow $1,000 to go on a family trip for fear of not being able to pay it back if something else went wrong. I didn't believe in spending a thousand dollars if I thought I could do it with a hundred! Through it all, today our children look back on those times and smile.

The only complaint they do still make is that they remember that if I would see a beautiful dairy farm, I often would stop and talk with the farmer. Meanwhile, they'd be sitting waiting in the car and saying, "Come on, let's go, let's go."

I admit that happened on several occasions. They probably viewed it as my pursuing my own selfish interests, and when I look back, I would agree that I should have been more considerate of their feelings and do more of my stopping and visiting at farms when they weren't along.

We didn't have a TV until Bonnie was in her teens, and I think we used to put it in the closet during the week, so the children would get their homework done first. Consequently, they never became addicted to TV and were all pretty good readers. However, I do remember one time we couldn't find Bonnie and discovered her hiding in the closet watching TV. That was so funny, so funny!

Until my parents were in their mid-70's, they lived next door to us. My dad was always concerned about the welfare of children, whether they were our neighbors' children or his own grandchildren. Once in a while he would come over and caution me about something, but he'd never do it with a negative attitude. Instead, he might say, "I don't know about them boys. Maybe you'd better warn them, as their actions are a little risky."

When our boys were around 15 years old, we got them a dirt bike. About that same time, there was a guy in the news named Evil Knievel, who did breathtaking stunts such as jumping over things while riding his motorcycle.

Lynn must have really admired him, because one day he parked the pickup truck right beside a big sawdust pile. When I was standing in that general area, along came Lynn flying on his cycle right over the sawdust pile, right over the pickup truck, and landing on the other side. Just seeing him go scared me to death! Then didn't he just come around and do it all a second time. He had timed it so that I would see him and he could show me he could do it. He had rigged it up and done it before I could yell "No!" He was really in gear to go.

Leon was a little bit that way also, but Lynn was the daredevil of the family when it came to taking risks. One time my dad saw him jumping over the sawdust pile with his motorcycle and he came after me. "Victor, you ought to make him stop that. He'll kill himself!"

"Yeah," I answered him, "I'll work on that, but I don't know quite how to slow the boys down."

"Well," he suggested, "you can always take the motorcycle from them."

But they were doing pretty good, and I didn't want to kill their enthusiasm! Ha! Ha! In time, as they matured, they did tame down a little bit.

One time when Grace and I were away, Grace's brother, Stanford Cox and his wife came to visit, and these boys almost scared the wits out of their uncle Stan. When they saw him pull in our driveway, the boys knew he would be walking toward the front of the house. One of the boys ran ahead, opened the large garage door, the kitchen door and the front door. Then Lynn rode the motorcycle in through the garage, through the kitchen, across the living room and out the front door, jumping over the steps along the way! Uncle Stan laughs about it yet today when he recalls that moment. "We knew those boys were sure up to something. As we approached the house, we heard this motorcycle all revved up, and the next thing we knew it was coming out the living room door and we were standing there watching it!"

It was several months before we heard about this incident. Then one day the boys talked about it, and Stan mentioned it, and of course, when we heard it, we had to laugh too. Those boys were a little risky, or as Grace would say, "daring."

On one occasion we were visiting our neighbor who was shut-in for a little while due to an illness. At that time, I had a new Ford Fairlane pickup truck, and our boys were 14 and 16 years old. We never took keys out of anything around the farm, and generally the boys would say, "We want to go to do so and so," but neither of them had a license yet. While we were inside the neighbor's house, we happened to look out the window.

"There goes our pickup truck! Who could that be?" I exclaimed.

When we got home, the pickup truck was in the shed where it was supposed to be, and the boys had gone to the barn and had started working ... and they were smiling. I forget how the conversation started, but I got around to asking them, "Who was the neighbor who was in trouble and needed to rent our pickup truck this afternoon?"

They just looked at each other and neither one wanted to talk. I didn't say much to them except, "Just be careful. I don't want to see that either of you can't get a license *legally* when you are sixteen."

At that time, in the late 60's and early 70's, traffic on the roads wasn't as heavy as today, but we wanted to honor the law. On a few occasions, when we were almost home, I would slide over and let 14-year-old Leon drive the last half mile. Generally, when we got to the edge of our farm, if anybody came toward us, we would just turn into our field and get off the road. We didn't want to endanger anyone. I always told them, "Remember, you might be driving safely, but if that other guy does something stupid and hits you, you're the illegal one. You're the one who's there without permission, without a license."

And they understood that. Basically speaking, they were fairly easy boys to handle.

A few months later my brother Earl arranged to meet someone at our house to carpool to go to a two-day meeting. At that time he had an orange Renault sedan which he left parked in our driveway. That same night, I went to a meeting at Allentown and left about 4:00 p.m. Shortly after I had gone, Lynn asked Grace, "Hey, mom, may we drive uncle Earl's car over to Bethel? Leon and I want to see someone there about buying a sheepskin?"

(However, they *really* just wanted to drive this car!)

Legally, Lynn could, because now he had a license. Earl had told us he was considering selling the car, and our daughter, Theresa, was thinking about buying it. So her brothers were also interested in "test-driving" it for their sister to see how it drove.

Well, they went over to Bethel, and it was a rainy night in springtime. Because there had been a storm earlier, at certain spots there were blossoms scattered all over the road. On their way home, when they approached an "S" curve, traveling at what they estimated to be about 30 or 35 miles per hour, the tires hit those wet blossoms which were as slippery as ice. The car spun up on the bank and rolled over, and the door flew open.

Leon said Lynn's face was down in the dirt with his hands outstretched. Since he didn't move, Leon thought he was dead. Leon found himself hanging onto a window, so he crawled out somehow on the other side, and ran up the road to an old bar, a rough-looking place, that had an outdoor telephone. He called our home, and no one answered, so he called the guy who worked for us in the dairy, Noah Sauders.

"Can you come and get us?" he cried breathlessly. "We had an accident, and I think Lynn is dead. I'm just bumped a little bit, but I have to get back to Lynn."

By the time Noah arrived, Lynn had come to, so Noah took both boys to the hospital. Fortunately, Lynn had just been knocked out and both had some brush burns, but neither had any

Grandpa Victor comforting a nervous ringbearer, Grandson Blake Ziegler, Lynn's son.

broken bones. I didn't get home from my meeting until around midnight, so I was not aware of the accident until a few hours after it happened.

The next day at school, as Leon told some of his friends about the accident, he broke down and couldn't handle it emotionally, so the school sent him home. "That was a terrible experience," he recalled. However, in a couple days, they were both fine.

That next day Lynn came to me and asked, "What are we going to do for uncle Earl?"

"Lynn, don't ask the question, what are WE going to do for uncle Earl? What are YOU going to do for uncle Earl?" I retorted. "You took the car without uncle Earl's permission, you convinced your mom to say 'yes' when she probably should have said 'no.' (He wouldn't have driven it if she had

2003 Graduating Grandchildren Daryl Myer, son of Ron and Bonnie Myer. Laura Ziegler, daughter of Lynn and Kathleen Ziegler.

insisted that he not do it.) Now it's a total wreck, and there's only one right way to handle this. You have to call your uncle Earl and tell him you drove his car last night and completely wrecked it and that he should go out and buy one right like he had and whatever the difference is, you will pay for it."

At this time Lynn was a senior and he had $720 saved up in a savings account. He admitted, "I don't have much money."

"Well," I suggested, "you can always pay it month by month or take out a loan. We're not going to let uncle Earl stick, because it wasn't his fault."

So he made the call and talked to his uncle Earl himself. I don't remember that I did any of the negotiating. A few days later Earl called back and said he had found one that suited him for $2,700. Since the insurance covered two thousand dollars of it, Lynn agreed to pay the remaining $700. Somehow, Lynn and Earl met together and the payment was made. I allowed Lynn to handle this whole business by himself so it could be a learning experience for him.

A few days later someone at school said to him, "It must be nice to be the son of a rich dairy farmer. You wreck your uncle's car, he gets another one, and you just go home and smile. It doesn't cost you a penny!"

"That's what *you* think," Lynn corrected him. "He cleaned me out! I gave up *all my savings* of the last 2 or 3 years."

"What do you mean? Didn't your dad pay for it?" his friend questioned.

"No," Lynn replied. He explained, "The person who is responsible pays the damages, and I was the driver."

If he wouldn't have had the money in savings, I would have helped him get the money. I probably would have taken him in to the bank and got him a loan. However, he *did* have enough, and although it cleaned him out, he doesn't hold that against anyone. When he talks about it now, he even agrees it was a great learning experience. It helped to make a difference in his life, making him a better person.

I reminded him afterwards, "You know, a lot of boys never got a second chance. Their life was snuffed out. In many cases, one stupid mistake cost them their life. Why the Lord chose to spare you, I have no idea, but I am thankful He did."

About two years ago I was passing the site of the accident with three of my grandsons, two were Leon's sons and one was

Lynn's. After pulling to the side of the road and stopping, I said, "See that locust tree over there with that big gouge or notch in it? That's exactly where the car hit and rolled down in the ditch. That is a landmark of where your dad's and your uncle's lives were saved when they were about 14 and 16 years old. You know, a lot of boys roll over and are dead instantly, but God chose to allow them to live."

There wasn't much conversation.

When I was growing up, all the children in our family went to school, worked on the farm, and helped with the chores until they were 18 years old. Any money that we earned was put into the family "kitty." After our 18th birthday, we either got a job or started to get paid for working at home and, for those times, that system worked well.

When my own children were old enough, they all participated in working on the farm as well, and really made a difference. However, they had several incentives. For one thing, I wanted them to learn to buy, sell, and keep track of their own expenses. By the time they were young teenagers, I wanted them to know how to buy their own clothes and understand how to handle money. So, I said to them, "Do you know what? We are going to start paying each of you."

When each one reached 12 years of age, we started to pay them—not a full-time wage, but a nominal fee so that they felt rewarded. At that time the IRS said you could pay members of your family up to $4,000 a year for duties done on your farm or in your business. I know when they were in high school, some of them reached that limit.

This worked out real good, as it gave them a little income, a little incentive. They learned how to make deposits in the bank, handle their own savings accounts, and started buying some of their clothes. We saw it as a learning process for them.

On top of it, although I was paying one of my children up to $4,000, it would have cost *double* that amount to hire an outsider. In addition, I could charge whatever I paid them as an expense, putting me in a lower tax bracket and keeping more money in the family, so to speak. So it was a win/win situation all around. We all benefited.

In today's society, I feel that parents should reward their children, as they are able. Don't wait until they are 17 or 18 and expect them to be able instantly to manage a full-time check when they get their first paying job. If they are fortunate enough to start out with a good job, without prior training in handling money, it can become "easy come, easy go." Parents should do more in helping them manage finances responsibly and understanding what a day's work and a dollar means. In the future they will really be thankful that they have learned those basics.

When our boys were in high school, they asked, "Dad, are you going to help us buy a car or truck?"

"Everybody pays their own way around here," I replied. Then I reminded them that my parents never gave *their* children many outright gifts of money or things, but they were always willing to sacrifice and work to help us achieve our goals. Some children never have those opportunities or offers of help.

In discussing this several years ago, Leon told me, "Dad, if you could afford to give me a farm for nothing, I wouldn't want it. I've seen so many of my friends inherit a half million dollars and still end up bankrupt, divorced, and so unhappy."

More often than not, we had extra people living with us and sitting around our dinner table. When our children were small, at various times we also had foster children, the senior citizens we cared for, and several young men out of prison who lived with us for brief periods. After our children grew up and left home, we sponsored the refugees.

We had been married only three years when the Neffsville Church of the Brethren Home put out an appeal for foster homes for children. Having been raised in a foster home herself, Grace felt this as a special calling.

Our first three foster children were from the same family, two boys and a girl, Mike, Simon and Jennie (not their real names). Because their parents were separated, they were placed in foster homes, and these three children just fit in with our own. Mike and Simon were a little older than our children were, and Jennie was the sweetest little girl. If you saw her working, you would never suspect that she was mentally slow. Grace always kept her dressed real nice, just like our own daughters.

Victor and his first great-grandchild, Jocelyn Dunham, daughter of Janelle Hower Dunham, whose mother was Victor and Grace's daughter, Theresa. Date: Dec. 2002.

One of Jennie's schoolteachers complimented Grace saying, "I'm really amazed that even though Jennie is your foster daughter, you take such good care of her."

"That's what it's all about," Grace and I thought to ourselves. We wanted to help these children and prepare them for life, so why shouldn't we love them and treat them like our own?

Today Jennie is married and has a family, but we haven't seen them for a long time.

Mike at 15 was such a nice, honest, hard-working boy, that he quickly became my favorite, almost like my own son. On June 7, 1957, we were just finishing up cutting our crop of hay. As I explained earlier, we packed our silage into trenches by driving over the cuttings with a tractor. Because of the danger, no one was ever allowed to drive the tractor to compact or roll the hay down except myself. It wasn't that risky for me. You could easily run down a slope but you had to remember you couldn't run up the slope or the tractor would go end over end. (With the new tractors today that have four-wheel drive and big front-end loaders, you can hardly do that.) I was operating the tractor and packing this silage and had to leave to go to town and get some parts. Mike came to me and said, "Victor, can I pack that down until you get back?"

Since he was such a good, safe operator, I agreed adding this warning, "Well, Mike, you can, but don't try to drive UP the slope because if, for any reason you spin your wheels, it crawls in the gears. The tractor will stay standing, and it will just walk the tractor upside down."

I was in Richland getting parts when I got the terrible news in a phone call. Ah, my, I was sick at heart! Till I got home, the state police and ambulance were both already there. You could see in the silage where Mike had come down, turned around, and in doing so, upset the tractor and he was under it. The steering wheel or something caught him, and his neck was broken instantly. That was a hard experience, really hard.

Phew! I could have sat and cried for days, but I knew that wouldn't do any good. When we told Mike's mom what had happened, she said, "You know, his dad has a mental problem. He fought in World War II and has suffered from shellshock ever since. He walks along the streets and roads, carrying a bag and is just a poor soul."

She herself had some mental problems also and that's why she hadn't been able to keep the family together. She did accept the news graciously though, saying, "God is in control. I know you and Grace did the best you knew how."

I assured her, "Do you know what? Mike was baptized and often talked about knowing the Lord personally. He wanted to go to Sunday School and church to worship, and I just know he is in heaven. There is no question in my mind about that, but that doesn't heal the pain."

With wisdom, she responded, "Well, time will be healing to both of us."

He had been with us about two years and was so intelligent. He could just do anything. You could explain anything to him, and he did it, just like a 50-year-old man. Anything! He'd come into the house and say to Grace, "I'll help you wash the dishes," or "Can I do anything for you?"

Oh, I'll tell you what, when that news hit, that boy was closer to me than any family member I ever had–first of all, because he had needed a home and secondly, because of his willing spirit. I have often wondered *why* God allowed that to happen. His mother also observed, "You know, he was such a wonderful boy, but maybe the Lord saw something down through the years and just took him home early to prevent the family or him from a lot of headaches and heartaches in the future."

I started getting gray hair the next day. I noticed it when I looked in the mirror. That's the way it affected me, and yet I didn't sit around and brood or even miss a day of work. I do remember that Enos Heisey, a friend who was a lay minister, came around and prayed for me.

Only a couple weeks later, one of the county commissioners called and asked if he could talk to Grace and me. When he came, he quickly got to the point by stating, "I have a 16-year-old nephew who ran away in Florida. He had been adopted by my sister, got in some kind of trouble and ran off, and if he goes back, he'll go to jail."

As his story continued, the result was that whoever was upset with him was not willing to give him a second chance, and this commissioner wanted us to take the boy into our home and see if we could turn him around.

"Oh, my," I exclaimed. "You know we just went through a tragedy."

"Victor, you can't live in the past," he reminded me. "If you take him, you just do the best you can."

We talked for an hour, but Grace and I were still reluctant. I said, "Oh, I don't know. Just what if . . . what if something dumb would happen?"

To assure me, he said, "Victor and Grace, if you are worried about that, I will write you a letter that I am totally 100% responsible for this boy, regardless of the circumstances, regardless of what happens, regardless of whether I made the right or wrong decision."

And immediately, he wrote out a letter (I believe I might have it yet in my filing cabinet) on the back of a county commissioner letter that "I, John Doe," (not his real name), "assume all responsibility in the event of ANY circumstance in the life of this boy. Victor and Grace Ziegler will NEVER be held responsible in ANY way, physically, legally, financially, or anything."

Although we still hesitated and had our doubts, there was another factor at work for this boy. When he was only three years old, his parents attended the Myer Church of the Brethren where Grace and I were married. Grace had known his mother and remembered this guy as the cutest little red-haired boy. Although years had passed and he was now 16 years old, because of these memories, Grace still held a warm feeling and fondness toward him. So, while leaning heavily on God for wisdom, we reluctantly agreed to take this boy, Greg, (not his real name), and see how we could help him.

During the short time he was with us, he did become a believer and was baptized. Although he was personable and could be kind, he had wild blood in him. We had to almost chain him down, you know. On the one hand, Greg could offer nice prayers when I would ask him, and he became a part of the family. But on the other hand, he was very headstrong.

From the start, I told him about the tragedy we had

experienced so recently, even *showing* him how Mike's accident had happened. I demonstrated and explained that if I drove the tractor up on the piles of silage and stop, letting the clutch fly out, this tractor will come right around and crush the driver. We talked about this often and I emphasized, "I *never* want another tragedy like that to happen here."

And would you believe it—on September 7, 1957, this kid, Greg, did the same thing! But he did it behind my back, without my giving him permission to be driving the tractor. In his case, none of his bones were broken, but the tractor pressed him into the soft material, the silage, and suffocated him. When we got to him, he was beyond hope, beyond help.

When his uncle John, the commissioner, came, he brought the state police with him and started ripping me out. I said, "Hold on here, John, remember our conversation of three months ago? I was scared, worried to death, so to speak, and you kept pressuring me by saying, 'Victor, you've got to help this kid; you've *got to help* him!' I asked you then, what if he does something dumb behind my back?"

"Well, yeah."

"Do you remember writing me a personal letter (and he had beautiful handwriting) taking full responsibility yourself and signing it with your signature?"

"Yeah." He hung his head, and there was a long pause. Then he looked me in the eye and said, "I'm sorry, Victor. I should have shut up."

And that was the end of it.

Greg's whole biological family came to the funeral and gathered around us. They said only good things about Grace. Even his adoptive parents, who hadn't been able to control him, told us, "We're so thankful you gave him a chance."

I can still see his uncle John, as we were walking out of the cemetery, telling me, "I just want to thank you one more time for keeping him out of jail, that he came to know the Lord and that we had such good reports about him during the time he was with you."

Those two tragedies were quite an experience!

You know, to this day, when I get up in the morning and look at the calendar and see it is June 7, the horror of that day flashes in my mind like big bold letters. It doesn't happen often, and it doesn't last longer than a minute.

I say to Grace, "Do you know what today is?"

And she says, "No."

"It's June the 7th."

"June the 7th?"

"Yeah, the day we lost Mike. And on September 7 the same thing happened." That two tragedies, so similar in nature, would happen on the same farm and so close together was just unbelievable. That all happened 47 years ago.

But, we don't look back. It was something to live down. For a whole year, I'd hear, "Victor moved too fast," or "Victor, you shouldn't be so sloppy."

When one guy told me that, I responded, "And you're one guy who wouldn't help anybody. You can condemn someone else, but you wouldn't risk giving a poor guy a dollar or helping to give a young kid a little direction."

When I'd start defending myself in that manner, they would all shut up and walk away. Some said, "Yeah, Victor, you did the right thing."

And those were their final words, "You did the right thing."

In looking back, I don't regret it, but *I do regret what happened*. All in all, we had more rewarding experiences than disappointing ones.

Sometime later, after a plea from the Neffsville Home, we agreed to take Harry, (not his real name), a 12-year-old boy. As an infant, he was left on someone's doorstep and never saw his biological mother and father. He was not too bright and wet the bed all the time. Grace used to make him wash out his own pajamas and bedding, thinking that would help teach him not to do it. Finally, we gave him a bedroom in the basement because we couldn't stand the smell in the house. He wet the bed until he was married.

During the first week Harry was living here, he told me one day that he was going to run away. "Tell me where you want to go, and I'll take you in the truck and drop you off," I suggested.

He never left.

I remember one time our kids played a joke on him. We had an outside toilet at the end of our cement walk, next to the garage. Our kids saw Harry go in it, and pretty soon they saw some smoke coming out. Then one of them got an idea, and the others went along with it. They ran and got a bucket of water, opened the door and threw the water inside. When they saw him, they acted surprised, and said, "Oh, *you're* in here! We saw the smoke coming out, and we thought there was a fire in here. We got some water to put it out, but it's just you in here . . . smoking!" Fortunately, he took it well.

When one of our foster daughters caught his eye and he began pestering her, we knew we had to make some changes, so a representative from the Neffsville Home had to come and move him to another home.

For a few years we lost touch with him, but we had heard he moved to New York state. Then one day he called saying he would like to come back and work for me if I had a job for him. I said he could and he was here for a while until I was able to get him a job in the community. We still see them occasionally.

The last foster child we had in our home was a 17-year-old girl who had been adopted by a family, and her adoptive mother never accepted her. Unexpectedly, the caseworker brought this girl and her adoptive mother to our house and asked us if we would consider helping her out for a couple months. It was a very awkward moment since we were approached out of the blue, so to speak, and the adoptive mother and the daughter were both present also.

Since the idea was so sudden, Grace sorta stuttered around at first and said, "Well . . . sure . . . ah . . . yes, we'll make something work."

About that time, I entered the scene and was told about what was happening. They were about ready to leave when the adoptive mother, Mrs. Lehman, (not her real name), spoke up and said, "Mrs. Ziegler, I want to tell you how bad my daughter is."

Before Grace could react, I interrupted and said, "Mrs. Lehman, we don't even *want to know* how bad your daughter is." (She had been shoved around to various foster homes and then was adopted by this family, but this mother didn't really want her and was always fighting with her.) "I already know one thing: God gave *every child* a gift or a talent. I believe in overcoming evil with good. We're going to find Lois' (not her real name) one good talent, and we're going to multiply that so much that it will bury every bad thing that has happened in her life. We'll do that by the grace of God."

It took three weeks. Within three weeks, Lois was a perfect angel, the nicest girl. She wasn't really that difficult to handle, even in the beginning, but she *was* scared. For about a week, until we got to know her, we didn't leave her in the house alone.

During her second week with us, Grace and I were going away one evening so I said to her, "Lois, I am expecting a phone call tonight. If anybody calls, would you take a message?"

"Yes, sure," she answered with a smile. "I'll be here studying for school tomorrow."

"Just get their name and tell them I'll be home after 9:00 or I'll call them in the morning whenever it suits them," I instructed.

While we were gone, she got two phone calls. The next morning when I returned the call of this one guy, he said, "Victor, who was I talking to last night? She was so courteous and gracious, but the voice was so young I knew it wasn't your wife. Did you hire a professional secretary?"

Of course, I couldn't wait to tell her what he said.

From that day on, she would do anything because she knew *somebody believed in her*. Although she struggled in most of her school subjects, she was good in art and really excelled in the culinary arts. She could really cook! In fact, after she left and got married, before my mom and dad moved away, I phoned her one day. "Lois, Grandpa's birthday is coming up and I remember that you made the best cakes. Would you be willing to make a cake for him? I'll pay you for the cake and for the gas for you to deliver it and visit him for an hour."

"I'll be glad to, and it won't cost you anything," she quickly agreed.

And she did and brought her husband along so we met him also. Now she has three children, and as far as we know, she's doing wonderful. She lives in middle Pennsylvania and we don't get to see them very often, but we always get a card from them at Christmas and Thanksgiving.

She had been with us about 1½ years. The most foster children we had at one time were three, and we must have had about ten or so in all, two of whom were retarded.

In raising our children, we encountered various scary moments. I remember the Sunday Lynn came home from church after studying in Sunday School about Jacob and his well. In trying to see what it was like for Jacob to get water, he went out on our back porch with a bucket in his hand, and leaned way over the banister so far that he toppled over it, narrowly missing hitting his head on a stone slab several feet below. If he had hit it, he could have easily been killed.

Lynn also gave us a scare when he tried skating for the first time on our pond wearing his new ice skates. He fell . . . hard, and as a result, had a concussion.

For many years, the cement walk between our house and the barn was really the top of a big stone wall. Beside the walk was a drop-off of about six feet, and down below was where we had our family garden. One day Bonnie was fooling around in the backyard with a bag over her head, pretending she was a blind person. Not realizing how close she was to the edge of the wall, she kept walking and suddenly stepped off the top of the wall into the garden. Fortunately, she walked away with only a few brush burns.

With our own five children plus the extra additions to our family and being involved in many farm, community, and Christian organizations, I was moving pretty fast. Leon said to me not long ago, "You know, Dad, the only thing I can fault you for as a parent was that you never had time to play ball or go along to wrestling and other sporting events."

And that is true. I didn't. I didn't.

Although I regret missing out on some of those activities with my children, my response was, "I'm so glad that where I messed up, the Lord covered up. Your mom always filled in. If it hadn't been for Grace and her strong faith, stability, and her heart filled with love, our children might not be who they are today.

At one point, one of the children told Grace, "Mom, you and dad take better care of the refugees than you do your own family!"

That sarcastic remark was a wake-up call and struck a note with me. I said to Grace, "We have to be careful that we don't go overboard."

You know it is easy to feel sympathy for distressed persons, and you see yourself and your family as being so blessed and doing well . . . but they see it through different eyes.

Four generations. Left to right: Grace Ziegler, Sharon Ziegler Martin, Melanie Martin Kirk, and Joanna Kirk, born in Mexico Sept. 30, 2004. (Victor never got to see Joanna, his third great-granddaughter.) Photo date: December 2004.

There may have been times when we were *too* enthusiastic and *too* occupied with service, but it all worked out tremendously. Today I couldn't have a more supportive family.

During his senior year of high school, Leon came home one day and said, "Dad, I want to leave three weeks before graduation."

Hiding my surprise, I simply asked, "Where are you going?"

"I'm going out west and joining a harvesting crew starting in Texas," was his ready answer. "I have to be there on May 18, and we're going to work all summer throughout the West finishing up in Saskatchewan, Canada, in November. I'll be getting back home near the end of November or the first of December."

"Is he really serious about this?" I wondered to myself.

Meanwhile, he kept talking about it. He was just 17½ years old, so although he was senior class president, he never graduated with his class! Never showed up for graduation.

I was on the school board at that time, and the superintendent called me and said, "Victor, what's going on? Your son is president of his class and you are on the school board, and he won't even be here for graduation?"

What was I to say? "You've got to know Leon," I responded. "When he sets his mind on something, there's nothing that can stop him."

I did try to get Leon to compromise saying, "I probably won't stand in your way, but you should be there to pick up your diploma at graduation."

"Aw, Dad," he disagreed. "I'll never look at it. Whether I get it or whether I don't, I'll still be the same person. If anyone on the board gives you a hard time, just tell them they don't need to sign my diploma. Just keep it on file. I don't need it. I'll go just as far without it as with it."

I could tell he was kinda "gung ho" about this, and of course, he did go.

I remember the week before he left, my dad expressed some fears by warning me, "Victor, don't you think you ought to keep him at home? What if he'd get in the wrong crowd and get messed up?" (We did know of a young fellow who had done this and ended up being a drunk, so pop's fears were not unfounded.)

However, my answer was, "Pop, the guy is 17 ½ and if we didn't teach him right from wrong and good Biblical principles by the time he's pushing 18, it's getting too late. At this point, I'd rather pray for him than stand in his way."

Leon had saved his money, and just before he left he bought a new 4-wheel drive Dodge pickup truck and paid for it in cash. (At that time, you could get them for around $6,000 or $7,000.)

The day he left I told him, "Son, we love you and we're going to be thinking of you and praying for you every day. Give us a call now and then and write us letters."

Then he took off in his new truck. He has since told me that he didn't even get 15 miles from home until he wanted to pull off the road, cry, and turn around, but he admitted, "I would have been ashamed to do that!"

So he went and came through it all right. Although he saw some ugly scenes that summer, his reaction was, "I was so glad I was saved from that kind of life. Some of the guys wanted to drag me into bar rooms and clubs, but I'd just go back to our trailer and go to bed or do something different."

His bosses were Christian, but there were a few guys who tried to drag him down. When he came home, he felt he had been treated pretty well.

During Christmas week, we got a phone call from the Dell brothers, the same outfit he had worked for during the summer. They asked, "Are you Leon's dad?"

"Yup," I answered.

"Hey, we want to talk to Leon about working for us next summer again," they declared, adding, "we need a guy like him."

"Well," I said, "I guess it's up to him."

So I put Leon on the phone. Pretty soon he came back all excited and told me, "Dad, they want me to name my own salary! They want to make me foreman of a 7-man crew. They are getting 3 or 4 new trucks and a couple of new combines, and they are giving them to me!"

"Do you know what, Leon?" I advised. "With the kind of people you are working for, although I never met them, I can tell you that you'll get more money if you don't quote your own salary. Let them give you what they want."

So, he went back to the phone and gave them his answer. "Hey, we can talk about the salary later. Mark me up, and I'll be there to work."

All that summer, they paid him a basic minimum, but at the end of the year I don't know how many thousand dollars they sent home with him. I'll bet he had $3,000 to $5,000 more than if he had quoted his own salary.

Leon felt the second year was harder than the first, but he was going steady with Donna then, the girl he later married.

Because of that he said, "Boy, I really wanted to back out." But he didn't, and it turned out real well. His bosses couldn't get done saying good things about him and his work.

Leon has turned out to be a better farmer than I was, and *I think all my children are doing a lot better than I did, but they should. What I learned from my dad, I passed on to them. Now they have the wealth and wisdom of TWO generations in their lives!* They can learn from our ideas and mistakes and go on from there, improving and building on them. Even though parents do well, it is so exciting to see young people move on further from there and excel even more.

The grandsons and I, Leon's three boys and I, were chatting one time and I said, "Do you know why you guys are so good? First of all, you've got a good mother and dad and secondly, your grandpa gave you all the good he had. If that isn't enough, you can take your dad's good and your mother's good and a little good from your grandparents, and man, you guys gotta turn out *wonderful.*" That got them going!

I had a funny time with my grandson, David, when he was about 13. He and two other grandsons of mine were working in the milking parlor when I opened the door and walked in. I exclaimed, "What a handsome bunch of fellows I see here. You can't go anywhere else and find three such handsome guys working together. Now, do you know where you got those handsome looks? I used to be handsome too, like you guys."

In a tone of shock mixed with sympathy, David asked, "Grandpa, what happened?"

"I'm so glad you asked," I replied, laughing. "It's obvious that I gave away my good looks because your grandma Grace kept hers!"

They got a kick out of that.

The Bible mentions in several places (Deut. 6:7, Titus 2: 2-5) that older men and women should teach the younger men and women the good ways of the Lord and righteous living. If there is anything in our society in which we are falling short, I think it is that. Many parents and grandparents live so far from their loved ones they don't see their children or grandchildren for a year at a time. I feel bad for those grandchildren because my family has been so blessed; we see our grandchildren every week or two. If it goes three weeks, we think it's long. If you can be located so that you can have family reunions oftener, that is a tremendous blessing. It is amazing what it does in building character in young children. The things money can't buy are the love of your family, your friends, good health, and the promise of eternal life.

Although I was only four years old or so, I still remember sitting on my grandpa's lap and combing his beard. He'd tell me stories of what happened fifty years before. That was exciting to a 4 year old. It might not have been to him, but it sure was to me.

Chapter Eighteen

Our Children Remember Their Growing-Up Years

"I am blessed more than I ever realized to have had him as my dad."
—Sharon Ziegler Martin

In June, 2004, our children got together to talk about things they remember about their "growing-up-years" in our home. Although I wasn't there that night, I was told that the conversation was hilarious, and I can believe it, because most of them are able to give quick answers that can come out pretty funny. All of them are parents themselves now, so that also affects their thinking.

Sometimes children can be our harshest critics as they see us at home, without any pretense or mask (although I don't think I ever put on a different manner in public than at home). For their own "protection," I will not identify who said what, although in some cases, their comments may give away who is speaking.

My children speak:

How the Daily Milking and Farm Work Were Their "Favorite" Things To Do

"As we got older and had to help to milk, Dad would always say, 'Go get started and I will be there.' Then we would wonder when would he

show up. Sometimes when it took really long, we would decide, 'We don't think he likes milking anymore than we do.'"

"In the mornings, when it was time to go to the barn to work, we would stay in bed as long as we could, and then suddenly, one of us would get up, dress as quickly as possible and run out to the barn. We had the rule that the first one there could be the first to leave and go back in the house. So we would race each other to get to the barn—not because we were eager to work, but because we wanted to be the first one out of there, the first one in the house and in the shower to get ready for school."

"Dad had the philosophy that nobody should ever be standing around, that idleness was really wrong, and everybody should always be busy at work. If he ever saw one of us not working, he would immediately give us a job to do. Consequently, when we saw Dad driving in the lane, we would run and hide. Now, occasionally when I want my son to mow the lawn or something, I can't find him. I know what is REALLY going on! I remember how it was."

"Dad never took the time to play with us, and I missed that. It was almost as though he had the idea: 'If you have time to play, there is work to be done.' In fact, I remember one Sunday afternoon about 16 years ago when I was pitching ball in my front yard with my own son and Dad pulled into the driveway. I actually felt a little funny, a little guilty, that he had 'caught' me playing! A carry-over from my own childhood."

How They Felt About Discipline and Punishments

"We don't really remember getting any whippings from Dad, but most of the disciplining was done by Mom, making us sit on a chair."

"Hold on there, I do remember getting a belt whipping from Dad one time."

"Was that out in the barn?"

"Yeah, that's where most of our work was done, and he probably caught me not working one time."

"Maybe it was more because of your wrong attitude."

"Yeah, I think that is right. I was probably somewhat rebellious and pushed him to his limit."

"*I don't really remember ever seeing my dad get mad—or my mom either. Both of them were pretty easy-going . . . except that they did make us work . . . not that it hurt us any.*"

"*It paid off in the future in that we all seem to enjoy doing the work we do.*"

Reminiscing About the Family Trips

"*When we took a family trip, the question was never asked of the children: 'Are you having fun?' We never had reservations made ahead of time. Instead, we drove as far as we could in one day (Dad LOVED to drive!) and often would get to a motel about 9:00 p.m.*"

"*We would beg our parents to stop at a motel that had a pool, and I remember getting to one (at 9:00 p.m., of course) in New England, and the water temperature was probably around 50 to 55 degrees. Although it was cold, a couple of us got in and swam anyway.*"

"*I was always afraid of water and hated it. I do remember getting to the motels late and often all seven of us would sleep in a room with just two double beds—to save money, of course.*"

"*Pop was not tight with money, per se. What I mean is Pop would never do anything frivolous on vacations, but on the farm he wasn't tight with money. Pop would pay whatever it took to do whatever he felt needed to be done.*"

"*Remember the time we saw Disney World in 2 hours? All Dad's friends and our friends would come back from Florida and rave about how wonderful Disney World was, that it was the highlight of their trip. So, when we were in Florida, we went early in the morning, so early that we were actually there before it opened. We bought our tickets, went in and went to the first two or three attractions before any lines had formed. By the time we had done that, everywhere we looked there were lines of people waiting, and none of us wanted to do that, so Dad said, 'Let's go,' and we agreed with him and we left.*"

"*As a matter of fact, I feel the same way yet today about Disney World!*"

Thoughts on Handling Responsibilities

"When I was around 16 years old, Dad and I took a 'cow trip' to Florida. When we got there, Dad had to attend some dairy meeting all day and he just told me to do whatever I wanted to do. I don't think I would ever give that kind of freedom to my son at that age. I guess he trusted me to stay out of trouble—and I did! I remember I was so naïve on that trip that I didn't know what a valet was. When this man came up to me and asked for the car keys so he could go and bring my car to me, I thought to myself: 'What is this? I can go and get my own car. I don't need you to do it for me!'"

"Back then, it wasn't like it is today. The dangers were so much less, and people weren't as quick to get violent as they are now."

"I don't know if Dad intended to make us grow up fast by giving us so much responsibility so young or what. I know I don't allow my kids to do near what I did at their ages."

"When I think of it—that when I was 12 Dad allowed me to drive equipment costing $75,000 through the fields—it still amazes me. I know it made me feel important and powerful to do these things, but today as I look back on it, it was quite risky—for him and for me—and I wouldn't allow my kids to do it. It did make me feel special to be allowed to do things that my cohorts or peers weren't allowed by their fathers to do. It probably helped tone up our driving skills also."

"On the other hand, I wouldn't want my boy hitchhiking 400 miles a day like I did back then. That wouldn't be so good today."

"We often disagreed on how to do things on the farm, but Pop would say, 'This is what my idea is, but we'll do it your way because you're the one who'll have to live with it.'"

"When it was time to buy a car, we bought the one I liked the best. It wasn't the most practical one, of course, but it was the one most pleasing to my eyes and Dad didn't disagree."

"When we got engaged, Mom and Dad never told me that because I was only 18, I was too young. However, if my daughter would want to do that at that age, I would think it is a bit too young."

Our family in August 2002. Seated left to right: Theresa Wickert, Lynn Ziegler. Standing: Bonnie Myer, Sharon Martin, Victor and Grace Ziegler, Leon Ziegler.

Their Co-Workers on the Farm

"*Some of the people Dad hired were questionable characters, to say the least. Some were easy to work with and others wore your patience thin.*"

"*There were a few women who were better at milking than the men!*"

"*I know Dad thought he was doing a good thing by helping out some guys who had been drug addicts and had been 'rehabilitated' by Teen Challenge or some guys who had been released from prison and couldn't find jobs. He would bring them to the farm to work. Most of them had been city guys and had no idea how to do the farm work, so we would have to redo their work or repair what they had done.*"

"*Not only that, it is a fact that older guys rarely learn things from younger guys, but instead younger guys often learn things from older guys. Dad never seemed to have given this fact a thought. These guys he would bring in told us things about life on the street and gave us a real education.*"

"Fortunately, our Christian upbringing outweighed the things these guys would say and was the greater influence in our lives."

Living with the Old People in the Nursing Home

"Remember when they had the old people there living with us, eating with us at every meal?"

"Yeah, the table was crowded with people. We really didn't have a time when we could talk and eat together privately as a family, sharing the exciting things that were happening in our lives."

"It was fun sitting and talking to some of those older ladies. I think some of them loved us as though we were their grandchildren. We had to be careful, though, that we talked to all of them and didn't show partiality."

"Most of the time it was nice having them there living with us, but there were a few times when we felt we were the ones who didn't belong there."

"Because of the way we were brought up, I always thought I would also try to raise my kids to enjoy being with all kinds of people, of all races, young and old, to appreciate older folks even though they themselves are young."

Memories of Their Grandparents

"I remember my grandparents (Abraham and Rhoda Ziegler) well. I always enjoyed going to their house in Reistville. They had a tricycle there, and I would ride it across the street and all around in their neighbor's driveway. I would think I was 'big stuff' to be able to do that!"

"Do you remember that little room they had upstairs next to their bedroom? I always thought that room was scary."

"Yeah. Me too."

"What was in that room? Did any of you ever go in it to find out?"

"Just a bed. At least, as far as I know."

"Grandma and Grandpa always served ice cream with pretzel sticks. We would eat it without spoons and use the pretzel sticks to scoop up the ice cream."

"Grandma and Grandpa would always listen to what we had to say. We could feel their love."

"I remember Grandpa as a real 'workhorse!' He loved to dig out tree stumps."

"Yeah, I remember when we made a fence and he chopped the logs for the fence. He was a real sweat machine."

Observations About Life with Their Dad

"Dad wasn't afraid of work either, but he was more of an organizer. He was the brains behind a project, the one with the ideas, an innovator."

"Yes, he would get the job started–tell everyone what to do, give everyone a job, and then he'd get lost. He wouldn't be the one doing the grunt labor. Later, he'd come back and see how you were doing."

"I often remember feeling kind of edgy when Dad would get up to talk, because I never knew what he was going to say or do."

"But then, don't most teenagers feel that way about their parents?"

"Maybe it was because Dad was never intimidated by anyone. He always just spoke out on any subject he had feelings about."

"Dad had the gift of being able to talk anybody into anything. If you believed something and knew you were right, and even thought he might have been wrong, if he talked to you long enough, he would convince you that his point of view was right and you had been wrong."

" If Dad had a nickname, it would be Victor Ziegler = 'Victor Digger.' This was an in-house name for him—among the family. My boys especially knew him by that name, and it wasn't meant to be derogatory. It was just a pet name because he just loved to run the pay loader and push dirt around. That was better than any nocturnal activities."

"With anything that they do, all people have certain strengths and weaknesses. With the pay loader, Pop could grade something by eye and do everything real good. His weakness was that he could always leverage that thing so hard, even though it was built like a tank. However, he also knew that if he leveraged it too hard, he could break something. If he *did, he would say, 'Hmmm, that engineer must not have built it tough enough.'"*

"You see, he could take a 10 ton truck and put 20 tons on it and say, 'Hmmm, why did that spring break?' And I would think, 'Now, come on, Pop, we know why it broke. You know why it broke.' He could frustrate you like that."

"He raked and leveled more concrete in the 70's than most people did as he made corn cribs, trench silos and other things."

"I brought a guy in to talk about putting up a free stall barn. He came and looked around and said, 'Well, there is a LOT of concrete around here.' That was Pop's thing."

"Concrete was always nice to work on. Everybody else was working in mud, but Dad poured concrete. He didn't spare on that. His theory always was, 'Pour it thin just in case you ever have to break it up!' (He didn't want to have to work too hard at breaking it up!)"

"He always was a progressive farmer, but then HIS dad was also in his day."

"Zieglers tend to not be too conservative when it comes to moving ahead."

"Think smart, work less!"

"I don't remember spending a lot of time with Dad when I was growing up. He was very busy with the farm and enjoyed a day's hard work. Looking back, I know that I had the security of knowing that I would be taken care of physically, that there would always be food on the table and clothing to wear, plus little extra surprises. My dad was a great provider."

"Our dad never had any hobbies. He just enjoyed people."

"He used to think it was so foolish and a waste of time when he heard of someone he knew actually going to a restaurant for breakfast. However, he has changed his opinion on that, especially since he has been sick."

"He actually told me the other morning he was going to the diner for breakfast, adding that 'Phares Eshelman will probably be there about this time.' He has even said that since he is having to slow down because of his illness, he is learning to enjoy some of these other things."

"I agree. He has learned to enjoy these things a little bit. Over the last year or two, I've called him now and then on the way to work and say, 'Where can I meet you this morning?' He would say, 'Where do you want to go?' Then we would get together at one of a half dozen local restaurants."

"I think he has learned over the years that relationships are more important than things."

"Dad had the gift of being an evangelist, always bringing the conversation around to the Lord. He sure had a way with words."

"When we were with Dad, it wasn't long before we would be laughing because of one of his stories or jokes. He sure kept us all healthy with laughter, and we all learned that laughter is good medicine."

"Dad could always take a joke as well as give it."

"In a negative situation, Dad had a way of seeing the best, the positive aspects. He would say, 'It could have been worse,' or 'That was a good learning experience.'"

"Did any of you ever see Dad cook . . . anything?"

"I don't think he knows how to boil water."

"I don't think he even knows how to make toast in a toaster!"

Some Days That Were Special

"I remember birthdays as a special time. We were always made to feel special because Mom always made us a cake, we would sing the Happy Birthday song, and there would be presents."

"Mom always made it happen."

"I think that was a project of Mom's—to make us feel special that

Our three daughters. Left to right: Bonnie, Theresa, and Sharon. August 1999.

day. Dad may have had some ideas about our gifts, and he paid for them, but Mom carried it out . . . made the cake, bought the gifts, etc."

"In some families, birthdays come and go and don't mean much, but in ours, celebrating them was a tradition, one that I do with my own family now."

"Mom often played table games with us, especially on Sunday afternoons, but Dad always took his nap then."

"If we didn't do that on a Sunday afternoon, we went visiting. We especially enjoyed going to homes that had children the same ages as we were."

Their Reactions to Their Mother's Abuse

"I am amazed that Dad could forgive the man. Most guys would be so angry they would go and fight it out with that person."

"I am just so glad that my parents stayed together and gave us a stable home to grow up in."

"I don't see how they survived this. Mom must have been just so scared! I'm not being critical because I have no idea how I would respond if I were ever put in that situation."

"I'm just so happy they stayed together."

"In today's world, they wouldn't have."

"People leave each other for a whole lot less."

Changes They've Noted Since Their Dad Has Become Ill

"He has more time now."

"He has a different perspective on things, a new insight into what life in the field of medicine is all about."

"Pop's first response when he learned he had lymphoma was like a deer caught in the headlights. He NEVER expected to go through anything like this."

"He expected to live healthy and die, and now he is caught in a quandary. Wow!"

"What he expected isn't happening. He is dealing with something here that he never expected to deal with in his life."

"*Everything that happens to us, even when we sin, God allows. I believe God allowed this in his life right now to teach him some things that maybe he would never have learned any other way, whether it is being more sensitive to certain things or what.*"

"*He was doing everything right. He ate healthy foods, avoided chemicals and artificial products and drugs . . .*"

"*We always kidded him: 'Eat healthy, exercise, and die anyway!'*"

"*At the present moment I am being blessed by my dad more than ever. His calm spirit in the midst of this situation just puts us all more at ease.*"

"*He knows where he is going and that is all that really matters.*"

Lessons Learned at Home

"*Over the years, one of the things they taught us is that you don't sit around waiting for things to be handed to you, you work for it. We were never taught to sit around and expect everybody else to do things for us. Maybe we weren't always taught how to sit down and relax or even to slow down, but they gave us a good work ethic.*"

"*The Bible teaches that 'to whom much is given, much is required.' (Luke 12:48) We have been blessed with a lot, whether it is wisdom, physical strength, abilities, or whatever it is, and it is all from the Lord. And if you have been given much, you are supposed to work with your hands to have something to give to those who are in need.*"

"*Dad will give money and advice and Mom is always willing to help anyone, anywhere, anytime. Both of them are compassionate and outgoing, using their own unique gifts to help others in any way they can.*"

"*That is part of the heritage they gave us. They taught us the joy of serving others. I get a real joy out of making someone else feel good.*"

"*I am so thankful for my Christian heritage that was passed on to me by my parents. They chose to follow God and I wouldn't be where I am today if they wouldn't have laid a foundation for me to build upon. I am just so grateful.*"

"*I can still picture their bedroom door hanging open and seeing Mom and Dad kneeling together by their bed at night, and I'm sure they were praying for us. We needed all the prayer we could get.*"

Chapter Nineteen

My Foundational Beliefs and Rules of Life

"I know whom I have believed, and am persuaded that He is able to keep that which I have committed unto Him against that day."
—2 Timothy 1:12b (KJV)

One of the most frequent questions that I get asked from believers as well as unbelievers is "How come all these funny, different, unusual and miraculous things happened to you, Victor?"

The miracles, the mysteries and the memories–you'd think I belong to the 3-M company! I really can't explain why God chooses one person and not another.

Although I am a poor reader, my parents gave me such a basic knowledge of the Scripture, I can quote almost anything. However, I usually need help from somebody to tell me where to find it.

When I go to give a speech, my notes consist of only four or five words, my key words, and they will each bring a mental picture to me so that I can talk on that block of words for five minutes or so. Then I will have another block of words, and that will keep me going until I want to wind down to a climax or whatever. I never wrote anything out yet for a speech or sermon, but I always got invited back, for some reason.

About 30 years ago Grace and I attended a Sunday School class meeting. During the evening we were sharing stories and having many belly laughs. I am the kind of person that if someone feeds me an idea or even just a word or two, that will trigger a whole story.

Anyway, we were telling stories and with me, the stories gotta be building or constructive or they've gotta stop. About 20 people were there and everyone was laughing.

Suddenly, one dear sister very seriously interrupted the mood with this question. "Victor, don't you know the Bible says you have to give an account for every idle word?" (Matthew 12: 36, KJV)

Looking her directly in the eye, I responded, "Sister, I didn't hear one idle word here yet tonight."

In shock, she objected, "Victor, how can you say that? How can you *say* that?"

"I'll tell you why I said it. During the last half hour we've been enjoying exchanging stories and family life happenings that are humorous and funny and everybody's been breaking out laughing. It went on so good that it takes me back to one of my favorite Scriptures, Proverbs 17:22a (KJV) that says, 'A merry heart doeth good like a medicine.' This means that Christians should smile and share the joy of the Lord and let the world know that nobody enjoys living more than we do. You know, I just saved you a $100 doctor bill. I'd be willing to split it in half and go 50/50 with you."

She shut up and joined in the laughter.

When I get out of bed every morning I say, "Lord, what's up today? Show me something or motivate me to do something or to say something that will make a difference in our family, in our community or in our church." Or I might say, "Lord, send someone to cross my path or stimulate my mind to think of something I can do for somebody to the glory of God, so I can have the joy of watching them progress and come to a new relationship with their family and the Spirit of God." I think it's all based on the simple faith of saying, "Lord, I believe, but I'm so weak, help my unbelief and help me to increase in my faith."

My greatest concern is that I am more enthusiastic than most people, and I don't want to turn an unbeliever off. So, I often kind of back off a little bit. As the saying goes, "You can lead a horse to water, but you can't make him drink." I try not to be too forceful in witnessing lest I lose them. Actually, if you are really sincere and looking out for their interests, that very seldom happens. However, I try to be sensitive that way.

Sometimes I have very bold expressions, and if I am around my brothers, I don't mind speaking frankly and forcefully because they understand it and we all have fun with it. But some people don't know me that well or aren't on the same wavelength, so to speak, and they misunderstand. Even if it comes out backwards, I'm willing to go back and apologize. Some of my best friends now are persons I stepped on 20 years ago and then told them, "I was wrong. That didn't sound right. What I said could have meant two different things, and I didn't realize it at the time. I am sorry." Then those people became my friends because they found out I was for real. They saw I wasn't just trying to be a smart aleck.

The more good things I express in life, the more good things seem to happen to me. I believe it is a basic scriptural principle. If you use one talent, then there will be two, and as you use those two, soon there will be three and so on. You don't realize it but they just keep building. After a while, you look back with wonder and say, "Wow! What happened?" As you use your talents, you keep getting more . . . and it's all given to you by the grace of God.

I definitely know I am not the greatest prayer warrior, yet I think if I skipped one day in asking for divine guidance, I would really be in trouble. Some people say, "You ought to spend an hour or two in prayer every morning."

Then I'd explain, "Well, it doesn't happen that way with me, but I have shared many a prayer and many a gospel hymn while plowing a field or driving 50 miles per hour down the road in a truck. I know some people, if they would have been riding with me, would have thought I was nuts because every once in a while my fist will bounce off the seat and I will shout, 'Hallelujah!' you know. And really, when I am alone and when it is appropriate, I have made it a practice to sincerely, expressively and verbally say, 'Thank You, Jesus,' a hundred times a day. I do it when I am alone because I do not want to offend unbelievers."

The attitude that you have about life is so important. I observed that in my dad in that I never saw him really discouraged. He would be optimistic about even the worst situations. One thing that sticks with me occurred after he had been hurt so bad in an automobile accident. When he was in the hospital in critical condition, there were several nights when I stayed in his room with him and slept on the hospital floor.

One morning about 2:00 or so, he suddenly sat up in bed and began describing what he was seeing. He described streets paved with gold and scenes straight from the book of Revelation. I thought he was dying. It was so impressive and I sat there totally alert and listened with both ears!

When I told him later on what he had done and seen, he admitted, "I'm not too sure that I remember all that." The memory had faded for him.

As time went on, he often made statements like, "Life has been so good. The Lord has been so good. *The darker the night, the brighter the light, so we have nothing to fear.* It doesn't matter what happens when you know where you are going. *When you know your destination, it doesn't matter which way you go home.*"

Many people never had a wonderful heritage like that, and aren't aware of God's wonderful promises.

A Mennonite preacher once asked me, "Why don't you come over to the Mennonite church? We need you in the Mennonite church."

"I would, but you ain't got enough water to baptize me," I answered him, adding, "in our church it takes nine barrels of water to baptize me, but in your church, it only takes nine drops of water to sprinkle you!"

The sad part is that on a Sunday morning if we get nine drops of rain, the Brethren all stay at home and the River Brethren go boating. They're not committed. Symbols of each denomination are wonderful if they really *stand for something*.

All of life is just like planting seeds. We think we got to water and we got to push 'em, but God waters and He gives the increase. All we must do is sow the seed. At times I've had to think, "How foolish did I look?"

More times than not, the very people that laughed at me later turned around in their thinking. For example, the minister's wife whom I met as we were leaving Russia who had laughed at me one night because I chose not to drink alcohol and then came the next day and asked if I would pray for her and her husband. What a tremendous feeling! To be made a fool of one day and then be so blessed that the same persons who called you a fool wanted you to pray for them when they were facing difficult moments.

So sticking by my beliefs wasn't done in vain. And it is never in vain! Sometimes the positive or good results happen more quickly or are more noticeable than at other times. The only times when it doesn't seem to work is when we are desperate about doing things *our way*, and we want human glory instead of giving God the glory. That's the only way it won't work. Then it WILL backfire on you. God overlooks a lot of things, but whenever we steal the glory from Him, the minute we do that, we lose the blessing.

I feel so strongly that I'd rather be a fool for God's sake in this world than make the foolish mistake of rejection, keeping silent, or not making a witness that many people do and they never get to enjoy the blessing. The beauty of it is, you don't have to wait for heaven to enjoy it; it starts right now and gets better and better and better. If people aren't told that, they will never know it. All of life has to be lived with that attitude.

It is amazing what happens when you recognize that. Hey, we are going to do whatever we can to the best of our ability and give God the credit and the glory and let the Lord determine the level of what happens. Whether it is just a small thing or a big thing, the attitude we have in doing it makes it equal in the eyes of God. In my opinion, an "attitude of gratitude" is the true key to success. At least, that's been my experience. Every time, if I feel I am tending to lose that gratitude, I kinda feel like my feet are slipping in deep water and I am gonna drown. Then I remind myself, "You will never drown praising the Lord. He will always keep your voice above the water because He wants to hear the glory!"

It is so enriching and energizing to think about all the people who have MUCH more capabilities than I ever had and what they *could be doing* to the glory of God. However, many persons end up being bored or "burned out," because their accomplishments are motivated by selfish interests in one way or another, with no enthusiasm, and are done for monetary gain or worldly fame. They never know the joy of commitment, and they are missing wonderful blessings!

I sometimes ask people, "Why do you waste your whole life cheating yourself?"

They question me, "What do you mean?"

"Well, there is *so much* out there waiting to be unleashed to the person who believes and wants to do something to the glory of God. Why would you cheat yourself of another blessing?"

Recently, Grace and I went into a restaurant and our waitress was a beautiful young lady who appeared to be about 19 years old. She wrote up our order and was very courteous, but didn't blink an eye or crack a smile.

When she came back, I said, "Ma'am, come here a minute. I got to tell you something."

And she came. Then I leaned toward her and said, "Tell me one thing: Why do you hide your million-dollar smile?"

She broke out laughing, and I continued, "If you would know the difference that makes! Think about what it does to you and how it enriches the lives of other people. I shouldn't really tell you this, but on top of all that, it is a proven fact that waitresses that smile get bigger tips than those that don't."

Of course, that was more fuel for the fire and just made her laugh a little more, you know. These waitresses are usually able to separate fact from fiction!

It cost me an extra dollar that day, but it was worth it. It was worth it! And you know what? If I ever get back to that restaurant again, I would *love* to walk in there and see that beautiful smile on that face again, because I know that smile couldn't leave her after that day. That just has a lasting effect.

She probably went home and told her mother, "I met a really crazy guy at work today!"

Nobody is convincing to others if he or she is always complaining, grouchy and down-in-the-mouth. We gotta be able to see sunshine on a rainy day because we see beyond the clouds. We know there is a reason for everything, and without the rainy season, we wouldn't enjoy the full fruit of the harvest. Once we understand that, then we have to tell each other and remind each other of all our blessings. If we don't, we will soon fall back into the same old trap of griping and being negative.

When people argue, "Well, I'm a Christian but I don't need to go to church." I tell them, "You're kidding yourself. You *can't* make it on your own. 'You are not to forsake the assembling of yourselves together as the manner of some is.'" (Hebrews 10:25a, KJV) If you want a real live illustration just go to the fireplace and take out a red-hot coal. In five minutes that coal is cold, gray and dead-looking, but if you put it back, it becomes revived from the warmth of the others. That's a perfect illustration of how we are to live. We can practice that in every area of our life, spiritually, physically and financially. You can believe this with confidence because it works.

It works every time because it is based on the instruction of the Bible. "All Scripture is given by inspiration of God, and is profitable for doctrine, for reproof, for correction, for instruction in righteousness." (II Timothy 3:16, KJV) If something in God's Word steps on people's toes, they say it contains errors, or has omissions and they want to rewrite it to their own satisfaction. However, in II Timothy 3:15, KJV, we read the Scriptures "are able to make thee wise unto salvation through faith which is in Christ Jesus." Once we surrender to that fact and to using God's Word as our guideline, we can really enjoy living.

I am also convinced that good attitudes produce good health. A mind-set of dissatisfaction, complaining, never seeing anything good in anybody just creates a lot of health and social problems. It's even been proven medically. People hate to admit it because they don't want to change. They think, "It's my right to have owned this grudge for the last 15 years, and I'm gonna continue to be mad at my sister."

I love to tell them to their face, "Well, your sister is enjoying life, but you're sure a miserable wretch. You're not hurting *her,* by not forgiving. If she has forgiven you and you keep harboring anger, spite, and revenge, you are paying a big price."

People need to be told that. That's why we keep preaching the Word. The truth is the only thing that sets you free, and the truth has to be repeated over and over again.

During my lifetime, as I worked in farming and business, one of the things that made life exciting was that I had a hard time planning my days in advance. When you are working with nature and the weather, you have to be flexible. So often you think you have everything planned that you are going to do on a certain day and then you get an outburst of clouds and rain and your plans all must be changed. Someone has said, "To make God laugh, make plans!" He can change your plans in the blink of an eye.

When that happens, you go to plan B, which might be getting your equipment ready so that when the sun does shine, you don't need to sharpen the knives, grease the machine or put fuel in the tank. You get everything ready to go. When the sun says, "Go," you're ready. You can always make up the lost time if you don't sit back, grumble and complain.

When you are enthusiastic and upbeat, it rubs off on your coworkers. Over the years I had several of my employees tell me that they were offered more money from other farmers, but they didn't accept those jobs because they enjoyed working where there was optimism and enthusiasm. When something went wrong at our farm, they didn't hear cursing and everybody getting scolded. Instead, our crew would say, "Let's find out why this happened and then maybe none of us will make that same mistake again next week."

Learning from the experience and taking steps to not repeat it are what really matters. You don't spend your time condemning everybody, but you study what went wrong. Then you say to your men, "Do you know what? If you do this and that, everything works right. But if you make one wrong move, it could wreck the equipment or even cost you your life." People soon pick up on that.

A mistake, regardless of how bad it is, is never the end of the world. It is just another opportunity to correct something and then move on. Instead of being a stumbling block, it can be a stepping stone. In fact, when I think about it, you can take a pile of rocks that look terrible, but when you roll the smooth side up, each one can become a stepping stone.

However, they *do* look awful in the rough. Everybody is gonna trip over stones like that, but they can become stepping stones to somebody who looks at them with a different attitude. And that is true in every facet of life. Without an optimistic attitude, it's just doom and gloom, and doom and gloom breeds more doom and gloom. After awhile there is no hope at all.

Life can be cruel and bad things happen, yet negativity just breeds more negativity. I haven't seen the film, "The Passion of Christ," yet, but I'd like to. But, do you know what? A lot of people died a cruel death like Jesus did, but there is one big difference. He carried the burden of the sins of the whole world. Therefore, I believe the psychological and mental grief must have been a lot more painful for Him than the nails and the torture. *None of it* was His own.

We read in the daily papers about people all around the world being tortured and terrorized and that must be terrible. The only way they can handle it is if they know "God's grace is sufficient." When they have that assurance, they are willing to

I loved to make my family laugh! Seated: Mae Patches. Standing left to right: Norman Kline, Vivian Ziegler, Verna Kline, Earl Ziegler, Grace Ziegler, Jake Kurtz, Victor Ziegler, Glen Ziegler. Photo date: Sept. 21, 2002.

die at the stake rather than surrender their faith in God. They know that the Lord Jesus Christ is their Savior, not only for getting them through today but for all eternity. We know that all of us were born to die, so we will have all eternity to praise the Lord and to be in the presence of God. That is certainly worth more than 70 or 80 years here! Nobody would trade a million dollars in cash for a little bit of interest money, but that is what so many people do. They trade away all the good things of eternity for a little bit of temporary satisfaction and momentary pleasures here.

I really believe there is something positive in every negative and many times it takes the negative to *bring out* the positive. It takes them both to make it work, and life is just like that. You can't enjoy the blessing of rain if you've never had a dry spell. You can't enjoy the mountain top if you've never been in the valley. And on and on it goes.

I always enjoyed life and appreciated it, but boy, I got a much deeper feeling and sense of the meaning of life the last 12 weeks than I ever had before. Now life *is* one day at a time. One day at a time. It's not one year or 20 years still to look forward to. When you're younger and you've never had a sick day, that's hard to comprehend.

One result of my little experience with illness is that it just makes me want to stand by a patient lying in a hospital bed or go and visit an elderly or sick person and give them encouragement. That makes me feel so useful and fulfilled.

Even though I did have financial losses, setbacks, a sick wife, accidental deaths of foster sons, ridicule, betrayals and disappointments, none of these things were ever a mental hindrance or blow to me to the extent that it would kill my enthusiasm. In those times of discouragement, the thought that went through my mind so often was, "The Lord gave and the Lord hath taken away. Blessed be the name of the Lord." (Job 1: 21b, KJV)

I was determined I am going to praise the Lord whether I have 50 cents in my pocket or $500,000. If the dollar volume affects my attitude toward God or my fellow man, who am I worshipping? Who am I holding in the highest esteem? I often have to think about that.

My *biggest* challenge is that people still call me and they'll say, "How does it feel to be a multimillionaire?" And I can't convince them! I don't want to go around spending a whole day going through the history and the financial statements to explain everything to them. They'll still believe what they wanna, you know.

So, I just say to them, "The Lord's been good. I always had enough to eat, the roof never leaked, I never had to sleep in a cold, damp house, and that's all that *really* matters. With all the things that went wrong, I always had a dollar left over for charity or a ministry or to help someone in need."

My pop was like that. If necessary, he would give the shirt off his back. To earn money to be able to give groceries to a poor family, he often chose to sweat it out and work hard. That was all I knew, the model I saw when I was growing up, and that was such a blessing.

I saw most of my dad's (what I would call) "wealthy" friends (in that day, if you had $100,000 you were considered wealthy) die ten years and more younger than he did. They were suffering in the hospital or struggling with family problems and weren't too happy. After observing that and reflecting on it, I thought, boy, I wouldn't trade living a life of faith in order to have all those material resources. How can a person be happy while having to hold on to all those "things" with a tight fist?

So, if I had my life to live over, I'd do it all over again. Next time I'd try to be a little more "wise like a serpent and still be harmless like a dove." (Matthew 10:16b, KJV) I do recognize that I made a number of mistakes. There are some people that the more you help them, the more you hurt them.

It's sometimes a tough job to decide–when you are helping this guy and when you are hurting him. Sometimes it's better to let a guy almost drown than to bail him out before he learns to swim! If you grab a person struggling in the water, he will never learn to swim. But if you get down underneath him and lift him up, he don't need help after awhile because he will have learned to swim. That's true in a physical sense as well as spiritually and financially.

A few of my mistakes happened because I was too quick to help. Perhaps these were caused by my sympathetic spirit, and then I always had $10,000 or $20,000 at my fingertips. I never had cash in the bank or a savings account. Oh, I'd pay a bill of $50 out of a checking account, but what happened more often was that I'd receive income of $50,000 and have $40,000 worth of bills with $10,000 left for myself. I never kept a large amount of money in a checking account because I didn't want the bank to make money on me! I considered it to be poor stewardship to give it to them interest free while I was paying 8% or 9% to them for a loan. I was cautious about that.

I warned people, "Don't ever let anybody kill your enthusiasm for helping but be sure to search for wisdom, because in many cases you may be 'entertaining angels unawares.'" (Hebrews 13:2, KJV)

However, sometimes the devil sneaks in the back door! You must pray for wisdom to discern. The devil is capable of putting you out of business, hurting your testimony, and causing much destruction.

Once in a while someone in my family would really kid me and say, "Look, you are helping this guy over here but you won't give me a quarter of a million dollars."

And they were right. I admitted it and said, "Do you know what? You're worth a whole lot more than he ever was! You're doing well financially, you have a nice family, a successful little business, and you are so blessed." And although they all recognize it, I'm glad they bring it up. It helps to remind me to keep praying for that wisdom, and I thank them for it.

I have a real concern that in our modern, affluent society we are all hurrying here and there, living in our plush homes and enjoying living, but don't give enough input to the next generations. In Psalm 71:18, TLB, it says: "Now that I am old and gray . . . give me time to tell this new generation (and their children too) about all your mighty miracles."

Not only in this verse, but in other Scripture texts also, we are given a mandate that the older we get, the more we are supposed to support our children and grandchildren and teach them the good things of life—whether it be about faith in God or the way to live, the way to eat, the way to respond. If we don't teach them and pass it on, nobody else will. If we lose just one generation to moral degradation, the whole world, the whole country, the whole church is doomed!

Although we are already starting to see a little bit of that happening, *there is still hope to reverse it!*

As long as we create moral awareness, good things can continue to happen. However, if good people remain silent, our society will not change for the better. Even though it may mean we will be ridiculed, we've *got to* speak out against the wrong and share our faith for the sake of the generations that follow us.

Chapter Twenty

Battling Lymphoma

"I don't want to get into the 'Guinness Book of World Records' for this!"
—Victor K. Ziegler (after the doctor tapped 8 liters
of lymph fluid from him)

(Note: This chapter was written based on recorded conversations
with Victor between March and June, 2004.)

At the annual Ziegler Christmas luncheon on December 13, 2003, my niece, Marie Kline Haynes, whispered to her husband, Ron, "What in the world is the matter with Victor?" She explained months later that she had noticed my strange ashen skin color immediately and the fact that I was thinner than usual. As a hospice nurse in Virginia, Marie was familiar with various physical signs of serious illness, and she spotted it in me immediately. Others in my family, who had seen me more often and who did not have that trained eye, never noticed a thing, and I myself didn't have a clue that anything was wrong.

In early January, 2004, after I had eaten a fairly small meal, I commented to Grace, "I feel like I've eaten a big dinner."

I was somewhat puzzled because I knew I had eaten only a small amount of food. I told myself, "Victor, you are just thinking wrong."

The next day I still felt full, but I didn't give it much thought. However, each day this feeling kept building and by the third week of January, my abdomen felt hard and looked like I had swallowed a football!

I also was feeling tired, a feeling I seldom had all during my life. In mid-January during a Sunday morning church service, I just didn't have the energy to stand up with the congregation to sing the closing hymn. "What's going on here?" I asked myself.

Finally, on a Friday night near the end of January, I went to the Outpatient Section of the Good Samaritan Hospital in Lebanon, PA, and met with a doctor there. After a brief examination, he said, "There are several ugly viruses going around that we don't know how to treat. I believe you have a lot of gas that is being caused by something which will probably correct itself."

Not quite satisfied with that analysis, three days later I visited a new doctor that I had never met before. Of course, I didn't have a family doctor so I just stopped in at his office in Myerstown around 7:30 p.m. since the sign on the door said he had office hours until 8:00. After explaining to his secretary that I just stopped in to see if the doctor could see me for ten minutes, and I'd be happy if he could do that, she responded that he had nobody scheduled from 7:45 to 8:00 so I would be able to see him. Another miracle!

So I just sat down and waited.

He frankly told me, "This is more than gas. This is something serious."

I was really glad he was honest with me because he set me on the right road.

"If you choose to go my route, I'd be happy to take you on as a patient and work with you, but if not, feel free to come back any time," he said.

He advised me to see Dr. Pilkington, a surgeon, and to get a CAT (computerized axial tomography) scan, and I did. That was the beginning of locating the problem. Although I wasn't a fan of the medical community and all the tests and drugs involved with it, I would never push any alternative too far away, because I always wanted to at least look at it. As I said earlier, *if you have everything to gain and nothing to lose, for goodness sake, try it*. You might learn something. If it didn't work, you would learn that it didn't work, and you can go on looking for something else.

The scan showed that I had a large lymph tumor lying on the end of my stomach and overlapping on the small intestine and attached to the outside wall.

When the surgeon saw it, he said "Wow! When you look at that picture, I would guess it weighs 5 to 10 pounds!" He continued, "What is *really* filling you up though, is lymph fluid which is pushing up toward your liver and kidneys and is coming up toward your lungs, and that is why you are so tired."

Then the surgeon tapped out the excess lymph fluid and said, "I want to biopsy that tumor."

They took me to the operating room and took a lymph node out of my groin, did another CAT scan and tapped the fluid. Because I was under anesthesia, I don't really know what happened, but I suspect they did a hurried job. They only took out 2 liters full. I still had more than that, of course, but then the tumor might have been that big that it pushed them.

When that was finished, Dr. Pilkington said, "Now, I would really like you to see the cancer doctor, Dr. Ludwig."

"O.K.," I agreed, thinking maybe I could learn something and improve my health.

Dr. Ludwig was a woman, about 55 years old, and for my first appointment with her, Grace went along. She was very business-like and said, "I've received this report from the pathologist, and they are so confused. It looks like you have a low grade lymphoma cancer but it is acting like the wildest one we have ever seen."

She went on to say that the experts don't know what to think, what to recommend or what to do. Then she said, "I'll send you to the Hershey Medical Center tomorrow morning to have them test your bone marrow and do this and do that."

"Dr. Ludwig, did you look at the report of the CAT scan that I did take?" I countered. "What results did that show?"

Her prompt reply was curt and short: "No, I'm not here for you to ask *me* questions. I am here to ask *you* questions!"

At this first encounter, she was like a snippy little bull dog. (However after that, she was so nice. Now she is so genuinely concerned about me that *she phones me* to see how I am doing!)

Finally, after I had listened to her for awhile, I said, "Dr. Ludwig, do you know what? It's not really killing me. I don't like it, but if the experts are all confused, I hate to see people shooting in the dark, and it is dark already. I've heard of people who shot in the dark and killed their best friend! I'm the kind of guy who feels that when the experts are all confused, we should sit down for a couple days until the sun comes out and the dust settles. Then we can all get around the table and take a new look at it, and we can see more clearly."

Sure enough, at the beginning of the next week she had a second report and she said, "It's not as bad as we had thought."

They had saved enough sampling so that they were able to do a second analysis. If I had let her go, they would have . . . One thing I learned about the corruption in the medical system: If you are over 65, they milk Medicare all they can. They keep pushing you to take this test, take that test, and it goes on and on.

Finally, I told them, "Look, I'm willing to take any test, but I am a tax-paying American citizen. I don't want to bleed the system just for the sake of going through the motions, but if you think it is necessary, I'll be glad to cooperate so you can learn and I can learn."

Right before this happened, when we got serious about this, she had said, "I could give you four treatments of a medium to low dose of chemotherapy, four days in a row, skip two weeks, and I believe that would shrink the tumor. All the surgeons agree that it would be better to shrink it than to surgically remove it."

Evidently, the lymph nodes are that important that they didn't want to chop that whole bundle out.

I was glad to hear they did not want to take the surgical route and told them, "I would agree with you on that."

So, they gave me some forms to fill out, and they found out I had no insurance, nothing but Medicare. (We dropped it 27 years ago–all our insurance, and we never missed it.) Anyhow, till it was done, the doctor, a nurse, and a social worker all stood around my bedside and wondered, "What will we do with this guy?"

One said, "This could end up costing $100,000!"

"Don't worry about it," I responded, trying to assure them. "I never had a bill yet in my life that I couldn't pay. I don't have too much to back it up, but I got a lot of friends. God always makes a way."

I was asked to meet with the social worker twice, and she gave me all the options: How to go to the welfare system, how to go here, how to go there . . . how to milk the cow! I learned so much that I was embarrassed to sign up. I told all my friends, "They *really* taught me how to milk the cow–it just depends which cow it is!"

Between the tumor and the filling up with lymph fluid, my stomach got so tight that I felt I could hardly eat anymore. Finally, they tapped all the lymph fluid off and that relieved some of the pressure, but my stomach didn't go down that much. It just took the pressure off temporarily and made my stomach softer again.

After a period of three or four weeks, I got tapped the second time. It had reached the point where I could only eat 2 or 3 tablespoonfuls of food. Although I could have eaten more, the pressure on my stomach was that great that I could feel it pushing up my esophagus. Fortunately, every day I had a good bowel movement, although I may have skipped a day or two when I was hurting pretty bad.

Then the doctors suggested that I take one "round of four" low to medium treatments of chemotherapy to reduce the swelling and shrink the tumor. They said these would be low doses and I wouldn't get sick and wouldn't lose my hair, and that was true. When I finished that first round, Dr. Ludwig, my cancer doctor, requested that I go through a second round of four treatments.

As I was going through this and beginning the second round, I sensed the doctor was a little discouraged.

"I am not happy with your progress," she told me. "It's not going down."

However, I assured her, "Well, doctor, I am. There's something good happening. I can *feel* it, I *believe* it, and I *know* it! There's something changing in my system. Everything is easing up a bit, and I feel a little better."

Then she said, "I wanted to go away for a couple days, but I wanted to be sure you are getting turned around before I go. Would you take another CAT scan on Monday? I am hoping to leave on Wednesday morning."

"Yeah, I will," I promised.

That next Wednesday morning she called me just before she left. "According to this last CAT scan, your tumor is shrinking significantly."

"What does 'significantly' mean?" I asked. "Twenty percent? Forty percent?"

"No, it's closer to 80%," she replied.

I said, "Wonderful! Another miracle's happening! No wonder I'm feeling so good."

"Would you let me give you another series of four low-dose chemotherapy treatments like that?" she suggested tentatively.

Well, the first eight had been so successful and I had had no side effects and I thought, "Maybe that's what it will take to get rid of the last 20%," so I answered, "Yes, I'll come in."

Until now, I have taken eight doses and yesterday, April 27, 2004, I started my third group of four treatments, so I'll have a total of 12. So that's what I'm doing now, in fact I just came from there. I could have been home earlier, but they have the best cafeteria in there where you can have all you can eat for $2.50, including such good soups and salads, so I stayed there and ate. Grace wasn't home anyway as she had taken a friend of hers to the doctor.

The beauty of this whole illness is that all my life I had *never* been sick. The week I finally went in to the hospital outpatient doctor, it had been 47 years since I had last been in a doctor's office!

The reason I know that exact time is that our youngest daughter, Theresa, is 47 years old. During the week that she was born, I caught a little pneumonia because I didn't listen to the doctor. He had given me some drugs for it, and I felt so good that I went right back to work and I shouldn't have. He had told me not to. I was too young to know that the drugs gave me a "quick fix" and they helped to turn me around, but that didn't mean I was cured. Since then, for 47 years, I never took an aspirin, never took a Tylenol, never skipped a day of work.

About 21 years ago, in October, when we had a four-way partnership with the farm operation, the boys took out life insurance. The life insurance company from Virginia called me and wanted me to have a physical examination. "What's it for?" I asked.

They said they do that to spot check and update their records.

"Well, what will it cost me?" was my next question.

"Nothing," they said. "We just want you to go to *our* doctor."

They sent me to Rohrerstown, Penna., near Lancaster where their doctor gave me an EKG (electrocardiogram) and a few other tests. When he had me wired up, he asked, "Victor, when did you have your last heart attack?"

"I never had one that I know of," I replied.

"Well," he said sounding puzzled, "let me run it again," and he did.

Then he said, "Victor, I don't want to scare you, but you should run home and see your doctor."

What he didn't tell me, and I didn't know, was that he called my doctor. Since I didn't really have a doctor, I told him that Grace goes to Doc Zimmerman in Scheafferstown.

Because we were in the middle of corn harvest from the middle of October to the first of November, after I went home I immediately changed clothes and jumped on the corn harvester and never went to the local doctor.

Three weeks later, one rainy day I came into the house and said to Grace, "I wonder if that doctor knew what he was talking about. It's a possibility that he could have. I'll call Doc Zimmerman and see what he thinks."

When I called him, he said, "Yeah, Victor, I was looking for you three weeks ago! The doctor in Rohrerstown told me you were coming right over to see me."

I didn't understand it that way. I thought he said I should go and make an appointment.

Doc Zimmerman then continued, "You ought to go to the cardiac center of the Good Samaritan Hospital and ask for Dr. Clemens."

I was scheduled for a Friday morning appointment. Two days earlier, at our Wednesday evening Bible study, I told our pastor that this guy claims that I've had a heart attack. Just in case he *might be right*, the Bible says in (to paraphrase in my version) James 5:14, "If anybody is sick, call the elders for the anointing service."

"Why don't we have it right here in our Bible study?" he suggested.

So we did, in the presence of about fifteen people who were there that night.

When I go to bed at night, I always fall asleep in about three minutes. However, on that Thursday night, for some reason I didn't get to bed until about 11:30. Twenty minutes later I was wide awake and looked at the alarm clock and saw it was 10 minutes before midnight, and I thought, "What's going on? I feel so wide awake I might as well get up and go to work."

About that time I broke out in such a sweat that I was wet all over. I walked over to the bathroom, and I remember that my feet were that wet on the linoleum floor that I could skate. I could look back and see my wet footprints! I looked in the mirror and thought again, "What's going on?"

Suddenly, I threw my hands up and said, "Praise the Lord. I feel so good. I feel 20 years younger! What's happening here?"

I was all excited and ready to go. I jumped in the shower, and when Grace heard the shower running, she came over and said, "What are you taking a shower in the middle of the night for?"

"I was sweating and was so wringing wet, even my hair was all wet," I explained.

After I finished the shower, I went to bed and slept like a baby. At two o'clock that morning there was a cow in the back of the house making noises. We kept all our cows that were expecting calves in a field in back of our house and slept with our windows open. I could tell by the way she was grunting that this cow was having labor pains and needed help. She had awakened me, so I got up, got dressed, went out and helped her deliver her calf and everything went well.

I came back in, took another shower, went to bed and got wide awake again at 4:30 a.m.

Then I got dressed and went down to the farm and told the boys all that had happened during the night. I concluded by saying, "You know, I kind of promised to go in to the hospital this morning to let them check me out, but I had a *miracle* happen during the night and I don't *need* to go in there."

Wisely, my son-in-law, Ronnie Myer, advised, "You ought to go in and let the doctor *prove* your miracle."

"Yeah, that's a good idea," I agreed with a smile.

I was scheduled to be there at 8:00 a.m. When I entered the waiting room, the one nurse asked, "Did you check in?"

"No, not yet."

"Well, sign in here," she instructed, shoving a lined tablet toward me.

Then she asked me to follow her into the room where they'd give the EKG. There was another nurse in there giving another guy a test. The nurses looked kinda puzzled at each other and the first one said with surprise, "Oh, you're using this. I thought I was scheduled to give Victor Ziegler an exam here."

The second nurse said, "That's what I'm doing now, giving Victor Ziegler his EKG."

I looked at this man and went over to him and said, "Good morning, sir. You know, I've traveled all over the world and met lots of people, but I never met another 'Victor Ziegler' except here in the heart station of the Good Samaritan Hospital."

When I said that, the second nurse picked up her folder, and I can still see her as she said, "Oh, my God! I have the wrong man."

She pulled all the wires off him real quick and said, "Sir, would you mind putting your shirt back on and going out and waiting in the waiting room?"

She was so nervous. She could have lost her job! It was so funny; I couldn't help but smile.

"Ma'am, don't worry about it," I consoled her. "We all make mistakes. I am a farmer. In fact, I just read an article that said, 'A farmer pays for his mistakes, a doctor buries his mistakes,' but it didn't say what nurses do!"

She could hardly smile as she was too upset.

Then I got serious and said, "This is no time to joke, when a person is hurting." So I backed off.

She left then and the first nurse took over, the one whom I had followed into the room. This nurse was supposed to get a blood sample, but she couldn't get any blood out of me.

To lighten the mood and make conversation, I said, "Well, the last time I donated blood I fell asleep. They thought I fell asleep because they had pumped me dry."

She stabbed me a couple times and then called the doctor down. In the meantime, while we waited for him to arrive, I had to tell her about this miracle I had experienced at midnight–how I had sweated it out and something passed, whatever it was. It could have been a plug. Who knows? But *something happened*, because I felt different.

When the doctor got there, I said, "Doc, I was just telling the nurse here about the miracle I experienced. Do you believe in miracles?"

"Yeah," he said, "my football team won last night!"

"No," I disagreed. "I'm talking about something altogether different."

Then he conceded, "We'll see, we'll see."

I agreed, "O.K., sounds good."

And you know, they couldn't find one thing wrong! They went so far as to make me drink chalk water to check my stomach, colon and intestines, and I thought, "This is getting ridiculous."

At that time, I believe I still had a little health insurance. I thought that since I have $300 or $400 or even $500 deductible (whatever it was) and I'll only be here a little bit, it isn't worth writing up. I planned to just pay the bill and forget about it.

Well, they kept me all day and spent almost $1,000 on me!

I'll never forget coming home and saying to the boys, "Now I'm not that dumb, am I, that if a guy has a heart problem, you don't check his rectum?"

And everybody laughed.

It was just so funny what they put me through. They were hunting for trouble and couldn't find it. Meanwhile, I was having fun playing the game, going through the motions and learning, but I didn't realize I was going to get billed a thousand bucks for it! Expensive fun!

Dr. Clemens, the heart doctor, called me around 4:00 p.m. and said, "Everything looks good. We couldn't find anything wrong."

"Doc," I replied, "I was telling you and the nurse about the miracle I experienced. There might have been something wrong, but now everything is corrected."

"Well," he said, without commenting on my miracle, "would you come back in 30 days?"

"Would it be all right if I would call you instead of you calling me?" I suggested. "If I notice something's wrong, I'll call you and update you."

Somewhat reluctantly, he agreed, "Well, that would be O.K., too."

And do you know what? I saw him now after 21½ years. When they told me I should get a heart check, I requested to see Dr. Clemens. I wouldn't have known him, and he didn't recognize me either.

"Doc, do you know why I am here?" I asked him. "I made you a promise 21½ years ago that if anything changes, I'd come and let you know. Now something has changed."

Before I had my first chemo treatment, the doctors wanted me to have a new heart exam test. Dr. Ludwig said she doesn't usually give chemo to persons who have less than 50% of their heart functioning, and this heart test showed that mine is down to 33%.

When she told me that, I asked her, "What are the chances that your machine doesn't work right in one case out of a thousand and maybe I'm the one?"

However, before she could answer, I added, "I'll believe it, and if you think more tests are gonna help, you don't need to wait for another test result. I'll cooperate with you."

Then Dr. Ludwig and the surgeon said they'd like to get another reading on my heart so I agreed to go in on Friday, May 4, 2004, for different tests. Dr. Clemens gave me several medications that he said he would like me to take to strengthen my heart, and I've been taking them.

Throughout this illness, I have developed more appreciation for the medical teams of doctors and nurses, the professionals, because I now understand that most of them are trying to do the best they can. I am looking for opportunities to talk to them about some of the things I am doing that they don't even know about.

In my particular case, when they gave me that heart test, and she told me my heart is only working 33%, I could see it scared her. I could tell she had a fear of giving me a full-dose treatment of chemo for fear it would kill me, shut my heart down, or something. And do you know what? I thank the Lord that that test registered like that, whether it was true or false. I think in the long run it will be false because I think the Lord is going to restore it to about normal. Even if I only have 50% of it, I don't have to dig ditches to witness to people. I can visit them one on one. I got awake many a night and thanked the Lord. That test result was a blessing.

I could tell that her first choice of treatment had originally been to attack this disease with "fully loaded guns," you know, the strongest stuff. She was determined to give me the heaviest chemo possible to knock it out of me, but I didn't want that. In my own mind and heart, I was trying to figure out how I could say "no" to her without offending her, so I just bit my tongue and went on. When that heart test result came, I thought, "Thank you, Lord, there's my answer."

I attribute most of the progress I am making toward recovery to a new Limu product I found and also to the Indian herbal remedy called essaic tea. I was selling it and recommending it to everybody but I never took it myself. On the third week of January I started using both of these products and by the time I got ready to go for my first chemo treatment three or four weeks later, I remarked to Grace, "Something's happening. I'm feeling so much better already. Something's changing in me and do you know what? If I didn't have an appointment with Dr. Ludwig, the cancer doctor, I wouldn't go. I am feeling so different already."

However, after I consulted by phone with the medical doctor associated with the herbal company, he told me that if I take low to medium doses of chemo, it might complement and enhance the effects of the natural products I am taking. For sure, it wouldn't hurt. With that in mind, I thought, "If it can't hurt me, I might as well not offend Dr. Ludwig and cancel. I'll just go and see what I can learn."

Three days before I took the first chemo treatment in this set I told Grace I'm gonna cancel the chemo because I could feel something good happening. It really started to change, you know.

"Well, you don't want to do that," she objected. "You don't want to be that stubborn!"

Then as I thought about it more, I agreed saying, "Do you know what? That doctor's trying hard and the medical doctors from the health product company said it won't hurt me, and Theresa, our daughter, is also urging me to do it, so I guess I'll go through with it."

I definitely have a good appetite these days and I feel good. I credit these results mostly to the essiac tea I am drinking and that new Limu product. I think they have helped me more on the road to bounce back than anything else I did. I also use the energizer, the magnetic thing here, and the electronic machine, and with all of them working together, I don't think I'll ever take anything away from what the medical doctors advise until I can give them something better. In due time I will comment to them that I am so glad that I took the low doses because I think they did me more good than the heavy doses that could have "fixed" me. That was the toughest thing for me because two years ago I would have said I would *never* take any form of chemotherapy.

I really liked the learning experience–to see what the procedures are and how they handle them. I've been enjoying every session with the chemo nurses as I see them oftener than I see the doctor.

Each treatment lasts about an hour and 10 minutes, more or less. On my very first treatment, there was such a lively conversation going on among the patients I couldn't believe it when my time was up. "Is it all done already?" I asked the nurse.

"Yeah," she answered.

I was amazed and said, "It only seemed like 10 minutes!"

On my second to last occasion, I fell asleep while receiving the chemo. I don't know if I bumped the needle or what, but anyhow it started seeping under the skin and my arm started to swell or get puffed up. I noticed it right away. My shirt sleeve fell down over it, and the chemo nurse didn't see it.

"Hey," I got her attention, "I fell asleep and something went wrong."

Immediately, she got all nervous. "My goodness, how did I miss that?" And she turned red in the face.

"Oh," I assured her, "this too shall pass. Don't worry about it. In a couple hours that will be all absorbed. I did that to a dairy cow once and in half a day, it had all dried up."

She just laughed and asked, "Do you see something good in *everything?*"

"Yeah, even in you. I think you are one of the nicest nurses around," I complimented her. I added, "One thing my mother and dad taught me is that *if you can't see anything good or say anything good, don't say anything.* Since I dozed off, it was probably my fault, so don't blame yourself. I see a lot of good in you because you're trying so hard to do the best job you can."

Of course, when she walked away, she was smiling.

I called after her, "Don't laugh too loud. I don't say that to everybody!"

I noticed that others who were sitting around me and receiving chemo also liked to encourage her, wish her well, and wish her God's best. As for me, I usually liked to lay low and if it got too quiet in the room, then I'd pick on this one or that one and ask, "Hey, where do you live? What are you doing here?"

About one-third of them were the same people who were scheduled on the same days that I came in. About half or more were new faces each time, and I could start learning to know them all over again. Most of them were very easy to have a conversation with once I got them started. I asked them about their family, their job, and things like that. Sometimes we had a real entertainment center going.

After a while I'd tell them why I was there, and I told them they should have seen me two months ago. I was beginning to look like I had swallowed a football and was kinda hurting. I admitted to them that 8 or 10 weeks ago, there were a couple nights when I thought, "Well, this might be my last day on earth." But that was all right with me. I was ready to "give up the ghost" and go to a better place, because "the best is yet to come."

People there would tell me what their physical condition was without my asking them–if I told them my condition *first*. There was a younger woman there who looked to be about 45. She looked so healthy it was hard to believe she was there taking treatments once a month and she's been taking them for some time. It sounded like she was doing this to keep her cancer in remission.

"Remission" is a term they use and its meaning is different from being cured. I believe it means the disease is sleeping or dormant. It's just not doing anything at the moment, but it could flare up at any time. It hasn't gone away.

I told the group that in my case, I keep praying for a miracle, and in fact, I believe I *am* experiencing a miracle. God is able to perform a miracle for anybody else also. We all don't experience the same things. *I do believe that we can ask, believe and pray for a miracle, but in the end, it is all up to God who is in control.* Basically, all I can change is what I do physically, such as my eating habits, my work habits, my resting habits. I have a strong belief that if I do my part, God will take care of the rest. Whether that means I have one more day left on earth or 21 more years doesn't matter.

There is a purpose for everything. When my time is up, what does the Bible say? "It is appointed unto men once to die." (Hebrews 9:27, KJV) Everybody has a different life span, and nobody can figure it out. That's what makes it exciting. If we knew the end from the beginning the way the Lord does, then we'd be "God" ourselves–or think we are!

What I am trying to say is, you can't really say you are *enjoying* going through this, but you are *thankful* that you've got the God-given grace to go through it without suffering depression or having a down-in-out spirit because of what it does for you when you come out on the other side.

Between my second and third rounds of chemo, Dr. Ludwig asked me to take a couple drugs, one of which was called bactrim, as a protection against pneumonia. She also said that people were sometimes apt to get shingles after problems with their immune system.

I took the bactrim one night and I thought, "Wow!"

Then I read the label and I said to Grace, "My goodness, that'll *kill me!*"

After about 15 minutes, I could feel my fingers stiffening and had to keep them moving. I didn't want them to lock up on me. Anyhow, I put the rest of the bottle on the middle of the kitchen table and hoped the doctor would never ask about it again.

Two weeks later, the nurse asked me, "How are you doing on those two drugs you are taking?"

"Oh, I'm doing wonderful," I replied with a smile. "They are so good that I set them in the middle of the table and I look at them every day and each day I feel better!"

But I didn't ever open the bottles again.

"Did you tell the doctor you're not taking them?" she questioned.

"No, and if she don't ask, I won't tell."

"Maybe you want to tell her," she suggested.

"I will if she asks," I promised.

Sure enough, on my second to last week, the doctor looked at me and asked, "How are you doing on these medications?"

"They sure are working good," I said, and then told her the story. I was going to tell her that I look at them and pray over them each day, and keep looking and praying over them, but I never opened the bottle, but I didn't go quite that far.

"Well, just keep me informed if things change," she concluded. She didn't get upset or scold me. I told her I understand that some people get shingles from chemo treatments, but I am getting an appetite like a horse. I can eat three times a day.

Through all this illness, I've been a strong believer in the anointing service. Such an interesting thing happened. I was considering calling Pastor Amos one Friday morning to ask his opinion about my being anointed either privately or publicly, it didn't matter to me.

When I reached him, he remarked, "Now that is interesting. My sermon this coming Sunday morning will be on the anointing service. I was just going to call *you* and ask if you'd be willing to sit and role play while I went through the procedures of how I would conduct an anointing service. It would be very appropriate to actually *do it*, since you wanted an anointing service anyhow, that is, if you are willing to go public with it."

"I'd be glad to," I assured him adding, "in fact, I have a strong feeling that if the senior citizens don't demonstrate their faith in the church and their belief in the gospel according to the Scriptures, how will younger persons ever pick up on it?"

"That will be great," he agreed saying further that he will tell the congregation that I asked to be anointed and that we are not having a "mock" service, but it will be the real thing. He planned to explain each step of what was happening as he lead up to and actually anointed me.

It turned out to be really nice. He called one of the elders up and Grace also and asked me some questions about being in the faith and if I felt good about all my relationships. He also offered an opportunity in case there was anything I wanted to share with any brother or sister in the church. I thought he handled it really well and it was a very meaningful service.

Then the pastor of the local Assembly of God Church came one day to visit me. When he prayed with me, he asked first if he could anoint me, and I said, "Sure." That was my second anointing.

I was anointed a third time at my request by Pastor Amos and my brother, Earl, in a private ceremony at my home.

All this was based on the passage in James 5:13-16 (KJV) which says, "Is any among you afflicted? Let him pray. Is any merry? Let him sing psalms. Is any sick among you? Let him call for the elders of the church; and let them pray over him, anointing him with oil in the name of the Lord: And the prayer of faith shall save the sick, and the Lord shall raise him up; and if he have committed sins, they shall be forgiven him. Confess your faults one to another, and pray one for another, that ye may be healed. *The effectual fervent prayer of a righteous man availeth much.*" I believe that.

The first time my brother-in-law, Monroe Good, visited me he said, "I can't believe this is happening to you, Victor. You were always so full of fire, never sick, always followed the best health practices, and yet you've been hit like this."

I responded, "Do you know what? I thought the same thing but now I have the answer. God is performing or improving a work in me that my friends and I don't understand. But I do know one thing: I never knew that I could have the patience that I now have. If somebody would have told me I could slow down, sit at home, drive the car, do a little visiting, answer the phone and do only those things for ten or twelve weeks, I would have thought, "HOW?" Yet, I enjoyed every day! I don't know how to tell people I didn't have even one discouraging day! I was always so busy that I didn't have much time to read a lot. Now I rest a lot more and even take one-hour naps, and that eats up a lot of my time. *If everything stopped, I would sit here each morning and say, "Praise the Lord–one more day!"*

One big blessing is that I don't have pain. It's just the *pressure,* similar to what pregnant women and obese people live with, that causes a little discomfort. I want to be able to help people who suffer from obesity–to help them with their diet and lifestyle. Although there are a few who need medical assistance, getting the physical body back in balance would help most people.

With it all, I am so convinced that God is allowing me to go through this for a reason. And all the wonderful times I've had with doctors and nurses . . ." I can really feel that the medical community has shown concern for me, and I've developed a much greater sensitivity toward them. They have a tough job because everyone responds differently and has different attitudes.

Another reason that I think God is allowing this to happen to me is to teach me what others go through and to develop in me a sympathy toward those who are suffering. When people complained to me that they were tired or not feeling well, I admit that I thought much of it was just "in their head." I didn't know what it was to be tired since I just never was! I know that's quite a statement from a person who is 71 years old! I couldn't believe it because I had never experienced it myself.

On some of my worst days, I just had to look for a chair or a sofa because I needed to sit down. If God allows me to live another 5, 10, or 20 years, it will be a lot different. First of all, I will understand more from the medical point of view and from other people's positions because they weren't blessed with a healthy body like I was.

Your body gives you a lot of good signals if you listen to it. Right now I have a tremendous appetite and I sleep like a baby. When they tapped me that first time, they took only two liters from me, but I think they could have taken another two liters. The next time, about two weeks later, they took four liters, then six liters, eight and one-half liters, and then eight liters, so they got 28½ liters from me which would be 56 to 60 pounds of fluid. Eight liters is 16 or 18 pounds. So far, I've been tapped five times. Each time they use a 6-inch needle and have to be very careful when they insert it so that it doesn't puncture any organs on the way.

I remarked to the doctor one day, "Doc, you are so good at getting that needle at the right place, but even more than that,

I believe you *know* you're not that good, but you are doing this with Divine guidance."

He responded, "You're right, Victor. You're right."

Then they put a plastic hose on the needle and they have these liter bottles that are full of vacuum. When the nurse attaches the hose to the vacuum bottle, it punctures the seal of the bottle and the vacuum in the bottle draws out the lymph fluid. It took only about a minute and a half until one bottle was filled. Then they switch bottles and fill the next one. The doctor told me the most he ever took out of a person at one time was 11 liters and I quickly told him, "I don't want to get into the Guinness Book of World Records for *this!*"

After I was tapped, my abdomen felt like a flat tire. I could feel my stomach and other organs repositioning themselves, trying to get back to "normal," because they had been pushed aside. One time I said to the doctor, "I need to sit here a moment."

He told me to stay until I felt comfortable. He suggested that I sit up slowly. When I did, I felt cramps in my abdomen. As I got dressed, I moved very slowly. By the time he took me out the front gate in a wheel chair, Grace was there with the car to pick me up.

Being tapped is a tremendous relief, and then, because my stomach had no pressure on it, I really felt hungry. The second to last time I was tapped my abdomen was so tight that I could only eat a couple tablespoons of food. The night before I went in, the pressure was so great that I could feel it pushing the food back up into my esophagus. I had eaten a little bit of tuna salad or soup or something and I said to Grace, "I dare not lie down because as soon as I do, I feel the food pushing back up." It felt better to sit at an angle. The last couple nights I couldn't go to bed at all because I felt the food pushing up. I guess what they call "an acid reflux feeling" is when you feel a little burning in your throat. If I stayed sitting, that didn't happen but the minute I laid down flat, I felt it. Getting tapped is a wonderful relief, but a person wouldn't want to keep doing it forever because each time you go in, there is the risk of hitting some of the organs with the needle.

One day the doctor mentioned that in a case similar to mine, he ran a shunt in a tube up under the person's skin and fed the excess lymph fluid into his jugular vein. It then went into his circulatory system and his blood took it out of his body through his urine. Somehow, I couldn't get too excited about that idea.

I did suggest that perhaps he could insert a needle and plastic tube in my abdomen that I could turn on whenever relief was necessary and the fluid would flow out and then I'd keep it turned off at other times. But he didn't seem to like that idea.

He said he thinks my big tumor squeezed the channels shut and the canals just haven't opened up yet. Right now I am feeling so good that I believe that something's opening up and I'm exercising more. The naturopathic doctor from Philadelphia told me, "Victor, you'll find that the more you exercise and use this machine, even two or three times a day, the more you will be stimulated."

And I *can* feel that it stimulates me.

Another naturopathic doctor located in Utah referred to a 3-foot circular stumper or trampoline (and I have one of those) as a "rebounder." He said, "You'll find that helpful. Start out easy and slow and if it feels good, do a little bit more every day. Using a 'rebounder' is the best way to stimulate lymphatic flow that there is. It works so well."

However, I didn't use this for perhaps six weeks. I didn't want to break this tumor loose or damage anything further. Something good is happening, because I can feel it. During the next 10 days I'll find out more as we'll see if I get another build-up of fluid again or not.

They claim that the whole lymph system's job is to filter out all the bad toxins and discharge them. I never realized that all your internal organs are lined with lymph glands and this is really your defense system. It's miraculous. I told one doctor, "I know now why your job is so tough. The Bible says that God created man (human beings) and we are 'fearfully and wonderfully made,' according to the KJV of Psalms 139:14. You guys have a tough job because every person is just a little different, and to figure out all these little intricacies takes a lot of wisdom."

For two weeks I was so weak that I was afraid to drive a car so Grace drove me around. Other than that, I've been out every day. Since I've been sick, I've gone to visit shut-ins, going here and there and doing little things. Then I would come home and sleep for an hour. After my chemo treatments, I often visited several people who were in the hospital. In one instance, I called ahead of time to see if this certain man was up to having company. His wife said, "Victor, I got to warn you: he don't talk much."

But when I got there, we had a nice conversation, and he even smiled a little.

There was a Mennonite guy, Dale, (not his real name), whose wife was ill with cancer. Just after I got so sick myself, I stopped in to see him to give him some encouragement. When I arrived, he was working in his garage, so we talked out there for a half hour or so. Then he said, "Victor, I don't want you to go home without meeting her."

Although they were a very reserved couple, he invited me in and I shook her hand and talked to her for about 30 seconds. I said I just wanted to come in and wish her well and ask the Lord to give her peace and a blessing. Then I added, "With your husband's permission, I can't leave without praying for you."

When she reached out to say good-bye by shaking my hand, I just held on to her hand and started praying. Then I left.

He called me three days later and said, "Victor, you don't know what that did for my wife."

She died two weeks later, but she had instructed her family that she didn't want to take any chemotherapy or radiation. Now he calls to see how I'm doing. He knew I was sick for a while and he was afraid I wouldn't feel up to it, so he'd call Leon, my son. Leon would assure him, "Oh, he'd be *happy* to chat with you."

So I called him back that night about 9:00. I said, Dale, how are you doing?"

"Oh," he answered, "you know, to celebrate our 45 years of marriage, I had just built my wife a new house and our son took over the farm. Now with my wife gone, I come home every night to a lonely house and a lonely heart."

I could really feel his pain and I said, "You know, Dale, I've never experienced that, and that is something I can't understand until it is my time."

We talked on the phone for ten minutes or so and then I suggested, "Dale, do you know what? I am feeling *so good* that I'm wondering if you could meet me for breakfast at 8:30 tomorrow morning at the Dutchway Restaurant?"

"I know it's only a couple miles away, but I was never in the Dutchway Restaurant," he admitted. His wife probably shopped there more than once a week, but he was one guy who never sat in a restaurant. I can understand that because up till about five years ago, I never sat down in restaurants much either.

We met there and had a wonderful time of sharing together. I assured him, "I could tell your wife was ready to go."

"Do you know what? What keeps me going is knowing that we *will* meet again. That thought gives me a wonderful peace," he affirmed. "That's the only answer."

Then I reminded him, "You know, if we would be married 100 years, it would still seem short! Sixty years is short! Forty years is short!"

When we were ready to leave the restaurant, he said, "Victor, I enjoyed this so much, your sharing and praying, that I want to take care of the bill."

"But *I* invited *you!*" I protested.

"No," he insisted, "I gotta do this."

So he picked up the bill. Then he leaned over to me and with a mischievous twinkle in his eye asked, "Hey, did I ever tell you the difference between a Mennonite and a canoe?"

I knew the answer, but I said, "I'd like to hear your version of it."

"A canoe tips and a Mennonite don't," he explained.

Then I told him that I have often used that joke with my Presbyterian, Lutheran, and Brethren friends. However, that showed that he still had a little humor in him yet, and that was a good sign.

The most frequent question I am asked is, "How do you take it so gracefully?"

Well, that's a good question for me. My answer is–if you live surrounded by God's grace, is there any other way to do it, you know? I'm determined in my own mind that whether I live or whether I die, the end result is the same, so therefore it really don't matter. I agree with what the Apostle Paul wrote in Philippians 1:21 (KJV) "For to me to live is Christ, and to die is gain." If I'm not in control, why don't we leave it up to the One who *is* in control?

Epilogue

Although Victor had his ups and downs during the first six months after being diagnosed with lymphoma, he reacted well to his chemotherapy treatments, kept his sense of humor, never complained, continued to visit shut-ins, and assured everyone that he felt "something good was happening" within him. The frequency of his being tapped of fluid became less and he had good color, a good appetite and no pain.

Sometime in August, he did reach a point when he felt it might be wise to be tapped once again and made an appointment. When he arrived at the doctor's office, his regular doctor was not in, so he was treated by an associate or substitute. As this doctor prepared to insert the needle, Victor showed him the spot under his left rib where the regular doctor would go in. This new doctor said, "No, I'll put it in here," indicating another area.

Again Victor protested, "I've done this often with cows, and I know it should go in here," and he pointed again to the familiar spot used so often by his regular doctor.

However, the new doctor refused to listen and continued to begin the procedure at a new location. Very little fluid came out, so the doctor tried again at another spot, but not where Victor was telling him to go. After several tries with little success, he gave up in frustration and sent Victor home.

By the time he got home, the whole side of his pants was wet. This had *never* happened before. The fluid kept dripping out. Victor went into the bathroom and holding his extended abdomen over the sink, massaged it, encouraging more fluid to come out. Finally he was able to expel enough that he got some relief from the tautness and pressure, but nothing like the full tapping he usually got with his regular doctor.

From that day on, his condition began to slowly worsen again. Although he tried hard to maintain an attitude of cheerfulness, he was uncharacteristically quiet at family gatherings, and instead of eagerly sharing stories would quietly smile as others told them. He began to lose weight but continued to have a hearty appetite. He thought that was a good sign, but his niece, Marie Kline Haynes, a hospice nurse in Virginia, said that was not the case. She observed sadly that he was simply "feeding the tumor" enabling it to grow bigger and stronger while his body grew thinner and weaker.

Around this time he also developed a cough after every spoken sentence or two. In spite of these signs of progress of the lymphoma, Victor still believed firmly that a miracle was happening and that ultimately, he would conquer this illness.

Ironically enough, during October, two of his sisters and their husbands had planned to leave for short-term mission work in Africa. Lena and Irvin Kreider were going to Ghana for a six-month period to help with cooking and carpenter work at a mission location there, while Ada and Monroe Good were returning to Nigeria where they had spent a large portion of their lives in missionary teaching, evangelistic and building construction work. After a family reunion in Africa, they planned to return to the United States on Christmas eve. When both sisters visited Victor, both felt they were probably seeing him for the last time on earth (and that hunch was right), and it was a very difficult visit for them.

At the end of Ada and Monroe's visit, Monroe led in a short prayer, especially requesting that God would touch Victor's body and make him whole again. At the end of Monroe's prayer, Ada suddenly became aware that Victor had started praying . . . for them! She was moved to tears to think that someone in Victor's physical condition still focused his prayers on the needs of others rather than his own.

As his energy slowly seeped away and his healthy skin color turned to an ashen gray, he persisted in believing there would be a turn-around toward health, but he was realistic enough to begin making preparations for his departure. Little by little, he explained their finances to Grace, telling her where things were and what was necessary to be done.

With his pastor, he began sharing ideas that he would like to be included in his memorial service, indicating those persons who should participate and even choosing the songs and the persons who should be asked to be soloists. He specifically expressed the wish that make-your-own ice cream sundaes be included in the meal afterwards.

Along with Grace and his family, he expressed the desire that his body might be used for scientific study so that more could be learned about the causes, progress and treatment of lymphoma. Working for the betterment of others was still his goal and he felt this was one final way he might possibly help succeeding generations.

After all that could be learned from his remains had been extracted, he requested that his body be cremated and that his ashes be scattered over the graves of his mother and father in the Heidelberg Church of the Brethren cemetery only about one-half mile from his home. His purpose for that choice was so that people would not gather around a casket to view the remains, the shell, the physical "house" in which his soul had lived. Instead, he wanted the theme of his service to give as much attention and *glory to God* as possible, praising Him for the abundance of joy and blessings Victor had experienced during his lifetime. His intent was to detract from himself as much as possible and focus on Christ much as John the Baptist's intent was when he said in John 3:30 (KJV), "He must increase, but I must decrease."

When he could no longer walk back to the bedroom to sleep at night, he slept on a recliner in their living room. At that time, the family decided to request the services of hospice, and Victor was quick to point out to visitors that that was not necessarily a "sign of the end." He stated instances when persons who had been served by hospice recovered, and those stories gave him hope. Although Grace was his primary caretaker, a hospice nurse stopped twice a week to see how he was doing, and his granddaughter, Katie, helped by shaving him. Through hospice they obtained an adjustable hospital bed which they kept in the living room.

In mid-November at his request Grace took him to the Richland restaurant where he used to enjoy going for breakfast. However, by the time they got home, he was totally exhausted. He continued to fill up with fluid and now it wasn't just in his abdomen but also his legs and arms and even his fingers were all puffy-looking and swollen. In all, during the 12 times he had been tapped, 110 liters of lymph fluid had been extracted.

However, his co-partner in the natural health products business, Ivan Martin, came one day with a new product that was to help rid the body of excess fluid. After he started to take it, Victor had the urge to urinate three times within an hour. As he started expelling more liquids naturally, he again had a surge

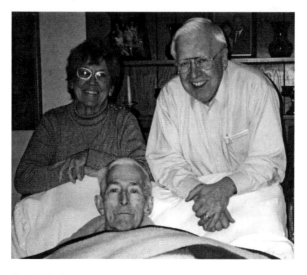

One of the last photos of Victor. Taken Nov. 10, 2004, the day before his 72nd birthday. Standing: Grace and his brother Earl.

of hope that perhaps this new product would accomplish the miracle, the turn-around for which he had been waiting.

As part of the family traditions fostered by Victor and Grace, Thanksgiving Day was a day when all the children and grandchildren gathered in the large basement family room of their home. Thanksgiving 2004 was no exception. While the family gathered downstairs, various grandchildren, children and in-laws took turns visiting Victor in the upstairs living room. He no longer had the energy to go up or down the steps to their basement family room and even if he had been carried down, he would have tired out too quickly from all the chatter and laughter which he had once so enthusiastically instigated and enjoyed.

In late November he received a lovely faith-declaring letter from his granddaughter, Melanie Martin Kirk, serving in Mexico doing mission work and the mother of Joanna, his third and youngest great-granddaughter, born September 30, who he was hoping to see for the first time during the Christmas season.

Earl visited him on Thursday, December 2, and Victor was too weak to speak above a whisper. Earl did most of the talking, but they did have a brief exchange in which Victor shared that he now has fluid in his lungs. Earl said, "Do you know what that means?"

"Yes," Victor replied softly, "and that's OK."

Family members took turns staying with him all night so Grace could get her rest. One night Victor said he heard singing that was so very beautiful and he was sure he was hearing the voices of an angel chorus.

On Saturday evening, December 4, Grace attended a meeting at the Richland Church of the Brethren but came home early. Although she had been gone only an hour, when she returned she could see a marked deterioration was occurring. Their son Leon, who was there at the time, noticed it also and together they decided to call the rest of the family. In the early hours of the morning all the children were gathered together in watchful waiting and prayer. Victor was conscious and around 4:30 a.m. he sighed saying softly, "Yes," as he arrived at the destination he had been traveling to all his life. From the time he accepted Christ as his Lord and Savior at age eleven, he had been on his way to heaven and now at age 72, he had arrived.

What a glorious final miracle!

"When all my labors and trials are o'er, And I am safe on that beautiful shore,

Just to be near the dear Lord I adore, Will thro' the ages be glory for me.

O That will be glory for me, glory for me, glory for me.

When by His grace I shall look on His face,

That will be glory, be glory for me."

—Charles H. Gabriel

"Victorisms" and Anecdotes:
Things We'll Always Remember About Victor

"We all have happy memories of good men gone to their reward . . ."

—*Proverbs 10:7a (TLB)*

"I was almost 90 when I first met Victor's sister, Mae Patches, six years ago when we were both widowed residents at the Landis Home's Retirement Complex. As we became close friends, I had a difficult time remembering the names of Mae's brothers and sisters and their spouses. One day Victor visited us, and as he left he went up the hall singing lustily, 'Victory in Jesus, My Savior forever ...' After that I had no trouble remembering Victor's name, associating the name 'Victor' with 'Victory.'"

—Jake Kurtz
Lititz, PA

Because Victor was such a big talker and never at a loss for words, Jean Kuhnert, a friend who traveled on several tours with Victor and Grace observed that "he must have been vaccinated with an RCA Victor Victrola needle when he was quite young and hasn't stopped talking since!"

"An attitude of gratitude is 90% of success." —A "Victorism"

"I never forget August 12, 1975, when my sponsors, Dr. and Mrs. Robert L. Barton, introduced me, my wife Kim (who was pregnant) and three children aged from 1½ years old to 6½ years old to the Zieglers.

In the living room of the Ziegler's house on their farmland, in the conversation I just tried very hard to understand what Victor said. He spoke too fast and have a different (?) accent (German maybe?), but I feel that he is very friendly and has the opened arms to help our family.

We moved in and lived in their basement for almost 1½ months before we moved permanently in our own home in Myerstown.

Every day Victor woke up very early (Grace told us), but at lunch or in the evening he always came down to the basement and asked how we're doing and do we need any help. He always smiles and has a very positive attitude. After many years went by, we love Victor very much. Victor is more than a friend—he is just our older brother.

One more thing before I forget—the first day when we're at their house, I did not get used to the odor of cow manure. Victor laughed and said, 'This is fresh country air. Very good for your health!'

We love Victor and pray God to help him as he always helped others."

—Nguyen Ta Quang and Kim Nguyen
Myerstown, PA

"I will always remember the time I met with Victor and Grace to interview them for serving on the SVPS (Susquehanna Valley Pregnancy Services) board. Victor told story after miraculous story of how he'd seen God provide financially for him and his family over the years. After Victor became a board member, he would look at any SVPS financial need as an awesome opportunity for God to raise up large donors who would gladly give toward God's work at SVPS. If we had a $100,000 need, for example, Victor would say, 'That's easy. We just need 10 donors who would each give $10,000. That's not hard for God!' His faith built our spirits, and made the financial need shrink in comparison to God's ability to provide."

—Lisa Hosler, Executive Director,
Susquehanna Valley Pregnancy Services

Because Victor always talked a lot, a friend teased him one day by saying, "You know, Victor, you remind me of an old pair of shoes that I have out in my garage."

"How's that?" Victor asked.

"Everything's worn out on them except the tongues!" his friend replied.

"God isn't ready for me yet."—A "Victorism" remembered by Pastor Jim Bauer, Richland Church of the Brethren

"At a social function, Victor moved through a crowd like a politician who was running for office, only he wasn't. He was just a friendly guy. Because he was always joking, I thought he might be shallow, but I quickly learned that he was spiritual, loved the Lord, liked to help and encourage people. He really blessed me."

—Constance Shea
Lebanon, PA

"How are you doing, Victor?" one of Victor's brothers-in-law asked him at a family gathering in April 2004. His answer: "I'd rather be well than be as good-looking as my brothers-in-law."

"Grandpa, I just want to thank you so much for the incredible legacy you have left to all of us who've come after you. Your life is one of passionate love for and obedience to Jesus. I remember when I was 15 years old and God really started to capture my heart and my relationship with Him became my own, I really began to notice that you were radical for Jesus and you didn't care what people thought of you. You inspired me, because I wanted to be like that. Thank you for being an example to me and encouraging me in my faith walk with Jesus." (In a letter she sent to Victor in November, 2004)

—Melanie Martin Kirk, Granddaughter
Youth With A Mission, Juarez, Mexico

"I first met Victor and Grace back in 1982 at Kennedy Airport in New York as we were waiting to board a flight for a tour of Australia and New Zealand hosted by his brother, Earl, and his wife, Vivian. On that trip I remember how Victor would always be talking to people along the way. It was obvious that he loved the Lord because his conversations would invariably include references to how good the Lord had been to him, but it was done in such a natural and genuine way that it wasn't offensive. One of the 'rules' Earl had set was that whoever was the last one on the bus would have to buy ice cream for everybody at the next stop. I am sure that Victor paid for more ice cream than anyone else on that trip."

—Jean E. Kuhnert
Chattanooga, TN

"Victor was a man in full gear. It was hard to slow him down to take time to smell the roses. One time he came in from working in the barn and headed for the shower, in which he always could be heard singing lustily, 'There Will Be Showers of Blessing.' After his shower, he prepared to brush his teeth. I had a tube of Diaperene lying on the vanity after changing one of the grandchildren's diapers. He picked up the tube and used it for toothpaste but quickly realized it wasn't toothpaste! It made his lips pucker up and he soon washed out his mouth. We had many good laughs over that."

—T. Grace Ziegler, Victor's wife
Myerstown, PA

"Victor visited us several years ago and on the way home he was stopped by a police officer for speeding. When he was asked if he knew how fast he was going, he replied, 'No, officer, I really don't, but thank you for stopping me and letting me know. You may have saved my life!' (He still got the ticket!)"

—Helen and Woody Frey
Lehighton, PA

"My son, James Adkins had been pastor at the Richland Church of the Brethren, and when he died, Victor came to me at his funeral and described him saying 'He was like a summer rain on parched ground.' That observation was such a blessing to me, and I'll never forget it."

—Barbara Adkins
Lititz, PA

"My fondest memory of Victor was hearing him say 'I'm just passing through Richland on my way to Heaven!' He would visit with each customer at the diner. Before he left, everyone would be blessed. I was happy just talking with him and now remembering our times together makes me smile and feel blessed."

—Sherry Sullivan
Richland, PA

"National Republican Congressional Committee Awards 2004 Ronald Reagan Republican Gold Medals. Washington, D.C.–House Majority Leader Tom DeLay (R-TX), NRCC Chairman Tom Reynolds (R-NY) and the National Republican

Congressional Committee (NRCC) announced today that Mr. Victor K. Ziegler has been chosen as a 2004 Ronald Reagan Republican Gold Medal Award winner.

Mr. Ziegler was selected based on unyielding support of the Republican Party, outstanding leadership in business and for displaying a commitment to President Ronald Reagan's vision for an entrepreneurial America. Only an elite group of business and professional people were nominated to receive the award before the awards selection committee reached a final decision.

Commenting on the selection, Congressman Tom Reynolds, Chairman of the NRCC, said, 'Mr. Ziegler has served as an Honorary Chairman of the Business Advisory Council and has provided much needed support. This award could not have gone to a more deserving candidate.'"

—Victor's wife, Grace, received this notification Dec. 9, 2004

"Victor was a special student of Arthur's–so talented and highly motivated–and Arthur felt fortunate to be Victor's high school agriculture teacher."

—Arthur and Mary Wolfe
York Springs, PA

"In 1979 my dad, Earl, suggested that it might be a wise financial investment for me to spend $10,000 to purchase an acre of land prepared for 1/3 acre building lots and later sell them at a profit. Since neither my dad nor I had any extra money at the time, Dad suggested that I ask Uncle Victor if he could help me. Because he was an astute businessman who liked to encourage young people, especially a nephew, his response was, 'Sure, I'd be glad to help you out, Randy.' With that loan I made a purchase of land near Pequea, Lancaster County, and in eighteen months I was able to repay Victor as I sold the three lots making better than 100% profit. I have never forgotten his act of kindness and generosity, and I understand this was just

one instance of the way he helped numerous persons who were young and/or in need . . . a way he put his faith into action."
—Randy E. Ziegler
Landisville, PA

"Victor had an ability to seize opportunity when it presented itself. It was obvious to me that God blessed him financially. The farm that I now live on was up for sale two and one-half years. No one bit. The owner tried unsuccessfully to sell lots by the highway for the same amount of time. Victor bought the farm and sold all the lots in six months."
—Ken Stoltzfus
First president of Jubilee Ministries

"I enjoy every day and tomorrow is always a better day."
—A "Victorism"

"Victor, Earl and I walked to Bible School at the Richland Church of the Brethren and as 'Junior Boys' we tested the patience of our teacher, Ray Kurtz. Walking home every day for two weeks at 11 a.m., we smelled the potatoes frying at the Betsy Ross Potato Chip factory. We could have eaten some then and there, but we never got any."
—Harold Keller
Mount Joy, PA

"Well, Saturday, December 11, 2004, came and went. And what a day it was! Nearly 600 people from throughout the eastern U.S. and Canada came to worship the Lord, pay their respect for our beloved brother, Victor Ziegler, and to comfort his family. I was honored to be able to lead the worship service and preach on one of Victor's favorite Bible texts: Philippians 1:21—'For to me, to live is Christ, and to die is gain.'

Earl Ziegler, Victor's brother, spoke three words that I'll never forget: 'Victor was fearless.' Then Earl shared about the time when Victor went to Cuba taking more than 1,000 English/Spanish New Testaments with him in suitcases. 'He could have been thrown into prison!' Earl recalled. But Victor, fully trusting that God would make a way, told the customs man that what he had in those suitcases would help Cuba more than anything else. And, praise God, the Bibles reached their destination!

I really believe that the reason Victor was so fearless was because he trusted God so much. And, you know what? I want to be like Victor! I pray that you do too! And, with God's help, we can!"

—Pastor Jim Bauer
Richland Church of the Brethren, PA

"When I had the pleasure of being invited to speak in the Richland Church of the Brethren, I arrived in Richland very early in the morning so I could get breakfast before the service began. When I entered the small café, one of the ladies came right over and quickly took my order. When she returned, she asked if I was on business in the area and I told her I was going to be the preacher at the morning service of the Richland Church of the Brethren. Very quickly she responded, 'Are you Rev. Phill Carlos Archbold?'

Quite surprised, I said 'Yes,' and added, 'How did you know my name?' 'Oh,' she said, 'Mr. Victor Ziegler was just here and told us you were speaking at his church this morning and he invited us to be his guests in the service.'

Victor believed in and practiced personal evangelism. No one was a stranger to him. All you had to do was watch him work a restaurant, many times knowing everyone there before he or they left."

—Phill Carlos Archbold
First Church of the Brethren, Brooklyn, NY

"Victor was very affectionate–especially with older people. My 90-year-old mother was at our house for a family picnic with the 'Cox clan' one August day in 1990. When we surprised her by singing 'Happy Birthday,' Victor thrilled her immensely by being the first to give her a hug and plant a kiss on her cheek."

—Grace Cox (Mrs. Stanford)
Lancaster, PA

"I would never buy a Chevy from a man who drove a Ford."

—A "Victorism"

"If I were describing Victor to someone, I would say he is the most energetic, ambitious, talkative and likeable person. He surely is a dedicated Christian. I remember working for Victor when he was expanding his dairy operation. My sons and I blasted rock and hauled dirt for the pond and fill for the barn. I enjoyed working for Victor as he came and went over what we were doing in a compatible manner. I often think of the many community projects he helped to accomplish. The Reistville Point project was finally finished with Victor's drive and patience. Praise the Lord!"

—Amos and Marian Zimmerman
Myerstown, PA

"Having always lived in western New York state, we appreciated it when Victor and Grace gave us a tour of Pennsylvania Dutch country. They described many of the idiosyncrasies of the Amish as well as the admirable qualities of these wonderful people. Victor himself often amused me when he would make a statement and then, raising his voice a little, would end his sentence with 'eh?' (Meaning 'Isn't that right?')

We traveled to New York state several times with Victor and Grace and enroute often we would all join in singing one hymn after another to the glory of God—not that we were that good singers but it expressed the joy we all had in our hearts that God had made us His children.

I believe that one of his most valuable services for his Lord has been the home visits he has made to the sick and needy. My husband was encouraged time after time when Victor 'dropped in' for a visit, and he made it his business. Before leaving, he usually offered prayer invoking God's blessing on us all."

—Vera Wilson
Myerstown, PA

"I remember the time Victor gave up his seat to someone else on a plane and for doing that was offered the best drinks on the plane. The stewardess came to him with all the special strong drinks. Victor glanced at them and said, 'I thought you were going to offer me the *best* drinks. Why, you don't even have milk! That's the best.'"

—David Keller
Lebanon, PA

During the last year of his life, when Victor was having good days, he enjoyed visiting shut-ins. One person he visited was Lisa, the wife of David Martin, who was struggling with cancer. After her death, David kept in contact with Victor as he coped with his own struggles. On one occasion, he shared a poem that his wife, Lisa, had written in longhand, and Victor found it to be very meaningful. Although we don't know if Lisa composed the poem or merely copied it from somewhere, we are including the last verse.

"I'm not going down, but upward,
And the path is never dim,

For the day grows ever brighter
As I journey on with Him.
So my eyes are on the hilltops,
Waiting for the sun to rise—
Waiting for the invitation
To the home beyond the skies."

"As a small guy in elementary school, Victor already liked action and exhibited a temper. One time he threw his glasses over the woodshed roof and another time, in anger, he threw stones at his brother, Earl. In looking back, I see that as the development of his peppy actions to get things done with enthusiasm. Victor was a visionary, a decision-maker, willing to lead and take risks. He was optimistic to the point that he told me that even in the worst years of drought and blight, he never lost money on a tomato crop, except the tomatoes he ate were very expensive."

—Harold Keller
Mount Joy, PA

"One day Victor and I were talking and he was sharing incidents about his family. He paused and said, 'You know, if a man didn't have a family, he would be poor.' (At that time Victor had several farms and several hundred head of cattle.)"

—Amos Cunningham
Brethren Village, Lancaster, PA

"When Victor was speaking to people about different religions, he would often say, 'There is no use worrying about what denomination you belong to because when we get to heaven, we'll all be united brethren.'"

—T. Grace Ziegler, Victor's wife
Myerstown, PA

"Victor and Grace gave time, money and encouragement to more ministries, churches, causes and individuals than anyone I know about except God."
—Harold Keller
Mount Joy, PA

"As we were taping the stories for this book, Victor and I were frequently interrupted by phone calls. Usually Grace took the call in another room, but one day she was gone and Victor answered the phone. The caller must have asked, 'How are you doing, Victor?' and although his body looked emaciated and sometimes was swollen with fluid, his instant joyful response was, 'I'm still praising the Lord–seven days a week!'"
—Vivian S. Ziegler
Brethren Village, Lancaster, PA

"My husband and I traveled with Victor and Grace several times. I always kidded him that I could *never* take a nap in the car while traveling with Victor–he was always talking–and there was never a dull moment. He always referred to Grace, his wife, as his 'Amazing Grace.' When entering a restaurant, he would make some remarks that would lighten up the waitress–(however, sometimes I felt like walking away as if I didn't know him!)"
—Rachel Z. Good
York, PA

"We first remember Victor as an outstanding FFA (Future Farmers of America) boy. Later we moved into half the farmhouse. We remember him as a very hard-working farm boy who knew the important information about the crops that were being planted and the breeds and types of animals being raised. Victor forced us out of our home! When we moved in, Mr. Ziegler, his dad, said we could rent there until one of the boys would get married and need a place to live. While we were living there, Victor and his cousin, Harold Keller, would often stop by late on Saturday nights with their dates and wonder if we had anything to eat. It was always a fun visit."

—Henry and Louise Wenger
Lancaster, PA

"One of Victor's favorite restaurant antics would occur when the waitress would be taking dessert orders. Victor would ask, 'Should we keep our forks?' Then he would spin a yarn that because he was told so often to keep his fork, he has a collection of hundreds of forks at home. During his last few months, he enjoyed the short story about a person who wanted to be buried with a fork in her hand. When asked why, she answered, because whenever she was eating out and was told to keep her fork, she knew that 'the best was yet to come.' The fork in her hand symbolized the eternal life awaiting her."

"Some years ago Victor and I and a mixed race boy attended a work camp in North Carolina. The three of us went into a restaurant and Victor introduced each of us, but when he introduced this boy, Victor explained, 'This boy's from Hershey, Pennsylvania, and his only problem is that they dipped him in the chocolate once too often.' (Fortunately, the boy wasn't offended and laughed as heartily as the rest of us.)"

—Norman Kline
Lebanon, PA

Victor got much fuel for his humor based on the name of his wife Grace, and the double meaning of its referring to the grace of God. His conversation was frequently peppered with references to his "Amazing Grace," statements such as, "God's Grace is sufficient for me," or comments about traveling with "Grace," living with "Grace," etc. The slogan for their health products business was "Gracious Living–The Way to a Victorious Life."

"When I was on a tour group, including Victor and Grace, traveling in Alaska, we visited the Arctic Ocean. At the shore edges, the water was frozen and Victor, being the daring adventurer that he was, decided to try walking on the ice. After just a few steps, the ice broke under him and he fell in. We all had a good laugh, not *at* but *with* him about that."

—Jean Kuhnert
Chattanooga, TN

"During the past 32 years my family and I have shared many special moments with Victor and his family. I traveled with Victor out west in his Volkswagen Rabbit to see this beautiful country while we were enroute to Seattle, Washington, to attend a Bible Conference. I can assure you there was never a dull moment. At one point we helped a victim of a truck accident and made many friends along the way. During this trip we discussed everything from politics, religion, education and also shared many jokes. Having to face many ups and downs of life, Victor always lifted my spirits by saying, 'Why worry when you can pray. Faith can move mountains.' . . . I am one of the blessed people who had two father figures, one from the East (my biological father) and one from the West, my dad, Victor Ziegler. I will *always* remember him." (Shared at Victor's Memorial Service)

—Samsudin Pabani
Toronto, Canada

"I remember how you would tell people things like 'I'm on my way to heaven and just passing through Myerstown,' (or wherever you happened to be that day). You always made Scriptures like 'Our citizenship is in heaven' and Hebrews 11:

13-16 real to me with how you lived . . . Thank you for teaching your children to love and serve Jesus, who in turn taught my generation, and I promise that I will continue that and teach my children. I know that you and Grandma haven't had easy lives and you've had your share of disappointments but look now at so many of your children and grandchildren who have surrendered their lives to Christ's Lordship and are serving Him! You can be proud—you have indeed left a legacy!" (In a letter to Victor in November, 2004)

—Melanie Martin Kirk, Granddaughter
Youth With A Mission, Juarez, Mexico

"I'm representing the 2 brothers and 4 sisters. While growing up in a large family, one experiences various emotions of love, joy and sibling rivalry. Victor and I shared the same bedroom while growing up and also the same zest for life. Even as a youth, every mountain or valley he experienced was a challenge and opportunity to grow. In his illness, he often said he is learning new lessons about life. He always saw the glass as half full, never half empty. Victor was a person of strong Christian ethics and integrity, not dissuaded by politics or expediency. Outspoken, he was sometimes at odds with the majority, even in our family discussions. He and his 'Amazing Grace' were givers, champions of the underdogs of society as evidenced in their refugee projects. His propensity in overcoming setbacks (and he's experienced many) and his desire to help others with his business acumen were motivating forces in his life. He was fearless. He was a great brother in the Lord and a best friend. Thanks, Victor, for teaching us lessons about victory, even in death. Victor was a man on a mission. His mission is now accomplished!" (Shared at Victor's Memorial Service).

—Earl K. Ziegler
Brethren Village, Lancaster, PA

"I have had so many good things happening to me that I *can't* count all my blessings."

—Victor K. Ziegler

In Appreciation To Those
Who Shared Memories

Adkins, Barbara

Archbold, Dr. Phill Carlos

Bauer, Jim

Cox, Grace (Mrs. Stanford)

Cunningham, Amos

Fisher, Steve

Frey, Helen and Woody

Good, Rachel Z.

Grander, Lloyd and Esther

Hackman, Warren

Hayes, Carol Johnson

Hosler, Lisa

Hurst, Elvin and Helen

Jackson, Joanne

Keller, David and Ruth

Keller, Harold

Kent, Pat A.

Kirk, Melanie Martin

Kline, Norman

Kuhnert, Jean

Kurtz, Jake

Martin, David

Martin, Ivan

Martin, Sharon Ziegler

Mummert, Ken and Betty

Myer, Bonnie Ziegler

Nguyen, Quang Ta and Kim

Pabani, Samsudin

Pabani, Zebunnisa

Reider, Paul and Fanny Ruth

Rogers, Dorothy

Rohrer, Erma

Shea, Constance

Shenk, Ernest and Marian

Stoltzfus, Ken

Sullivan, Sherry

Van Lieu, Richard, Carol and Ann

Wenger, Henry and Louise

Wenger, Jesse

Wickert, Theresa Ziegler

Wilkinson, Josette

Wilson, Vera

Wolfe, Arthur and Mary

Wolfe, Vernon and Florence

Ziegler, Earl K.

Ziegler, Leon

Ziegler, Lynn

Ziegler, Randy

Ziegler, T. Grace

Ziegler, Vivian S.

Zimmerman, Amos and Marian

Chronology of Events in the
Life of Victor Ziegler

1932	– Born on November 11, 1932 at Richland, PA
1936	– First memorable event–death of brother Lee, June 25, 1936
1938-1946	– Attended 1st–8th grades at Richland Elementary School
1946-1950	– Millcreek Twp. High School, Newmanstown, PA
1950	– Began farming in partnership with parents
1952	– On August 24, 1952, married Theresa Grace Cox
1953	– A year of learning to live together
1954-1984	– Purchased my parent's 160-acre dairy farm with 35 dairy cows and built it to over 500 head of milking cows and over 600 acres of crop land
1954	– Birth of our first child, Bonita Kay, on March 5, 1954
1955	– Birth of Sharon Marie on Oct. 1, 1955
1957	– Birth of Theresa Elaine on January 31, 1957
1958	– Birth of Lynn Victor on July 11, 1958
1960	– Birth of Leon Eugene on January 29, 1960
1960	– Purchase of 2nd farm, 67 acre Harvey Hoover farm, in March
1960	– In August, brucellosis struck our herd and Grace had surgery
1960-1970	– Served as member of Lebanon County Soil & Water Board
1962	– Introduced free stalls in the dairy business to Eastern PA farmers
1964	– Built a double four milking parlor (milking 80 cows) and increased herd to 100 cows
1964	– Built two 24'x70' concrete silos with bottom unloading

1965-1970 – President of Lebanon County Farmers Association

1965-1971 – Sunday School teacher & youth advisor,
Heidelberg Church of the Brethren

1965-1972 – Grace operated an Assisted Living Home for 8
to 12 senior citizens in our home

1968-1972 – Member of Lebanon County Extension Board

1970   – Built a new free stall barn for 70 cows, doubled
the size of milking parlor to double 12

1970   – Built new ranch house; moved into it in
November

1970-1985 – Chairman of Agway Farmers Cooperative,
Lebanon Co.

1970-1986 – Board member for Teen Challenge ministries

1970   – Elected to Lehigh Valley Milk Producers board
of directors

1971   – Introduced liquid manure in Eastern PA;
increased herd to 200 cows

1972-1977 – Treasurer of Lehigh Valley Milk Producers
Cooperative, Allentown, PA

1972   – Built a new 200-cow free stall barn and added
100 more cows

1973   – Increased dairy herd to 400 milking cows

1974-1980 – Served on ELCO school board

1974-1999 – Board member (president for 7 years) for Jubilee
Ministries, Lebanon County (prison ministry)

1975   – Lawsuit with Lehigh Valley Milk Producers

1975-1990 – Sponsored 11 refugee families from Vietnam,
Cambodia, Africa, Hungary, and Russia

1977-1982 – Served on Maryland Milk Producers Cooperative
board, Baltimore, MD

1978   – Took a farm tour group to Hawaii

1979   – Took 2 week agricultural tour to Germany

1980   – Took tour to Hawaii with Richard Canfield

1980-1988 – Served on Church of the Brethren Youth

Services (COBYS') original board

1980-1990 — President of Lighthouse Ministries, a home for
            unwed mothers, in Richland, PA

1981   — Toured 3 weeks in U.S.S.R. with Farm Visits
            group

1982   — Directed a 3-week tour to South America

1982   — Went on tour to Tahiti, Australia and New
            Zealand

1983   — Served 3 weeks in South America on a study
            tour for Heifer Project International

1983-1998 — Served as trustee and Agricultural Consultant
            to Farmers and Agri-Businesses in Lebanon,
            Lancaster, and York Counties

1985-Death (2004) — Board member for Children & Youth
            Services, Lebanon County

1985   — Spent 2 weeks in Honduras as support person
            for Mission Medical Team

1986   — Took 15-day tour to Alaska

1987   — Served 2 weeks in Nicaragua with a Manchester
            College (IN) Youth Exchange team

1990-Death (2004) — Member of the board of First
            National Bank of Fredericksburg, PA

1990   — Retired from full-time farming. Sold the farm to
            my youngest son, Leon Ziegler

1991   — Spent 10 days in Cuba distributing Bibles in
            churches

1993-Death (2004) — Appointed to Millcreek Twp. Planning
            & Zoning Board

1994   — Joined post-Annual Conference tour from
            Wichita, KS via Branson, MO

Note: All this made possible by God's Grace! My good wife!

1990-2000 — Part-time assistant on my son's farm

            — Part-time driver for the Manheim Auto Auction

   – Part-time escort driver for High Steel Co.,
      Lancaster
   – Part-time husband
But enjoying – FULL-TIME LIVING!
Never a dull moment . . . and the **best** is **yet** to **come!**

God Bless You All!